Comparative Politics
AN INTRODUCTION

We work with leading authors to develop the
strongest educational materials in Politics,
bringing cutting-edge thinking and best
learning practice to a global market.

Under a range of well-known imprints, including
Longman, we craft high quality print and electronic
publications which help readers to understand and
apply their content, whether studying or at work.

To find out more about the complete range of our
publishing, please visit us on the World Wide Web at:
www.pearsoneduc.com

Comparative Politics

AN INTRODUCTION

PETER CALVERT

Professor of Comparative and International Politics

University of Southampton

Longman

An imprint of **Pearson Education**

Harlow, England · London · New York · Reading, Massachusetts · San Francisco
Toronto · Don Mills, Ontario · Sydney · Tokyo · Singapore · Hong Kong · Seoul
Taipei · Cape Town · Madrid · Mexico City · Amsterdam · Munich · Paris · Milan

Pearson Education Limited
Edinburgh Gate
Harlow
Essex CM20 2JE

and Associated Companies throughout the world

Visit us on the World Wide Web at:
www.pearsoneduc.com

First published 2002

© Peter Calvert 2002

ISBN 0582 438233

British Library Cataloguing-in-Publication Data
A catalogue record for this book is available from the British Library

Library of Congress Cataloging-in-Publication Data
A catalog record for this book is available from the Library of Congress

10 9 8 7 6 5 4 3 2 1
06 05 04 03 02

Typeset in 10/12pt Giovanni Book by 35
Printed by Ashford Colour Press Ltd, Gosport

Contents

Lecturer support
There is an Instructor's Manual available for download from www.booksites.net/calvert

List of Figures

List of Tables

Acknowledgements

The author and publishers would like to thank the following for their valuable help at various stages in the development of *Comparative Politics: An Introduction.*

Steven Bastow (Kingston University)

Georgina Blakeley (University of Huddersfield)

Werner Bonefeld (University of York)

Ben Clift (Brunel University)

Alvin Cohen (Lancaster University)

Philip Giddings (University of Reading)

Carl Levy (Goldsmiths College, University of London)

Don MacIver (University of Staffordshire)

Cas Mudde (University of Edinburgh)

James Newell (University of Salford)

Marke Pennington (Queen Mary and Westfield College, University of London)

Yumei Zhang (University of Luton)

We are grateful to the following for permission to reproduce copyright material:

Figure 2.1 after figure from *Comparing Political Systems*, Weidenfeld & Nicolson, (Blondel, J., 1973); Table 2.2 adapted from table from *A Preface to Democratic Theory*, University of Chicago Press, (Dahl, R.A., 1964), copyright © 1964 University of Chicago Press; Table 7.5 from *Sunday Tribune, November 1992*, Tribune Newspapers plc, copyright © 1992 Sunday Tribune (Ireland); Table 8.1 produced from information from *Essence of Decision: Exploring the Cuban Missile Crisis*, Little Brown, (Allison, G.T., 1971), by permission of Pearson Education Inc.; Table 10.4 adapted from table from *Military Rule in Latin America*, Unwin Hyman, (Remmer, K.L., 1989), by permission of Thomson Learning; Table 10.5 adapted from table on p. 85 from *Democracy in the Third World*, Lynne Rienner Publishers, (Pinkney, R., 1994), Figure 11.1 adapted from figure on p. 119 with the permission of The Free Press, a division of Simon & Schuster, Inc. from *Violence and Repression in Latin America: A Quantitative and Historical Analysis* by Ernest A. Duff and John F. McCamant, with W.O. Morales, Copyright © 1976 by the Free Press; Figure 11.2 adapted from figure from *'Towards a Theory of Revolution'*, in *American Sociological Review*, *Feb 1962*, American Sociological Association, (Davies, J.C., 1962); Table 11.2 produced from information from *Keesing's Record of World Events, Volume 35, 1989*, (Keesing's Worldwide LLC).

We are grateful to the Financial Times Limited for permission to reprint the following material:

House arrest in style for the playboy president, © *Financial Times*, 9 June, 2001; Court rules on land control, © *Financial Times*, 10 January, 2001; Fischer predicts EU will become federation, © *Financial Times*, 16 May, 2001; Russia: Mixed outcome to devolving power to the regions, © *Financial Times*, 10 May, 2000; Why Blair deserves to have Thatcher's hair, © *Financial Times*, 16–17 June, 2001; Change of mood paves way for reforms, © *Financial Times*, 7 December, 2000; Market slump greets Koizumi election triumph, © *Financial Times*, 30 July, 2001; Yucatan's poll dinosaurs are threatened with extinction, © *Financial Times*, 26–27 May, 2001; An Early Victory, © *Financial Times*, 28–29 April, 2001; Wanted: enforcer to keep Fox cabinet in line, © *Financial Times*, 12 July, 2001; Dissent grows within Tokyo cabinet team, © *Financial Times*, 3 August, 2001; Military chiefs in Peru to vow to take a back seat to democracy, © *Financial Times*, 21–22 April, 2001; Indonesia's transition is a boost for democracy, © *Financial Times*, 28 July, 2001; The Political spat that brought economic policy to a halt, © *Financial Times*, 24–25 February, 2001.

In some instances we have been unable to trace the owners of copyright material, and we would appreciate any information that would enable us to do so.

World Map

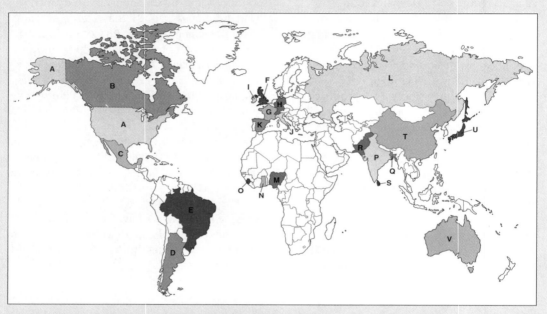

Country descriptions featured in the text

A	USA	20	**G**	France	50	**M**	Nigeria	83	**S**	Sri Lanka	186
B	Canada	21	**H**	Germany	51	**N**	Ghana	83	**T**	China	187
C	Mexico	21	**I**	Ireland	52	**O**	Sierra Leone	84	**U**	Japan	188
D	Argentina	26	**J**	Italy	52	**P**	India	184	**V**	Australia	213
E	Brazil	27	**K**	Spain	53	**Q**	Bangladesh	185			
F	UK	49	**L**	Russia	173	**R**	Pakistan	185			

PART ONE **Introduction**

Why Politics?
Why Comparative?

CHAPTER ONE

Learning Objectives

By the end of this chapter, the reader should be able:

- to establish a definition of politics and other key terms;

- to explain why the comparative method is essential to its understanding;

- to acquire a basic understanding of the various approaches to the subject and how they differ from one another;

- to follow the approach used in this book and the reasons for the emphasis on the themes of liberalisation, globalisation and democratisation;

- to evaluate the utility of the study of comparative politics.

Definitions

Why did Aristotle describe **politics** as the 'master science' (Aristotle, *Ethics*, I, 1, 1094a, in 1968, p. 354)? It was simply because politics is the key to everything else that human beings do. Literally everything that happens in society is the result of a political decision.

Politics, therefore, is the *making of decisions* in society. Politics is not action, though, but interaction; it is both what decision-makers do to people, and what people do to try to influence the decision-makers. Hence it is to be found everywhere in society where decisions have to be made, but nowhere more so than where the most fundamental and crucial questions have to be resolved.

The principal institution of any society dealing with political matters, and the key to understanding its politics as a whole, is its **government**. A government is an organisation which has established a *successful claim to have the legitimate monopoly of the use of force* (Weber 1965, p. 154). Once secured, this monopoly ensures that in the last resort the decisions of government can be enforced. In other words, a government has **power**.

By force is meant any use of physical coercion, whether by government, other groups or private citizens. By power is meant *the ability to get others to do what you want*. Hence it is the central concept in politics. However, as Steven Lukes (1974) has made notably clear, like many other concepts in politics, power is 'essentially-contested'; that is to say, it is a concept on which *by definition* agreement is impossible (Gallie 1955–56). A second 'face' of power, therefore, is *the ability to stop issues from being discussed by with-holding them from the political agenda* (Bachrach and Baratz 1962). The third of Lukes's three 'faces' of power consists of the *underlying 'bias of the system'*, which is sustained by 'socially structured and culturally patterned' practices (Lukes 1974).

Power in the modern state rests on the sanction of force, though in practice the sanction is never completely secured – there will always be 'crime' and there will always be dissent. In addition, there are always a number of (subordinate) levels of government in a political community of any size. There is no such thing as an absolute dictatorship. To get what they want, dictators have to act through underlings. Even if we do not accept fully what rational choice theory tells us (see below), that people will be constrained to act in their self-interest (North 1986), we can reasonably expect that self-interest will at least play an important part in determining their actions.

The organised community within which a government claims obedience as of right of all citizens has traditionally been known as a **state**. Present-day states, covering a relatively wide area, are commonly termed nation-states. Originally, this was to distinguish them from earlier forms of political organisation covering relatively small areas, such as tribes or city states. In modern states the majority of inhabitants generally identify themselves with one another, by the possession of a common language, religion and/or culture. A people with this sense of identity is a **nation**. However, the term 'nation-state' is a misleading one, for there is no exact correspondence between state and nation. There are states with more than one nation (Britain), nations with more than one state (ethnic Albanians, Hungarians, Serbs, etc.), states with no definite national identity (Chad) and nations with no definite state (the Palestinian Arabs) (Seton-Watson 1977).

It was in nineteenth-century Europe that there emerged the concept of **nationalism**, the belief that the only appropriate basis for a state was the nation. To this day, therefore, states which lack a sense of national identity try very hard to inculcate it, as the

United States (Lipset 1979) did when it encouraged the study of **political science** by its future citizens.

The study of the relations between states is commonly known as **international relations**, and forms an academic discipline so closely allied to politics that the two are normally taught together. Indeed, the fact that the disciplines have become separated is largely fortuitous, and there is everything to be gained by bringing the study of comparative politics and international relations as close together as possible. The fact is that the practice of international relations was established in a political climate which held that states were in every sense quite distinct and separate from one another, treating with one another as equals, and owing no duty to any outside earthly authority. This notion, which is termed **sovereignty**, has been regarded as one of the attributes of a state since the time of Jean Bodin (Frankel 1964, p. 13). It has two important implications. Within the state, the state's rules are supreme, in that all other sets of rules must be compatible with those of the state. Externally, the state's boundaries may not be changed, nor its jurisdiction within its own territory challenged, by any outside authority without its own consent.

All state governments are, in theory, still sovereign. Taken literally, this would mean for the people whose destinies they control that there was no appeal to any higher level. However, the concept of sovereignty is not 'real', but simply a convenient, and indeed very important, legal fiction. In practice, ever since the concept of the state emerged, in or around the sixteenth century, states have interacted with one another and so at least to some minor extent have been dependent on others. And in the twentieth century, and especially since 1945, states gave up substantial proportions of their former freedom of action to **intergovernmental** and **supranational organisations** and, indeed, to one another. And these states are therefore bound by international obligations to respect certain minimum standards of behaviour and to avoid certain types of action.

Yet this should not lead to the belief that there is a general decline of the state. On the contrary, there are more states now than ever before, and in almost all of them the spirit of nationalism seems as strong as ever. And, since the whole inhabitable world is now parcelled out between them, it is quite impossible for anyone to ignore their existence, or escape from the influence of one or another of them (Frankel 1964, pp. 28, 126, 156). And with modern communications the actions of different states are now so interpenetrated that international relations, in the old sense, has had to expand its boundaries to include all sorts of relations with and between **non-governmental organisations (NGOs)**. This term is a wide one, ranging from **international organisations (IOs)** with technical responsibilities such as the Universal Postal Union (UPU) to pressure groups such as Greenpeace and the Worldwide Fund for Nature (WWF).

Sovereignty is intimately bound up with two other ideas – those of legitimacy and authority, with which it is often confused (Friedrich 1972, pp. 14–15, 47–8).

Legitimacy means that a government is generally recognised to have the right to do what it does. It depends, therefore, not on what the government claims, but on whether or not that claim is recognised. The fact that a government is recognised as legitimate, whether by its own citizens or by its peer states, gives it authority, which is the assurance that its commands will be obeyed.

Authority itself, however, is not absolute or unlimited. To have authority to do something is the right to do that thing, and be obeyed; it is not a general grant of power to do anything you want. Authority, therefore, can be delegated, divided or shared. In fact, all operation of complex governments depends on this fact, since the delegation, division or sharing of the tasks of government depend on it.

Authority and Power

The question of authority was treated by Max Weber as being central to the evolution of the modern state (Weber 1965, pp. 132, 324ff.). Originally, Weber believed, the authority of government stemmed from what he termed *charisma*: that is to say, the outstanding personality or personal qualities of an individual. In more developed societies, charisma was 'routinised', or subjected to legal forms and controls, thus enabling the society to survive a change of leader. It could be either *traditional* (accepted because it had always been accepted) or *legal-rational* (accepted as being conferred by formal rituals involving some kind of choice or recognition by or on behalf of the society as a whole). Weber therefore distinguished these three types of authority, charismatic, traditional and legal-rational, from one another, while treating them as 'ideal types' which were not necessarily found in pure form. Thus a person of outstanding personal qualities may come from an old family, which lends traditional authority, and legally be elected president, a position which confers legal-rational authority. An interesting example of this duplication was King Norodom Sihanouk, heir to the kings who built Angkor Wat, who in the 1950s gave up his throne to become prime minister of Cambodia. In 1991 he resumed the throne as the one figure in that unhappy country who could command a measure of general support.

The fact is that in all but a few modern states there was a specific moment in time when a government seized power, and all other governments after that time claim part or whole of their authority by virtue of being successors to that government. Even in states such as Australia and New Zealand, which achieved independence peacefully, conquest formed the basis of the colonial state. In Canada and Malaysia self-government was conceded because of the threat that the territory might otherwise succumb to force. In Nigeria and Ghana, Pakistan and Bangladesh force has been used since independence to install a series of military governments. All Weber's forms of authority, therefore, amount to the same thing, the habit of obedience. The collective habit of obedience gives a tendency to inertia in social systems. Social systems, once established, will tend to continue unaltered until either society decides to change them or it discovers that it has forgotten any need for them. By extension, the longer a social institution continues in existence, the longer it is likely to continue.

So it is with the key social institution, that of government itself. The habit of obedience is perpetuated the more easily since very few people, if any, see or are in the habit of seeing the government as a whole, and thus may be, and frequently are, protected by encapsulation from the attentions of the government. All that is not central to them is regarded as being peripheral. So the bulk of governmental operations survive war, invasion, revolution, civil war, earthquake, flood or pestilence, joining together after the event to repair the damage as best as possible in the accustomed mould. And changes of major importance in government only take place either incrementally, by slow changes over a long period of time, or, as in the case of Japan or Eastern Europe after 1945, by imposition from without.

It is important to stress that the initial seizure of power does not confer either authority or legitimacy. Nor are the motives relevant. Governments which seize power always claim to be acting under the authority of some superior law – be it divine right, the will of the people, or the mission of the armed forces to protect the state. But such arguments have to be recognised as fallacious. No modern government has legitimacy purely from the fact of its past history, and all governments depend on the active or passive consent of their subjects to their actions. Sadly this gives them a lot of scope to coerce their subjects into accepting those actions.

Politics as a Social Science

Politics can be regarded as an art, because for those who practise it (**politicians**) that is what it is, a skill which they generally learn by trial and error, and not by study. But the study of politics is termed political science, and those who study it professionally are known, correctly, not as politicians but, rather awkwardly, as political scientists. When the term 'political science' was brought into common use in the earliest years of the American Republic (Crick 1959) the word 'science' covered all forms of systematic knowledge – as the German term *Wissenschaft* still does. More recently the term has come to be associated particularly with the so-called 'exact' sciences: e.g. physics, chemistry, biology, which are based on experimental evidence from which they derive regular laws giving them the ability to predict future events.

Clearly the study of human political behaviour cannot be reduced to propositions with the inflexible regularity of the so-called laws of Nature. There is scarcely a rule of politics that is not broken successfully at one time or another, and there is no reason to suppose that there are in fact any that cannot be broken. Statements about social phenomena cannot be predictive in the 'If A then B' sense (Runciman 1963, pp. 2–3). All statements in the social sciences are statements of probability. Consequently, any statement about human behaviour can be true only for individuals in groups at the most, and can say nothing about the certainty of action by a single individual. Additionally, in dealing with human beings as opposed to natural phenomena, knowledge of the results of an investigation into a pattern of behaviour will lead to changes in that behaviour pattern in the future – assuming one were able to discern a pattern in the first place.

Hence philosophers such as Winch (1958) have asserted that there is no possibility whatsoever of developing a predictive science in the social sciences. Is it true then that political science cannot be scientific? No, for two reasons.

First, not all sciences can make such predictive statements, and, in fact, the belief that they can stems from a common failure to understand the nature of the so-called exact sciences. Medicine, for example, is undeniably a science, and what is more, it works. Yet many statements in medicine about the effect of one or another treatment can only be couched in terms of probabilities (Lessnoff 1974). It can be said that a treatment usually helps patients with a certain condition to a complete recovery, but it cannot be certain that it will help any *one* patient to whom the treatment is administered.

Secondly, as in medicine, the weighing of probabilities in politics is seldom a simple matter; the more serious any problem is, the less likely that it will occur on its own, and the more likely that it will occur in conjunction with other problems to which it is closely related (Brodbeck 1968; Przeworski and Teune 1970). In such circumstances, a decision on one problem will necessarily have consequences for the others which may well make their solution much more difficult, and in extreme cases it may seem very difficult to make any useful decision at all. Just as the exact sciences (including medicine) have had to build up their basic store of information over many generations, and often by trial and error, so too political scientists are doing the same. The fact that the road may be a long one is no excuse for not setting out on it boldly. As the Chinese proverb has it: 'The journey of a thousand *li* begins with a single step'.

In what respects, if any, then, should political science be regarded as a science? There are broadly three factors.

First, it has a defined and unique field of study. It is not, for example, history, sociology or philosophy, though it has both borrowed from and contributed to each of these disciplines in what has been a fruitful interchange for each.

Secondly, it does seek to build up a body of knowledge which is as *comprehensive* and *exact* as techniques permit (Parsons and Shils 1962; Easton 1957; Stanyer 1976; Mayer 1989).

Comprehensiveness is limited by two problems. Political phenomena are very short-lived, and it requires very intensive study to keep up with a developing political situation. As with the politicians themselves who are actively involved, it may occupy all one's working day for days on end. In addition information is constantly getting out of date. Hence books on politics cease to fulfil their original purpose and soon become history books. (Sadly, the reverse is not the case, so historians get a lot of free books.)

Exactness is limited by the very nature of the art of politics. In so far as political activity is to be realised in the form of decisions, it involves the amassing of a given amount of support. There is no dictator so powerful that his or her decisions do not have to be carried out by others. In an assembly, a committee, a meeting, or an election, support may take the very specific form of committed votes. The stock-in-trade of the successful politician, therefore, is the recollection from moment to moment of the balance of advantage or disadvantage to his or her own side, together with the tally of obligations amassed in the course of bargaining for support. However, this knowledge is in itself a valuable part of the ability to bargain, and so is jealously guarded. Hence the political scientist in this respect too is aware of a barrier of information. Other difficulties exist too. With many actors come problems of collecting, maintaining and above all recalling large amounts of information culled from many different sources. This information has to be reduced to a standard form. Much of it is not numerical, but in nominal form; that is to say, certain information is either present in a given category or it is not. This restricts the range of possibilities for analysing it. But in themselves, none of these problems is strange to the exact sciences.

Thirdly, political science makes use of the *hypothetico-deductive method* to derive regular principles from observing the behaviour of both individuals and groups. It is possible to understand enough about the motivation of politicians to be able to make reasonably reliable predictions of their most likely courses of action, together with the probable consequences of alternative courses of action or inaction. Even if it is true that a politician may break all the rules of politics and get away with it, nevertheless to say this is to say that there are rules that do apply to the majority of cases. In the long run, it may even be possible to discern regular laws. In the meanwhile, politicians can do something much more alarming. They can (and do) use detailed survey evidence to tailor their public statements and actions in order to maximise support and win elections, and the evidence from the United States since this first emerged as a possibility in the 1960 presidential election shows that they have become increasingly successful in doing so.

The Comparative Method

Politics has to be studied comparatively because there is no other way in which to obtain the raw data on which to base informed judgements (Lijphart 1971). It is certainly possible and, indeed, most desirable for political philosophers within particular societies or political systems to think constructively about how people ought to act in ideal situations. It is, in fact, the only way to explore the full range of possibilities implicit in any given situation to think about it as an abstract problem. But this can only be done in the light of general principles about human behaviour which are derived from experience, as in the problem itself. At best that necessary experience will be a broad one, but the more systematic it is, the broader it is also likely to be.

In one sense, then, there is no study of politics that is not comparative (Dogan and Pelassy 1984). All political science, as all other sciences, involves learning by measuring and examining events which are comparable, so that first impressions of how the results might vary from one case to another (hypotheses) may be tested, and, if supported, gain acceptance as regular statements of future probability (theories). Only the comparative method, moreover, shows up regular patterns in the behaviour of both individuals and groups. It must begin therefore with a careful choice of case studies according to clear criteria for selection (Yin 1989, 1993).

The difficulties outlined above dictate the choice of method. The comparative method is the clinical one: to examine cases of the phenomenon which is to be investigated, cases which will be complicated by irrelevant information and misleading statements by the participants involved, and by a wide range of other differing factors which just have to be tolerated (Landman 2000). Where the investigator begins is largely a matter of individual choice. The subject matter is, after all, the same from whichever direction it is approached. To be fully effective, however, any study must seek to take place in an informed knowledge of the range of possible variation that can take place. It must also embody a sufficient depth of historical knowledge to show how the society and its political system have evolved and are evolving, and this means awareness not only of the techniques of the political scientist but also those of the historian. This done, the student then orders the resulting set of findings by the use of shorthand expressions for general concepts such as are implied by the use of technical terms and systems of classification.

Hence what value any research may have depends entirely on the adoption of a satisfactory research design (Allan and Skinner 1991). This has a number of stages.

First, formulate clearly what is the problem to be investigated.

Next, establish hypotheses that are to be tested. These hypotheses, however, must be capable of being analysed in terms of the data that has been obtained and will be sought in the future. These hypotheses will have to be formulated in such a way that a precise relationship can be identified between the **dependent variable**, the change to be explained, and the **independent variables** which are believed to affect it.

Next, the validity of hypotheses must be tested against the data. In political science, as in sociology or weather forecasting, it is very seldom possible to use either of the two methods by which validity can be ascribed to scientific research. Experiments are rarely possible, both for reasons of time and for ethical reasons, and for the same reasons the researcher cannot arrange for observations, other than in surveys of individuals, to be randomised, a procedure designed to eliminate interference in the results by the choices of the observer. So the choice of analytical techniques must reflect the limitations of the material, though this does not mean that political scientists should not at all times strive for greater accuracy (Marsh and Stoker 1995; Yates 1998).

In the end, the results of the work must then be set out clearly and made available to other researchers, showing how and why those conclusions have been obtained.

Schools of Interpretation

The study of comparative politics rests on a fundamental assumption. It is that human behaviour is broadly speaking constant: that it will be the same in the same circumstances, regardless of time and space. Without this assumption the philosophical problems of studying politics in a comparative context would be immensely complicated, if not, indeed, rendered impossible. However, this is not in itself sufficient reason for making that assumption. The overwhelming weight of evidence is that *homo sapiens* is a very homogeneous species (Howells 1971; Dobzhansky 1971). Such differences as exist between the populations of different parts of the world are trivial, and such as exist are in any case easily accounted for by accidental factors, such as the relatively temporary isolation of small units of population on remote islands. And between the sexes such differences as exist appear minor compared with those of many animal species. Hence variations in fundamental behaviour patterns between different communities in different parts of the world are likely to be so slight that they may be safely ignored in planning comparisons even between widely separated communities.

Such similarities of behaviour, however, are often concealed by the fact that they are described in a very different way in different languages. This is the first and most important reason why political science needed to develop a standard vocabulary in which to talk about politics in a comparative context (Almond and Coleman 1960; Almond 1968; Sartori 1970). The act of comparison, too, will help researchers in turn to escape from the assumptions of their own times and their own society (Dogan and Pelassy 1984, p. 5).

Political scientists have prejudices like other people, and the most persistent of these are their own political views. It comes as no surprise to find, therefore, that their writing on politics can be grouped in the main in one or another of four competing schools of interpretation: historical/descriptive, Marxist, behaviouralist/functionalist, and rational choice.

Historical/descriptive

Despite criticisms that have been levelled at the historical/descriptive method by the supporters of other schools, it lies still at the basis of all case-study work in political science, and, it may be said with confidence, provides 90 per cent of the information on which all the more ambitious approaches in each of the schools depends. Work that neglects the basic principles of historical research produces valueless data, so political scientists, if their work is not to be helplessly dependent on others, must understand the value and significant features of different historical sources.

They will learn from the best historians three things: to take account of all the information available to them, even if they do not agree with it or it with them; to give due weight to the factor of time in the development of events; and to show clearly to the reader the source of their ideas.

On the other hand many historical studies seek to explain only specific sequences of events as they have happened over time, in their own terms (historicism). What political scientists seek to do is to obtain general theories purporting to explain human behaviour. That is, through their work, they seek to derive sets of propositions describing the conditions under which specific types of behaviour will take place. These propositions will then be valid for all times and places and not just for some specific sequence of historical events.

Interestingly enough, in the historical/descriptive tradition, propositions of this kind about governments have often been supplied by lawyers, though legal terminology was in the first instance developed for very different purposes.

Marxist

Marxism contributes to modern interpretation an emphasis on the economic basis of human society, a new and widely held definition of class as the fundamental division in society and a belief in human betterment. It is distinctive too in its powerful and seductive idea of a common path of development for all societies. This is not an original idea, but it was one which gained considerable impetus from the onset of the industrial revolution, since Marx himself, who asserted the primacy of economic causes in determining human behaviour, was the first to seek to explore these in relation to an overall philosophy of history, which he hoped – and repeatedly asserted – had in itself a predictive value.

Two points are of the greatest value to the study of comparative politics: the fact that the political cannot be detached from the economic and social aspects of a community, and the need for hard data as the essential foundation for any serious future research.

The main weakness of the Marxist approach is that its scientific basis has become hopelessly confused with the political programme of Lenin and the Bolsheviks in Russia. Under Stalin Marxism-Leninism was used to justify an authoritarian regime and appalling atrocities committed in the name of progress, while in the West a variety of writers and thinkers collaborated in the trivialisation of Marx's most interesting propositions by unthinking repetition. Where Marxism is most fruitful is where it has been incorporated into the general body of human knowledge, of which no one school of thought has a monopoly.

Behaviouralist and functionalist

Behaviouralists derive from the natural sciences an emphasis on clinical study of behaviour in very small groups and in the individual. This fills an essential void in Marxist theory, which is concerned above all with very large groups and movements. As has been demonstrated by biologists, propositions derived from the behaviour of one size of group are simply not valid for other sizes of groups (the so-called ecological fallacy). And, as much of politics involves small-group behaviour, the political scientists' use of the work done in this area, which has been slow to be accepted other than at the most superficial level, is hardly excessive, though it is also true to say that obsessions with methodological purity have had a stultifying effect on actual research.

Behaviouralism has, however, had an important effect on the way we look at politics. Its belief that individual behaviour is invariably rational in some sense has been queried, though it has provided the basis for *rational choice theory* (see next section). As Goodin (1976, p. 13) says, 'the only entirely satisfactory response to this query is a practical demonstration of the power of the theory'. He cites evidence from European countries which confirms the theoretical argument that political parties will tend to form only the minimum size of coalition required to win (Taylor and Laver 1973). If predictions are tolerably correct then the model probably mirrors at least some essential features of the real world (see also Buchanan and Tullock 1962; Downs 1957; Olson 1965).

Biology has specifically contributed to political science the concept of social entities as *systems* performing specified *functions*. Again this is not a new idea, for the notion of the 'body politic', familiar in medieval times, is but an earlier version of the same idea. The expansion of the concept of system in political science and the rise of the function-alist school coincided with and was aided by the cybernetic revolution and the success of engineers in developing artificially intelligent machines. Though it may not look like it at first sight, 'cybernetics' comes from the same Greek root as 'government' and means 'the science of steering' (Weiner 1967, p. 11). And a *political system* is simply that common whole of related parts and functions that is concerned with the making of decisions within a society (cf. Almond and Powell 1996).

System concepts have considerable advantages over traditional terms derived from legal terminology. They can be applied on any scale, to a local community or to a whole modern state, utilising the concepts of regionally or functionally distinct subsystems within one common whole of interrelated parts (Dahl 1964a, p. 9). Increasingly, there-fore, political scientists have come to talk of political systems rather than of states.

Systems analysis has contributed to political science in addition two essential ideas. First is the notion of *function*. A function is simply a task performed by a system that con-tributes in some way to its survival. The same functions may be performed in different systems by different structures – a worm, for example, 'sees' with its skin (Almond and Coleman 1960, p. 13). Second is the idea of *structure*. A structure is any recurrent pattern of behaviour in a political system that persists over time. It is function that determines structure.

A weakness of the functionalist approach is that it has too readily been assumed from this that all structures will have useful functions. In fact they do not necessarily do so, since they may merely represent the residual traces of a function that is no longer per-formed, as in the case of the appendix in human physiology, and the American Electoral College in politics. But the main weakness is that it assumes that political systems 'need' to survive. There is no reason to suppose that this is the case, certainly not in the sense that a plant or animal needs to survive.

Rational choice

Rational choice theory is a development of behaviouralism which seeks to apply eco-nomic models of rationality to the making of political decisions. It is a normative theory. 'It tells us what we ought to do in order to achieve our aims as well as possible. It does not tell us what our aims ought to be' (Elster 1986, p. 1).

Its basic assumption is that human beings invariably choose rationally, hence their observed behaviour will always fall into a consistent pattern. This assumption is put in its clearest form in the economist Paul Samuelson's Weak Axiom of Revealed Preference, which holds that if a person 'chooses x when y is available, then he will not choose y in a situation in which x is also obtainable' (Sen 1986, p. 61). The problem with this assumption is that human life is so complex that precisely the same situation seldom if ever occurs, if only because it has already happened. It also makes two other assumptions which can be challenged: that full information is available on which the choice can be based and that this includes the future consequences of the person's actions. If x is bread and y is soup, choice might be affected by whether or not one had just eaten.

Let us assume for a moment, however, that these conditions are all fulfilled and that the individual makes a rational choice. Does this mean that collectivities, such as families, firms or political communities, also choose rationally? No, since Arrow's Impossibility Theorem demonstrates that this is not the case (Arrow 1963). Hence though political scientists can and do use rational choice theory to try to understand some of the policy choices made by governments, they find that in practice they have to take account of a variety of non-economic factors to explain outcomes.

There are three main applications of rational choice theory in politics. Game theory defines rational behaviour in game situations. Some of these, such as the Prisoners' Dilemma, have a number of applications in politics, and are a branch of decision theory, properly the theory of rational behaviour under risk and under uncertainty. Classical economic theory assumes certainty, and in the form of the rational actor model has useful applications in the field of public policy. More widely, rational choice can also be used to explore problems in ethics, in so far as moral judgements involve rational choices of preference based on impartial criteria, and provide a theory of the common welfare of society (Harsanyi 1986).

The Political System

Modern states are so large and complex that at any one time only a few comparisons can be selected for study, either because of their importance (general value to society) or their salience (urgency to find a solution to a problem). The first task is to specify the boundaries of the political system. The political system might be regarded, as Talcott Parsons did, as one of a number of subsystems of the overall social system; or, with Easton, it can be distinguished as an entity for study on its own, engaged in transactions with the social system which constitutes the nearer part of its environment (Davies and Lewis 1971, pp. 22–3). The choice is an open one. Whichever is selected, it must at all times be remembered that the political system is not a real entity, but a conceptual one. The political system is not a group of people, a huddle of buildings, or even a carefully constructed machine. It is a set of social relationships, and its boundary is set by the limit of those relationships, wherever that happens to fall.

It is partly for this reason that the broader concept of political system is attractive, since that way its boundary appears to coincide with that of the state, and from the point of view of a student of international relations this would seem to be convenient. But unfortunately it is misleading for the student of comparative politics, in two ways. On the one hand, the political system of many states – for example, Brazil – does not impinge directly on the lives of a significant fraction of its inhabitants. They live their lives in what the anthropologists call an encapsulated society: one which exists within the territory of the state without forming part of it (Vogt 1969, p. 582; cf. Rose 1971, pp. 27, 31). On the other hand, the boundary of the nation-state of today, as already noted, is penetrated from outside by many different influences and affected by

globalisation (Herz 1959, p. 64). Indeed, over the past two decades it has been increasingly common to regard domestic and international politics as only aspects of one interrelated whole.

The term political system here, therefore, will be used as a synonym for government – that is to say, that system of interaction which forms the fundamental control mechanism within a society. The boundary between it and the rest of society is not a clearcut one. It runs not between individuals, but between the different roles they play. Most people do not participate in making demands in politics most of the time. But they cannot opt out of it when it makes demands upon them, at a minimum when they are called upon to pay their taxes. Politics is an essential part of modern societies; it is certainly never absent.

The political system is political because it is concerned with the making of decisions about the allocation of *power resources*. And this allocation is disputable because power resources are limited. By power resources is meant those things which people want, which if controlled by governments enable them to maintain their power over those they rule. In material terms this means food, clothing, housing and energy, or the equivalent cost of those items, the supply of which is, at any given point in time, itself limited. Control of such resources gives political *power*, which in turn means the ability to use force to control them, the habit of exercising authority which is referred to as *status* (Turner 1988), and the limitations on access to authority which are often loosely and inaccurately termed *class*. Class, status and power can be traded off one against another.

The political system is that part of the social order in which the ultimate decisions of society are made. Approaching the problem of steering mechanisms from the viewpoint of cybernetics, Deutsch identified important properties of any political system. A cybernetic system is a self-steering mechanism guided by analysis of consequences of its own decisions. Knowledge of these consequences, which is termed *feedback*, is literally 'fed back' from the output to the input side of the process. Hence just as inputs are converted into outputs, in turn the outputs are monitored for specific inputs. Deutsch points out that a mechanism such as a gunsight will have to have the capacity to anticipate what the future course of events may be, and to modify the information received by the input side accordingly. The gun must fire, not at the aircraft, but in front of it, so that by the time the shell arrives the aircraft will be at the correct position in space to be hit by it. In this instance this correction is known as *gain*, an allowance for the delay in response to a decision which is known as *lag* (Deutsch 1966, pp. 90, 106).

To be able to 'steer', there must be two categories of *inputs* to the system. On the one hand there will be *demands* on which the decision-makers are asked to to act, and information to enable them to decide. On the other, they must also receive *support* of various kinds for their decisions. This consists both of personnel to make the decisions, and a great deal of resources, both material and moral, with which to make them effective. The decisions themselves, the rules by which they are enforced and the way in which they are interpreted, form the *outputs* of the system.

A similar reasoning lies behind Easton's (1957) model of the political system (Figure 1.1), which forms the basis for many later variants. The first attempt to adapt the systems approach for the purposes of comparative politics was made in 1960 by Almond and Coleman (1960, p. 17). As they pointed out, the outputs of government were already familiar as the 'powers' set out by the makers of the American Constitution, and since followed by most other constitutional lawyers. However, to distinguish the functions

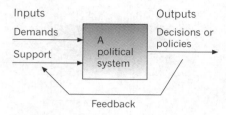

Figure 1.1 The political system (after Easton)

from the bodies set up to embody them, Almond and Coleman labelled them, rather than the legislative, executive and judicial powers, the functions of rule-making, rule-application and rule-adjudication. By doing so they made it easier to discern that, for example, when Congress, which is formally a legislature, impeaches the president of the United States, it is actually exercising the function of rule-adjudication. There are many other such examples of overlapping functions in all constitutions, some deliberate ('checks and balances') and some accidental.

Almond and Coleman broke new ground when they turned to the inputs, as these had been largely ignored by earlier writers. One of them they termed political communication (cf. Deutsch 1966). This strictly speaking, however, is neither an input nor an output, but a method by which inputs and outputs are conveyed. It will be dealt with separately in Chapter 4. Almond and Coleman's other three categories of input are: political socialisation and recruitment; interest articulation; and interest aggregation.

- **Political socialisation and recruitment**, which are rather odd but not incompatible bedfellows, consist of the process of formal and informal shaping of citizens' attitudes to politics; and those structures that exist for the recruitment of people into political or administrative office.
- **Interest articulation** refers to the process by which people express their needs and wishes. It can be divided into demands upon the system and expressions of support for it.
- **Interest aggregation** means the process of linking together various interests into a more or less coherent programme of action on which a decision can be taken.

In a later adaptation of this classification, Almond and Powell (1966, 1996) distinguished interest articulation and interest aggregation, together with political communication, and the three output functions of rule-making, rule-application and rule-adjudication, as *conversion functions*: that is, those processes which enable the political system to convert demands and supports into political decisions (Figure 1.2). Among these decisions are some, undoubtedly, affecting political socialisation and recruitment, which are seen by Almond and Powell as *pattern maintenance functions*. The efficiency of the system in doing each of these things they describe as its *capabilities*.

What is not at all clear, however, even in the revised model, is just why these, *and not any other categories*, should have been chosen. It does recognise that inputs may arise within the ranks of the decision-makers themselves, termed variously 'withinputs' and 'intraputs'. But there remains an impression that the initiative for political action comes in the main from outside.

A simpler, and more effective way of looking at inputs to the political system is simply to regard them as *positive* and *negative* (Table 1.1). Positive inputs, which enable

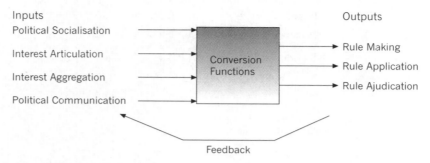

Figure 1.2 The political system (after Almond and Coleman)

Table 1.1 The political and social systems

	Input	Output
Political	P+ Support	F− Power resource extraction
	P− Demands	F+ Input control
Social	Q− Taxes	E− Negative interest arbitration
	Q+ Subsidies	E+ Positive interest arbitration

Source: after Calvert 1969

the government to perform its functions at all, include support in the widest sense, but more particularly the resources to make decisions. Negative inputs are demands on government for action or payment.

There are also only two main types of outputs. Political decisions as such are not outputs, any more than a tap is water, or a switch electricity. Positive outputs are *rewards*; negative outputs are *sanctions*. The prime 'purpose' of the political system is to survive, but only because that is the prime objective of the people who make the decisions. Like any other system, it can either adapt to changes in its environment, it can change its environment to suit it, or it can, and usually does, do both. It utilises its outputs to maximise support for it, and to minimise the demands made upon it, within the parameters of the society in which it operates, and under the general constraint of the principle of economy of effort. Given unlimited resources there would be no problem in maintaining support indefinitely. But scarcity, population growth, natural disasters and international influences limit resources in almost all modern political systems, so that the allocation of resources is the fundamental task they face. It is the curious characteristic of politics that a very small amount of power, correctly used, can be sufficient to gain control over a very large quantity of resources, both physical and human. To understand fully how any individual government is actually operating, therefore, it is necessary to trace the direction and intensity of all the possible functional flows, and of their interactions – a simple equation of power between government and society would not only be misleading, but meaningless. To trace them, they must first be identified and labelled.

The government puts *out* resources to perform the function of *power resource extraction* by which, in turn, it takes in 'necessary' *support*. Being challenged continuously concerning its right to do this, it puts *out* more resources in *input control* in order to regulate and where necessary screen out *demands* coming in.

It will, further, regulate society in its own interests, through the general function of interest arbitration which can be either positive or negative. By *positive interest arbitration* it strengthens interests and thus attaches them to itself, at the same time depriving the society at large of the resources implied; by *negative interest arbitration* it does the reverse. However, the strengthening of interests soon implies a challenge to the authority of the government itself and will lead to corrective action being applied, so that the two processes are in fact continuous. The principal means employed can be simplified into taxes on the strong and subsidies for the weak, but since the resources for the maintenance of the system in each case are drawn from the social system and the political system of itself produces nothing, the maintenance of the political system in its existing form is only possible for so long as sufficient groups within the society have an expectation of getting something out of it.

In Table 1.1 the symbols P and F refer to inputs to and outputs from the political system respectively; Q and E to inputs to and outputs from the social system with which it is conterminous. The symbols + and − (read 'positive' and 'negative') identify the direction of flow (Calvert 1969).

The principle of economy of effort – that an organism or organisation will generally try to make the minimum response required to meet a situation – goes right to the heart of the system, however. Thus though all governments owe their origins at some time, and their continued maintenance ultimately, to their faculty of coercion, they do not choose to operate in the coercive mode for most purposes because it involves a disproportionate drain on their resources and weakens them for their ultimate task, their own defence against an external attack or natural disaster. What happens when they do will be the subject of Chapter 9.

Basically, however, a government depends on force in the way that banks depend on their reserves. When a customer deposits money in a bank it is not simply placed in a numbered envelope in the vault; most of it is lent out again and only a small proportion retained. If there were to be a 'run on the bank' the bank would have to send out for more cash or risk a serious crisis of confidence. Governments, therefore, insist on banks keeping enough money in their reserves to be able to meet any but the worst crises, and even they can be surmounted if the reserves of the central bank are brought into play. In the same way, no government has anything like enough force at its disposal to subdue all its citizens if they all rise in revolt simultaneously. But since they rarely, if ever, do so, governments can continue to operate for very long periods of time with very small reserves of support, and the longer they have operated, the greater the confidence that they will continue to do so, and the greater the degree of actual positive popular support on which they can count.

Popular support will be maximised if, in addition, the government can be seen to be doing visibly useful things for its citizens. However, to do so requires a great deal of money, and in consequence the first task of government is to extract from the society it governs the resources it requires not only for its own maintenance but for its chosen programme. The principal way in which this is done is by taxation, which in the modern state has almost completely superseded the system of individual fees and charges for specific services which earlier governments used (for a more detailed treatment of the economic bases of politics and the role of taxation see Chapter 5). Taxes are not paid voluntarily; they are extracted from citizens more or less painlessly with the aid of a series of bargains to supply remedies for specific demands which the citizens or their representatives present, but they are extracted nevertheless, and the first task of a successful government is to maintain the function of power resource extraction. The art of taxation, as Jean-Baptiste Colbert, Louis XIV's finance minister, put it, is 'to pluck the goose so as to get the maximum number of feathers with the minimum amount of hissing'.

Given adequate resources, the government can then embark on a strategy of maximising supports and minimising demands in which its use of positive and negative outputs is very keenly attuned to the needs of the situation. A government which in this way is keenly aware of the desires of its citizens is commonly called a *democracy*; one that does not is loosely termed a *dictatorship*, particularly if coercion is used to limit demands upon the system. The problems of classifying systems, however, will be dealt with further in Chapter 2.

The Game of Politics

Whatever type of political system it is, it will be bound by rules. These rules (which may or may not be formally enshrined in a constitution, laws, etc.) are the rules of a game, the game of politics. The game is a complex one, for it consists of competition within the state boundaries for access to each of the principal resources. Part of the complexity stems from the nature of the resources themselves, for it is necessary to point out straight away that the first has a unique property – that people are divided into two groups each in competition for the other. From a male point of view, women are resources, but they are also players; and to women, men are not only players, they are also resources, though men may find it beneath their dignity to think so. The value of women as resources to men is the key reason, in Marxist feminist theory, for the establishment and maintenance of patriarchy through the legitimation of force.

A second complication arises from the fact that the various resources may be traded off between players, not according to their 'intrinsic' value, but according to the saliency of the need for each felt by the players in question, in each of the series of transactions of which the game of politics consists. Since the game of politics lasts a very long time – much longer than any human lifetime in fact – there develops a very complex awareness of the network of bargains and consequent relationships involved which acts as the fundamental underpinning of all other human relationships within society.

And why does the game take so long? It is tempting to answer: because without it life cannot go on, or the species be reproduced – but that seems too great an oversimplification. In pre-modern times there seems little evidence that people had to participate in politics simply in order to live. This is not to say that politics did not intrude itself upon them, and more frequently as time went on, but simply that unless one lived in a city there seems to have been little need, simply to earn one's livelihood, to take part in politics at all. Nor, for the reproduction of the species to have been quite effective over a space of more than 100,000 years, was it necessary, it seems, for mankind to develop settled communities. One is forced back to the explanation that people take part in politics not because it is essential to them, but because they like it; that, in short, it enables them to *structure time*. Human beings are a long-lived species (among animals only the blue whale lives longer, if human beings let it), and even the older amongst us have already forgotten how hard we had to work to structure time before television was invented.

For politics is not just a game, it is the ultimate game: a game played with real people and real things. Consequently, as Bailey points out, its rules are different in nature from other games in that you as a player have three options about how to treat them. You may play according to the rules and seek to win that way. You may seek to bend the rules in your favour, or even to break them when others are not looking, for there is no umpire to tell you that you cannot. Or, you can work to change the rules, so that you can make the game more congenial (Bailey 1969, pp. 32–3).

| Case Study | House Arrest in Style for the Playboy President |

It was one of those days that define a nation's history. Carlos Menem – Argentina's president from 1989 to 1999 and the current head of the opposition Peronist party – was under arrest, accused of illegal arms sales during his first term in office.

In theory, it should have come as no surprise. Following a six-year investigation into the clandestine weapons shipments to Ecuador and Croatia, Judge Jorge Urso had arrested two of his former aides and the former army chief. Newspapers had speculated for days that Mr Menem's detention was a possibility, and the judge appeared in unforgiving mood, denying Mr Menem's request to travel abroad on honeymoon.

But Argentines inured by decades of official impunity were convinced that the wily Mr Menem would find a way out of this jam as he has so many times before.

As disbelief began to fade, many Argentines began to feel a sense of pride in what they saw as a sign of the growing maturity of their democracy. Despite the efforts of some demonstrators, the only havoc was caused by the gangs of paparazzi besieging the former president.

The biggest surprise was that Mr Menem could be arrested and things continue to function normally.

Mr Menem had long sought to tie the country's fate to his own. As the case against him moved forward, he sought to remind the country of his influence, telling Argentines to buy dollars because a devaluation was around the corner.

Once upon a time, such a warning at such a sensitive economic juncture could have brought the country to its knees. This time, it merely brought him condemnation from all parts of the political spectrum.

In fact, what was surprising was just how little support Mr Menem could garner.

The judge now has just over a week left to decide whether to charge Mr Menem formally with masterminding the illegal arms sales to Croatia and Ecuador.

Following that, there could be a lengthy trial and several appeals. Even if acquitted of the charges, analysts say he could spend up to three years under arrest. If convicted, the president could face a sentence of five to 10 years.

In the end, Argentines were left to ponder the strange trajectory of a complex and remarkable man. During his 10 years in office, Mr Menem profoundly transformed the country, selling off state enterprises, ending hyperinflation and restoring civilian control over the military.

His election in 1989 had horrified sophisticated residents of Buenos Aires, who watched him stride into the capital wearing a poncho, giant white sideburns and flares. But over the years, he titillated as well as embarrassed a society obsessed with celebrity.

Few other presidents have so obviously enjoyed the trappings of power. He had a new private motorway closed down for several hours so that he might test out the top speed of a red Ferrari donated by Italian businessmen. When reporters questioned him about it, he roared off shouting, 'It's mine, mine, mine!'

He was a famous womaniser. He threw his wife out of the presidential residence in front of gathered television cameras. He suspended state engagements for visiting supermodels. He made even Madonna blush as she met him to get permission to film in the presidential palace.

But Madonna was not the only beneficiary of his hospitality. During his two terms in office, Mr Menem received a long line of celebrities, pop stars and sporting heroes including Princess Diana, Claudia Schiffer, Michael Jackson, Diego Maradona, Pele and the Rolling Stones.

Even under arrest, he should not be too lonely. Under Argentine law, people over 70 years of age can serve out their sentences under house arrest. And Mr Menem's new prison must be among the most luxurious in the world: a beautiful colonial-style home on the outskirts of Buenos Aires set in 5,600 square metres of lush green. For his first evening in captivity, Mr Menem had dozens of visitors to dinner with his wife of two weeks, a Chilean former Miss Universe half his age.

Source: *Financial Times*, 9 June 2001

North America

THE UNITED STATES OF AMERICA

Official name: The United States of America
Aka: America, the United States, the USA
Type of government: Federal presidential republic
Capital: Washington, DC
Area: 9,372,614 sq km
Population (2000): 271,645,000
GNP per capita (2000): $29,340

Evolution of government: Representative government established in British North American colonies after 1689. Following long period of neglect, attempts to tax led to revolution and successful secession of colonies (1783) under loose confederation. Need for stronger central government and unified currency and economic system led to new Constitution (1787) and establishment of federal republic led by George Washington (1789).

Main features of government: First written Constitution with 'dual federalism', a sharp division of powers between federal and state governments, and a separation of powers with checks and balances (Chapter 2). Type example of presidential republic with president both head of state and head of government and key to decision-making (Chapters 2 and 8). Two-party structure supported by single-member single-ballot electoral system and indirect election of president (Chapter 7). Party structure loose and decentralised and divided control brought 'gridlock' in 1990s. Congress powerfully transformative (Chapter 8). Supreme Court has power to interpret Constitution including the power in specific cases to overturn Congressional acts (Chapter 2). Powerful independent media (Chapter 3). Because of its superpower status, the USA since 1947 has given unusual prominence to intelligence agencies (Chapter 10).

CANADA

Official name: The Dominion of Canada
Type of government: Federal parliamentary monarchy
Capital: Ottawa
Area: 9,970,610 sq km
Population (2000): 31,000,000
GNP per capita (2000): $19,290 (PPP* $21,860)

Evolution of government: French colony of Quebec conquered by Britain 1759; linked with Ontario under British rule after 1783 but subject to border threats from USA. Fear of American conquest triggered Confederation in 1867 (Chapter 1) establishing new pattern of full internal self-government within the British Empire. Canadian Pacific Railway finally linked Maritime Provinces to Pacific province of British Colombia. Almost all of the population live within 100 miles (160 km) of the US border. Independent since 1931.

Main features of government: Monarchy not an issue: Canadian-born governor-general represents queen of Canada. Two-party system; single-member single-ballot system gives strong swings with volatile electorate (Chapter 7). Considerable tension between provinces; special problem of Quebec separatism. Federal government with extensive responsibilities for vast Arctic region.

* Purchasing Power Parity (PPP) is a method of comparing monetary values on the basis of what they can buy, as opposed to the existing exchange rate between the currencies concerned.

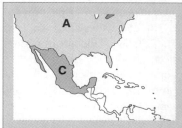

MEXICO

Official name: The United Mexican States
Type of government: Federal presidential republic
Capital: México, DF
Area: 1,958,000 sq km
Population (2000): 97,000,000
GNP per capita (2000): $3,970 (PPP $8,190)

Evolution of government: Core of present state dominated by Aztecs before arrival of Spaniards 1519. Struggle for independence began 1810, effective 1821, federal presidential republic established 1824. In nineteenth-century wars lost half its national teritory to the United States; the long dictatorship of Porfirio Díaz (1877–80, 1884–1911) introduced economic liberalism but demands for political reform triggered agrarian and labour unrest. The Mexican Revolution of 1910 (Chapter 11) was followed by far-reaching social reform and single-party dominance 1929–2000 (Chapter 6).

Main features of government: Constitution of 1917 established important social rights in programmatic form (Chapter 2). Single-member single-ballot system modified to give proportional representation to opposition parties (Chapter 7). Strong presidency increasingly restrained by bureaucratic immobility (Chapter 8) under long period of one-party dominance. Weak legal system. Thirty-two states with a common constitution each have elective governor and state legislature, contention for which paved way for breakdown of one-party rule.

Comparison

The basic unit of study in comparative politics, then, is the state or political system. There are quite a number of them – 189 are currently (2001) members of the United Nations. However, politicians are seldom consistent for long and three anomalies exist: some long-established states (Monaco, San Marino) are not members of the United Nations (UN), one territory (Palestine) is recognised by the UN as a state but does not yet have autonomy, and some territories (Taiwan, Western Sahara) are not members of the UN because they have been unable to gain international recognition as states. On a more practical level, more than 200 entities were represented at the Olympic Games in Sydney, Australia, in 2000. This number is in theory quite large enough for meaningful analysis in statistical terms. However, the universe of states is not a random sample. By a **random sample** we mean a sample of a population (of persons, things, etc.) which we wish to study, selected by a method which eliminates human choice (as by the use of a table of random numbers) in such a manner as to render the sample statistically representative of the whole. The members of the world community in fact differ drastically in all kinds of most obvious ways.

At one end of the scale there is the gigantic Russian Federation (Rossiskaya Federatsiya). It stretches across eleven time zones, and covers 17,075,000 sq km, or one-eighth of the world's land surface. In 1999, it was estimated to have a population of 147 million. At the other end of the scale is the smallest UN member state, the Pacific island of Nauru, with a population of 9,460 (1999 est.) on an area of 21.3 sq km (2,130 hectares), most of it bare jagged coral (*Statesman's Yearbook*, 2000). Clearly any comparison between Russia on the one hand and Nauru on the other must be almost meaningless, even if the formal legal status of each is the same. The disparities are, in fact, so great that a small handful of cases – the United States, the Russian Federation, China, Japan and India, for example – invalidate the generalisations about the rest.

Hence, having first defined the unit for study, the second general principle of comparison is to ensure that as many variables are held in common as possible. One could compare, for example, the United States and the former Soviet Union, and it soon becomes clear why the former has survived and the latter has not. Britain (area 241,705 sq km, population 59 million (1999 est.)) is comparable with France (area 543,965 sq km, population 59 million (1999 est.)) because they are, by world standards, very similar in population and basic levels of development, located in the same temperate region of the world, have many similar geographical features, share a common historical tradition, exhibit rather similar economic and social structures and have banded themselves together in an association called the European Union (EU). There are many interesting generalisations that can be made about all Western European states, both big and small, for similar reasons (Gallagher, Laver and Mair 1992). But there can be considerable problems in trying to make comparisons between widely separated states even where they have some obvious similarities: between, say, France and Thailand (area 513,115 sq km, population 61 million (1999 est.)), or Ireland (area 68,895 sq km, population 4 million (1999 est.)) and Sri Lanka (area 65,610 sq km, population 19 millions (1999 est.)).

Political scientists, therefore, have suggested a number of possible strategies or approaches to the general problems of comparison, and one of these may well have advantages over all the others in considering any given problem.

1. **Whole unit approach**. The examples given so far are of a whole unit approach. Their authors try, more or less successfully depending on the space available, to compare all relevant structures in two or more modern states that have important aspects in common. However, when comparing more than two countries at a time (pair-wise comparison), the whole unit approach generates so much information that handling it can be very troublesome.

2. **Competing power centres approach**. Other writers have borrowed from anthropologists the technique of comparing different societies known as the competing power centres approach. This involves, for politics, identifying centres of political power in given societies, and finding out with whom they compete and for what. Certain patterns recur again and again, the best known of which is generally known as the conflict between the **core** and the **periphery** (Galtung 1971; see also Clapham 1985; Migdal 1988). Here the term 'core' refers to the region in which both political and economic power are concentrated. Conflict between core and periphery is a basic pattern operating both between states and within states.

In the latter case it commences whenever political unification takes place, whether this is by the voluntary linking of states in alliance or confederation, the federation of states of common heritage, or the conquest of imperial possessions by a colonising power. Generally speaking, the stronger the resistance put up by the periphery to the pretensions of the central authority, the weaker the structure of the whole. Hence, by examining more closely the nature of the competing centres, greater insight can be gained into the special conditions that gave rise to federalism in the United States or Germany, as opposed to its abandonment in Colombia or Venezuela, federalism being, in fact, a very special case of a stalemate in the conflict between centre and periphery. In Switzerland the balance between core and periphery is weighted much more decisively in favour of the periphery, while in the European Union the bulk of the strength of the institution continues to reside with the periphery and the core has only very limited powers for specific purposes. There is, for example, no *general* power of the Union to intervene in individual planning disputes, and provided that the state concerned has conformed to the specific requirements of the treaty, it can otherwise do what it likes. Consequently the Union cannot as yet be regarded as a state in its own right.

Alternatively cross-national studies of specific problem areas not only further the explanation of the problems in question but also illuminate general understanding of the nature of politics. The most striking example of this has been the impact of feminism, as a result of the better understanding of the position of women in different societies (see, for example, Norris 1987).

3. **Local community approach**. Another level again is the local community approach. In this, reasonably sized areas defined as forming communities with some sort of individual coherence are compared across national boundaries. Valen and Rokkan used this technique to identify differences in size, scale, potential for political organisation, specialisation, etc., which have obvious implications for the comparison of the countries concerned (Valen and Rokkan 1974, p. 315). Studies of towns in different countries have been made for various purposes, usually by geographers or town-planners, and these too can contribute much to the understanding of comparative politics (see, for example, Goetz and Clarke 1993). An obvious weakness, however, is the very different organisation, powers and capabilities of units in different countries.

In this book, examples will be drawn from a wide range of states world-wide, as seems most appropriate. However, for the convenience of users, four groups of states

Table 1.2 Selected states, basic data, 1997

Country	Area (sq km)	Population
Argentina	2,766,890	36,000,000
Australia	7,687,000	19,000,000
Bangladesh	144,000	126,000,000
Brazil	8,512,000	165,000,000
Canada	9,970,610	31,000,000
China	9,600,000	1,248,100,000
France	544,000	59,000,000
Germany	357,000	82,200,000
Ghana	240,000	18,000,000
India	3,387,000	980,000,000
Ireland	70,280	3,750,000
Italy	310,000	57,500,000
Japan	378,000	126,000,000
Mexico	1,958,000	97,000,000
Nigeria	924,000	121,000,000
Pakistan	804,000	130,600,000
Russian Federation	17,075,000	146,000,000
Sierra Leone	72,000	5,000,000
Spain	505,000	40,200,000
Sri Lanka	64,500	19,000,000
United Kingdom	244,100	59,000,000
United States	9,372,614	271,645,000

Source: World Bank 2001

will receive particular attention. Although they include some of the world's best-known countries, they differ quite considerably in size, population and resources (see Table 1.2):

- the USA, the type example both of a presidential system and of a federal state, and large states such as Canada, Mexico, Argentina, Brazil and Australia which adopted some or all of the features associated with presidentialism or federalism;

- the UK, France, Germany, Spain, Italy and Ireland, as parliamentary systems and fellow-members of the EU;
- Russia and the former communist states of East-Central Europe now seeking entry to the EU;
- Nigeria, Ghana and Sierra Leone in West Africa and India, Pakistan, Bangladesh and Sri Lanka in South Asia as former colonies and representatives of the states of the South or 'Third World' (see page 73).

Themes

Three themes run throughout this book. They are the forces shaping political systems today: liberalisation, globalisation and democratisation, which will be discussed in greater detail in Chapter 3.

Liberalisation refers to two different concepts, which are not necessarily related to one another. In politics it refers to a loosening of control over demands made on the political system, and thus extending the range of rights and freedoms available to the citizen, such as may precede successful attempts at democratisation. In economics, which is the main sense in which it is used here, it refers to the idea that governments should not play an active role in economic matters. Their task, many now accept, is merely to set the scene for the free operation of the market. The privatisation of public corporations and the deregulation of economic activity both come under this heading. The purpose of liberalisation is, its proponents argue, to promote economic development (see Chapter 5).

Globalisation is the 'intensification of world-wide social relations which link distant locations in such a way that local happenings are shaped by events happening many miles away and vice versa' (Giddens 1990, p. 64). In other words, the process of globalisation entails a decline in the degree to which geography, or physical location, limits what can happen in any given part of the world. There is widespread agreement that it is happening; there is less certainty, however, about whether what is happening is important and precisely how and where it is happening. It results from the spread of the global economic system originally created by and now sustained by the advanced industrial countries and is most evident in the world-wide marketing of products such as soft drinks, hamburgers, clothes, trainers and CDs. Among its consequences are claimed to be: a greater integration of peoples, the phenomenon of the 'shrinking world', the blurring and even disappearance of boundaries, and the rise of technocracy (rule by those possessing certain skills). Whether it promotes economic development is disputed (Held 2000).

Democratisation refers to the spread and consolidation of democracy in the Third World and the countries of the former Soviet bloc. Huntington dates the beginning of what he terms the 'third wave' of democratisation to 1974 (Huntington 1993a, b). In the narrow sense this means establishing certain procedural requirements (e.g. free and fair elections, a government responsive to the popular will). In the wider sense it refers to the process of establishing a 'civil society' characterised by active participation in politics by the widest possible number of people.

Finally, it is, of course, quite legitimate to study any one country or any one aspect of politics on its own, in the hope that one's findings may be interesting in themselves. It is a sobering fact that at least a third, and probably over half of all published work in 'comparative' politics is still of this kind (Mayer 1989). But such studies will be much more valuable if they are done in the awareness that there is value to others in recording results in a form that will make later comparison easier. There is also an advantage to oneself in using knowledge of other countries to formulate a wider range of questions to ask of the data. There is no advantage to anyone, however, in piling up so much material that no one handling it can do anything useful with it, or, on the other hand, spending so much time deciding on how to start that a potentially fascinating journey never begins.

The Utility of Comparative Politics

Why then should we study comparative politics? For this reason: in a world of nation-states, anyone who may at any time, for any reason, seek to venture outside their own

South America

ARGENTINA

Official name: The Argentine Republic
Type of government: Federal presidential republic
Capital: Buenos Aires
Area: 2,766,890 sq km
Population (2000): 36,000,000
GNP per capita (2000): $8,970 (PPP $10,200)

Evolution of government: Spanish settlement began 1536 but present territory was never fully settled; autonomy proclaimed by Buenos Aires 1810 and independence for greater part of former Spanish viceroyalty 1816. Civil wars between Buenos Aires and interior temporarily arrested by dictatorship of Juan Manuel de Rosas (1835–53). At fall of Rosas, federal presidential regime established but tension between Buenos Aires and interior ended only in 1870s with federalisation of capital. Boosted by immigration, spectacular economic growth under oligarchical regime 1876–1930 when armed forces stepped in. Politics since 1943 dominated by attitudes towards personalist regime of Juan Domingo Perón (1946–55) culminating in return of Perón and outbreak of serious unrest. Thousands died under military-led 'Process of National Reorganization' 1976–82 when armed forces defeated in war for the Falklands/Malvinas and return to civilian rule 1983.

Main features of government: Constitution of 1853 survives substantially unaltered. Peronists have remained party with the majority tendency; elections by d'Hondt system (Chapter 7) produce relatively few parties and stable coalitions in Congress, which remains essentially an arena (Chapter 8). Weak judiciary subject to executive interference. President Menem (1989–99) made extensive use of decree powers (Chapter 9) to bypass Congress and impose his will on provinces but handed on a major economic crisis to his successor (Chapter 5).

BRAZIL

Official name: The Federative Republic of Brazil
Type of government: Federal presidential republic
Capital: Brasília
Area: 8,512,000
Population (2000): 165,000,000
GNP per capita (2000): $4,570 (PPP $6,160)

Evolution of government: Coastal Brazil settled by Portuguese from 1500; independence 1822 as Empire ruled by heir to Portuguese throne. Abolition of slavery triggered military revolt and fall of Empire 1889, when federal parliamentary republic established. Military revolt in 1930 paved way for fascistic 'New State' under Getúlio Vargas in 1930s, but Brazil's participation in the Second World War aroused armed forces to country's weakness and in 1964 the armed forces seized power and established a military developmentalist regime (Chapter 10) led by a 'modernising oligarchy' (Chapter 2). After a long period of 'decompression' elections were conceded and civilian rule restored in 1985.

Main features of government: Executive presidency with extensive powers. A highly fragmented multi-party system results in shifting coalitions in the highly transformative Congress (Chapter 8), which can and do frustrate executive initiatives. History of rapid economic growth accompanied by persistent inflation; economic liberalisation measures under the 'Washington Consensus' (Chapter 5) have failed to stabilise the economy but led to an increasingly wide gap between rich and poor.

country, whether to do business, to travel or to go on holiday, will benefit from a better understanding of the very considerable variety of state systems of which the modern international world is still composed. But it is no less important in broadening the general standard of civic understanding, and so enabling the citizen to play a more informed, and hence more effective part in public debate.

Comparative politics is concerned with identifying both similarities and differences. Above all, it teaches to do so *in a systematic way*. And it is this that demonstrates just how much the political scientist can help the practitioner of politics, the politician.

Like many other professionals, politicians over the years develop abilities to size up and guide a situation. These abilities, which, as noted above, are generally self-taught, are often of a high order, but they are not without their faults. Apart from those errors which creep in unconsciously over the years, as they grow tired or careless, politicians have a specific limitation to their knowledge in that they are trained to think in adversarial terms, and a general limitation that the deeper their knowledge is in their chosen field, the less adequate their knowledge will be in others. These other fields political scientists have the freedom to explore, and in other countries or in other times they can seek out and examine patterns of behaviour generally rare or unknown in the politician's society, but ones with which – in changed circumstances – the politician may some day have to deal.

And political scientists, while they cannot answer all the questions a politician might wish to put to them, can answer, or help to answer, some very useful questions.

- How can we choose a leader who will have the support of most of the people?
- Will the next elections give the right result? Can we make sure they do?
- How can we decide a difficult political issue and avoid responsibility for the outcome?
- Why do other people seem to get all the money? How can I get my hands on some?
- Can formerly hostile groups live alongside one another in close proximity?

These are only a few of the questions the comparative study of politics helps to answer. It is obvious how practical they are.

Summary

Politics is concerned with the making of decisions in society and an understanding of political processes is essential to all else that happens. We study it comparatively because observation alone will not tell us much and we cannot use the experimental method.

As with other disciplines, we need to define key concepts before we can set to work to build up a systematic body of knowledge capable of enabling us to make predictive statements. However, owing to the complexity of social processes at best these statements will be probabilistic, i.e. they can tell us whether or not there is a high probability that certain consequences will follow but they cannot say that they definitiely will.

The subject matter is the same but different understandings of how politics works mean that there are several different approaches to the subject. This text takes a modified functionalist approach. To ensure continuity and compatibility it is organised around three themes characteristic of the politics of the first years of the twenty-first century. These themes are liberalisation, globalisation and democratisation.

Key Concepts

authority, to have the right to do something or to instruct others to do something

'core', the region in which both political and economic power are concentrated

democratisation, the spread and consolidation of democracy in the Third World and the countries of the former Soviet bloc

dependent variable, the change to be explained

globalisation, the 'intensification of worldwide social relations which link distant locations in such a way that local happenings are shaped by events happening many miles away and vice versa' (Giddens 1990, p. 64)

government, an organisation which has established a successful claim to have the legitimate monopoly of the use of force

independent variable, a change believed to explain changes in the dependent variable

intergovernmental organisations, organisations created by agreement among states which can act only with the agreement of all member states

international organisations (IOs), supranational or intergovernmental organisations created for specific purposes by agreement between states

international relations, the study of relations between states

Key Concepts continued

legitimacy, the fact that a government is generally recognised to have the right to do what it does

liberalisation, in the political sense, loosening of control over political demands; in the economic sense, attempts to ensure that governments play a minimal role in economic matters

nation, people identified by the sense of possession of a common language, religion, culture or ethnic origin

nationalism, the belief that groups termed nations, supposedly distinguished by language, religion or culture, exist and should be organised as independent states; inclusion of those who share perceived common traits and those who do not

non-governmental organisations (NGOs), organisations having an existence independent of government

periphery, areas outside the region in which political and economic power are concentrated, and subject to exploitation by it

political science, the study of politics

politicians, people who take an active role in politics

politics, the making of decisions in society

power, in politics, the ability to get others to do what you want

random sample, a sample of a population (of persons, things, etc.) selected by a method which eliminates human choice (as by the use of a table of random numbers) in such a manner as to render the sample representative of the whole

sovereignty, the belief that states are in every sense quite distinct and separate from one another, treating with one another as equals, and owing no duty to any outside earthly authority

state, the organised community within which a government claims obedience as of right of all citizens

supranational organisations, organisations created by agreement between states which can take decisions which are binding on a member state even if the state or states concerned oppose the decision

Sample Questions

The purpose of these questions is to give readers some idea of the sort of questions they might be asked in an examination. Inevitably this assumes that they will undertake supplementary reading and especially items recommended in the lists attached at the end of each chapter.

Candidates should expect questions on a comparative politics paper to be explicitly comparative. If a question names a specific country, they can expect the question to be designed to test their knowledge of a specific problem area. In all cases, however, they should expect to *compare* and *contrast* two or more political systems (or types of political systems) in such a way that they demonstrate awareness of the wider issues involved. They will also get credit for showing an understanding of current events relevant to the question. They should therefore also choose one or more countries or areas on which to focus special attention and read a good newspaper regularly, daily if possible.

Candidates should be careful to note whether the syllabus allows them to draw upon examples from countries outside the list of those specified for more detailed study, though as ever the examples would have to be relevant to the topic under discussion.

Some possible topics for examination questions on this chapter would be:

- What is the comparative method, and how can we apply it to the study of politics?
- Can the study of comparative politics be 'scientific'?
- What are the differences between government, state and nation?
- How far can a typology of political systems contribute to our understanding of them?

Further Reading

An excellent general introduction to politics is A. Heywood (1997). On the definition and scope of politics, see also Arendt (1958), Runciman (1963), Crick (1964) and Leftwich (1984), among many others. Dogan and Pelassy (1984) give a crisp and interesting overview of the comparative method at work. An advanced treatment of the various approaches to comparative politics can be found in Lichbach and Zuckerman (1997).

The functionalist approach is dealt with by Almond and Powell (1996) and used in a different way as the basis of analysis in Almond *et al.* (2000). Alternative approaches incorporating some of its insights are used by Lane and Ersson (1991) and B.G. Peters (1999). Sartori (1970) reminds us of the necessity for accurate identification of concepts. On the differences between state and nation see Seton-Watson (1977).

Methodology and research design in the social sciences generally are dealt with in Allan and Skinner (1991), Landman (2000) and Marsh and Stoker (1995); see also Ragin (1996). The student should be encouraged from the beginning to seek and find the most up-to-date data available. The most comprehensive ready reference, published annually, is the *Statesman's Year Book*, used above. Both the United Nations and other UN organisations such as UNESCO publish regular yearbooks or similar compilations of statistics on a comparative basis. Unfortunately, however, not all countries publish their own statistical yearbooks, such as the *Annual Abstract of Statistics* in the United Kingdom, and many countries fail to report important data even to the UN, for example unemployment figures or the national rate of homicide. It is also absolutely crucial for the would-be student to show an awareness of current developments, which can all too easily take people by surprise. So there is a need to read at least one serious newspaper on a regular basis and follow current news stories on television and radio. Remember that the internet gives easy access to current newspapers across the world so that you can and should if possible follow up a story on elections in Chile in *El Mercurio* or on atmospheric pollution in Malaysia in the *Straits Times*.

Studies of individual countries and regions form an essential basis for any comparative study and the reader will find any or all of the following useful.

On the United States see McKay (1997) and Bowles (1998). On Latin America generally, see Calvert and Calvert (1994). On Mexico see Needler (1990).

On Europe generally, see Lane and Ersson (1991), Gallagher, Laver and Mair (1992) or Gowland, O'Neill and Dunphy (2000); on the place of women in public policy see Lovenduski (1986). On the European Union see George (1991). On the UK see Coxall and Robbins (1998) and B. Jones (2000); on France see Stevens (1992), Safran (1995) and Elgie and Griggs (2000); on Germany see Larres and Panayi (1996) and Stent (2000); on Spain see P. Heywood (1999), Newton and Donaghy (1997) and Lawlor and Rigby (1998); on Italy see Gundle and Parker (1996), Koff and Koff (2000) and Newell (2000).

On post-Communist systems generally, see Dawisha (1997) and Kitschelt (1999). On East-Central Europe see Agh (1998) and White *et al.* (1990). On the former Soviet Union an extensive literature includes Conquest (1961), Hazard (1964), Hill and Frank (1983), Hough (1977), Inkeles (1968), Lane (1978) and McCauley (1993). On the former East European Communist states see Lovenduski and Woodall (1987), Ionescu (1967), Fejtö (1974) and Rubenstein (1965). On Russia see Brown (2001); on Poland see Millard (1999); on Ukraine see Kuzio (1998).

On Third World politics generally, see Calvert and Calvert (2001) and Clapham (1985). On Nigeria see Ihonvbere (1994), Aborigade and Mundt (1998) and Joseph (1987); on Ghana see Nugent (1996); on India see Gehlot (1996).

Democracy and Its Rivals

CHAPTER TWO

Learning Objectives

By the end of this chapter, the reader will be able:

- to understand the basic features of liberal democracy;

- to identify alternative forms of government and to show how these forms have been categorised and how they relate to one another;

- to clarify the differences between, for example, authoritarianism and totalitarianism;

- to develop understanding of the emergence, development and modern practice of confederation, federalism and federal government.

Liberal Democracy

The overwhelming majority of modern states claim to be 'democracies'. We call this form of democracy **liberal democracy**. On the one hand, liberal democracy is *representative*, distinguished from the older classical notion of 'direct' democracy in that, under it, citizens do not govern themselves directly but choose representatives to govern. On the other, it is *limited* – the government is restricted in what it can do. Liberal democracies are states in which government is limited in its powers by a written constitution, a system of law and/or an independent judiciary, and is responsive to the popular will as expressed through free and fair elections. Under such a government certain basic freedoms (often termed *civil rights*) will be guaranteed to the individual (Holden 1993). In the political sense, *liberalisation* means extending the range of rights and freedoms available to the citizen, and it is important to distinguish between this usage and the so-called liberalisation of an economy by removing constraints on investment and trade. *Democratisation* refers to both the process by which other forms of government evolve (or are transformed) into democracies and the process by which existing democracies become more democratic, as for example by improvements in electoral representation or the defence of civil rights.

However, democracy is an 'essentially-contested' concept, that is to say, a concept on which *by definition* agreement is not possible. Democracy is about a contest for power and the outcome of that struggle colours people's perception of it. Hence it is not possible to determine *with certainty* which states are liberal democracies and which are not. There are broadly three working possibilities.

An *inclusive* definition allows the label to all governments which call themselves democratic and can claim to have been chosen by the people. Lincoln spoke of 'government of the people, by the people, for the people' (*Gettysburg Address*, 1863) but the United States of 1863 would not be accepted as a liberal democracy today. Schmitter and Karl hold that democracy does not consist in a single specific set of institutions. 'There are many types of democracy, and their diverse practices produce a similarly varied set of effects' (Schmitter and Karl 1993, p. 40).

A *procedural* definition focuses on the way in which this process of choice is achieved. 'The democratic method is that institutional arrangement for arriving at political decisions in which individuals acquire the power to decide by means of a competitive struggle for the people's vote' (Schumpeter 1943, p. 269). It is easy enough to tell whether or not an election has been held, but it is another matter to tell whether it has been 'free and fair' (see Chapter 7). A criticism of this approach is that it can lead to low standards being applied and the acceptance of 'low intensity democracy' (Gills, Rocamora and Wilson 1993) as an adequate substitute for the real thing.

An *exclusive* definition concentrates on determining whether or not features exist that are incompatible with free popular choice: there must be no military intervention, no armed repression of the opposition or of minorities, no secret police, no limits on candidature at elections and no ballot rigging. In addition some claim that there must be a vibrant civil society/civic culture. The point is that consent in itself does not make a government democratic (Partridge 1971; Ginsburg 1982) – citizens may see no alternative to passive consent to oligarchy or dictatorship.

Schmitter and Karl warn us not to expect too much. Democracies are not necessarily more efficient economically than other forms of government, they argue. They are not necessarily more efficient administratively, either, and they are not likely 'to appear more orderly, consensual, stable, or governable than the autocracies they replace'. Lastly, 'democracies will have more open societies and polities than the autocracies they replace, but not necessarily more open economies'. What they will have, however, is a much better chance of delivering, in the end, a stable, peaceful and prosperous society (Schmitter and Karl 1993, pp. 49–51). And Diamond points out that three tensions or paradoxes are inherent in the very nature of democracy: conflict v. consensus, representativeness v. governability, consent v. effectiveness (Diamond 1993).

Those of us who live in the English-speaking world take democracy so much for granted that we easily forget just what a modern phenomenon it is. Liberal democracy originated in a much older concept of representation: the idea that it will be easier to get people to pay taxes if their representatives are asked to agree to do so first.

Representative government was achieved before it became general practice to allow all citizens to vote, displacing the older idea that only the well-to-do had a stake in society. Hence there is general agreement that the appearance of democracy is associated with a certain minimum level of economic development. Here, however, agreement ends.

Again there are broadly speaking three alternative views of the relationship between economic development and the change to democracy. Those who take the *modernisation approach* believe that at a certain stage of economic development democracy becomes possible, and that, in the words of Seymour Martin Lipset, 'the more well-to-do a nation, the greater the chances that it will sustain democracy' (Lipset 1960, pp. 49–50). The reasoning is clear: since the seventeenth century it has been recognised that sufficient economic resources to bring a certain sense of security are needed for people to take part in politics, and the better educated they are the more likely they are to be able to participate successfully. The emergence of an educated middle class has therefore been seen as a precondition for the emergence of liberal democracy.

Those who take a *structural approach* see the nature of structures of class and power as central. The accumulation of wealth gives rise to a middle class. But at a certain point in time it is the class as a whole that challenges the old elites for a share in political power, if necessary by force. Or, as Barrington Moore put it, 'no bourgeoisie, no democracy' (Moore 1969, p. 37). This would imply that liberal democracy was in practice an instrument of class rule and that its institutions function to maintain the rule of middle-class elites and to disempower ordinary citizens. A growing disenchantment with democracy seems evident in the steadily declining turnout in US elections (already very low by European standards) since the 1960s.

The *transition approach* sees the agreement to democratise less starkly, as a matter of elite choice, bargaining and negotiation, the impetus for which comes from the historical conflict over scarce resources. 'A people who are not in conflict about some rather fundamental matters would have little need to devise democracy's elaborate rules for conflict resolution' (Rustow 1970, p. 362). Again the question is: why do these conflicts arise, and how far do the mechanisms that purport to resolve them actually work to do so?

Liberal democracy is well established in Western Europe, North America, Japan and other leading countries. However, economic development is not a prerequisite for people to want democracy, as is demonstrated by the persistent reappearance of the liberal tradition in Latin America over the past century and a half, and some striking examples from South Asia, the Middle East and the Caribbean. Liberal democracy has proved adaptable and responsive to the pressures of survival in a competitive world, and with the collapse of the rival Soviet model, it currently has no effective competitor. However, this does not mean that all liberal democracies are the same.

Since the nineteenth century, it has been a widespread assumption, particularly in English-speaking countries, that stable democratic systems required a high level of social consensus. Where this was achieved, political stability was enhanced and society unified. Where it was not, there was a tendency for political order to break down and democracy to collapse. For some time it has been accepted that the key determinant of political stability is the number and nature of *social cleavages* in society (Lipset and Rokkan 1967; Rae and Taylor 1970; Lane and Ersson 1991). There are many factors dividing groups in all societies. If the dividing lines between these groups do *not* coincide with each other, competitive democratic politics can and does take place without endangering the whole structure. The problem comes when they do coincide with one another and a major split opens up, as in Belgium between the Flemings and the Walloons.

However, there are several states which are among the most democratic in Europe in which, on the contrary, a high level of agreement is obtained in divided societies. Hence special interest attaches to what is now termed **consociational democracy**, a term originally formulated by Arend Lijphart, as a result of comparative studies by political scientists from Austria, Belgium, the Netherlands and Switzerland (Lijphart 1969, 1974, 1977; Lembruch 1967; Steiner 1972, 1974).

Consociational democracy, Lijphart argued, exists in societies which are clearly and apparently permanently divided vertically into a number of communities, whether ethnic, religious or linguistic. These communities, after Dutch practice, are often referred to as 'pillars' and their division as 'pillarisation' (*verzuiling*). It is characterised by an elaborate process of *negotiation* between the elites of the different 'pillars' leading to *accommodation* and *compromise*. Four basic principles are used to diffuse and to resolve conflict:

1. **executive power-sharing**: the executive is not vested exclusively in one group; all pro-system groups are represented in the government;
2. **autonomy**: each group has a right to regulate its own affairs in certain respects;
3. **proportionality**: jobs are shared in proportion to representation in Parliament or Congress;
4. **minority veto**: the minority have a right to veto any proposal which they regard as violating their basic interests.

In fact, as Table 2.1 shows, Lijphart's argument is that it is the behaviour of the elite that makes this system possible. What is of particular interest is whether the strategy of seeking agreement is really successful, or whether its apparent success in the Netherlands was simply the necessary product of coalition government in a highly fragmented party system. It is true that it has not served to maintain a unitary state in the highly

Table 2.1 Lijphart's typology of democratic systems

	Political culture – homogeneous	Political culture – fragmented
Elite behaviour – coalescent	Depoliticised democracy	Consociational democracy
Elite behaviour – competitive	Centripetal democracy	Centrifugal democracy

Source: after Lijphart 1969

unpromising circumstances of Belgium, where ethnic, linguistic and religious cleavages between Flemings and Walloons coincide with a clear-cut geographical split. It is also true that with depillarisation in the Netherlands it seems to have come to an end (van Mierlo 1986). But it seems to have worked well both there (see Gladdish 1991) and in Austria (Gerlich 1987) over a substantial period and there is evidence that where the same strategy has been adopted in other states – Germany in Europe, Canada in the Americas, Malaysia in South-East Asia – it has achieved a much higher degree of political stability than might otherwise have been expected. Conversely its abandonment in Colombia, Cyprus, Lebanon and Nigeria has led to political instability, unrest and even civil war.

This reminds us that all states, even liberal democracies, exist in an evolutionary context and may well have diverged considerably from the ideal types they profess to represent (cf. Macpherson 1977). Moreover on many occasions in recent years rulers have argued that for reasons of national security, or otherwise, they have found it 'necessary' to suspend or dispense with any or all of the notions of individual rights, limitation of government power or the right to a fair trial.

Identifying alternative forms

From the beginning of the study of politics, observers have tried to order their ideas by the use of various systems of classification. Modern systems utilise the basic concept of participation, in conjunction with other criteria. However, political systems are in constant evolution. Static typologies are therefore of little use compared with developmental models.

Classification as a means of organising information is essential, and the first system of classification propounded for states was that used by Aristotle himself, who divided them between those ruled by the one, by the few, and by the many (Aristotle 1968, p. 113). This distinction, even though it was not developed for use on modern complex states at all, is still useful, but only in a limited sense. It appeals to the most important of popular feelings about politics, the sense of how far – if at all – the system appears to respond to one's own individual wishes. In an age when democracy is almost universally espoused as the ambition of each and every political system, it still operates as the chief criterion for determining just how far any given state or political system can be truly regarded as democratic.

But the mere number of the rulers (read decision-makers) in a modern system is not an adequate guide to the way in which the system as a whole actually operates, even assuming that the exact number could be determined. Concepts such as the few and the many are irritatingly imprecise. One of the few definite things that can be said, for example, about the 'Fourteen Families' traditionally said to control El Salvador is that intermarriage and breeding combine to make the actual number quite meaningless. For another thing, the capacity of the ultimate decision-makers is determined by their effectiveness. This depends both on the amount and accuracy of the information that reaches them, and on their capacity to implement their decisions once taken. Even 'Ramfis' Trujillo of the Dominican Republic, who in 1962 personally shot his political prisoners with a machine-gun, had in other, more complex respects to depend on others to act on his orders and so found himself forced to flee the country regardless (Diedrich 1978, p. 248).

Once a ruler depends on others, autocracy is qualified, and so, in practice, the rule of the one becomes the rule of the few. Not only must the others continue to render their services, but they may and do act in the name of the one person who bears the responsibility for all decisions of government. To understand other countries, therefore, one has to identify a set of criteria by which they can be sorted into recognisable categories.

Participation

The key concept for this purpose is the concept of **participation**. Almost all states nowadays consider that they are either democratic or aspiring to democracy. That is to say, their rulers believe that under their form of government, as far as human fallibility allows, the ultimate decisions are either taken by the people at large, or will be, as soon as they can be taught how to do it. Unhappily, there are two basic strands of thought as to what is meant by democracy. The fact that these differences involve differences of technique rather than belief makes them of as much interest to the student of comparative politics as to political philosophers, and indeed they reflect the observations by those who first formulated them of the political systems of their own day.

Both views are concerned with the process of choice by which the people select their representatives and that by which people or representatives reach decisions on specific issues. The older view, represented in ancient times by Roman practice, and in modern theory by the writings of Rousseau, see both as aspects of what Rousseau termed 'the general will' (*volonté générale* – Rousseau 1958, pp. 20, 22–30). The general will of the people is not just the will of the majority, nor even of all individual people, it is a coherent expression of the feeling of the society as a whole. It is therefore possible to say that the general will cannot be understood and interpreted by a series of individual choices, but that anyone who can perceive what the general will is can point it out and advocate its support to his or her fellows. This was the view of Robespierre and the Jacobins during the French Revolution, and it is one congenial to individuals or groups under the 'mixed' constitutions of most modern societies.

The more modern view, represented by Locke and Mill among theorists, is that all government is a process of compromise, and that the general will – if it exists – cannot be arrived at except by approximation. This approximation can be arrived at by accepting the decision of the majority in all processes of choice involving large numbers, but in the self-restraint also of that majority in tolerating the views of the minority (Locke 1956, pp. 49–50, 95–8; Mill 1958, pp. 102–3). Thus a series of shifting coalitions becomes possible on individual issues. Recent American writers, beginning with Dahl (1964a, b) and Kornhauser (1959), have increasingly emphasised the importance of keeping the process of choice essentially one of bargaining in a 'free market' of ideas.

Competitive v. non-competitive systems

Like the Jacobins, Russian and Chinese Communists believed that there could be no antagonistic conflict within their states, but have gone further in claiming that their party, as vanguard of the proletariat, was therefore the sole body able to interpret the general will correctly. A similar argument has been used by various self-appointed rulers to justify their actions as being guided by a superior form of legitimacy. Writers on these aspects of government have therefore propounded a number of schemes of ideological classification which take these facts into account. Some have chosen to focus on the location of power in the system, others on the degree to which theory is reflected in a valid attempt to replace counting heads by a system for reaching a consensus of views.

Thus Talmon distinguishes between 'representative' and 'totalitarian' democracy in his study of the conflict of the emergent ideas in the French revolutionary period (Talmon 1961), while Almond and Coleman distinguish in Asia and Africa between 'Western' systems based on the acceptance of majority decision, and 'non-Western' systems in which attempts are made to include criteria of value on the process of decision, and to promote the solidarity of turbulent states by making decisions only when they command universal assent (Almond and Coleman 1960, p. 17). Both terminologies, however, are highly unsatisfactory, and '**competitive**' and '**non-competitive**' are better.

Whatever the terminology employed, the fact is that structures of similar names perform different functions in each type of system. Thus political parties, which for some 'competitive' systems are largely concerned with articulating and aggregating interests, are for the 'non-competitive' systems primarily a means of mobilising support. 'Non-competitive' systems, abhorring overt conflict, do not allow for interest groups openly to operate as pressure groups, abolish or co-opt competing parties and predetermine the result of elections by various devices designed to monopolise political power for those favoured by the regime, often with the ideological justification that, because of their special knowledge, such matters should be the preserve of a small group or elite. But these facts are not the product of the differences in terminology; the terminology has been selected to reflect just those differences.

Participation may be either *qualitative* or *quantitative*. A football match involves twenty-two players, a polo match eight. That is a quantitative difference. But a football match may also involve the participation of a handful of spectators, if amateur, or of thousands, if professional, but the differences may have little impact on the performance of the players compared with the quantitative difference in the teams themselves if a member of one is sent off the field. And participation can be further restricted or enhanced, other than by simple, clean-cut numerical criteria. Thus the fact that a goalkeeper's function is to remain within a defined area of the field is counter-balanced by allowing him increased freedom to handle the ball, while the fact that other players have greater freedom on the field is limited by the fact that the goal is only of a certain size, and so on.

In politics the most important differences between modern states are the number of *levels* on which, and *channels* through which, participation can take place.

There are many possibilities of participation in European states short of taking part in government itself, the actual decision-making process. These include: first of all, interest in politics; secondly, voting; thirdly, political organisation – taking part in some kind of mechanism designed to influence the political process, party membership, possible candidature for the assembly, and actual choice to be a member of the government itself. These are all *levels* of participation involving greater involvement in the system and a greater say in what goes on.

But at each level, except at the top, there are a number of alternative *channels* through which participation can be effective, and include elections or referenda, interest groups, political parties and local government organs. The same is true even in such apparently unpromising instances as, for example, China under the Cultural Revolution, but there the channels included such unfamiliar devices as the wall poster, the Red Guards, and the revolutionary committees (Robinson 1969). And when one system is compared with another, what varies is not simply participation, but what is considered to be political. In other words, political participation varies with the definition of what is properly the concern of politics and what the proper way of being political is.

It is for this reason that one has to make a functional separation between one aspect of government and another, rather than a purely institutional one, because what is defined as being one thing in one country may be defined as being something quite different in another. To take the obvious case, in almost all modern countries people 'participate' in elections. But what this *means* in terms of the individual varies from country to country, depending on what the actual likely outcome of the vote is – that is, the degree to which it is connected to the rest of the political process.

Authoritarianism

It was in the age of the Cold War (1946–90) that a new term, **totalitarianism**, came into use in the West to describe a syndrome of features believed to be characteristic of both fascism in Hitler's Germany and communism in the Soviet Union, China and Eastern Europe. These states, it was thought, differed from all previous states as having both the will and the ability to exercise unlimited control over their populations (Friedrich and Brzezinski 1975) and will be discussed further in the next section. By contrast an older word, '**authoritarian**', gained a new popularity as a convenient term to designate more traditional dictatorships. The beliefs which underpinned those systems designated as 'authoritarian' systems included: belief in the transcendental importance of the principle of authority; an emphasis on the exclusive use of political power, unfettered by juridical restraint or civil liberties; and a tendency to excuse the excesses either of arbitrary decision-making or of despotic methods of political and social control.

Consequently, various writers have since 1960 sought to identify a number of criteria by which to distinguish between the two broad types of political system, democratic and authoritarian, which they see as opposites.

Thus Dahl, who began with the Aristotelian criterion as his point of departure (Dahl 1964a, p. 26), first distinguished between two broad types of political system which he termed *polyarchies* and *hierarchies*, according to criteria such as the existence of a separation of powers, the independence or otherwise of the judiciary and civil service, the existence or otherwise of competitive parties, and formally organised pressure groups with open access to the decision-makers (Dahl 1964b, pp. 84–7). Subsequently he went on to divide the categories using two criteria, *competitiveness* and *inclusiveness*, the extent to which the system encourages popular participation. The result is four categories: closed hegemonies, low on both criteria; inclusive hegemonies, high on participation but low on competition (Cuba, for example); competitive oligarchies, low on participation but high on competition; and polyarchies, with high levels both of participation and competition (Table 2.2). This generates three categories of authoritarian systems and is still widely used.

In a key study Linz defined the new authoritarian states as 'political systems with limited, not responsible, political pluralism; without elaborate and guiding ideology (but with distinctive mentalities); without intensive nor extensive political mobilization (except at some point in their development); and in which a leader (or occasionally a small group) exercises power within formally ill-defined limits but actually quite predictable ones' (Linz 1970, p. 255).

On the basis of Linz's definition it is possible to distinguish as he does between new and old authoritarian regimes. The longer established an authoritarian regime is, the less it needs to rely on the overt use of force and the more it tends to develop new forms of legitimacy. However, for Linz authoritarian government is always a transitional state,

Table 2.2 Dahl's typology of political systems

	Competitiveness low	Competitiveness high
Inclusiveness low	Closed hegemonies (hierarchies) Saudi Arabia	Competitive oligarchies Nigeria
Inclusiveness high	Inclusive hegemonies Cuba	Polyarchies France

Source: after Dahl 1964b

either towards democracy or towards totalitarianism. In his recent work with Al Stepan (Linz and Stepan 1996, pp. 42–51) they defend the concept of totalitarianism as still having meaning, while proposing a new category of 'post-totalitarianism' to designate many of the countries of the former Soviet bloc. At least one of these, Romania, is however categorised as 'sultanistic' – a term originally proposed by Max Weber to identify the most extreme form of patrimonial state.

Alternatively, Sahlin (1977) suggests, it is also useful to distinguish between protective authoritarianism and promotional authoritarianism. Protective authoritarianism is the argument of those who intervene by force simply to protect the status quo and the position of those who benefit from it. Following a traditional military coup, which has only the limited aim of displacing the existing government, a period of emergency rule normally follows in which the armed forces emphasise the power available to them, their limited ambitions in making use of it, and their intention to return the country to civilian rule as soon as possible. Some regimes of this type, for example that of Franco's Spain, do survive for a long period and, Sahlin notes, become 'old' authoritarian regimes in Linz's terms, gaining a degree of legitimacy through force of habit, and, generally, needing to depend less on the overt use of force. However, their principal aims remain the same: the de-politicisation of issues and the demobilisation of the masses.

Promotional authoritarianism, by contrast, is characterised by a desire to promote change, by supplanting the existing government and establishing one which will stay in power for a period of years to pursue certain stated aims. Chief among these aims is economic development, the desire for which is in itself rooted in a nationalistic belief in the value of a strong state. But this requires a certain degree of mobilisation of the masses in the interests of productivity. For such neo-authoritarian regimes this can most safely be achieved by appealing to nationalism. However, even this does not resolve, but only postpone, a fundamental conflict between the desire for economic mobilisation and the fear of political mobilisation. There are two possible ways in which this can be done; in each case, significantly, they involve maintaining and not jettisoning the forms of democracy.

Some authoritarian regimes are prepared to mobilise the popular sector for both political and economic purposes, and to live with the consequences. Regimes of this rare type can be classed as authoritarian populist regimes. The classic case of such a regime is to be found in Argentina under General Juan Domingo Perón (president 1946–55, 1973–74). Its success can be gauged by the fact that ever since the coup that displaced the regime in 1955, no government has long survived that did not come to terms with the Peronists. Despite his authoritarian ideology and emphasis on the role of the leader (known as 'verticalism'), Perón was constitutionally elected and re-elected, and it took several attempts for the armed forces to overthrow him (Calvert and Calvert 1989).

Other regimes have been able to achieve such a degree of economic success that their citizens are prepared to wait for democracy. It is probably not just coincidence that the so-called 'tiger' economies of East and South-East Asia – Singapore, Taiwan, South Korea, Malaysia and Thailand – are in states where for a variety of reasons and in varying degrees the governing style, and often the substance, is authoritarian. However, as we shall see later (Chapter 5), there are other explanations for their apparent success.

Oligarchy or totalitarianism?

Other writers have sought to utilise the concept of totalitarianism. The word 'totalitarian' was originally coined by Mussolini to designate a state in which the power of the state worked without hindrance and the individual citizen had no rights at all. Friedrich (1972) distinguishes totalitarian states from others, by six criteria:

1. an official ideology, to which everyone is supposed to adhere;
2. a single mass party usually led by one man, organised hierarchically;
3. monopoly of the effective use of all weapons by party and bureaucracy;
4. monopoly of the means of effective mass communication;
5. a system of terroristic police control;
6. central control and direction of the economy (Schapiro 1972, p. 18).

In the late 1960s the concept of totalitarianism came under strong attack, both from writers in Eastern Europe and from specialists on Eastern Europe. The former pointed out that the six criteria were chosen to link together three principal historical instances: Mussolini's Italy (1922–44), Hitler's Germany (1933–45) and the Soviet Union under Stalin (1928–53). They rejected this linking as propagandist, principally (though not entirely) because they saw the purpose of the Soviet Union as being entirely opposed to that of the other two instances. The 'leadership principle' was not, they argued, a basic principle of communism, but an aberration. The latter, on the other hand, had failed to find evidence that the overwhelming control claimed for the state by the proponents of the model did in fact exist in the Soviet Union at that time. They were able to identify a limited number of competing power-centres and interest groups within Soviet society (Skilling and Griffiths 1971; Hough 1976; Kelley 1976) and some even argued that a degree of **pluralism** existed (the view that the will of the individual is best served by the multiplication of competing groups – Solomon 1983). Hence they could dismiss the totalitarian model of Soviet decision-making as the product of a single authoritarian will (essentially a 'rational actor' model) in favour of a scheme which saw decisions as being the product of competing individuals and interests within government (a 'bureaucratic politics' interpretation; see Allison 1971, p. 5; Gustafson 1980; Dawisha 1980; and Chapter 8, this volume). Other Eastern European states, notably Poland and Hungary, had diverged from the model substantially on the criteria of centralised control of the economy, and acceptance of the ruling ideology (Ball and Millard 1986).

A more serious problem is presented by the difficulty of distinguishing between 'true' democracy and what Finer (1970) called '**façade democracy**': that is to say, a system that is nominally democratic, but in fact oligarchical. Where does the dominance of an elite end and **oligarchy** begin?

This problem is well illustrated by Shils's early model which formalised concepts widely used at the time in speech and in the press (Parsons and Shils 1962). He distinguished, on the one hand, the rule of the few, which he called oligarchy, from the rule of the many, democracy. He then proceeded to subdivide these types by two different criteria: what he took to be the actual effective degree to which the concept is applied, and for what purpose the government concerned advocated it.

He thus derived two types of democracy: *political democracy*, that is to say liberal democracy, such as exists in Western Europe and the United States, characterised by free elections, competitive parties, pressure groups, and so on; and *tutelary democracy*, such as was characteristic of Pakistan under Ayub Khan (1958–68), where the government holds many rights in abeyance on the pretext that the people need to be educated before being ready for political democracy. This category might include many military governments that, as in Bolivia, Ecuador, Peru and Brazil in the 1970s, promise free elections once they have ended illiteracy, taught everyone who to vote for, and given them an official party to support – but there must surely be serious doubts whether democracy is the right word for it.

And it is in fact very difficult to distinguish tutelary democracy from the first of Shils's three categories of oligarchy, which he calls *modernising oligarchy*. This is where the rulers justify their restraint on public self-assertion on the grounds that to do so will promote economic development. Naturally modernising oligarchy can be made to look attractive, particularly if judiciously contrasted with its old-fashioned counterpart, *traditional oligarchy*, where nothing is ever done because the rulers like things the way they are. Lastly, however, Shils offers a third category, that of *totalitarian oligarchy*. This is rule from the centre directed by an ideology which justifies it on the grounds that it is in the true interests of the masses and backed by a coercive apparatus which demands positive and not merely negative acceptance.

Although these three types correspond to popular ideas of differences between states – and especially to types which were fashionable in the 1950s when the scheme was outlined – the way in which the differences are drawn is not really up to the strain of actual classification. Was Brazil under General Medici (1969–74) a modernising oligarchy, as it professed to be, or a totalitarian oligarchy, as Amnesty International tended to regard it? Not only is there, it seems, no very hard-and-fast line to be drawn between democracy and oligarchy, but the divisions between the subtypes are just as uncertain. And the scheme makes no mention of perhaps the most fruitful subtype proposed: *totalitarian democracy* (Talmon 1961). The so-called people's democracies of Eastern Europe after the Second World War ruled in the name of the people, and claimed to be much more democratic than the liberal democracies, precisely because they set out to give the people what they believed they needed, not what they actually wanted. Talmon was not of course the first thinker to warn of the dangers of the dictatorship of the majority.

For unfortunately in the meantime the word 'totalitarian' continued to be widely used, and indeed still is, otherwise it would not be necessary to have this discussion here. By loosening the definition somewhat, Crick extended to eleven the number of criteria by which he distinguishes between *autocratic, totalitarian* and *republican* regimes (Crick 1973, pp. 44–81). This raised two new problems. First, extending the number of criteria makes for a very unwieldy typology, and the aim of classifying should be to make things clearer. Secondly, it does not enable us to distinguish authoritarian regimes; in fact by preferring the word 'totalitarian', it confuses the boundary between the two. And it is authoritarian regimes that we need to clarify, since even those who have employed the totalitarian model have never been able to argue that outside its specific time-frame it was worth distinguishing.

The notion of totalitarianism enjoyed a brief renaissance in the 1980s, when it was incorporated in the notorious distinction of Jeane Kirkpatrick between 'totalitarian' governments and 'moderately repressive authoritarian' governments (MRAGs). She argued that their control mechanisms were such that 'totalitarian' states could not evolve into liberal democratic states. The United States should therefore, she argued, be prepared if necessary to support 'moderately repressive authoritarian' states, such as Pinochet's Chile, rather than run the risk of allowing a state to succumb to totalitarianism (Kirkpatrick 1982). The collapse of Soviet power in Eastern Europe in 1989 and the disintegration of the Soviet Union two years later has exposed the specious assumption on which this argument was based.

Static Typologies

The problem is, however, one common to all *static typologies* of political systems (see Table 2.3). The best approach would be to return to first principles and determine a number of *clearly defined criteria* by which states can be categorised and the different labels employed by politicians and others related to one another. Blondel (1969, p. 40) has pointed out that three axes of classification could enable us to link all such criteria: a radical–conservative dimension, a democratic–monarchical dimension, and a liberal–authoritarian dimension (see Figure 2.1). The importance of this approach is that it makes us think clearly, not just why some 'cells' of a given typology are full, but why others are empty, and it will be helpful to bear in mind in what follows. For this book is based on an approach which is rather different, but is, nevertheless, based on the same imperative, to relate the universe of states to underlying processes. The problem is twofold. On the one hand, the number of possible axes of classification is potentially infinite. On the other, all classifications, however detailed, will be actively misleading in so far as they distinguish categories only at one moment of historical time. For within the universe of states order can be found only if it is understood that all static typologies

Table 2.3 Static typologies of political systems

Aristotle	Shils (1962)	Dahl (1964b)	Finer (1970)	Crick (1973)
Monarchy Tyranny			Dynastic state	Totalitarian
Aristocracy Oligarchy	Modernising oligarchy Traditional oligarchy Totalitarian oligarchy	Hierarchy	Military regime Façade democracy Quasi democracy Totalitarian regime	Autocratic
Polity Democracy	Political democracy Tutelary democracy	Polyarchy	Liberal democracy	Republican

Dimensions of ideology

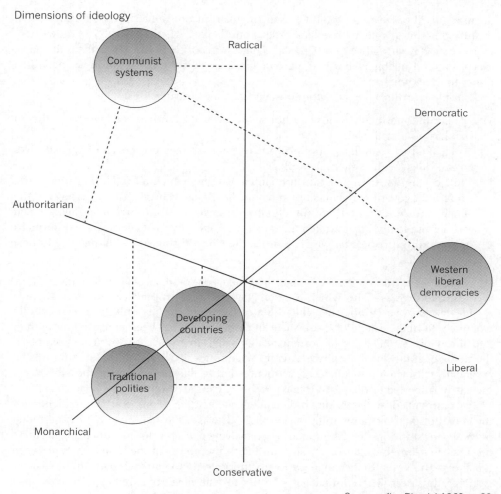

Source: after Blondel 1969, p. 39

Figure 2.1 Blondel's three dimensions of classification

are only 'snapshots' of an evolving pattern, and that the confusion stems from the conflict of two principles:

1. Each political system has some freedom to evolve according to its own internal political dynamics.
2. All political systems have been shaped by the influence of two successive periods of political evolution which have occurred in the last 200 years, each of which has altered (in ways that are not wholly compatible) prevailing ideas about the relationship of the individual to the state.

Constitutions

Since 1787, it has been customary to draw up a written document called a Constitution which provides the ground rules for the operation of the political system. Here such a document will be given a capital C, to distinguish it from the term constitution which is still sometimes used to refer to these ground rules whether written or unwritten. However, today virtually all modern states have Constitutions (the UK is the only major exception, and in this case it is more correct to say that the constitution is uncodified rather than unwritten).

Four basic features are to be found in virtually all Constitutions:

1. A **preamble**, stating on whose authority the Constitution has been written – this in itself has no legal force.
2. The **text**, which establishes political institutions, assigns powers to them and gives ground rules for the system to work.
3. A **Bill of Rights**, stating certain fundamental rights which all individuals have and listing what governments may not constitutionally do to breach them. (However, the French Constitution of 1958 initially did not have constitutional guarantees, which were subsequently incorporated from its predecessor by the Conseil Constitutionel.)
4. An **amending procedure**, which enables the Constitution to be changed to fit new circumstances.

Lawyers have in the past distinguished between rigid and flexible constitutions according to the ease with which they can be amended. In practice, however, there is a wide range of variation. The United States Constitution has only been successfully amended 26 times since 1787; the Mexican Constitution has been amended more than 330 times since 1917. The important thing is that amendment should be possible – the first Constitution of a united Italy, the Piedmontese *Statuto* of 1859, could not be amended, with the unfortunate consequence that Italian politicians of the Liberal era increasingly tended to disregard it, paving the way for Mussolini.

Governments of states gaining independence after 1945 soon became impatient with the constitutional restraints imposed on them. It was not long, therefore, before many of these Constitutions were scrapped or extensively rewritten to introduce an executive presidency, formalise a one-party state and curb the power of the judiciary. Experience has shown, however, that changing a Constitution to try to entrench partisan provisions is a risky business. The temptation is strong for the next government to write a new Constitution, thus inaugurating an era of *faction constitutionalism* such as plagued Latin America during the nineteenth century – Venezuela, the most striking example, has now (2001) had 23 Constitutions. There is also a strong temptation to incorporate *programmatic provisions* which deal not just with what the form of government should be but also with what it should do. These are to be found in both the Italian Constitution of 1947 and the German Basic Law of 1949 but the classic example is the Mexican Constitution of 1917, which contains the basis for the later land reform programme (Article 27) and Labour Code (Article 123) and even a provision empowering the president to expel any foreigner from the country whose presence he finds inconvenient (Article 33).

Two other features of Constitutions have a continuing relevance. These are the **separation of powers** and *checks and balances*. Because both are well-known features of the US Constitution, it is particularly interesting to see how they may turn up in a very different form elsewhere.

The differentiation between the **executive** and the **legislative** 'powers' was first formulated by Locke, but it was Montesquieu who in his visit to Britain in 1739 popularised the notion by describing it as a basic principle of British liberties (Montesquieu 1966). The framers of the American Constitution in making it the basis of their document

Case Study Court Rules on Land Control

The US supreme court yesterday curtailed the power of the federal government to regulate local land and water use, in a decision closely watched by business groups and environmentalists. The court split 5–4 along lines which have become familiar in its battle over the balance of power between the federal government and the states.

The court found the federal government, under the landmark Clean Water Act, did not have the power to prevent a group of Chicago localities from building a landfill on seasonal ponds used by migrating birds. But it stopped well short of a broader challenge to the authority of Congress to regulate the environment under the constitution.

Congress did not intend the legislation to cover such small bodies of water, Chief Justice William Rehnquist wrote for the majority. 'Permitting the (government) to claim federal jurisdiction over ponds and mudflats would also result in a significant impingement of the states' traditional and primary power over land and water use,' he wrote.

Writing for the four traditional dissenters on federalism matters, Justice John Paul Stevens criticised the decision: 'Today the court takes an unfortunate step that needlessly weakens our principal safeguard against toxic water,' he wrote.

The US Chamber of Commerce, which argued in support of the Chicago localities, welcomed the decision as striking down an instance of 'regulatory overreach' by the federal government. The ruling will free property developers from one kind of federal intervention, and will potentially give farmers, mining companies and other businesses more say over how they use their land.

Source: *Financial Times*, 10 January 2001

also arranged that there were some formal links between executive and legislature (the president has to report annually to Congress and could veto legislation, the Congress has to approve taxation and could in the last resort impeach the president). They were wise to do so, since without these checks and balances the system could not have worked at all. It is because in practice the powers are not rigidly divided that Almond and Coleman preferred rather to identify the functions of rule-application and rule-making.

Federalism

Locke also spoke of a third 'power', but this one has scarcely ever been specifically incorporated into the Constitution of any modern state, though it is implicit in the structure of all states. This was the **federative power** – the power to conduct relations with other states (Locke 1964, p. 383). An exception was the former Soviet Union, where the 1936 Constitution was amended after the United Nations was created to give individual Union republics the right to conduct direct relations with other states. This enabled Moscow, through branch 'foreign offices' in Bielorussia (now Belarus) and the Ukraine, to have three votes in the UN instead of one, for there is no recorded instance of either state voting independently of the Union as a whole as long as it lasted. The federative power never aroused much interest in other theorists, who were very reluctant to apply it to the actual study of states. It appeared that the federative power, such as it was, was exercised either by the executive, or, worse, by the army. However, the question of the distribution of powers did arise, and was of particular importance when a number of states joined together to form a larger union. The simplest form is what we may term a *league* of states, each retaining the full power to act but joining together to create institutions for specific purposes. This was the position of the American colonies under the Association (1774) or of the European Economic Community (EEC) when first established in 1957.

A closer union, in which a range of powers are given to a central government, but most powers remain with the constituent states, is a *confederation*, such as Switzerland before 1848 or the United States under the Articles of Confederation (1777). In practice, however, many people regard Switzerland today as a **federal system** or *federation*, along with Australia, Canada, India, Malaysia, etc.

The situation is enormously complicated by the fact that for some purposes the term 'federal' has come to mean exactly the opposite in Britain and the United States from what it does in Continental Europe. In France 'federation' means *decentralised* government; in the 'Anglo-Saxon' terminology it means *centralised*. The problem arises from the fact that in *The Federalist Papers* (1987) Alexander Hamilton chose to use the term 'federal' to refer to the new central government he was advocating for the United States.

The problem that the framers of the American Constitution sought to solve was how to maintain representative democracy over a vast area divided into at least thirteen different states surrounded by potentially hostile powers. They came up with the concept of the division of powers which is characteristic of the Constitutions of all true federal states. In a federal system, powers are divided between a central ('federal') government and a number of regional ('state') governments, each of which has the full authority to act within its own boundaries in all matters assigned to it (Wheare 1963; Duchacek 1970). There are therefore four categories of powers assigned under the US Constitution: *enumerated*, clearly stated to be assigned to the federal government (the power to coin money); *concurrent*, available both to the states and the federal government (the power to tax); *reserved*, allowed to the states but denied to the federal government (administration of criminal justice); and *denied*, permitted neither to the federal government nor to state governments (imprisonment without trial). In the US system the presumption is that any unspecified powers belong 'to the States respectively, or to the People', a phrase whose guileless simplicity has caused a surprisingly large amount of trouble.

The history of independent states in the nineteenth century was one of constant struggles to define their identity. In these struggles the major factor was the struggle between centre and the periphery of the newly emergent states, as the centre sought to extend its control over the periphery and the peripheral provinces sought autonomy or even independence. This struggle continues today. Though Belgium is in some respects an exception, it is still probably true that all true federal governments have been created by the unification of separate states and none has ever been created by the *devolution* of powers from a central government. The Russian Soviet Federated Socialist Republic (RSFSR) formed in 1918 was not a true federal state; 'Russia's "federalism" was essentially administrative and formal, with its constituent parts lacking constitutionally protected autonomous powers' (Lapidus 1995, p. 85). Unlike the Soviet Union, in which it was merged in 1922, it was not created by a formal federation treaty, and since 1991 the new Russian Federation has not allowed any of its components to go their separate ways.

Yugoslavia's federal structure was initially imposed at the end of the Second World War by Marshal Josip Tito. It was subject at all levels to control by the Communist Party operating under the principle of 'democratic centralism'. It was then transformed by

Case Study | Fischer Predicts EU Will Become Federation

The European Union is set to develop into a federation of nation states, according to Joschka Fischer, Germany's foreign minister. 'I would dare to prophesy that things will go this way. Certainly, not without crises or problems, but the pressure is in that direction,' the Green party member predicted. Mr Fischer said such a federation seemed the only effective way to handle a European Union with up to 27 member states once its expected enlargement got under way from 2004.

He said in an interview with the Financial Times: 'We have three possibilities – intergovernmentalism; federalism; or a federation of nation states. In the light of experience, it would seem advisable to seek the third option as our next step even if the second has my full sympathy.'

He cited November's speech by Tony Blair in Warsaw – in which the prime minister put forward a model in which national legislatures would provide delegates to a future second chamber of the European parliament – as a decisive contribution to the debate on Europe's future.

'Irrespective of my agreeing with all of it, for a British prime minister, he made the most important speech since Churchill's landmark speech on Europe' in Zurich in 1946, said Mr Fischer, referring to Sir Winston's call for a united states of Europe.

Mr Fischer's comments come a year after his landmark speech at Berlin's Humboldt university setting out a vision for the future of Europe.

He said on Wednesday: 'I'm a convinced believer in the federal state. But visiting Westminster, I understood for the first time Britain's resistance above all to a transfer of the sovereignty of the House of Commons.

'As I see Britain as an essential part of Europe and the EU, my question was: how should an integrated Europe be constituted, so that even England could cross this bridge? Or France, where nation cannot be divided from state?'

Mr Fischer's thinking has developed in the light of reaction to his speech, especially with regard to the role of the Council of Ministers in the balance of power with the Parliament and the Commission.

A year ago, he put forward alternatives for an executive – developing the Council into a fully-fledged European government or expanding the Commission, including direct election of a president. Today, he is convinced the former is the only answer.

'The Council must become the executive, with the Commission, and give up its legislative responsibilities to the European parliament. Otherwise we will slide back into intergovernmentalism and have the problem that, in a union of 25 or 27 members, stagnation or negotiating difficulties will dominate.'

Source: *Financial Times* (FT.com), 16 May 2001

the 1974 Constitution designed by Edvard Kardelj into a unique 'system of delegation' which at one and the same time turned not only the six constituent republics (Slovenia, Croatia, Serbia, Montenegro, Bosnia and Hercegovina, and Macedonia) but also two autonomous areas within Serbia (Kosovo and Vojvodina) into eight proto-states with their own presidencies and parliaments, enhanced the rivalries between them and atomised the federal government by replacing it with a collective presidency and a parliament almost destitute of powers. Once Communist Party control had also been lost, this unusual arrangement simply disintegrated (Dyker and Vejvoda 1996, pp. 16–17). It too, however, was not a true federal system.

Constitutional courts

The Americans also adopted the concept of a discrete **judicial power** originally hailed by Montesquieu as characteristic of Britain (Montesquieu 1966). It is fair to say that when Montesquieu visited Britain in 1739, by contemporary standards the British judiciary was indeed unusually independent. The 1787 Constitution of the United States, therefore, speaks of three powers: the legislative, executive and judicial. The judicial power has been transplanted into modern terminology by Almond under the functional name of rule-adjudication, and this reminds us that in two respects the United States is an exception. In most states, the judiciary is part of the executive branch of government, even where the belief exists that there is an abstract entity called law existing independently of the power of government. And under the US system of '**dual federalism**' (McKay 1997, pp. 69–70) federal and state governments have dual sovereignty and there are separate and overlapping judicial systems of federal and state courts. Each of the fifty states has a separate constitution, its own courts and its own system of local government.

Changes in the Federal Constitution require the approval of two-thirds of both houses of Congress as well as three-fourths of the states. Since 1796, however, it has been taken as read that the federal Supreme Court and Circuit Courts have the power to declare state law unconstitutional as repugnant to the Constitution of the United States as a whole, and, following the precedent set by *Marbury* v. *Madison* (1803), the Supreme Court subsequently successfully asserted that it could also declare federal law invalid. In other federal systems, such as those of Australia and Canada, the doctrine of parliamentary sovereignty (see below) leaves much less room for judicial interpretation. Understandably under the American system many of the key decisions have been concerned with the distribution of economic powers, which were matters which were not clearly spelt out in the Constitution (see Peterson 1995).

There are three distinctive features of the role of the United States Supreme Court as interpreter of the Constitution:

1. The Court is an ordinary court with original jurisdiction in a few specified matters and appellate jurisdiction (acts as a court of appeal) in all other matters. It is not a special administrative court whose sole task is to interpret the Constitution.
2. It does not give advisory judgments or opinions on hypothetical cases. Hence if no appropriate case comes before it, it is unable to rule on the constitutionality of laws. Hence they remain constitutional.
3. For most of its existence the Court has operated under the doctrine of 'judicial self-restraint'. Only in the most unusual cases has the Court questioned the constitutionality of a law and it has frequently shown great skill in avoiding having to do so.

The German system of **collaborative federalism** is radically different from the American. The sixteen *Länder* do not have separate constitutions. Under the 1949 Basic Law a special Constitutional Court interprets the Basic Law and rules on the validity of legislation. Constitutional changes require the agreement of the Bundesrat, the upper house of the federal legislature. The powers of the federal and *Land* governments are not distinct but shared: it is the responsibility of the sixteen *Länder* to enforce federal law under the principle of *subsidiarity*. Hence the federal government passes 'framework laws' which are developed and enforced by the *Land* governments. As in the United States, federal and *Land* governments have concurrent powers in a number of areas, e.g. transport, and the

The European Union

THE UNITED KINGDOM

Official name: The United Kingdom of Great Britain and Northern Ireland
Aka: UK; Great Britain; Britain; England (incorrectly)
Type of government: Constitutional parliamentary monarchy with some regional devolution of power
Capital: London
Area: 244,100 sq km
Population (2000): 59,000,000
GNP per capita (2000): $21,400 (PPP $20,640)

Evolution of government: In England medieval assembly began to meet c. 1260; merged with Parliaments of Scotland (1707) and Ireland (1801). Emergence of representative government after Civil War and 'Glorious Revolution' of 1688 (Chapter 11); evolved into liberal democracy after extension of the franchise 1832, 1867, 1884 but votes for women conceded only after struggle 1918. Leading colonial power despite loss of American colonies in 1783 (see USA); after independence for India (q.v.) in 1947 systematic decolonisation followed. Welfare state introduced after 1945 under influence of Labour Party backed by unusually strong trade union movement. Globalisation's impact evident in uncritical acceptance of US influence and belief in 'special relationship'. City of London however remains a major centre of finance capital and Thatcher government (1979–90) pioneered deregulation, privatisation and economic 'liberalisation' (Chapter 5).

Main features of government: Constitution uncodified (Chapter 1). Single-ballot single-member electoral system (Chapter 7) gives party system in which two dominant parties have shared power (Chapter 6) for more than two centuries. Unarmed civilian police introduced 1829 (Chapter 10). Civil service introduced 1850s widely admired and copied but for ideological reasons (Chapter 4) undermined and made less accountable by transfer of power to agencies in 1980s. Strongly centralised decision-making system created in two World Wars modified by devolution of powers to Scotland and Wales in 1997 (Chapter 8). Parliament an arena. No separate system of administrative courts.

federal government uses equalisation grants to iron out regional differences. But unlike the United States, Germany does not have separate laws and judicial systems for each *Land*. There is a unified judicial system, in which the higher courts and judges are federal and the lower courts and judges are *Land*-based, and the civil service is organised on similar lines.

France too has a special body charged with interpreting the Constitution, the Constitutional Council (Conseil Constitutionel). Under the 1958 Constitution either the president, the prime minister, the president of the National Assembly or the president of the Senate may request an opinion from the Council on the constitutionality of an

FRANCE

Official name: The French Republic
Type of government: Unitary semi-presidential republic
Capital: Paris
Area: 544,000 sq km
Population (2000): 59,000,000
GNP per capita (2000): $24,940 (PPP $22,320)

Evolution of government: Medieval assembly disunited and ceased to meet in early seventeenth century. Financial crisis of government led to summoning in 1789 and beginning of French Revolution, type example of a 'great social revolution' (Chapter 11). Imperial rule under Napoleon I (1804–14) marked by militarism (Chapter 10) which paved the way for imperial expansion in later nineteenth century. Parliamentary republic emerged as compromise in 1875 but discredited in 1930s by scandal and defeated by Germany in 1940 when a dictatorship was established (1940–44). The Republic was restored in 1944 but following a crisis of decolonisation in Algeria and the revolt of the army in 1958 (Chapter 10) General de Gaulle was recalled to power and Fifth Republic established. Major centre of opposition to globalisation in the form of US ('Anglo-Saxon') influence; similarly resisted economic liberalisation throughout the 1990s.

Main features of government: Constitutional Council has only limited powers to check constitutionality of laws (Chapter 2). Semi-presidentialism: president has reserved sphere in defence and foreign affairs; prime minister and Cabinet responsible for day-to-day administration (Chapter 2). Unitary government in which continuity of policy maintained before 1958 through powerful and well-trained civil service (Chapter 8) which transcends ideology (Chapter 4). Traditional multi-party system effectively modified 1958 by introduction of single-member second-ballot system (Chapter 7) for National Assembly, which lost most of its power to challenge governments. A separate system of administrative courts handles grievances.

item of legislation. They must do so within a fixed period of time after its approval. If they do not do so, or there is no decision, the law is constitutional, whether it appears to be or not, and there is no further appeal. In this way in 1962 General de Gaulle was able to call a referendum on extending the powers of the president, without first getting the approval of parliament.

Spain's Constitutional Court was established by the 1978 Constitution. Like the German one, it is *concentrated*, dealing exclusively with the interpretation of the Constitution, and *abstract*, in that, unlike the Supreme Court of the United States, it does give advisory judgments. Initially it could be asked for a decision before the event (*a priori*), but in 1985 this possibility was abolished except for the special case of international treaties, since it resulted in delays which were assiduously exploited by the opposition to hold up legislation. A large number of authorities, including lower courts, have the power to refer cases to the Court but some 90 per cent of its work comes from individuals

GERMANY

Official name: The German Federal Republic
Type of government: Federal parliamentary republic
Capital: Berlin
Area: 357,000 sq km
Population (2000): 82,200,000
GNP per capita (2000): $25,850 (PPP $20,810)

Evolution of government: The multitude of German states in existence before 1789 were partially consolidated by Napoleon and linked in a customs union after 1815. The 39 remaining states were eventually incorporated in 1871 in a German Empire led by Prussia. The Weimar Republic created in 1918 was displaced in 1933 by a Fascist dictatorship led by Adolf Hitler, which is often taken to be a type example of totalitarianism (Chapter 2). Hitler led Germany to a disastrous defeat at the hands of the United Nations in 1945. Under the influence of the Cold War two German states emerged, the German Federal Republic in the West and the German Democratic Republic in the East. They were re-unified by general consent with the agreement of the Soviet Union after the fall of the Berlin Wall in 1989 (Chapter 11).

Main features of government: The Basic Law of 1949 continues as the constitution of the re-united Germany. It was designed to limit the powers of central government. System of 'collaborative federalism' (Chapter 2) in which central government makes framework laws implemented by state (*Land*) governments under principle of 'subsidiarity'. Chancellor (prime minister) chosen by popular vote independently of parliamentary majority and can only be overthrown by 'constructive vote of no-confidence' (Chapter 2); president has largely ceremonial role. 'Mixed' proportional electoral system for lower house, the Bundestag (Chapter 7), introduced under Basic Law 1949. Elements of consociationalism and neocorporatist features (Chapter 6) in economic policy-making have limited social conflict.

who have exhausted all other remedies. The twelve judges are chosen by the Congress (four), the Senate (four), the Cabinet (two) and the judiciary (two).

The problem with giving judges the power to decide on the constitutionality of legislation is that it is hard to justify in terms of democratic theory, particularly where (as in the US case) they are appointed and not elected. The problem is compounded when the judgment is one which the majority of voters do not support. In 1985 the Spanish Court, on the casting vote of its president, gave a conditional approval to a 1983 law permitting abortion in the first twelve weeks of preganancy. Following German experience, the law was very limited in its effect and carefully drafted with a view to resisting the challenge which came when the opposition Alianza Popular (AP) referred it to the Court. Hence though it did uphold the constitutionality of the measure, the Court laid down conditions which were to be followed, thus venturing into areas which the minority argued were properly the province of the legislature (Barreiro 1999).

IRELAND

Official name: Ireland ('Eire', though often used in the UK, is simply the Irish for Ireland and 'Republic of Ireland' is incorrect)
Type of government: Unitary parliamentary republic
Capital: Dublin
Area: 70,280 sq km
Population (2000): 3,750,000
GNP per capita (2000): $18,340 (PPP $18,340)

Evolution of government: As part of the UK after 1801 developed movement for Home Rule in later nineteenth century. Failure to grant this led to abortive revolt in 1916 (the 'Easter Rising'); transformed into fully developed movement for secession following its suppression. In 1918 representatives elected seceded from Westminster Parliament and established their own (Dáil Eireann). In 1922 the Anglo-Irish Treaty granted 'Dominion status' (full internal self-government) to 26 of the 32 counties, the remainder remaining part of the UK. In the Civil War that followed the republicans were defeated but came to power with an electoral mandate in 1932 and their 1937 Constitution limited residual British influence. In 1949 Ireland was declared a Republic.

Main features of government: Directly elected presidency with largely ceremonial powers. Parliamentary government; executive power with Cabinet appointed by prime minister (Taoiseach) elected by Dáil. Despite highly proportional electoral system (STV – Chapter 7) has evolved system dominated by two main parties.

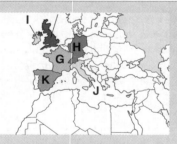

ITALY

Official name: The Italian Republic
Type of government: Unitary parliamentary republic with limited regional devolution
Capital: Rome
Area: 310,000 sq km
Population (2000): 57,500,000
GNP per capita (2000): $20,250 (PPP $20,200)

Evolution of government: Italy was unified between 1860 and 1870 under the House of Savoy as a constitutional monarchy. The Piedmontese Constitution could not be amended and was increasingly disregarded. After the First World War discontent with government paved the way for the rise of Benito Mussolini who became prime minister in 1922. Mussolini used his party militia to establish an authoritarian (and would-be totalitarian) regime (Chapter 3) which lasted until 1942. Discredited by its association with the dictatorship, the monarchy was deposed in a referendum and Republic established (1946).

Main features of government: From 1946 on a long period of dominance by the Christian Democrats (DC) supported by Cold War polarisation and funds from the USA (Chapter 6). Extreme multipartism sustained by Imperiali largest-remainder system of proportional representation, replaced in 1990s by a less-proportional mixed system (Chapter 7). One-party dominance led to prevalence of clientelism and corruption (Chapter 9).

SPAIN

Official name: Kingdom of Spain
Type of government: Constitutional parliamentary monarchy with substantial regional devolution
Capital: Madrid
Area: 505,000 sq km
Population (2000): 40,200,000
GNP per capita (2000): $14,080 (PPP $16,060)

Evolution of government: Absolute monarchy until invasion by Napoleon in 1807; influence of French Revolution brought Liberal revolt against restored government in 1820 and institution of representative government. Carlist civil wars of early nineteenth century however were accompanied by rise of militarism (Chapter 10), and influence of anarchism in late nineteenth century brought ideological polarisation (Chapter 4). In 1931 the king left the country and a Republic was proclaimed but in 1936 the armed forces revolted and after a bitter Civil War (1936–39) General Francisco Franco established a dictatorship. On his death in 1975 the monarchy was restored and personalist dictatorship gave way to liberal parliamentary democracy.

Main features of government: Parliamentary government. Elections to lower house (Cortés) by list system on provincial basis (Chapter 7). Considerable degree of autonomy since 1978 for 17 self-governing regions, notably two problem areas of the former Republic: Catalonia (Catalunya) and the Basque provinces (Euzkadi).

Developmental Typologies

Once the bases of classification have been clarified it should be easier to see how political systems change over time. *Developmental typologies* are those that take the time dimension into consideration (see Table 2.4).

The oldest of these typologies was that of Aristotle, as modified by the historian Polybius, who saw governments as following an endless chain of evolution: from monarchy, to aristocracy, to democracy, and then by way of tyranny, back to monarchy.

Marx's typology is one of economic systems, but each has a corresponding political order. He argues that human society will ultimately go through four stages. It began with an era of 'primitive accumulation', in which people start to garner resources from the world around them. With the rise of powerful families, powerful hereditary rulers use force to compel the peasantry to work for them and so concentrate land and wealth in their own hands. This 'feudal' society is organised in a pyramid of power based on landownership. With the rise of commerce and industry, economic power passes into the hands of those who own capital, the bourgeoisie. In the great bourgeois revolutions, the English and the French, they seized political power from the decaying aristocracies and created a new and much more powerful form of state based on their ability to expropriate and then to control the surplus labour of the industrial workers. Finally, in the last

Table 2.4 Developmental typologies of political systems

Aristotle/Polybius (c. 146 BC)	Marx and Engels (1962 [1848])	Almond and Powell (1966)
Monarchy Aristocracy Democracy Tyranny Monarchy etc.	Primitive accumulation Feudal Bourgeois Socialist	Patriarchal/patrimonial Feudal Premobilised modern Mobilised modern Democratic
	Primitive accumulation Oriental mode of production ???	Patriarchal/patrimonial Historical bureaucratic Premobilised modern Mobilised modern Authoritarian

stage, the industrial workers will then in turn rise in revolt, overthrow the rule of the bourgeoisie, establish the dictatorship of the proletariat, and build a socialist society.

Almond and Powell (1966, 1996) proposed a developmental model of politics, and their structural-functional analysis continues to be employed to structure their view of comparative politics (Almond *et al.* 2000). Their developmental model rests in the first instance on the concept not of power but of authority, and follows the distinction made by Weber between patriarchal, patrimonial and feudal authority (Weber 1965, p. 346).

For feminists, **patriarchy** is a form of rule characterised by male dominance and the subordination of women. The purpose of the state is to maintain this subordination, without which men cannot control marriage and with it the assurance that their property will be transmitted to male heirs. As Engels noted in the nineteenth century, it was not a universal characteristic of primitive societies, some of which were matriarchal and some of which lacked established hierarchies. For Weber, however, patriarchal authority means simply authority vested solely in the representative of the lineage and patrimonial authority depends on the possession of goods, or lands having value. Feudal authority involves a bargain between the holders of each of these concepts for a series of reciprocal obligations of service and protection. In other words the representative of the lineage that holds centralised authority holds power only by agreement with other people who have a right to authority within their own limited areas.

Out of the patrimonial states there has been developed, in turn, what has been called the *historical bureaucratic state*. This is Eisenstadt's (1963, p. 4) term for a state in which the system of government has become so routinised that, within limits, it operates regardless of the competence of the nominal ruler. Every so often, human biology being what it is, either the inheritance fails or there is a 'time of troubles' when there are many contenders for the throne. But the bureaucratic structure by that time is such that decisions continue to be made, the system continues to work, the field boundaries are still delimited, the harvest is still gathered, a tenth is dished out to the priests, and a pittance is dished out to the poor (if they are lucky). And it is out of this historical bureaucratic system that modern states have derived.

Almond and Powell provide a special category for the *secularised city states*. These are very small states such as Liechtenstein, San Marino or Monaco, but probably not

Andorra or Luxembourg, because they are too large, or the more recently independent island states such as St Vincent or St Kitts in the Caribbean, or Kiribati, Nauru or Tuvalu in the Pacific. Secularisation refers simply to the fact that the religious element has, in modern times, been taken out of their government, which presumably excludes the Vatican City State, but it is very hard to see why.

It will be noticed that Almond and Powell do not, as is done here, stress the duality of the origins of government. They accept the fact of government, and with it, implicitly, the assumption that it is beneficial to society. But there are always two elements in conflict in government: government and the people, the claim to power and its acceptance, or reward and punishment. Government is interaction, not action. From this point onwards, moreover, they view development as a process of *political mobilisation*: that is, the bringing of more and more people into the political life of the community. Certainly the mobilisation of individuals does mean at the same time taking account of their interests. To bring them into the political system, they have to be getting something out of it if they are going to be required to continue to put something in to it. It is, of course, possible to find, even today, systems in which large sectors of the population are not incorporated in the structure, and so a category is provided for pre-mobilised modern systems.

Finally, they conclude with two categories of mobilised systems, in which mass participation is both required and encouraged, and so is qualitatively different. One is the democratic state in which the desire of the people to produce inputs is fully accepted and channelled, even when it is a question of demands rather than supports. The other is the authoritarian system, where the support is wanted but demands are not.

To summarise, therefore, Almond and Powell see the evolution of modern states as following a historical path from the patriarchal-patrimonial level, through the feudal states and the historical bureaucratic states, to the pre-mobilised modern states – modern, that is, in that they still exist in today's world, but are not mobilised in the sense that the mobilised modern state requires or permits. And in these mobilised modern states, the common factor is that people participate widely in politics, some because they want to do so, some because they are made to do so, and some for both reasons.

Executive and legislature

For the present writer the possibilities are somewhat more complex (see Table 2.5). The categorisation has two distinctive features. First of all, the dualism which Almond and Powell discern as coming into evolution of states at the division between the authoritarian and democratic states of today is here seen as running throughout the whole

Table 2.5 Varieties of government

Primitive	Agrarian	Imperial	Assembly	Apparat
Tribe	Kingdom	Empire	Presidential	Party
	Theocracy	Tyranny	Caesarism	Praetorian
Band	Horde	Feudal	Federal	
	City	Anarchy	Parliament	

course of human history. Indeed, this conflict, natural because politics is institution-alised conflict, provides the basic dynamic for all experimentation with political forms. People in Western Europe or the United States may have forgotten or become habitu-ated to the essentially violent and self-imposed way in which their governments first emerged. But the facts are still fundamental to their understanding of how they work today. All governments exercise just as much power as they believe they can get away with. It is in the extension or, conversely, in the limitation of these powers that all modern governments have been shaped. Governments who try to mobilise their peoples in order to get them to work harder and pay their taxes soon find that the people will demand a greater say in government in return.

Secondly, precisely because this dynamic is continuous and fundamental, it is con-sistent with the observation that the process of political change ebbs and flows. It does not follow a cycle of change from one form of government to another, returning to the beginning, as Plato and later Polybius suggested (Calvert 1970a, pp. 40, 43–4). Nor, as the Victorians (including Marx) would have it, is there an irresistible progress in the sense that political systems evolve along a single line towards a predictable future state. Of course, human beings learn by experience, but even with books to aid them, mem-ories grow cold and old men die. Hence the revolutions in Eastern Europe in 1989 should have come as a surprise to no one, least of all to those who were most surprised by them.

All modern states derive their basic political structures from a period of violent dis-ruption and reconstitution. Such a period of disruption may either take the form of an independence struggle, international war or revolution. The phenomenon of revolution is covered in detail in Chapter 11. Here the term is used in the usual sense to refer to political and social changes accompanied by violence, such as people associate particu-larly with England, the United States, France and Russia (Brinton 1952), and in modern times with countries as diverse as Mexico, Turkey, China, Egypt (Leiden and Schmitt 1968), Cuba, Iran and Nicaragua. In all of these instances an important feature of these changes has been the attempt to claim power by people claiming to act directly on behalf of the masses, and in the majority of cases this claim has momentarily led to direct rule by a convention (Verney 1961; see also Brogan and Verney 1963), a special type of **assembly** claiming complete control over every aspect of political and social life.

Convention theory

Most liberal democracies today are of one of two types: the parliamentary or the pres-idential system. But a developmental perspective reminds us that both are historical variants of what Verney called the 'convention theory' state (Verney 1961, pp. 3, 57). By **convention theory** Verney means a rare and short-lived, but historically very significant form of government, in which all conversion functions are exercised by a represent-ative assembly (a 'convention', after the French Revolutionary Convention). This form of government has existed historically after certain major social revolutions, e.g. England 1649–51, United States 1777–89, France 1793–95, Russia 1917–18 ('all power to the Soviets'). However, it has not done so for long and in practice has invariably been modified. At the time of the French Revolution, all power was vested in the National Convention (assembly), and all other centres of authority were for a time destroyed, neutralised, or subordinated. The chairman of the Convention was its servant, not its master. The execution of its policies was entrusted to committees created for that purpose. Thoughout its existence, including the period of the Terror (1793–94), the notorious Committee for Public Safety was re-elected monthly. In the parallel instance in England under the Commonwealth (1649–53), Parliament did not delegate even the ceremonial function of receiving ambassadors. Each was brought before the entire House to be formally introduced, and to bow and be bowed to. Remnants of these and similar practices were still embedded in the Constitutions of communist states, notably those of the USSR (1936), China (1949) and Cuba (1975). In practice, even in those instances, the system was substantially modified in certain well-defined ways.

A second characteristic of convention theory government is a unifying political culture which seeks to make equal that which is not already equal. The consequence, therefore, is a conflict between centre and periphery, and more particularly a conflict between two principles – the principle of *representation*, which favours having a big assembly so that representatives are as close to their constituency as possible, and the principle of *efficiency*, which favours small groups for taking day-to-day decisions. In practical terms this means that under the pressure of business the assembly sits for longer and longer hours, and in the end many of the representatives are tempted to hand the burden of work over to someone else. And popular pressure for them to do so may by then be very great, particularly where, as in the French case, the political system is threatened by attack and a speedy response is called for.

If an assembly is to survive for a long time as an effective and working instrument, it must not only develop a system of committees, it must delegate effective power to them. Such a development is most strikingly illustrated by the United States Congress. However, in the United States the creation of a separate executive has created a **presidential system**. Where, on the other hand, one of the committees has come to assume the executive power while remaining within the assembly, as in Britain, the result is a **parliamentary system**. Both represent compromises by which a government, limited in its powers of decision, is in return guaranteed the right to extract a sufficient quantity of power resources from the society it governs. There are important differences, however, in the terms of the two compromises (see Table 2.6).

Parliamentary systems

In Britain, almost uniquely, the parliamentary system was not embodied in a single written Constitution. Hence what became the prototype statement of the rules of the parliamentary system for most of the rest of the world was the Belgian Constitution of 1831, which was specifically modelled on British practice. Present-day examples of working parliamentary systems include not only Britain and Belgium, but also Australia, Canada, India, Israel, Malaysia, the Netherlands, Sri Lanka, Germany and Japan. There is an independent origin for the parliamentary systems of the Nordic countries in Sweden in the eighteenth century (Verney 1961, p. 18; cf. Hawgood 1939, pp. 145–6); and much earlier than that for the Althing of Iceland and the House of Keys in the Isle of Man. However, despite promising beginnings parliamentarism failed to develop in Poland (as, today, in the European Community) because of the veto each of its individual members could exercise.

In a parliamentary system the functions of rule-application, nominally derived from a *head of state*, are in practice vested in a committee of the assembly, consisting of ministers appointed by the head of state, but responsible to the assembly for their political actions. In countries such as Britain or the Netherlands, where the head of state is a

Table 2.6 Convention theory, parliamentary and presidential systems

Attribute	Convention	Parliamentary	Presidential
Head of state	Chairman	Monarch or president	President
Head of government	Chairman	Prime minister	President
Executive	Committee elected by assembly	Appointed by prime minister from assembly	Secretaries of president
Executive members of assembly?	Yes	Yes	No
Executive can dissolve assembly?	Yes	Yes	No
Fixed term for executive?	No	No	Yes
Assembly checks executive?	Yes	Sometimes	No
Focus of power	Assembly	Parliament	None
Assembly controls own business?	Yes	No	Yes

Source: after Verney 1961

hereditary monarch, his or her functions are ceremonial only. In a state with an elected head, such as Iceland, Ireland or Italy, the president (as s/he is rather confusingly called), may have rather more power, though once elected s/he is expected to stand above the political struggle. And in most states, exceptions being Japan and Sweden, the head of state has to sign documents giving effect to laws, and retains in this, and the choice of a first or prime minister, reserve powers which may be activated by some unexpected crisis.

The prime minister, as *head of government*, chooses the executive committee, or ministry (Weller 1985). This must normally consist of elected members of the assembly. This is not the case in the Netherlands, Luxembourg and Norway and the way in which they are chosen varies a great deal. In Israel the prime minister is separately elected by popular vote; in Germany each party must present its chancellor-candidate at elections; in Britain the sovereign by custom has to call first on the leader of the largest party to form a government; in Italy, with frequently changing coalitions the norm, presidents have played an active role in forming governments, one of the few major prerogatives they enjoy. However, in all cases the government can only survive as long as it can command a majority in the assembly, though in Germany it can only be overthrown by a 'constructive vote of no-confidence' naming someone who is prepared to take on the job of chancellor. This device has only been used successfully once (Larres and Panayi 1996, pp. 74–5).

It is the assembly which normally elects the head of state, where this office is not vested in a hereditary monarch. Five countries that are exceptions are Austria, Finland, France, Iceland and Ireland. There the presidents are directly elected by the people, and in the case of Finland (as in semi-presidentialist France) the president has an important

Table 2.7 Leagues, confederal and federal states

LEAGUE/ASSOCIATION	
European Union 1993	United Arab Emirates 1971

CONFEDERAL STATE	
Switzerland 1291/1849	

FEDERAL STATES	
Parliamentary	Presidential
Canada 1867	United States 1787
Australia 1900	Mexico 1824
Austria 1919	Argentina 1853
India 1947	Brazil 1889
Germany (1871) 1949	Yugoslavia 1945
Malaysia 1957	Micronesia 1990
Nigeria 1963	
Russian Federation 1991	

independent sphere of authority in foreign affairs. However, even there, all power has in practice to be exercised through parliament, the collective entity formed by the head of state, the ministry and the assembly.

The fact that all power decisions pass through parliament has been confused in the past with the idea that power rests in it, or even, more misleadingly still, in the assembly itself. But like any other organisation, a parliament's effective power is limited, sometimes dramatically so, by the constraints of time and space. Hence the powers of the ministry, which is only indirectly responsible to the electorate, may well not be effectively checked by the assembly either.

Presidential systems

The other favoured compromise is the presidential system. This differs fundamentally. The prototype is the 1787 Constitution of the United States. But not only has this been amended substantially over time (Neustadt 1964), as a model it has only been taken up throughout the world since 1946 and in a form which differs substantially from the original intentions of the framers of the American Constitution.

It was perhaps natural that in the first three decades of the nineteenth century, presidential systems should have been adopted by most of the newly independent states of the Americas, with the exception of part of Haiti and of Brazil, which remained a parliamentary monarchy until 1889 (Needler 1963). Only one other presidential state dates from this period: Liberia, a colony for freed American slaves, independent in 1847. After that there was a long gap, until the rising power of the United States created Hawaii (1892; annexed by the United States 1898) and Cuba (1901).

It was only after 1946 when the Philippines, under American tutelage from 1898 onwards, became independent, that the presidential system came to sweep across the rest of the Third World, beginning with the Middle East and North Africa, and spreading throughout Africa south of the Sahara in the wake of the dissolution of the British, French and Portuguese colonial empires after 1960. So powerful was the urge to imitate it that even established parliamentary systems such as those of Pakistan and Sri Lanka were modified in the direction of presidentialism. But few of the systems that have resulted are true presidential systems in the constitutional sense.

In the prototype presidential system the assembly remains separate and distinct from the executive. Rule-making remains the function of the assembly; rule-application is entrusted to one person, the president, elected directly for a limited term, who appoints officials to assist him, which though they are also commonly called a cabinet, are not a committee of the assembly, and are not politically responsible to it. And in the United States the potential conflict of function between president and legislature is met by a variety of devices, but most distinctively by the creation of an independent system of rule-adjudication with power to rule on the constitutionality of specific actions of either of the other two branches of government.

Since there is no focus of power, this system is dynamically unstable, and its invariable tendency has been for the president to destroy the compromise by assuming, often with the aid of force, control over all functions of government. To be a true presidential state, therefore, three conditions have all to be observed.

1. The president must be *elected by the people* according to agreed rules generally regarded as fair. The president must not be a hereditary ruler, be self-appointed, come to power by a military coup, or be nominated by the chiefs of a military regime.
2. He or she must be *elected for a definite term*. There is some difference between being elected for a series of definite terms and being in power indefinitely, but in practice one tends to lead to the other. Consequently constitutional provisions limiting presidential terms are normal, though they are often abused, if necessary by the systematic rewriting of constitutional provisions, as with the Somozas in Nicaragua (Diedrich 1982). Assumption of the presidential office for life invites the corollary that the shorter the life, the shorter the term. In practice, of the eight presidents of Haiti who have been elected for 'life', only Dr François Duvalier actually died in office; his predecessors and his successor were deposed. 'Papa Doc' did realise this might happen and one of the ways in which he ingeniously circumvented the restrictions on re-election was to hold municipal elections in 1961. At the top of each ballot paper was the president's name, and after the votes were counted Haitians were told that they had unwittingly given him an overwhelming vote of confidence (Rotberg 1971, p. 232).
3. The president *must not be able to dissolve the assembly* (or suspend its powers) during its fixed term of office. In practice this is often done, as in Uruguay in 1973, by the leaders of military or military-backed regimes, making use, in most if not all cases, of emergency powers, which will be considered further later (Weinstein 1975, pp. 132–3).

In Switzerland there is a collective presidency in the Council of State, the members of which take it in turns to chair meetings for one year. This example was copied in Uruguay on two occasions, more recently between 1952 and 1967, in a deliberate attempt to weaken presidential power. In principle the sharing of executive as well as legislative functions between parties should be a good thing; however, the case of Bosnia in 1992 showed that the system is particularly vulnerable when rivalries between the parties render decision-making impossible (Silber and Little 1995, pp. 232–3, 239).

Semi-presidentialism

If, in a presidential state, secretaries (see p. 63) become ministers by being given the power to sit and vote in the assembly, they become to an extent responsible to it, and the result is a mixed system which is neither presidential nor truly parliamentary. However, a more recent, and in other respects anomalous example is France. **Semi-presidentialism** is characterised by a dual executive, consisting of an elected president with defined political role and a prime minister and cabinet responsible to the assembly.

Experiments along such lines are not new – among presidential states Chile (1891), Peru (1860) and Cuba (1940) have at different times adopted elements of parliamentarism such as a prime minister and the interpellation of ministers while keeping the executive presidency. Peru, before 1968 and after 1980, is an example which has had a long history (Bourricaud 1970, p. 270).

However, the Constitution of the Fifth Republic in France (1958) did the reverse. It was designed to stabilise the faction parliamentarism of the Fourth Republic by establishing an executive presidency which General de Gaulle would want to occupy (Cerny 1980, p. 32). The Constitution of 1958 was deliberately designed to weaken the powers of the National Assembly as far as possible, while giving the president a substantial area of prerogative power in defence and foreign affairs. In both, the tendency is to make the president one of two foci of power, whereas in the true presidential system there is no focus of power. The president is able to make full use of his or her ability to command attention from the media to set the agenda for government, though in his later years, weakened by terminal illness, President Mitterrand tended rather to react to events (Cole 1997b, pp. 46–7). Moreover the president is able to deal with high-profile matters of international politics while the prime minister retains responsibility for the everyday matters of government – as de Gaulle said, 'the price of milk'. However, the distribution of political power is seldom constant for long. The prime minister not only continues to exercise important powers in concurrence with the president, there are also many functions that the prime minister alone holds (Ardant 1991; Elgie 1993).

The main weakness of the system is the possibility of conflict between the president and the parliamentary majority, especially where (as in France) they are separately elected. In the French case this has already resulted in three periods of 'cohabitation' when the president's party has been opposed by a majority in the Assembly: President François Mitterrand with Jacques Chirac (1986–88) and Edouard Balladur (1993–95), and President Jacques Chirac with premier Lionel Jospin (1997–). These periods have proved to be much less contentious in practice than in theory, since in 1986 President Mitterrand seems to have accepted the convention 'that the leader of the majority party or coalition had the right to be called upon to form a government' (Cole 1997a, p. 41). However, though Mitterrand did withdraw to some extent to a superior position as arbiter above the political battle, it is also true that he continued to intervene from time to time, not only in his reserved domains of defence and foreign affairs, but elsewhere, and not always predictably. One of his most surprising decisions was to dismiss his old rival Michel Rocard in May 1991 and appoint Edith Cresson as France's first woman prime minister. Though she shared the abrasive style of Margaret Thatcher, she lacked her popular mandate and was dismissed in April 1992 (Cole 1997a, p. 49).

Other criticisms of the system have also been made. One is that the direct election of the president instituted in 1962 has made the presidency too responsive to public opinion. Another is that it has made the system too 'leveraged' – a relatively slight move by the president has a considerable effect on the rest of the system so there is a tendency for every matter to be referred right to the top (Wahl and Quermonne 1995). The reduction of the excessively long presidential term from seven to five years should do something to alleviate the latter problem, though at the cost of accentuating the former.

Since the fall of communism in Eastern Europe both Poland (1989) and Russia (1993) have adopted semi-parliamentary systems, though the latter gives the president a much wider range of powers than does the French. In his later years, afflicted by illness, Boris Yeltsin exercised only spasmodic control over government and replaced prime ministers from time to time to create the illusion of activity. To general surprise, the last of these, Vladimir Putin, after heading the Russian punitive campaign against Chechen separatists, was elevated to the presidency when Yeltsin resigned on New Year's Eve 1999. But when the president and premier are unable to agree on a common programme and the premier has too much independent power to be dismissed, the result can be the complete paralysis of government, as in Slovakia when in 1995–96 the two were not even on speaking terms with one another.

Poland emerged from communist rule in 1989 with the 1952 Constitution still in place (though much amended) and in principle 'unified authority' in the Sejm. The shift in 1990 to direct election of the president gave the new democratically elected leader of Solidarity a separate source of authority to make use of the powers to propose and veto laws and a restricted power to dissolve parliament. The so-called 'Little Constitution' of 1992 (which supplemented rather than replaced the 1952 Constitution) extended the president's powers and established a dual executive. The president was given specific powers in foreign affairs and defence by being designated the 'guardian of the Polish Constitution, the protector of Poland's national sovereignty and security and the integrity of its territory; and the safeguard of its international political and military alliances' (Art. 32[2] cited by Millard 1999, p. 40). Some of those who had previously supported President Walesa's call for a strong presidency, however, became disillusioned by his constant struggles with the fragmented majority in the Sejm. Hence the tendency of the 1997 Constitution was on the contrary to weaken the presidency and strengthen the premiership, while retaining the dual executive and establishing the formal separation of the legislative and executive powers. The presidency lost its primacy in defence and foreign affairs, and the presidential veto was restricted, but President Kwasniewski regained the sole right to appoint the chief of staff and senior commanders of the armed forces and the presidents of the Constitutional Tribunal and the Supreme Court (Millard 1999, p. 46).

The struggle for power

The struggle for power takes place throughout a political system and at a number of levels. The continued working of a liberal democracy depends on some kind of balance being maintained, between executive and legislature, between the chief executive and his/her colleagues, and between the government and the people.

As we have seen in Chapter 1, the key is the balance between executive and legislature. In presidential systems the balance is perhaps easier to maintain when, as happens at regular intervals, the president is elected at the same time as the assembly. Even then, different political parties may, as in the United States between 1981 and 2001 or in Brazil since 1990, be chosen to represent the people in each of the branches of government. In Chile after 1963 the timing of the respective terms was such that political conflict between the branches was actually made worse (Gil 1965, p. 208). Though the Christian Democratic majority in Congress in 1970 properly accepted the verdict of the popular vote and ratified the election of the Marxist President Salvador Allende, he in turn was unable to achieve a popular majority for his proposals for radical reform.

Though there must, if government is to function at all, be a close relationship between the two areas of competence, executive and legislature, summed up in the American phrase 'checks and balances', they must be reciprocal and there must be limits on the president's ability to influence the assembly. This is not as easy as it seems. The executive president is both head of state and head of government, owns no superior, and can – and does – convert the duties of his or her ceremonial role into political power. Speaking on behalf of the government as a whole (particularly in foreign policy or in times of national crisis or disaster), making use of the resources of the media, and in particular being seen visibly associated with concrete evidence of achievement in the form of new roads, airports, dams or military installations, all can be used to generate or to strengthen existing support. And, as Montesquieu observed: 'It is an invariable experience that every man who has power is led to abuse it; he goes on until he finds limits' (Montesquieu 1966, p. 151).

The executive president, unlike the head of government in a parliamentary system, is not limited in the power to recruit and to appoint heads of departments by the need to draw them from the ranks of the assembly. Once appointed, the heads of department are the president's subordinates – his secretaries, literally. They seldom have any independent power-base. If the president's power to choose them is limited to an extent by the need to obtain congressional approval, the power to dismiss them is not, and there is a limit to how long any assembly, however powerful, can go on blocking presidential nominees.

In parliamentary systems, on the other hand, the balance between executive and legislature involves the balance between the chief executive and his/her colleagues. Research into ministerial careers suggests that there is less to choose between the parliamentary and presidential systems than this would suggest. Both are characterised by a very rapid turnover of ministers, some two-thirds of whom hold office for less than a year (Blondel 1985). By reshuffling her Cabinet annually, Mrs Thatcher, prime minister of the United Kingdom 1979–90, was able to achieve an exceptional degree of ascendancy over her colleagues. However, since she had to choose among her colleagues, who each had separate and distinct electoral bases, there came a time when this process brought retribution.

Conversely it has time and again been demonstrated, notably in two World Wars, that in time of crisis the parliamentary system can manage an effective response to the challenge. Nor is there any truth in the suggestion that the parliamentary system is somehow unfitted to manage a programme of economic growth over a long period. In fact, Japan, for forty years the world's most successful state in the economic sense, has managed its economic growth since 1945 through a parliamentary system, and the German system is both parliamentary and federal.

In the Weberian sense, the parliamentary and presidential systems, as described here, therefore, are 'ideal types'. Even in its homeland, the United States, in the age of the 'Imperial Presidency' and in particular under President Richard M. Nixon, there were noticeable deviations from the strict constitutional assumptions of the presidential system. The parliamentary system does not depend on such a rigid set of criteria, and, as the case of the United Kingdom shows, it can evolve within a relatively short period of time. But there must be limits to this process. The president of a republic in a parliamentary system such as France can be given more power. A monarch can be rendered virtually powerless, as occurred in Sweden in 1975 (*Annual Register* 1975, p. 151). Yet such is the complexity of modern political systems that no one could deduce from these facts alone either that the French president or the Swedish Riksdag has become all-powerful. The visible constitutional structures are only a partial guide to the real structure of power and decision-making.

Summary

Liberal democracies are states in which government is limited in its powers by a written constitution, a system of law and/or an independent judiciary, and is responsive to the popular will as expressed through elections.

There are two main forms of government in liberal democracies: parliamentary systems and presidential systems. Both derive from a theoretical model in which power is concentrated in a representative assembly and in the former communist states (and some others) all three forms have been modified by being brought under the control of a ruling party organisation. A substantial number of modern states continue to be under authoritarian rule, either of a traditional ruler or of a military dictator. However, the concept of totalitarianism, though still widely used by politicians and press, has little value.

Some 40 per cent of the world's population live under some form of federal government, a form of liberal democracy characterised by the division of powers between a central government and a number of 'state' governments. These systems emerged from the confederation of a number of smaller units and afford citizens an enhanced ability to participate in politics at more than one level.

Key Concepts

authoritarian, government or state characterised by very limited participation and strong emphasis on the right of the rulers to give orders

collaborative federalism, system in which the powers of federal and state governments are not divided horizontally (as in the USA), but are shared, decisions typically being made at the lowest practicable level according to the principle of subsidiarity

competitive systems, political systems in which a degree of free competition of ideas is permitted, e.g. by competitive elections

consociational democracy, for Lijphart, a political system characterised by strong and long-lasting political cleavages and an elaborate process of negotiation between the elites of the different 'pillars' leading to accommodation and compromise

convention theory, for Verney, a rare form of government in which all conversion functions are exercised by a representative assembly

dual federalism, a federal system characterised by dual sovereignty, in which federal and state governments have separate and distinct constitutions, courts, legislatures and powers

executive power, those persons or bodies whether elected or appointed who are able to make and to enforce binding decisions within the existing structure of rules (laws)

façade democracy, for Finer, a system that is nominally democratic, but in fact oligarchical

federal system, one characterised by the division of powers between a single 'federal' government and a number of 'state' governments

federative power, the power to conduct relations with other states

judicial power, those persons or bodies who have been chosen to decide whether in specific cases rules (laws) have been breached or to resolve disputes about the application of those rules

legislative power, those persons or bodies who are able to make rules (laws) which are authoritative, i.e. can in principle be enforced

liberal democracy, states in which government is limited in its powers by a written constitution, a system of law and/or an independent judiciary, and is responsive to the popular will as expressed through elections

mixed constitution, for Aristotle, a political system that combines elements of monarchy, aristocracy and democracy

non-competitive systems, systems where free electoral choice either is not allowed or does not exist in practice

parliamentary system, a governmental system characterised by the unification of powers, the executive power being vested in a committee of the legislative assembly and so responsible to the assembly

participation, the extent to which citizens take part in politics

patriarchy, for feminists, a form of rule characterised by male dominance and the subordination of women

pluralism, for Dahl, a political system characterised by the free interaction of many competing interest groups in the making of policy; by extension, the belief that this is a desirable state of affairs

presidential system, a governmental system characterised by the separation of powers, the executive power being vested in a president and the legislative power in a separate assembly

oligarchy, for Aristotle, government by the few; systems in which a closed group has a virtual monopoly of political power; generic term of abuse applied to traditional landed elites in Latin America

semi-presidentialism, system in which power is shared between a directly elected president with a reserved sphere of power in defence and foreign affairs and a prime minister and cabinet accountable to the assembly

separation of powers, the belief, popularised by Montesquieu, that the executive, legislature and judiciary should be separate and able to act independently in their own sphere of responsibility

'totalitarian', a term coined by Mussolini to designate a state in which the power of the state worked without hindrance and the individual citizen had no rights at all (see **authoritarian**)

Sample Questions

Candidates should be familiar with a representative selection of typologies of states which have been proposed since the major expansion of comparative politics got under way in the 1960s, and be prepared *critically to analyse* the strengths and weaknesses of each. Given their special relevance to liberal democratic systems, typologies of political parties are common in the literature and a favourite subject for examination questions (e.g. 'How useful is a typology of states to our understanding of comparative politics?'). Other questions could focus on specific issues relating to liberal democracy, participation or applications of the concepts of authoritarianism or totalitarianism:

- What do we mean by the term 'liberal democracy'? Is Britain still a democratic country?
- How useful is the concept of 'totalitarianism' in understanding the nature of traditional communist political systems in the 1970s and 1980s?
- 'The essence of Marxist-Leninist political systems is mass participation combined with the "leading role" of the communist elite.' Discuss.

Further Reading

On the principles of liberal democracy see Holden (1993) and for its philosophical basis Plant (1991a). Lijphart (1969) is the classic formulation of the notion of 'consociational' democracy. Lane and Ersson (1991) discuss social cleavages in the Western European context. Dahl (1964b) is the best starting point for the pluralist model. An excellent overview of competing theories is Dunleavy and O'Leary (1987). Various typologies of states discussed are presented in detail in *inter*

alia Parsons and Shils (1962), Almond and Powell (1966), Finer (1970), and Blondel (1973).

For 'totalitarianism' see Schapiro (1972), and for a critique of its application to Eastern Europe before 1989 see Ball and Millard (1986). For 'authoritarianism' and other important political concepts see Foley (1993).

For comparative treatments of federalism Wheare (1963) is dated but sound; see also Duchacek (1970).

PART TWO **Environment and Development**

The Global Environment

CHAPTER THREE

Learning Objectives

By the end of this chapter, the reader will be able:

- to locate politics in its environment;

- to determine how far that environment today is the product of human economic development and what influence this has had on politics;

- to investigate what is meant by the notion of political development.

The Environment

The history of human political organisation has been shaped by the **environment**. By environment is meant two things: generally, the world and all that is in it, and specifically, that part of it in which a specific political system is located. It can be divided into the natural environment, the built environment and the social environment.

The *natural environment* consists of the physical topography of a country, its climate, its soils, its water resources and its vegetation. However, much of what people today regard as the 'natural' environment has in fact been determined by human activity. The deserts of Iraq and the Sahel, the great American dustbowl and the Dorset heathlands are all the end-product of imperfect farming techniques. The bare hills of Croatia or the Philippines were once covered with forest. They are quite as artificial as cities such as Rijeka or Manila.

The *built environment* of cities and towns is designed for human comfort and convenience, though with ever-increasing size it frequently falls short on both counts. The one thing it lacks, however, is the ability to produce the food on which its residents depend. To control supplies of food it must control the countryside.

The *social environment* both determines and is determined by the physical environment, whether natural or artificial. With the development of human societies the social environment for all has changed accordingly.

Government and Territory

Government begins by some individuals establishing a claim to the monopoly of the use of force over others. It seems only prudent, therefore, to ask whether or not there is any natural predisposition in human beings towards the use of force. Among philosophers, Thomas Hobbes in particular believed that there was. Without strong government, therefore, human beings would soon relapse into savagery – 'the war of all against all'. Some modern ethnologists agree that human beings, in common with other animal species, have an innate instinct of **aggression**.

Lorenz (1966) saw aggression as an essential drive which defines the community and protects it against outside attack. In other words, if the community has a boundary (and it may be a highly mobile boundary), that boundary is defined as the line at which the aggressive response is triggered off by an intruder. It is a fail-safe mechanism in that it is safer to respond aggressively to someone who turns out to be a friend, than it is to accept as a friend someone who turns out to be an enemy.

This seems a highly plausible argument, and a simple mechanism of this kind could be a reasonable explanation of the aggressive actions of animals. But there are weaknesses in it. First of all, for animals aggression does not mean actual fighting. Baboons, for example, get up every morning to go down to the edge of their territory and jump up and down and howl at their neighbours for half an hour. But they rarely come to blows with them. This aggression, therefore, is ritual aggression, and a similar ritual element can be observed in human societies. Significantly these rituals are not innate, they are *learned*. For there is abundant evidence that one of the great characteristics of primate species is their social organisation. Social behaviour, which requires *co-operation*, not only enhances the chances of survival for the group as a whole but also for every member of it. What applies to other primates is even more true of humans, for the long period it takes for a human baby to become an adult gives even more opportunity for behaviour to be learned.

Hence few modern psychologists would agree that there is an innate instinct or drive of aggression. The opponents of the idea of the aggressive drive argue that human beings are instinctively underdetermined – that is to say, there are very few things they *must* do. They go on to argue that there is really no evidence that human aggression is instinctive. The evidence is entirely consistent with aggression being socially conditioned. It derives from an unfavourable environment, and in particular from overcrowding.

Many of those who reject the idea of an aggressive drive follow the view of John Dollard and his colleagues, who asserted that 'aggression is always a consequence of frustration' (Dollard *et al.* 1939). The frustration-aggression thesis has been used by Ted Gurr to develop a theory of how internal conflict arises in a political system (Gurr 1970, p. 24). Though such lines of research still look promising, they present in fact considerable difficulties, since the concept of frustration is a very subjective one. Overcrowding and bad social conditions can undoubtedly be very trying. But circumstances which one person finds frustrating may strike another as perfectly reasonable.

In any case, why should overcrowding and bad social conditions necessarily lead to an aggressive response? Alternative possibilities exist: withdrawal, accommodation, or, in extreme cases, mental breakdown. The point is, surely, that people do behave aggressively in certain social conditions, and the relevance today is that these are the conditions in which modern societies have to function. And aggression begins with their personal relations with one another, so the ways in which those relations may be modified are of fundamental importance to their political development. If 'an Englishman's home is his castle', does the separation from his neighbours which this brings help him to develop a society in which his level of aggression is relatively low? Or can he shrink his horizons to the walls of a French, American or Russian apartment and still get on well with the people next door, and vote accordingly? Certainly there is some evidence that alteration of the physical environment in which people live can bring about a marked decline in violence.

The modern phenomena of competition for the control and use of territory, they would argue, are to a great extent the artificial product of human social conditions and can be explained under the frustration-aggression thesis by competition for food in conditions of growing scarcity and serious overcrowding (Crook 1973, pp. 183ff.)

Overcrowding in giant cities has been the most striking social development of the twentieth century, as the continuing growth of Tokyo, Shanghai and Mexico City bears witness. Overcrowding may indeed lead to sudden complete biological collapse in some species – rabbits for example. The correction of such problems is a vast political problem, with implications for government control and use of land throughout the community. Most developed countries in Europe and North America have in the past fifty years come to realise some of the problems involved, and have adopted elaborate systems of planning and control of development, or zoning as it is known in the United States. However, during the 1980s many of these controls were abandoned, in the belief that all such matters could safely be left to the free market. The major disturbances in Los Angeles in 1992 suggested that they could not, and in the 1990s European states have generally been much more cautious about relaxing controls, regardless of how much they wished to do so.

Landownership and reform

But the expansion of towns is only a special case of the control of land and its capacity to generate wealth. The industrial revolution was preceded, and made possible by, an agricultural revolution which increased the productivity of a given amount of land dramatically. Control of political power was used to take productive land away from country-dwellers and to create large estates. In turn the industrial revolution gave rise to transport systems which made possible the conquest of the countryside by town-dwellers. As this control was extended in the twentieth century, it resulted in the industrialisation of agriculture (agribusiness). The impact on the environment of the internal colonisation of the countryside can be plainly seen in the replacement of traditional subsistence agriculture by large farms or plantations managed for export and/or commercial sale of a single product or limited range of products (Calvert 2001).

There is no *direct* relationship between unequal landownership and dictatorial government. Australia, a democratic country, has one of the most unequal land-distribution patterns in the world. However, landownership had historically given rise to a degree of political control over others which they could not effectively challenge. Hence the redistribution or reorganisation of land has been a major factor in breeding resentment against incumbent governments over the last two hundred years, and all reform programmes have had to take account of it. Land reform after 1945 was an important element in the rapid economic development of South Korea and Taiwan.

The Marxist model called for the common ownership of land as with other forms of property. However, things did not go in practice as Marx had foretold. In the Soviet Union under Stalin (1924–53), agricultural land was reorganised into collective farms under state ownership. Great suffering was occasioned to millions of peasants, and a catastrophic drop in production followed, bringing hardship and even starvation to many parts of the country. Peasants living on collective farms were, however, permitted to retain a small plot for their own use, and during the 1980s these private plots contributed a disproportionate amount to the overall level and variety of production. In China, however, during the Great Leap Forward (1958–61) private property in agriculture was wholly abolished by the formation of communes, only to be restored by allowing private plots openly from 1961 to 1966. During the Great Proletarian Cultural Revolution 'rectification campaigns' were used to induce the peasants once more to surrender their plots, with some success, but evidently not without cost in terms of economic disruption. Then under the 'open-door' policy of economic liberalisation promoted by Deng Xiaoping, peasants were again allowed to sell produce from private plots, with a significant increase in their standard of living as a result. In Cuba no allowance was made for private plots, and the country has conspicuously suffered from a serious decline in levels of pre-revolutionary production. Even during the 1960s it had to import black beans, a staple food in the Caribbean area (Goldenberg 1965, p. 227). In the 1990s the intensification of the US blockade led to a partial liberalisation of production as the country strove for self-sufficiency.

A common charge against land reform schemes is that they lead to inefficient production. It is true that (in theory) this problem can be solved and more food produced from existing land for a considerable time into the future. However, this is not a solution, for three reasons. First, it requires high inputs of energy which the world ecosystem is just not capable of absorbing. Secondly, it will exhaust the soil, and once that happens the situation will get steadily and irremediably worse. Lastly, in the meanwhile the existing levels of inequality will have to be maintained. Conflict, therefore, can arise in part from the fact that advanced industrial development is at least partly a positional good (Hirsch 1977): that is to say, something whose desirability to others stems from the fact that only a few people at a time can have it.

This global conflict arises, in part, from the external colonisation of the rest of the world by the European powers, between the fifteenth and twentieth centuries. It is natural to blame colonisation, despite the subsequent collapse of these empires, for the present very unequal pattern of economic development among today's independent states. Under this assumption, it was common in the 1970s to group states in one of three 'worlds', according to their level of economic development.

The advanced industrial nations of Western Europe, the United States and Canada, Japan and Australia formed what was termed the 'First World'. These states continued to dominate the world economy and, if anything, to become richer in relation to the others. The 'Second World', consisting of the Soviet Union, its allies in Eastern Europe and elsewhere, and China, had effectively isolated themselves from the world economy. They claimed to have an effective alternative model of development which other states could follow. All other states formed the **Third World** (Calvert and Calvert 2001). Most but not all were former colonies. What they tended to have in common was that they were relatively poor and dependent on the production of primary products for the world market for what income they did have. Once independent, their prime aim was to follow the same path of economic development as the advanced industrialised nations had previously done.

The end of history

Following the end of the Cold War, it has been widely argued that liberal democracy and the free market now reign supreme. In the United States, Francis Fukuyama has gone so far as to say that in a Hegelian sense we are witnessing 'the end of history'. Liberal democracy is the best form of government attainable (Fukuyama 1989). How much credence should we place on these claims?

Certainly a principal objective of Western European states, in the tradition established at the time of the French Revolution, has been democratisation, the spread, consolidation and maintenance of pluralist, representative democracy. The characteristic feature of modern political systems was the emergence of the **assembly** as the prime instrument of mass mobilisation. As we have seen, the systems generated by this development have in many cases more recently undergone further modification. Such modifications usually result from the attempts of governments to substitute for the assembly forms of representation, such as by a party or the military, more easily directed in the perennial task of mobilising the population in support of its government, and in the performance of tasks which many of its members do not really want to perform. Occasionally this brings about a successful reaction among the population for a greater say in their own government. Sometimes, as at the fall of Ceauşescu in Romania in 1989, this is gained by popular uprising, and very rarely, as in former East Germany and Czechoslovakia, is it grudgingly conceded.

But the irruption of the assembly into the political structure of France in 1789 has had such wide consequences that it still forms the basic point of departure for all later developments. This is because its claim to power is based on a very simple principle, its representation of the people.

The establishment of pluralist democracy has coincided with first a decline and then a revival in the belief in the market economy. However, it is quite incorrect to believe, as some have argued, that these two objectives are necessarily connected or that one is dependent on the other. As Hannah Arendt points out, political liberty is an absolute good and hence its own justification (Arendt 1963, pp. 219–20). To believe either that liberty will necessarily result in prosperity, or that an unregulated market economy is a prior objective and a requirement for liberty, would be in each case to make a most serious mistake.

There are two reasons for this. First of all, as is now all too clear, the sacrifice of freedom in the Soviet Union did not result in prosperity and the attainment of freedom will not necessarily do so either. A market economy may or may not be a desirable goal in itself, but it is an objective quite separate from that of political liberty.

Secondly, in recent years the proponents of the market economy have presented a wildly romantic picture of the 'free market' as an independent force, superior to the power of the state and not in any way to be trammelled by state regulation. In fact this picture is not only misleading, it is the exact opposite of the truth. No market can exist without political power to regulate and protect it (see Chapter 5). An unregulated market is no market at all, since the essence of a market is a bargain which both parties know is going to be kept. It is because political authority is able to give this stability and assurance to private individuals that in turn it is able to demand of them their obedience.

Historically markets originated in a variety of ways and had a variety of patrons, but in the modern world the whole world is parcelled out among nation-states. It is they and they alone which issue money, create credit and provide the legal framework within which the market can operate. But for most of the world the fact that their states are weak and unpredictable puts citizens at a considerable disadvantage, both politically and economically, compared with their more fortunate neighbours.

All governments seek to the best of their capacities to be efficient, rich and successful. This in turn means external obligations such as maintaining a surplus on their balance of payments on overseas trade, and keeping their currency strong against the US dollar (unless, of course, they already have dollars). And for internal reasons they want, as visible signs of their success, such things as new motorways, airlines, shipping fleets, oil wells and public buildings.

But there are two problems. All of these things cost money and inconvenience people, so there is a latent conflict between what people need and what they would vote for if they were actually asked – if, for example, they were yachtsmen, railway users, householders or gardeners. Since it is impossible to build a motorway with a kink in it to avoid someone's cabbage patch, or to allow people to eat Swiss chocolate if it unsettles the balance of trade, governments tell their citizens that their sacrifice is necessary for the good of the nation at large. However, they are not always convinced, and sometimes they become sufficiently aroused to try to do something about it, when they may well find themselves being offered some form of compensation in order to placate them.

Secondly, therefore, there is an innate conflict between the desire for economic success for the society as a whole and the narrower needs of the political elite themselves. What this means, in plainer terms, is the maintenance of the government itself in its existing framework of political obligation, by promises to benefit those who support them at some unstated time in the future. The problem is, unfortunately, that most governments are not very good at keeping their promises. This does not matter too much in a very rich country. But in a very poor one it is a recipe for disaster.

The North–South divide

The disappearance of the Soviet Union has not helped diminish the North–South divide, and of the majority of the world's states, in what is still widely referred to as 'Third World', many are still autocracies, and a substantial number can be confidently said to have a long way to go before they settle down as stable liberal democracies.

There are three problems with the term 'Third World'. It was originally adopted to refer to countries which were aligned with neither superpower in the Cold War. With the end of the Cold War this meaning is no longer valid. By then the term had already evolved into a concept of **development** (Worsley 1967). However, there are different sorts of development and levels of development, so that it is unlikely that any two states will exhibit comparable levels of development on all indicators. On the other hand, to use the term 'developing world' instead is to accept unchallenged the claim that the so-called 'developing world' is in fact developing, and this view can certainly be challenged. Hence many specialists prefer to use a different term and for many the division between North and South has replaced the Cold War division between East and West. But the older term is so widely known and so convenient that it is still used and therefore still has meaning (Thomas and Wilkins 1999; see also Calvert and Calvert 2001).

The North–South divide is an economic division and not a political one, as between democracies and autocracies, but it often looks that way. Even in Latin America, most of whose states have enjoyed political independence for more than a century and a half (longer than Italy, or Ireland, or Israel), political democracy has yet to come to Haiti and has recently been under serious threat in Peru. One-fourth of the world's population live under the authoritarian system of the People's Republic of China, and it is not at the time of writing showing any signs of emulating its neighbours in the former Soviet Union.

However, even this powerful state cannot suspend the laws of nature, and the remorseless pressure of population growth is driving its citizens into the extreme form of the Third World 'short-termism' which has seriously degraded the environment of Mexico, Thailand or the Philippines and now threatens Malaysia. In such countries political control is purchased by allowing unrestrained exploitation of land and forests. The immediate returns are promising, but soon the inevitable happens and irreplaceable soil washes away in the tropical rains. Disconsolate settlers abandon their holdings and swell the crowds in the shanty towns on the edge of the great cities, where despite all their efforts the pressure of space creates an unhealthy and dangerous environment, fertile of resentment and ready to be mobilised in support of any populist leader who promises a quick and easy solution to their problems.

Ethiopia was once one of the most fertile countries in the world, and the seat of civilisation for thousands of years. Today (2001) much of it is a dustbowl, and while its people are starving, its government has been waging war against neighbouring Eritrea. In neighouring Somalia public order broke down in 1992. While tens of thousands starved, the state ceased to function and until 1999 there was no central government to bring under control the hordes of independent leaders, armed with Soviet and American weapons back in the days of the Cold War.

In these circumstances it is, unfortunately, all too easy for elites to divert attention from their own shortcomings by blaming 'foreigners' for all their country's problems. It is much more satisfying to believe that one is the victim of vast external forces. Furthermore the rulers of the rich countries have everything to gain in the short term from looking after their own domestic political support, keeping taxes down and allow-ing their companies to make money abroad. The future of the former East European states is still very much an open question. The same sort of forces that have led to the semi-unification of Western Europe may yet lead to the reconsolidation, not of the old Soviet Union (that has certainly gone for ever), but of a new regional grouping in North Central Asia. Other regional groupings are emerging in other parts of the world. But future relations between these regions, and the states of which they are composed, are still very unclear. One thing is certain: political conflict existed for centuries before Marx was born or the Soviet Union was invented. It can confidently be expected to be with us for a long time yet.

Economic Development

Economic development refers to a process by which societies increase their capacity to produce. In practice economists tend not to draw distinctions between what they pro-duce, so that the standard measure of economic development is the gross national prod-uct (GNP), the sum total of all that is produced by economic activity in a single year. Since states vary so much in size and productive resources, it is often best to distinguish between more or less 'wealthy' states in terms of their GNP per capita.

This immediately shows that the world is a much more complicated place than the 'Three World' model would suggest. First of all, it makes clear that the majority of states are indeed very poor and there are relatively few rich ones. However, in income terms they form a continuum, not a set of separate categories, though the World Bank has found it useful to divide them into four groups: low-income countries (including China), lower-middle-income countries, higher-middle-income countries and high-income coun-tries. Reliable data on GNP for the 'Second World' has only recently become available. However, where it is available, the figures suggest that the 'Second World' is a political, not an economic concept, a view supported by the collapse of the Soviet Union and with it the notion of a distinctive path to economic development. Today, therefore, for a variety of reasons, it is more usual to speak of two main categories according to their rough positions on the globe: the 'North', the advanced industrialised countries, and the 'South', the rest, but the older term has the advantage of familiarity.

Globalisation

There is no doubt that the industrial revolution, which began first in Britain, then spread to other parts of Europe and later to the rest of the world, marks a radical transforma-tion in economic processes and a major step in economic development. For us, states that have achieved this level of economic development are 'modern'; the others are not. The question of what happens next, however, is still hotly debated.

Older theories of national differences in terms of economic development were based on the concept of *modernisation*. This was a unilinear model which envisaged develop-ment as a single continuum, along which societies moved slowly from traditional to modern. As modernity, mainly in the form of technology, industry and capital investment, was diffused to the less-developed countries (LDCs), it was once generally believed that they would achieve similar levels of development.

In the model advanced by the economic historian W.W. Rostow (1960, 1971), the process of economic modernisation takes a considerable, though diminishing time to get under way, but accelerates into self-sustaining growth after a certain stage of development (the take-off point) has been reached. In theory all countries should be capable of attaining self-sustaining growth. However, not all countries do achieve this, and the classic example is Argentina. It reached what Rostow believed was its take-off point in the 1920s and was at that stage among the half-dozen richest nations in the world. By 1990 it ranked 80th (*Buenos Aires Herald*, 15 July 1990).

It is no coincidence that it was in Argentina and Brazil, where economic development was expected but failed to take place either in the way or to the extent expected, that writers proposed an alternative model of development generally known as *dependency theory* (Cardoso and Faletto 1979). Drawing some of its inspiration from the Marxist critic Paul Baran (1957), it was soon widely adopted in Europe, Asia and Africa. The basic theory takes the nation-state as its unit of analysis and its methodology is historical. It argues that, contrary to the belief of the classical economists, countries that have not yet developed cannot simply follow the example set them by the advanced industrial countries (AICs). The reason is structural: the prior existence of the AICs actually stops other states from developing. The AICs are at the 'core' of the world capitalist system; it is they who have the resources to invest and the power to call the terms of trade. Countries on the 'periphery' of the system have no such freedom of choice. To develop they must attract inward investment from the AICs. However, this investment will not take place unless they fulfil conditions which effectively stop them from developing: opening up their markets to competition from the AICs, abolishing tariff barriers, maintaining convertibility so that corporations can repatriate their profits to the AICs etc. The effect of these conditions is that capital is drained out of the periphery into the core.

One variant was offered by André Gunder Frank (1978), who drew an important distinction between *undeveloped* and *underdeveloped* countries. Accepting the basic premises of the core–periphery relationship and arguing that the rich Western nations were now the global 'bourgeoisie' exploiting the Third World 'proletariat', he claimed that capitalism was actually *causing* underdevelopment. Underdeveloped countries had economies that had actually been *distorted* by capitalism. Capitalism, for Frank, promotes uneven growth in the form of both national and regional polarisation. Funds flow, not from the rich nations to the poor as aid agencies would like, but rather from the poor nations to the rich, as they pay for expensive imported manufactured goods and the multinational corporations who operate on their territory repatriate their profits. Far from being destined to follow the same pattern of development as the industrialised countries, the LDCs are the victims of the world economic system. Their lack of development is not something natural; it is actually caused by the existence of the developed economies, which has ensured that they remain suppliers of the primary raw materials the developed economies need. Only through a major change in the balance of power in the world system and a radical shift in the terms of trade in their favour can they be enabled to break out of this condition of dependence.

However, in 1973 the Organisation of Petroleum Exporting Countries (OPEC) tried to engineer just such a change by restricting production and forcing up the price of crude on the world market. Though this brought about a brief recession in Western Europe and the United States, both this first 'oil shock' and the second that followed in 1979 had a much more serious effect on the majority of Third World economies that did not have petroleum. By 1990, despite a failure to implement effective conservation measures, the AICs had become much less dependent on imported petroleum, and the collapse of the world coffee and sugar agreements, which had existed since the 1930s, demonstrated that similar attempts to maintain prices in other commodities were even less likely to be successful. On the other hand, the so-called 'tiger' economies of Singapore, Thailand, Taiwan and South Korea, developed in co-operation with the AICs on the basis of low-cost production, had brought about very rapid rates of economic growth and a substantial degree of prosperity for the peoples of those countries.

A second variant explains this. In world systems analysis the focus is on the world system. Again historical example is used to identify both cyclical rhythms and secular trends. These suggest a long-term trend to move production out of the AICs and into the periphery, in order to save labour costs. The result is the emergence in the last quarter of the twentieth century of a 'semi-periphery' as a result of the 'dependent development' of states such as the 'Asian tigers'. States can however move both up and down within the complex structure of the world economy in response to changing economic conditions in the world system.

Certainly economic development depends on a number of preconditions, and the variety of the world's states means that no one pattern is likely to be applicable to all. On one hand, the pessimism of the dependency theorists appears to be misplaced. It is possible for states in the Third World to develop. On the other, it seems clear that some of this development at least is 'dependent development'. Krugman and Young have shown that the rates of development of the 'Asian tigers' were not so exceptional and that they can be adequately explained by the very high level of input into those economies (Krugman 1994; Young 1994). And the conditions in the Asian tigers have not, so far, been replicated in Latin America, with the possible exception of Mexico, which is uniquely dependent on the US economy. There, as in many parts of the Third World, the gap between most people's living conditions and those of the inhabitants of the AICs is continuing to widen. But the figures presented in Table 3.1 make clear just how much variety there is between the experiences of different states despite very similar levels of economic development. This suggests that the decisions made by Third World governments can make a significant difference to economic outcomes.

Many writers argue that older ideas of difference are outdated because the whole world is now influenced by the process of *globalisation*. Globalisation has been defined by Giddens as: 'Intensification of world-wide social relations which link distant locations in such a way that local happenings are shaped by events happening many miles away and vice versa' (1990, p. 64). There are four main themes which emerge from the literature:

1. There is a steady integration of peoples. As people move from place to place in search of work, to get away from conflict or simply in search of new experiences, the cultural differences between societies have been eroded. Blue jeans, baseball caps, trainers, Coca-Cola, McDonald's, horror movies, pop music and many other staples of everyday life have been internationalised.
2. Communications and travel have been speeded up. The farthest points of the planet can be reached in hours by air, while electronic communications transmit text, pictures and sound all but instantaneously. In the 'shrinking world' it is no longer possible to say something in one place and assume that it will not be heard in another.

Table 3.1 Selected states, GNP per capita in US dollars, 1997

Country	GNP per capita (US$) 1997
Argentina	8,970
Australia	20,300
Bangladesh	350
Brazil	4,570
Canada	19,290
China	750
France	24,940
Germany	25,850
Ghana	390
India	430
Ireland	18,340
Italy	20,250
Japan	32,380
Mexico	3,890
Nigeria	300
Pakistan	480
Russia	2,300
Sierra Leone	140
Spain	14,080
Sri Lanka	810
United Kingdom	21,400
United States	29,340

Source: World Bank 1999

3. Boundaries between states have become increasingly blurred and for some purposes, especially the movement of money, have practically ceased to exist. Long before the collapse of the Berlin Wall East Germans could watch West German television. By converting their currency to the Deutschmark they gained the freedom, not just to cross the old frontier, but to buy goods and to travel throughout Europe and beyond.

4. All these things have, however, been purchased at a price. World-wide there has been an increasing tendency to embrace technology as the solution to social and political problems. The claim of experts to know better than others has resulted in technocratic dominance not just in scientific matters, such as computer science or medicine, but social scientific areas such as economics and psychology.

The cultural effects of globalisation are obvious. The United States has been the main source of influences in the twentieth century through the desire to emulate the lifestyle of Hollywood by buying its products. One of the few exceptions is the world-wide dominance of football (soccer), but even this has now reached the United States itself.

However, it is the zeal to consume that sustains the world-wide economic system, within which it is not just the products that matter, but the way in which they are sold. Fast-food outlets and supermarkets have broken the traditional link between seller and buyer. No less importantly they have broken the link between the production of food and its consumption, creating a world in which what you buy is a matter of what you are prepared to pay. In 1700 even King William III could not buy fresh peas out of season; in 2001 they are a staple of frozen food cabinets in British supermarkets and the diligent shopper can choose between Israeli oranges, Brazilian mangoes and Kenyan sweet potatoes. Satellite television offers the world a choice of sensation and package tourism enables people for the first time to encounter cultures very different from their own and to do so in numbers sufficiently large to have a significant effect on the economies of many smaller countries. Most recently, the internet affords the opportunity to select for oneself from an unparalleled range of information and, with the linking up of the internet and television, also entertainment.

Liberalisation

Not surprisingly, therefore, post-Marxist writers stress the economic effects of globalisation. The first and most important of these has been the new assertiveness of the world capitalist system since the collapse of communism in 1991. This world system is governed (if at all) through the Bretton Woods institutions: the International Monetary Fund (IMF), the World Bank and the World Trade Organisation (WTO). The first two of these international organisations (IOs) have the power to control national spending by *setting terms for* treasuries and central banks (*conditionality*). The third has the power to regulate trade in goods and services and to punish countries which breach its rules by authorising other countries to inflict financial harm on their manufactures. Yet even the countries which suffer from this process do not challenge the legitimacy of the system under which they deprived themselves of the possibility of making decisions. In Gramscian terms, the so-called 'Washington consensus' has achieved **hegemony**. Governments in Europe have voluntarily embarked on a process of economic liberalisation: deregulating economic activity, privatising state industries, weakening trade unions and cutting down on social security provision.

There have been three main consequences:

1. The bipolar world of the 1980s has given way to a tripolar world, characterised by the exercise of economic power across fading national boundaries by international organisations and transnational corporations.
2. The distinction between centre and periphery has been blurred (or neoliberalism encourages the emergence of multiple centres and peripheries). New regional economic groupings have emerged enabling regional hegemons to exercise their influence more effectively.
3. The periphery itself has become differentiated, notably by the emergence of 'dependent development' in several parts of the former 'Third World'. Among those countries which have a special position in this process are the oil-rich Middle East (Saudi Arabia, Bahrain, the United Arab Emirates); the 'Asian tigers' and their imitators (South Korea, Taiwan, Singapore, Malaysia); and small island developing states such as St Vincent and St Lucia in the Caribbean, the Maldives in the Indian Ocean and Kiribati in the Pacific.

Case Study — Russia: Mixed Outcome to Devolving Power to the Regions

Boris Yeltsin has earned himself a unique place in Russian history for many reasons. But perhaps the most striking aspect of his eight-year rule was in willingly giving away part of his powers.

Under the constitution he drew up in 1993 Mr Yeltsin made provision for the direct election of 89 regional governors and ceded them considerable autonomy. These regional leaders were also granted the right to sit in the Federation Council, the upper house of parliament, which acted as an additional check on the president's powers.

Last spring, for example, Russia's political establishment was riveted by the clash between Mr Yeltsin and the Federation Council over the fate of Yuri Skuratov, the prosecutor general who was investigating allegations of corruption in the Kremlin. The regional governors, who owed their political careers to Mr Yeltsin, twice exercised their constitutional right to confirm the prosecutor general in office – in spite of the president's vehement opposition.

In some respects the new constitutional deal between Moscow and the regions has worked surprisingly well, introducing some checks and balances into a political system, which historically has always been dominated by the executive branch of power.

Some regional centres, such as Novgorod and Samara which have been run by dynamic governors, have seized the opportunity to chart their own destinies and have attracted investment to help regenerate their local economies. Other republics, such as the central Russian regions of Tatarstan and Bashkortostan and the far eastern republic of Yakutia (Sakha) which boast big non-Russian ethnic populations, have also won a high degree of autonomy, helping to defuse separatist claims.

However, other centres, such as the city of St Petersburg and the Primorsky region in the far east, have stagnated as the local authorities have become intertwined with shadowy economic interests. Moreover, many governors have grown almost feudal in their exercise of power, dominating their local companies, media, and courts. As the tragic fate of the Caucasian republic of Chechnya has shown, Russia's flexible constitutional arrangements also have their brittle limits. There is now a decidedly murky pattern of regional relations across Russia's 11 time zones.

The two most acute problems that bedevil Moscow's relations with the regions are fiscal and legal. Crudely put, the regions have the right to spend money but have

Case Study   Continued

little responsibility for raising it while the central government can struggle to enforce the most basic of federal laws. There is a consensus that Russia's federal relations need to be changed; as yet, however, there is no agreement about precisely how this should be done.

Yevgeny Yasin, the former economics minister, says that many governors have entrenched themselves in their regions to such a degree that they have become an obstacle to much-needed structural reforms. 'Every governor and every leader of a republic is a small oligarch,' Mr Yasin says. 'There is no difference between a Boris Berezovsky (the Kremlin powerbroker) and Yuri Luzhkov (the mayor of Moscow). They simply have different positions and they do the same thing from different angles.

'They both use administrative resources to control federal property and seize control of financial flows. This means there is no free market and prevents reforms from working,' he says. 'Either we pursue nomenklatura capitalism and lose 10 to 15 years or we create a free market.'

Mr Putin's team is clearly keen to strengthen what Russians call the 'vertical of power', enabling them to enforce the will of the central government throughout the regions. The president has already initiated a series of arm-wrestling matches with many of the governors over how to rebalance their respective powers.

Minitmer Shaimiev, the president of Tatarstan, says Mr Putin has told the governors he wants all members of the Russian federation to live under one common system of laws, taxes, and budgets. Mr Shaimiev acknowledges this would curtail some of the special privileges that Tatarstan has enjoyed over the past few years thanks to the separate constitutional treaty it signed with Moscow. But the Tatar leader says he is prepared to compromise as long as the federal government fulfils all its financial obligations in the republic.

'In a federal state it is impossible to object to the argument that we should all live within one common legal space,' Mr Shaimiev says. 'But to try to manage Tatarstan's economy or that of any other subject from the centre is not only problematic but contradicts the very laws of a market economy.'

For the moment, the governors retain considerable powers within their regions and are in a strong position to resist the Kremlin's centralising impulse. Many observers thought it significant that Mr Putin backed away from a direct confrontation with Vladimir Yakovlev, the governor of St Petersburg, who is standing for re-election this month. The Kremlin had earlier supported Valentina Matviyenko, the social securities minister, to run against Mr Yakovlev. But she dropped out of the race once it became clear how tough the fight would be.

Some observers argue that Mr Putin may only be ducking such challenges until he has consolidated his power. Although the president has rejected the idea that the Kremlin should revert to appointing governors, he has made his long-term intent fairly clear. 'Russia was founded as a super-centralised state from the very start. This is inherent in its genetic code, traditions, and people's mentality,' Mr Putin said before the presidential elections.

Yegor Gaidar, the former prime minister, says the federal government has been unsustainably weak over the past few years and it is clear there will be some degree of recentralisation under Mr Putin. But he warns of the dangers of dismantling Mr Yeltsin's democratic experiment altogether.

'It is much easier to run a unitarian state than a federal state. But the fact that Russia is a federal state is very important for its long term stability. I hope Putin understands it would be a mistake to push recentralisation too far,' he says.

Source: *Financial Times*, 10 May 2000

FT

West Africa

NIGERIA

Official name: Federal Republic of Nigeria
Type of government: Federal presidential republic
Capital: Abuja
Area: 924,000 sq km
Population (2000): 121,000,000
GNP per capita (2000): $300 (PPP $820)

Evolution of government: British colonial control of coast region with capital at Lagos, extended to Protectorate over Muslim North in 1907 under system of dual mandate. Independent 1960; parliamentary federal republic of 4 states 1963 but military coup by northerners 1966 led to attempt of Igbo (Ibo) of the coast to secede as 'Biafra' and to civil war 1967–70. Under continuing military dominance several unsuccessful experiments in constitution-making before present return to civilian rule 1999.

Main features of government: Federal system of 36 states with state governors and legislatures. Central government a presidential republic led by former soldier and military president, General Olusegun Obasanjo, elected president 1999. Continuing strong role of the military. Serious unrest followed first introduction of Muslim Shar'ia Law in Northern state of Zamfara 1999. Despite being a major oil producer, the country's economy remains in crisis and is notorious for clientelism and corruption.

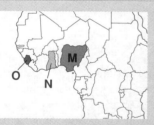

GHANA

Official name: Republic of Ghana
Type of government: Unitary presidential republic
Capital: Accra
Area: 240,000 sq km
Population (2000): 18,000,000
GNP per capita (2000): $390 (PPP $1,610)

Evolution of government: Internal self-government established in colonial period; at independence 1957 a parliamentary republic. Prime minister Kwame Nkrumah, however, transformed into presidential system under his own leadership with East European touches (Chapter 4). In 1966 Nkrumah was overthrown by army and police, inaugurating long period of military dominance and intervention (Chapter 10). Flt Lt Jerry Rawlings seized power in a coup in 1979 and shot three of his predecessors before restoring civilian rule; in 1982 he again seized power on behalf of a Provisional National Defence Council. In 1989 a slow move back towards liberal democracy began. Rawlings was elected president in 1992 and 1996 but his designated successor failed to win in 2000.

Main features of government: Presidential republic (Chapter 1). Strong presidency established by charismatic leader with populist appeal (Chapters 6, 9). Liberalisation followed by democratisation (Chapter 3); having failed to discredit elections, opposition has now successfully contested power. Independent judiciary. Ghana is heavily dependent on the changing world price of a single crop: cocoa.

SIERRA LEONE

Official name: Republic of Sierra Leone
Type of government: Unitary presidential republic
Capital: Freetown
Area: 72,000 sq km
Population (2000): 5,000,000
GNP per capita (2000): $140 (PPP $390)

Evolution of government: Freetown and coastal settlement established by British philanthropists as settlement for freed slaves 1788; colony established 1808 and interior proclaimed a protectorate 1896. Independent 1961; proclaimed presidential republic under one-party rule by Siaka Stevens 1971. Role as base for regional peacekeeping mission in neighbouring Liberia precipitated an invasion by insurgents sponsored by Charles Taylor. Savage civil war followed marked by mutilation of captives and civilians and impressment of child soldiers, often under the influence of drugs. By referendum 1991 officially returned to multi-party government under elected president but the civil war has been slow to die down.

Main features of government: Presidential republic with strong executive presidency. Government ineffective in hinterland, where armed bands supported by Liberia continue to dominate the diamond fields and other key areas. Country's infrastructure has collapsed and there is acute poverty in both Freetown (swollen by refugees) and the countryside.

Politically, centres of power now lie outside the nation-state and in most cases lie beyond its control. The keenest advocates of the globalisation thesis argue that the process goes much further than this, that national boundaries are disappearing and for the first time in human history there has emerged a truly global economic system. This system is subject only to global market forces and individual states no longer have the capacity to govern the transnational companies that are its main actors (Ohmae 1990). Neostructuralists argue that the state can no longer control its own economy, and is subject to the unpredictable play of market forces. It is therefore restricted in what it can do and interest groups, political parties and legislatures have to come to terms with but seek to avoid the consequences of their own powerlessness.

However, Hirst and Thompson argue that this argument is overstated. They draw a sharp distinction between a truly globalised economy and one that is merely 'internationalised'. Transnational corporations are indeed powerful and we would be wise to remember that. But they are not 'stateless'; they trade from a base in a national economy and their national identity continues to be important to them, providing a structure of law which regulates their actions, a common culture which gives them their competitive edge over less integrated companies, and the backing of a powerful patron which can afford a variety of forms of concealed support. Europe, Japan and North America remain the main providers of direct foreign investment. Together they exercise a considerable degree of control over world financial markets, though for ideological reasons they may well choose not to exercise the power they have (Hirst and Thompson 1999, pp. 2–3).

If they do not, democracy, previously challenged by the Cold War, superpower dominance and the national security state, has achieved a new level of acceptance, only (paradoxically) to have to meet a new threat posed by the neoliberal paradigm, which says that whatever the people want, they are not necessarily going to be allowed to have.

Political Development

It was, inevitably, tempting to try to analyse the development of political systems in terms of modernisation. The theme espoused by modernisation theorists, that all societies tend to move from more traditional forms of organisation towards a single, more modern form, is to be found in the work of Marx, Weber and Durkheim, among others.

Building on the work of the eighteenth-century economists, Marx and Engels (1962) [1848] argued that the political order derived directly from the prevailing mode of production. Hence there would be an appropriate political order for each stage of economic development, in a linear progress towards modernity, though one cut across with specific moments of transition. For them, societies were scattered at various stages along the road leading to socialism, but all were moving at greater or lesser speed towards the same place, a place where satisfaction of material needs would rest on the large-scale production associated with industrialisation. Thus the economic stage of primitive accumulation characterised by nomadic society was, they argued, displaced when slave labour became generally available by feudal society. This in turn gave way to capitalist society, in which, by a revolutionary seizure of power, rule passed from the aristocracy to the new bourgeoisie. Capitalist society, however, would in turn bring its own nemesis. By calling into existence an industrial working class, the proletariat, it created the class which would ultimately supplant it, and build on its ruins a socialist society in which 'the exploitation of man by man' would come to an end.

For Weber (1965 [c. 1919]), the tendency towards the complexity of mass industrial society increasingly required societies to move from traditional and charismatic forms of authority towards legal-rational authority and bureaucratic organisation. Durkheim (1964 [1893]) saw modern society as increasingly characterised by a division of labour and interdependence. These themes come together in the work of the post-Second World War structural functionalists, working under the influence of the American sociologist Talcott Parsons. For Apter (1965) *political modernization* was a process of adaptation to the changing needs of economic development. The starting point was traditional society, which proved strongly resistant even to the impact of Western colonisation. 'Secular-libertarian' societies tended to emerge because of the particular needs and requirements of industrial society.

But political modernisation proved a very troublesome concept to define, let alone to apply systematically. Perhaps as you read this you are looking out on the glass, steel and concrete of a college, factory or block of flats which represent, in visual terms, a stage of the development of building techniques. As you look, you are aware that in turn this depends on a process of economic development, involving such trends as the growth of corporations, economies of scale, mass production, greater use of machinery, and substitution of natural products by synthetic ones. But it is not clear that the government of the town in which that building stands, or indeed the political system of any country in the world, has changed in the sense that builders have changed from the use of stone and wood to the use of concrete and glass, and the growth in size of political units is not in itself a guarantee of greater political effectiveness, and may well be the reverse. The term 'modernisation' was increasingly seen in the late 1960s as ethnocentric and misleading, even by those who continued to use it (Kautsky 1972). The emergence of authoritarian regimes in post-independence Africa and in Latin America was seen as an alternative route to modernisation, and the notion of the universality of liberal democracy as a model seemed to be discredited (Huntington 1968; see also Lenz and Shell 1986; Apter 1987).

Political development, the term that took its place, was from the outset a controversial term, with many definitions (Huntington 1965). There was, and is, moreover, a tendency to assume that political development must in some way be related to if not actually *caused* by economic development. The theme that rational economic production required a well-educated and democratically controlled workforce was strongly in evidence in **convergence theory**, which argued (against very strong opposition on both sides) that the political systems of the USA and USSR were bound in time to get more like one another (Brzezinski and Huntington 1964). After a long eclipse, a somewhat similar view has been enjoying a new vogue in the aftermath of the changes in Eastern Europe and the collapse of the former Soviet Union.

Convergence suggests that all societies are *en route* to industrialisation and hence that similar Western-style democratic political systems will displace authoritarian and state-socialist arrangements. The emerging societies will reflect the 'logic' (or needs) of industrialism, including urbanisation, advanced technology, well-developed communications, enhanced educational opportunities and high social mobility. Increased economic interdependence and increasing cultural similarity will reduce conflict between states and make the world a more stable and peaceful place.

Of course there are arguments that can be raised against the convergence model. There are many societies in the world that it would be difficult to see as moving towards industrialisation. Many parts of the world – Africa south of the Sahara, for example – have so little infrastructure (good roads, railways, adequate power supplies etc.) and so many social problems (not least, feeding their populations) that industrial development must be very limited for the foreseeable future. Industrial development itself, in any case, takes many forms and the oil-producing states of the Middle East vary markedly in social structure from the 'high-tech', manufacturing states of the Far East, such as Taiwan and South Korea. Both are different, again, from older industrialised nations. Which professional and technical experts are accorded most respect in any hierarchy of occupations varies a good deal too, as does the degree of status attached to education. Education is often least valued in the most industrialised nations and the convergence model does not explain this. Authoritarian and personalist rulers remain, and only when they openly and flagrantly violate international law, as in the case of the 1990 Iraqi invasion of Kuwait, do they attract much attention from the world community. The emergence of fundamentalist Islamic regimes in countries such as Iran and the Sudan has also provided evidence against the convergence hypothesis.

Nevertheless the convergence argument, in a rather specialised form, is still being used by the proponents of the so-called *free market* in both Western and Eastern Europe.

Not only do they believe that the free market is a prerequisite for democracy, but they argue that the existence of the market in itself renders democracy inevitable. Better knowledge of a century and a half of Latin American political history suggests that this idea should be treated with the greatest possible caution.

Democratisation

However, there are two senses in which it is still not only possible but necessary to talk of political development as a common theme which links together the political systems of the modern world within a historical framework. First of all, with time there has been a tendency for political systems to become more *complex*. Secondly, over the past two hundred years most, if not all, systems have been modified to allow for greater *participation* by the general mass of the people.

In fact the concept of sovereignty in the modern sense is inseparable from the idea of the representation of the people, in an *assembly* which has successfully asserted its right to take part in the making of new laws. By 'assembly' is meant here a grouping together of people representing the society as a whole. They do not have to be elected by any specific system of election. There only has to be general acceptance that the assembly as constituted represents the people as a whole. It stands for all classes and all interests and acts on their behalf – and they must obey it (Verney 1961, p. 3).

However, for democracy to exist there has to be more than this. There is a general consensus on five basic requirements:

- government chosen by the people;
- free and fair elections;
- freedom of expression;
- civil society;
- rule of law.

What therefore has to happen for these things to be attained? At the time of the French Revolution, and for long afterwards, the starting point was a divinely sanctioned monarchy. In modern times the target of efforts at democratisation has usually been a military dictatorship or other authoritarian government. Following Huntington, most modern writers identify three stages in this process:

1. **Liberalisation**. In this stage there is a gradual relaxation of political and social control. Increased freedom of expression is either tolerated or happens without effective resistance from government. The release of political prisoners is frequently a first step towards trying to negotiate popular acceptance for the continuation of the regime. Other than in Romania, this was a general feature of events in Eastern Europe in 1989, as it became increasingly clear that the Soviet Union neither wanted to nor was able to maintain unpopular pro-Moscow governments in power.
2. **Transition**. When it becomes clear that the issue is not how long the regime can survive, but whether it can survive at all, the government seeks to reach an agreement with the opposition, possibly brokered from outside. The central point of the agreement is when and how elections will be held for the formation of a new government. However, the reason for reaching it is to protect the members of the outgoing government against possible reprisal. Following the ousting of General Suharto in

Indonesia, the interim government of President Habibie presided over elections which resulted in a new parliament. This body did not, however, choose the leader of the largest opposition party, Megawati Sukarnoputri, as president, but instead selected a prominent and respected Muslim leader who had the trust of the army and the support of Suharto's official party, Golkar. He in turn was ousted in 2001 (see p. 308).

3. **Consolidation**. Following the inauguration of the new government there follows a long period of consolidation. Unlike the other two stages this has no definite limit, and in recent years the 'consolidologists' have tried with some difficulty to define it more closely. It is during this stage that there emerges a new sense of civil society and even of a civic culture which supports a democratic government. There will be general acceptance of new order and regular elections will become normal. Huntington himself has suggested a stringent test of successful consolidation. This, the so-called 'two-turnover test', requires political power to have changed hands from government to opposition twice by means of elections. Though this seems reasonable at first sight, there are some surprising exceptions. Post-war Germany did not fulfil this condition until 1997, because Chancellor Kohl did not originally take power as the result of an election but because the Free Democrats changed coalition partners. Post-war Japan has yet to fulfil the condition. Yet no one seriously imagines that democracy has not long since been consolidated in both countries.

Three waves of democratisation

It has become commonplace in the literature to refer to the regimes that emerged in the most recent period of democratisation in Europe, Asia and Latin America as the 'third wave' democracies. This usage stems from Huntington's historical analysis of the process of democratisation, which suggests that the course of democratisation can be seen as three 'waves' of democratisation, broken by two short 'reverse waves' of reversion to authoritarian government (Shin 1994).

Between 1828 and 1926, the first 'long wave' of democratisation, Huntington argues, resulted in the emergence of the old democracies: the United States, Britain, France, Italy, Argentina, Canada, Australia and New Zealand. Then, between 1922 and 1942 there was the first reverse wave. Italy, Germany, Spain and Portugal in Europe and Argentina, Brazil and the majority of the Latin American states were all affected. Then starting in the middle of the Second World War, in 1943, and lasting until 1962, there was a second short wave of democratisation. The major states that adopted democratic government during this period – India, Israel, West Germany, Italy, Japan, etc. – have retained it ever since. However, others, such as Greece and Turkey in Europe and Argentina, Brazil and Chile in Latin America, succumbed to a further 'reverse wave' of authoritarian rule at various times between 1958 and 1975. It is only since 1974 that the third wave of democratisation has swept across Portugal, Spain and Eastern Europe, and much of Latin America, Asia and Africa (Huntington 1993a, b). However, despite a favourable international climate, democratisation is not necessarily a very rapid process, and the example of Ghana is instructive (see Case Study).

Case Study Democratisation in Ghana

Background

Ghana, the first country in Africa south of the Sahara to become independent in 1957, has had a turbulent history since. At independence it was a parliamentary system led by the charismatic Kwame Nkrumah, whose idea of 'African socialism' derived from a mixture of British labour politics and American Black radicalism. Under Nkrumah Ghana was turned into a 'one-party state' with himself as president supported by a Convention People's Party (CPP) organised loosely on Marxist lines. Unchecked by criticism, a great deal of money was squandered on a range of prestige projects which the country could not really afford.

In 1966, while he was out of the country, Nkrumah was overthrown by a coup organised jointly by the army and police, who overcame the East European-trained Presidential Guard in a savage battle. A National Liberation Council was set up chaired by the leader of the coup, Col. A.A. Afrifa. The ruling apparatus of the one-party state was dismantled and some market-oriented reforms followed, before in 1969 elections were held and the country was returned to civilian rule under Dr Kofi Busia. However, with the falling price on the world's markets of Ghana's principal export, cocoa, the government was soon in financial difficulties and in 1972 the army stepped in again.

For the next three years Col. I.K. Acheampong ruled with the assistance of a National Redemption Council. In 1975 he concerted his government into a military dictatorship and this in turn was displaced in 1978 in a further coup led by Lt Gen. F.W.K. Akuffo. He and a Supreme Military Council continued to hold power while nominally preparing the country for return to civilian rule. However, before this could happen there was an unexpected development. The junior officers of the armed services, led by Flt Lt Jerry Rawlings, overthrew the senior officers in 1979 accusing them of corruption. The Armed Forces Ruling Council purged the government and on Rawlings's orders three former heads of state (Afrifa, Acheampong and Akuffo) were shot on the beach outside Accra as a warning to others. Then, equally unexpectedly, elections were held and a civilian government returned to office under Dr Hilla Limann.

By 1981, Rawlings decided that civilian government too had failed and seized power again. Over the next nineteen years he was to continue to head the government while experimenting with four different approaches to the problem of governing Ghana.

The first period, 1981–83, was a period of *radical populism*, reminiscent in some ways of the Nkrumah period. The new Provisional National Defence Council did not hold elections but instead created local organisations on the Cuban/Libyan model. Economic policy involved a return to price and wage controls, and a self-reliant 'socialist' development strategy.

During 1983–89 the regime evolved into a more *pragmatic authoritarianism*. Despite its military origins, the government remained separate from the military establishment; in fact it proved able to control dissension among the armed forces through the popular committees it had established. Its Economic Recovery Programme of April 1983, moreover, was an orthodox stabilisation package, which could have been prescribed by the International Monetary Fund. By 1986 it appeared that the economic decline of the country had been halted. In 1987–89 further structural reforms took place with the phasing out of the state monopolies which had been a feature of the system since the earliest days and banks began once more to invest in Ghana. The cocoa farmers gained as a result but the condition of the poor worsened. Rising discontent brought a measure of liberalisation with the election of district assemblies and a move back to a more democratic system began.

Case Study   Continued

Liberalisation

Between 1989 and 1992 therefore the country entered a phase of *political liberalisation*. There was a further extension of participation leading up to a referendum on the reintroduction of a multi-party constitution in April 1992. The result was a landslide win for the constitution and for the ruling National Democratic Congress (NDC). In the 1992 elections Rawlings was elected president under the new constitution. Critics regarded the elections as a sham but the opposition was divided and had rashly boycotted elections in the hope of gaining foreign sympathy. Instead observers certified them as fair.

Although, given Rawlings's undoubted personal popularity, there is no reason to disagree with this opinion, the Fourth Republic inaugurated on 7 January 1993 was initially at most a *limited democracy*. Rawlings remained as commander-in-chief of the army and the security apparatus remained in place, while Rawlings's NDC dominated Parliament. The opposition, on the other hand, soon came to accept the new institutional arrangements, particularly after the revival of the concept of an independent judiciary.

Transition

Full transition to a working liberal democracy came at the earliest in 1996, when Rawlings was re-elected with 57.2 per cent of the votes cast, to 39.8 per cent for John Kufuor of New Patriotic Party (NPP), which won one-third of the seats in Parliament and was able to constitute itself as an effective opposition. Again there was no allegation of the results having been obtained by fraud. In 2000 Rawlings did not run for re-election and the NDC nominated his chosen successor, John Mills. There was a number of violent clashes when NDC supporters tried to disrupt voting in the first and especially in the second round of voting, when an NPP MP was killed. But observers judged the elections broadly 'free and fair' and Mills was defeated, the results of the two-stage process being as shown in Table 3.2.

Consolidation

In parliamentary elections Kufuor's NPP won 98 seats and narrowly failed to gain an overall majority in the 200-seat assembly, results for the other parties being: NDC 93 seats, People's National Convention (PNC) 4, Convention People's Party (CPP) 1, independents 4. In January 2001 Rawlings stood down as promised and John Kufuor succeeded him as president. Though his party lacked an overall majority in Parliament, it was expected to be able to govern reasonably effectively.

Ghana has therefore had one successful 'turnover' of power but it remains to be seen how long it will take for democracy to be consolidated.

Table 3.2 Results of presidential election in Ghana, 2000

Candidate	% of vote first round	% of vote second round
John Kufuor (NPP)	48.3	57.0
John Mills (NDC)	44.9	43.0
Edward Mahama	2.5	—
George Hagan	1.8	—
Others	2.5	—
Total	100.0	100.0

Summary

Present-day politics can only be understood in a developmental context. Modern complex societies are built up out of relatively simple elements. The relationships within modern complex societies obviously reflect the nature of economic production, and the overarching framework of the global system determines the economic relationships not only between but within modern states. However, there is still substantial room for variation in the political arrangements within any given society, and the influence of political ideas such as freedom and participation has been so great as at times to override considerations of economic productivity. Political development, therefore, is a term which should only be used very carefully.

Key Concepts

aggression, propensity to use force

assembly, a group of people representing society as a whole

convergence theory, the view that the logic of industrialisation is that all societies will become more alike

development, in economics, the increase in a society's capacity to produce; in politics, the tendency of political systems to become more complex

environment, generally, the world and all that is in it, and specifically, that part of it in which a specific political system is located

hegemony, for Gramsci, the successful representation of the interests of the ruling class as the interests of society at large; more generally, the power of an ideology to gain general acceptance and so constrain all thinking about politics and society; dominance so potent that it appears natural, and questioning it seems subversive

Third World, those countries that are neither advanced industrial countries nor part of the former Eastern bloc

Sample Questions

Examination syllabuses require candidates not only to show that they know how systems work now, but to explain why, in terms of the historical, social and economic development of those systems. Candidates are unlikely, however, to be required to answer questions on political anthropology or primitive government, unless the syllabus specifically indicates that this is likely.

Where examination questions concern an aspect of the politics of only one country, it is still generally true that the categories used will have a wider comparative context, and awareness of the relevant debates would be an advantage.

- How do we know when a democratic system has been consolidated?

- How far can a developmental perspective enhance the understanding of politics?

- 'Communism is essentially a programme for the economic and social development of backward countries.' Discuss.

- Is the nation-state in Western Europe a historical anachronism?

- Account for the rise of the 'third wave' democracies.

Further Reading

On the global environment and its crisis see C. Thomas (1992) and Calvert and Calvert (1999). The concept of the environment in political analysis is discussed by Easton (1957) and Deutsch (1966), as well as by other writers. Early warnings of today's environmental crisis came from Falk (1970) and Meadows *et al.* (1974).

Political anthropology is a specialist field not easily accessible, but Bailey (1969) uses an anthropological approach and introduces the concepts of rules and of the 'game' of politics. A clear and well-organised introduction to 'Third World' politics and society is Calvert and Calvert (2001). On economic development Gauhar (1983) forms a useful introduction, while Rostow (1960) and Myrdal (1972) are classic statements of developmentalist theory. On the notion of political development see Huntington (1968) and Lenz and Shell (1986). Cardoso and Faletto (1979) was one of the first statements of dependency theory, and retains its interest well despite many later critics, while C. Thomas (1987) discusses the nature of present-day economic constraints on Third World states in the international arena.

The Social Sources of Power

CHAPTER FOUR

Social Power

The social sources of power involve communication, political culture and ideology. Communication is the vehicle by which politics is carried on. The range of systems of communication available and the way in which they are used help determine the nature of politics. Political culture describes the way in which politics is carried on. It forms part of the collective memory of a society, and is largely determined by the dominant ideology. This is the system of ideas which is taught – consciously or subconsciously – as part of the socialisation of new members of the society.

Communication

Communication is the transmission of a signal through a channel from a sender to a receiver (Miller 1963, p. 6). The signal, sent in the form of an economical statement known as a code, does not arise accidentally, and it must be recognised and interpreted by the receiver into a pattern of actions or statements. Communication therefore normally includes a process of coding and a process of decoding, as well as the act of transmission, which may be either direct or through third parties. An essential prerequisite, therefore, is that the code should be known to the parties at both the sending and receiving end. Lastly, a communication may cause the receiver either to act on their own account, or to tell others to act according to a predetermined plan or code of conduct. This is the pattern that characterises the relations between central and local government. In the UK, for example, the Department of Local Government gives general instructions which have to be carried out locally according to local circumstances. Students of politics should be warned that such communications cannot necessarily easily be understood or accurately interpreted by outsiders, since the codes in which they are transmitted may be complex, obscure or deliberately restricted to a select few (see below).

Communication is the foundation of society. It begins with language itself. The many human languages provide a sophisticated means of communication that differentiates human beings from other animals. With the exception of the cetacea (e.g. whales and dolphins) no other animal appears to have a 'vocabulary' of more than some twenty 'words'. Nevertheless, the existence of simple communication systems among animals shows that they fulfil the needs of the animals using them. Much the same kind of lesson can be drawn from human society. For each type of society, good communications are appropriate communications. A small rural community can be well integrated and interact fully by direct speech; a city such as New York or Tokyo would disintegrate under the same conditions. But conversely the same number of farmers deprived of direct speech and dependent for integration on television and radio would not be a community at all. In fact it is just this reliance in modern states on the mass media which leads to that decentralised and demoralised condition which has been termed 'mass society'.

The fact that it originated with direct speech is the key to another property of language, particularly everyday language. People may all be talking at the same time and so have difficulty gaining attention. Hence, in any given communication, much of the content is redundant. To put it another way, the same thing is said more than once. Part of the content is only there to make the sense of the rest clear.

Communication serves a wide range of different purposes. It is possible, however, to distinguish between eight different categories into which individual sentences can be classified: phatic communion, prevention of communication, recording-transmitting, instrumental, affective, catharsis, magic and ritual (Miller 1963).

1. **Phatic communion**. This is the technical term applied to formal exchanges which open up the possibility of communication between two people who have just met, e.g. 'Hello. How are you?' 'Fine. How are you?'

2. **Prevention of communication**. The converse of phatic communion is a statement indicating unwillingness to communicate, usually coupled for reasons of politeness with an expression of willingness to communicate later, as e.g. 'Hi there.' 'Hi. Sorry, can't stop now. See you later.'

3. **Recording-transmitting**. The simplest example of a communication that is concerned only with the recording-transmitting of information is dictation. However, substantial wodges of such material are to be found in formal statements to parliaments and congresses and form the staple filler of many political speeches, which otherwise would be unbearably short.

4. **Instrumental**. Instrumental statements are statements which result in physical movement or action on the part of the person addressed. A patient entering the consulting room is greeted by the doctor with a series of instrumental statements: 'Come in. Sit down. Now what seems to be the trouble?' An explicit statement in a political speech calling on members of the audience to vote for the speaker is also instrumental, as is a call to give active support or money to a political party.

5. **Affective**. However, in political speeches, particularly (but not exclusively) at election time, politicians angle their statements in order to generate emotion rather than action. In addition, many political messages are sent for the purpose of deliberately confusing or misleading receivers. Appealing to a wide audience can easily involve preventing them from drawing the correct conclusions from a pattern of actions or statements, or, as we now say, putting the best 'spin' on them. At times of national stress or emergency the use of emotive language is particularly valuable, since it distracts attention from inconvenient facts. The way in which President Bush of the United States told the American people he had given orders to invade Panama is an outstanding example (see Case Study).

Other specialised uses of communication may be less obvious, but no less important.

6. **Catharsis**. Powerful emotions, once aroused, can be hard to handle and the experienced politician will know when and how to discharge powerful emotions, such as pain and grief, in a way that consolidates their own political leadership. The ability of Bill Clinton, president of the United States 1993–2001, to empathise publicly with suffering and loss was a key factor in his continuing popularity, despite the relentless attacks of his political opponents.

7. **Magic**. A rain-maker who repeats often enough that it is going to rain is quite likely to be right some of the time; if so (such is the waywardness of human nature) those are the times that are remembered. Similarly politicians who have little or no ability to influence events positively often resort to the incantation of formulae which are indistinguishable from the magic of the rain-maker. In the early 1990s there was widespread alarm in Britain that the appearance of bovine spongiform encephalopathy (BSE) might endanger human life. Despite the fact that they had no justification

Case Study · Bush Invades Panama

Background

On 20 December 1990 US troops invaded Panama to overthrow the government of General Manuel Noriega. This action was in breach of the Charters both of the United Nations and of the Organisation of American States. Hence when President Bush spoke to the American people on nationwide television he used strongly emotive imagery to justify his action:

What he said

'Last Friday, Noriega declared his military dictatorship to be in a state of war with the United States and publicly threatened the lives of Americans in Panama. The very next day, forces under his command shot and killed an unarmed American serviceman, wounded another, arrested and brutally beat a third American serviceman, and then brutally interrogated his wife, threatening her with sexual abuse. That was enough' (*Congressional Quarterly Weekly Report*, 47, No. 51, p. 3534).

What was misleading

In fact it was not Noriega, but the Panamanian Congress, who had said they regarded themselves as being in a state of war with the United States. There had already been a substantial previous build-up of American troops there. The American serviceman shot was unarmed because he was in civilian clothes. He had driven through an official checkpoint without stopping. There was no evidence that specific orders had been given by Noriega to Panamanian troops 'under his command' to harass Americans. The alleged threat of sexual abuse was never substantiated.

What he did not say

Bush did not observe that Noriega's regime, though corrupt, was less brutal than previous Panamanian regimes the US had supported. He did not disclose that Noriega himself had not only been an informant for the US Central Intelligence Agency (CIA) for many years but had actually been commended for his work for the US government. He failed to mention that had Noriega's regime survived for just ten more days it would have had, under the Treaties of 1977, the right to appoint the first Panamanian Chair of the Panama Canal Commission.

What happened next

In the war that followed, 26 US soldiers were killed and 323 wounded. The Panamanians lost 314 soldiers and more than a hundred wounded, and there were literally thousands of civilian casualties. Noriega was persuaded to surrender to US troops. Though a soldier, he did not receive the protection of the Geneva Convention. Instead he was taken to the USA and sentenced by a US court to a long term of imprisonment for actions which, if they had taken place, had not been carried out under US jurisdiction.

Source: Calvert 1990c

whatsover for doing so, Conservative agriculture ministers repeatedly declared that British beef was 'safe': in May 1990 John Gummer said that it was 'completely safe' and as late as 1996 Stephen Dorrill said that eating it posed 'no conceivable risk', something for which to his credit he subsequently apologised (*The Guardian*, 27 and 28 October 2000).

8. **Ritual**. Ritual, both physical and verbal, serves a number of useful purposes in politics. The complicated circumlocutions obligatory in the British House of Commons, and the requirement to address the Chair, rather than one another, serve to slow and so cool the process of debate. 'Madam Speaker, the Hon. Member for Stoke

Newington South has undoubtedly been guilty of a terminological inexactitude'
means exactly the same as 'You are a liar', but with reasonable luck will not lead to
bloodshed.

Many people feel impatient with the slow and tortuous course of democratic debate.
However, what is the alternative? It is not so many years since two Uruguayan politicians
fought a duel, or a Mexican deputy opened fire with a pistol on an opponent on the floor
of Congress. And in 1980 a speech by Archbishop Oscar Romero urging the government
of El Salvador to listen to the complaints of its citizens was followed by his assassination, in the act of saying Mass, by armed gunmen belonging to the extreme right
(Romero 1985).

Metacommunication

Face-to-face communication has the additional advantage that we interpret the spoken
word by taking note, consciously or unconsciously, of **metacommunication** – information gained from signs such as context, body-language or gesture (Condon 1966, p. 9).
Signs differ from symbols in that they are not consciously created.

However, though the interpretation of signs is easy in theory, it can be quite difficult
in practice. The idea that one can walk down a street in a strange town and look at it
for the evidence it gives on the lives of those who live there is not a remarkable one.
Whether the street is swept, what sort and size of houses it contains, whether they have
gardens and what sort of plants they have in them, whether the houses are well painted,
what sort of curtains show at the windows, the presence of garages, lawnmowers,
scooters, bicycles, cars and children's toys – all these, given experience of that society,
inform the passer-by of the social standing, income, occupation, taste and even the
political sympathies of the residents. But only up to a point.

In a society in which governments are on the alert for manifestations of discontent,
of course, people may take great care to assume a uniform outward appearance. Besides
they may, and frequently do, live in flats or apartment blocks; the presence of a concierge, security guard or electrically operated door here can be a sign of the degree to
which those within feel it necessary to defend their position against the outside world.
The French concierge and the Russian *dezhurnaya* have on the other hand each been useful to the state when it wished to keep an eye on the residents.

Similarly there is some body-language that appears to be universal – a politician
who is lying, for example, will be unable to control the rise in his blink-rate. But some
is specific to the individual's society and culture. And some forms of communication –
notably the telephone – screen out metacommunication almost completely, making the
task of interpretation correspondingly difficult.

Distortion of communication

Otherwise all communication is subject to distortion, specifically of three types (Pierce
1962, pp. 25, 29; Condon 1966, p. 51; Miller 1963, p. 257). It may be subject to bias,
interference or overload.

1. **Bias** is selectivity to certain signals rather than to others. It may occur because no one
   within the system recognises the significance of certain signals. Or it may result

within the system from the choice of information to be passed on to the decision-makers by the selectors who first receive the communication.

2. **Interference** is the obscuring effect of the general mush of background noise, coming in the case of politics from the wider social environment: information on subjects such as the weather, sporting events or cultural activities which engage the attention irrelevantly from their very volume and persistence.

3. **Overload** selectively limits the capacity of the network to handle information flows. The problem of it is its random effect on individual communications within the total volume of messages being passed.

The German critical theorist Jürgen Habermas argues that systematic distortion of communication is in itself a way in which control can be maintained over a society, and that this distortion is the product of the dominant ideology of that society (Habermas 1979).

Levels of communication

The extent and effectiveness of each and all of these types of communication depends on the level at which it takes place. At the simplest level of understanding there is face-to-face communication, that is to say, direct speech between two human beings. It is at this level that government alone becomes truly real to the individual person. Therefore it is not surprising to find that the essence of government to most people is not the orderly but impersonal operation of the postal service or traffic lights, but the occasional but often potentially conflict-laden encounters with policemen, local government officers or civil servants, such as welfare officers or social security clerks. These are the people with whom citizens deal directly, and it is on them that resentments tend to get discharged.

Face-to-face communications are direct, real, present. They are the necessary foundation of systems in which interaction, characteristic of them, is replaced by action. The only other means of communication with the characteristic of interaction is the telephone, which transmits speech directly, and which like direct speech leaves no written record.

The problem has been compounded by the arrival of the mobile phone. Previously it could be assumed that the percentage of households in a country that had a telephone was a useful measure of development, and the countries at the top of the table – Canada, the United States and Germany – were all prosperous (see Table 4.1). It could also be assumed that such countries would be more democratic. It is difficult for a society to be a completely closed one if its citizens have telephones, though in the former Soviet Union this feature of the telephone was minimised as far as possible by the absence of a satisfactory telephone directory. Yet even with this limitation the former Soviet dissident Andrei Sakharov could, through the use of the telephone, retain access to the outside world and hence to world public opinion as long as he was not actually in prison. On the other hand, it is also true that before the Revolution in 1959, Cuba, though a dictatorship, ranked fourth in the Americas in the percentage of telephones and towards the top on a whole variety of other economic indicators.

Undoubtedly, in open societies, telephones have a great advantage for citizens over physical presence: properly used, they enable them to penetrate to a much higher level

Table 4.1 Telephones per 1,000 households, 1999

Country	Telephones per 1,000 households, 1999 (*1998)
Argentina	201.0
Australia	520.0
Bangladesh	3.4
Brazil	149.0
Canada	655.0
China	85.8
France	582.0
Germany	590.0
Ghana	8.0
India	26.5
Ireland	478.0
Italy	462.0
Japan	558.0
Mexico	112.0
Nigeria	3.8*
Pakistan	22.1
Russian Federation	210.0
Sierra Leone	3.8*
Spain	410.0
Sri Lanka	36.4
United Kingdom	567.0
United States	664.0

Source: World Bank Development Data 2001

of decision-making than would otherwise be possible. As in face-to-face discussion, too, refutation can be advanced directly, specific points confronted, and statements demanded which cannot easily be evaded.

However, there are limitations of scale: interaction is not a feature of a mass meeting, even though communication is by voice and face-to-face. Questions may be offered, but even when answered immediately need not be revealing: the practice of gathering questions together and answering them in a supplementary oration gives all the advantage to the speaker. 'Heckling', as systematic barracking of a speaker is known in Britain, is forbidden in many countries; in others, such as South Africa, it can be accompanied by a high level of violence that at election times has long been taken for granted (Butler 1959, p. 261).

Mass communication is the distinctive characteristic of modern societies. Mass communication by voice, the radio broadcast, is now proportionately very cheap and has extensive uses in spreading government propaganda both at home and abroad. The role of Radio Cairo in inflaming opinion in Algeria in 1954–56 is considered to have been a major factor in the response of the Mollet government at the time of Suez, but it was undoubtedly just as important in integrating post-revolutionary Egypt itself (Nutting 1967, p. 21; H. Thomas 1966, p. 22). On the other hand, by the 1980s people in the former German Democratic Republic (GDR) could receive not only radio but also television broadcasts from West Germany, thus informing them about life in the West and building up popular pressure for eventual reunification.

Television has a particular appeal to members of governments attempting to put over their point of view to the largest possible number of people. Mass communication by television was extensively used by Fidel Castro in the first fifteen years of his rule in Cuba to communicate his views to the public. However, as there were no elections before 1975, there was no equivalent method of communicating the views of the public to the political leadership (Huberman and Sweezy 1968, p. 152).

Today both the number of television transmitters and the number of receivers are commonly given as indicators of economic development (see Table 4.2). They can also be used, with appropriate caution, to judge how far a country has evolved towards mass society. The impact of television has been much quicker and more widespread than expected because each set is usually watched by quite a large number of people. This can have negative consequences: the Peruvian earthquake of 1969 killed thousands because they were inside, huddled around the television, watching the national team play in the preliminary rounds of the World Cup; the 2001 earthquake, although more violent, caused a much lower death toll.

The immediacy of television has given it a special place in the folklore of politics, perhaps not entirely justified by the facts, since it has important social consequences which may not be so easy to control. Direct personal conversation may increasingly be invaded by shared television experiences, but equally the same experiences facilitate the education of young children and provide topics of conversation for people of all ages who hitherto had nothing in common (McQuail 1969, pp. 71ff.).

Visual communications apart from television depend, except in rare instances, for most of their effect on the use of writing. Writing is a code for expressing on paper or other material the sounds of the code that is language. Knowledge of this code is however not a normal part of each individual's basic home instruction, and is imparted by specialists as the first part of a process of formal education. Literacy is therefore not a political attribute as such, but it does arise only as part of the attribute of formal inculcation in the values of society. This point is important, since the existence of such values determines the interpretation of written material as certainly as they do the interpretation of photographic or pictorial material.

The extent of adult literacy is not only an indicator of social development, but of the extent to which citizens have been empowered to make use of the legal and political

Table 4.2 Television receivers per 1,000 households, 1997

Country	Television receivers per 1,000 households, 1997
Argentina	223
Australia	554
Bangladesh	6
Brazil	223
Canada	710
China	321
France	595
Germany	567
Ghana	93
India	65
Ireland	402
Italy	528
Japan	686
Mexico	272
Nigeria	66
Pakistan	22
Russian Federation	410
Sierra Leone	12
Spain	409
Sri Lanka	84
United Kingdom	521
United States	806

Source: World Bank Development Data 2001

opportunities available to them (see Table 4.3). It is not necessary to be literate to understand a political argument and to be able to assess the varying merits or otherwise of candidates for election. However, to be a candidate, to organise a club or a political movement, to be able to assess critically a sale agreement, a lease or other legal document, it is essential to be able to read and write. Sharp differences in this as in other

Table 4.3 Adult literacy, 1999

Country	Adults illiterate, male %	Adults illiterate, female %
Argentina	3.2	3.3
Australia	—	—
Bangladesh	48.3	70.7
Brazil	15.2	15.1
Canada	—	—
China	8.8	24.5
France	—	—
Germany	—	—
Ghana	20.6	38.5
India	32.5	55.5
Ireland	—	—
Italy	1.2	2.0
Japan	—	—
Mexico	6.9	10.9
Nigeria	28.7	45.8
Pakistan	41.1	70.0
Russian Federation	0.3	0.6
Sierra Leone	NA	NA
Spain	1.5	3.3
Sri Lanka	5.7	11.4
United Kingdom	—	—
United States	—	—

Source: World Bank Development Data 2001

respects exist between urban and rural communities. This in turn affects the balance of political power in those societies.

Individual visual communications are primarily letters and similar messages; mass communications include, apart from posters and handbills, newspapers and even books, all forms where the same text is multiplied by printing press or photographic means.

Societies vary a great deal on the extent to which communications are controlled. By their nature written and printed communications can be controlled and even monopolised almost completely by governments. This is particularly true of newspapers. As they used to say in the former Soviet Union: 'There is no news [*izvestiya*] in *Pravda* and no truth [*pravda*] in *Izvestiya*'. Even clandestine printing presses are of little avail if the supply of newsprint or ink is a state monopoly. Moves to create similar state monopolies in Chile under Salvador Allende (1970–73) (*The Economist*, 20 November 1971) and Peru under Velasco Alvarado (1968–75) (*The Times*, 20 January, 10 February 1970) were regarded with great suspicion by journalists and helped generate opposition abroad in each case. In Albania and Romania before 1989 every typewriter had to be registered lest it be used for the dissemination of propaganda against the regime. Nevertheless as in the former Soviet Union *samizdat* (literally 'self-publication') circulated in other East European countries long before the liberalisation of means of communication which marked the last stages of the collapse of the regime.

The internet has opened up new possibilites for political opposition. It was developed as a means of communication which could not be interrupted in the event of war. The insurgent EZLN in Chiapas, Mexico, were the first to use a website not only to bypass government control of other forms of communication, but to use it to co-ordinate pressure by outside lobby groups. In China the government is very sensitive to possible criticism on the web and has been actively seeking to deny access to specified sites. In Cuba access to the web is tightly controlled and all email messages have to be channelled through a limited number of computer terminals, enabling them to be checked for political orthodoxy before being passed on to their recipients.

Communications and decision-making

The way in which communications are used in the process of decision-making can be dealt with under three headings: inputs, internal communications, and outputs.

1. **Inputs**. These can in turn be divided into two categories: input communication in general, that is, all influences from the environment; and feedback, the response monitored to actions by the decision-makers themselves.

The first step is regulation of the input, both to reduce the pressure to manageable proportions, and to distinguish the first from the second. The effect upon decision-makers of wholly unregulated input communication can hardly be imagined. It has occurred, however, for only brief periods, as after the collapse of communism in Europe in 1989. Suffice it to say that no one – whether individual or group – could possibly exercise any functions of decision-making if exposed to a continuous unregulated flood of inputs. It is all one whether they are pestered by people with demands, or by people with offers of support, since the one generally turns out to be conditional on the other.

Equally it would be fatal for governments to be too effectively screened. In particular, a government must have information on the effects on the environment of its own actions. Unlike an organic body, it has no other compulsion than conscious choice to do so, but equally so its actions could be taking place in a void. For this purpose, therefore, governments find it necessary to devise systems by which they can admit the inputs they wish to admit, while continuing to exclude unregulated calls upon their time. Such role-bearers include secretaries, 'spin doctors', bodyguards, trusted party organisers and workers, and on occasions the police and intelligence agencies. David Easton termed them the 'gatekeepers' (Easton 1957).

In a democratic society, the decision-makers themselves will be expected to be seen going among the people: in President Lyndon B. Johnson's words, 'pressing the flesh' (T. White 1965, p. 366), and obtaining apparently spontaneous responses of joy to the presence of someone associated with government policy as a whole, or a crucial sector of it. This is certainly useful as far as it goes, but as an output of government enabling a higher level of extraction of effort rather than a genuine input mechanism.

2. **Internal communications**. Assuming that the process of regulation of inputs has been assessed, the next task is to look at the means by which the decision-makers handle communication among themselves. Decision-makers are people. Decisions are made by people, even if they are made by omission more often than by commission. And these people may, and often do, form a particularly close group; that is to say, they form an elite which can be identified either subjectively or objectively or both. The strength of an elite lies in its ability to communicate. They compensate for the greater mass of information they have to handle by taking advantage of their ability to communicate directly, face to face. This gives them not only an advantage against the mass of society, but also against the bureaucracy which may otherwise all too easily overwhelm them with its rigidity and resistance to change.

The decision-makers do not have it all their own way, however, in dealing with the general public. Members of the public only need the opportunity to communicate, to be able to put their case. The decision-maker has to rely on the assumption that his or her brief comments will go on record and may cause trouble in the future.

3. **Outputs**. Much of the process of internal communication is concealed by governments until no longer of great current interest to scholars. The importance of output communication is thus disproportionate to us, as the sector of the communications net most easily accessible to the investigator as political scientist. Given enough records, the investigator can analyse its characteristic pattern. This varies according to the direction, the volume and the content of the communication flow, and specifically in the ways set out here.

Outputs may have two different effects. They may act directly, by delivery to a desired individual or group with a calculated emphasis and association of political pressures. Or they may, as we have already seen, act indirectly, through the instrumental effect that they cause others to act in state or local government. Local government structures often are formally independent, but respond to central instruction. This type of action is most important because without it the operation by decision-makers of a modern administrative machine would be quite impossible. Its own articulation, its internal routing of messages, is therefore of fundamental importance in assessing its effects, for the way in which it affects the outside world is more often indirect than direct. In the UK the freedom to act of local government was almost wholly eroded between 1979 and 1997 by limiting the power of local government to raise funds through local taxes (by the end of the century over 80 per cent of local government funding came from central government) and imposing very strict limits on how local representatives could spend the money that they raised. The Greater London Council (GLC) and the six metropolitan councils were summarily abolished, leaving London the only one of the world's major cities without a central authority (though the power of the Mayor of Los Angeles is minimal). Interestingly at the same time the French government abolished the *tutelle*, the power of departmental prefects to exercise control over the decisions of communal governments, and actively encouraged the voluntary merger of communes into larger and more effective units.

Restricted codes

The crunch comes at the most important part, discovering what (if anything) the messages are actually about. This involves understanding the **code** in which they are written.

As already indicated, it is in the nature of communication that messages are transmitted in code; it is not just an accident of time or place, and codes are not cyphers, that is to say, they are not meant to be secret, so there is no fundamental reason why a trained observer cannot learn them.

The first step obviously is to learn the language. For a student of comparative politics learning languages can become a major task in itself, for the language reflects the society which uses it; indeed it shapes society, a flexible language such as English taking on new concepts to the point of meaninglessness, while an exact language such as French implies a closer correspondence of ideas in the mind of speaker and hearer. The shaping effect of language is felt at those points at which ideas are taken for granted. Students of politics have long been locked into an earnest debate as to whether Marx expected the state to be 'transcended' or 'abolished'; the German word which he used (*aufheben*) inconveniently meaning both, and indeed also lifted, picked up, arrested, kept or preserved (see also Merritt 1970, pp. 152–3).

Then, beyond the dictionary definition of words, societies employ general codes of social communication, in which words such as 'crown' or 'flag' carry wide-ranging overtones of political responsibility, and phrases such as 'the common law' in England, or 'the Fourth of July' in the United States, are heavy with meaning which the individual words of which they are composed totally lack (cf. Eysenck 1963). Understanding of the general code of each society is, therefore, the understanding of the nature of political education.

Beyond these in each society lie restricted codes, applicable only within certain sectors of that society (Bernstein 1973–76). Communication within these sectors is conducted for most purposes in terms of the restricted code. Bernstein himself is interested in the way in which working-class children are both identified and restricted in their possibilities of expression by their restricted code. Full access to power, he suggests, is only possible through learning the general code of society as a whole.

However, there are even more limited examples of restricted codes. The classic instance is the code employed by the armed forces, characterised by a small vocabulary in which each phrase has a very precise meaning ('quick march!', 'right turn!', 'slope arms!', 'rapid fire!'). This has two advantages that ensure the general use of such a code by the soldiers of any country. One is that each order given to a soldier means one thing and nothing else. Under conditions of severe stress – under fire or danger from mines or aerial attack – the soldier given a command will respond instinctively without having to make a conscious and potentially fatal choice. The other advantage is that the limitations of the code deliberately leave him no room for concepts not covered by it, such as fear of flight (the latter being termed a 'tactical retreat'). Indeed the deficiencies of the code are such that the soldier tends to supply his own two or three all-purpose words to fill gaps.

Restricted codes are most important for this quality of exclusion characteristic of all forms of professionalism, and nowhere more so than in government. That can indeed be implanted generally by education in political matters, so that the subject is bound to an official ideology, and is less receptive to destabilising stimuli. This can in turn be used to strengthen distinctions of status, or to impart values suggesting certain types of social patterning rather than others.

This was strikingly important in communications within and between communist systems. For the former USSR a phrase such as 'proletarian internationalism' meant 'limited sovereignty for other communist states', while for the Chinese 'Hold High the Banner of Marxism-Leninism' meant 'oppose Maoism' (Hong 1978). But it is also found in liberal democratic political systems. Under Harold Wilson, for example, the phrase 'social contract' was used in the UK to refer to the control of wages by government without the formal passage of legislation, but had the additional political benefits (other than deliberate vagueness) of suggesting agreement and social value (Bosanquet and Townsend 1979, pp. 7–8). In the United States the phrase 'pro-life' means forcing unmarried mothers to have babies, by denying them the right to undergo an abortion. At worst political debate may come to be filled with a series of nearly meaningless catch-phrases, as in Sukarno's Indonesia, where many of the slogans chanted by the crowds included English words, such as 'ritulin' (retooling), known to Sukarno as an engineer, but not familiar to his audience.

The use of a special restricted code within the administrative system combines all these qualities. It depends on its capacity and precision to carry large volumes of meaning in a short space, and ensure accurate response on the part of its servomechanisms. A circular on building standards will be complied with by local authorities in a similar fashion, but with the necessary adjustments for regional variations of soil, climate, and so on. But when the same communication falls into the hands of a person who does not know the restricted code, a misinterpretation of it may lead to confusion.

By extension, tortuous and jargon-filled codes may be employed deliberately to restrict the circulation of information to administrative circles, while continuing to permit the public, in theory if not in practice, full participation in the processes of government. They form, therefore, one of the many means by which participation is actively restricted. The use of simple language, coupled with the availability of good civics classes in school or adult education, has just the reverse effect. Beyond this, though not intentionally, the use of restrictive codes can handicap feedback processes. Here the problem is that the code used within the system is not able to carry the range of meanings used by the plain language of those outside it whose opinions are being canvassed. Often this can occur because a wide range of views are reduced to a single formula. Since a great deal of uninformed hostility to government arises from just this feeling of not being understood, it is not surprising that codes play a major role at particularly crucial moments such as the consolidation period of revolutions (see Chapter 11).

Semantics and politics

Sadly, insufficient attention has been given in the past to semantic analysis in political discourse, and, rather disappointingly, little progress seems to have been made as a result. The science of semantics, it is not too much to say, is in its infancy as far as the understanding of political concepts is concerned, but without its aid cross-national comparisons involving socialisation or ideology are unlikely to be valid. Even as between

Great Britain and the United States – 'two nations divided by a common language' (Oscar Wilde) – the structure and implications of the English language vary greatly. So much we know. But how it varies, and where it varies, and what implications the variations have for political communication, is a problem for semantics.

In the late 1950s psychologists interested in semantics devoted much effort to the precise location of concepts in what, with Osgood, Suci and Tannenbaum (1957, p. 25), can be termed 'semantic space'. Questionnaires submitted to volunteer subjects called upon them to assess the position of words and phrases in terms of pairs of opposed qualities. Some extremely interesting results emerged. It even became possible, using related techniques, to build on identifications of concepts in two or more areas or regions – as in one study between the United States and Mexico – and compare their values in terms of a single attribute such as 'respect', maintaining semantic correspondence between the concepts used to assess variations resulting from purely societal differences (Díaz Guerrero 1975, pp. 89ff.) However, there is a long way to go before this laborious technique can be applied to politics in general.

It has however been possible to make content analyses of speeches or statements by leading politicians, and to assess from elimination of ancillary matter and purely functional expressions the presence or absence of qualities such as 'hostility' or 'aggressiveness' (North *et al.* 1963; Pool 1957). So far these techniques have mainly focused on ascertaining what politicians are actually saying – no small task in itself – though some writers claim to be able to construct a 'cognitive map' of the decision-makers' perceptions and values. Given a sound semantic foundation, however, great expansion could be foreseen in the use of all these techniques in the new century. The result for the study of comparative politics, and for political science in general, would be wholly beneficial.

Political Culture

The term 'political culture' is a controversial one. However, in making comparisons between different societies, it is hard to avoid coming back to the concept of '**culture**'.

First of all, it must be clear what the term means. To a political scientist, as to an anthropologist or a sociologist, a 'culture' is the entire pattern of behaviour of a given society. In this sense, therefore, individual behaviour within that society will in some sense be determined by that culture, and that of politics is no exception (Rush 1992).

In everyday use, the term 'culture' often has a much more restricted meaning. Culture in this sense, sometimes termed 'high culture', refers to specialised forms of self-expression in art, literature, music, etc., produced by an educated stratum of intellectuals, knowledge of which acts as a strategy of 'social closure' to define this group. By **social closure**, Frank Parkin (following Max Weber) means 'the power of one group to deny access to reward, or positive life-chances, to another group on the basis which the former seek to justify', in this case educational credentials (Parkin 1979; Murphy 1988). Despite their relatively small numbers and isolation from the rest of society, in all ages intellectuals have tended to believe that intelligence entitles them to hold and control political power. Since writers on politics are themselves intellectuals they tend to share and propagate this belief. However, education does play a key role in most societies in regulating access to the 'leading strata' (Aron 1967), from which the political elite in due course will be drawn.

The inclusive definition of 'culture', however, has its own difficulties. The problem arises with Marx's insistence on the primacy of the mode of production as determining the nature of society. Even non-Marxists have long accepted that economic processes, and the consequences of economic growth, urbanisation and industrialisation, play some role in determining the nature of society. But the dominant tendency in Marxism has long been to insist on a rather deterministic view, in which culture forms only part of the 'superstructure' of society resting on an economic 'base', and this view was part of the official ideology of the Soviet Union down to its collapse in 1991. Despite this, for some years previously in other parts of Eastern Europe, Marxist thinkers had increasingly come to accept, as Marx had probably originally intended, that the culture of a society also affects and shapes its capacity for economic production. Hence the terms 'base' and 'superstructure' were actively misleading. This idea was not, of course, foreign to non-Marxists familiar with Weber's famous argument that North European puritanism, for a variety of reasons, provided a particularly favourable climate for the development of industrial capitalism (Weber 1974).

The political culture of a society, then, is that part of the dominant culture of that society which establishes the values and norms of political debate and decision-making. It was to ascertain whether or not the existence of democracy was related to the nature of what they called the 'civic culture' that Almond and Verba conducted their celebrated comparative study of political attitudes in five selected states (Almond and Verba 1963), which has gained additional notoriety by being selected by the philosopher Alistair MacIntyre as an example with which to damn the whole comparative enterprise (MacIntyre 1983).

MacIntyre was arguing that the social sciences cannot be regarded as sciences because human beings have the freedom to make decisions for themselves. Therefore their behaviour cannot be predicted and no general laws can therefore be formulated about their conduct. We have already dealt with a number of general objections to this argument (Chapter 1); the question here is whether or not the Almond and Verba study was a fair example to pick. This study was based on a common questionnaire administered to a panel of respondents in each of the states in their own language. That technique has, of course, valuable possibilities. However, there are serious linguistic problems in administering a questionnaire in more than one language. Consequently unintended differences of meaning may, and some have argued do, arise, undermining confidence in the interpretation of the results. Certainly this sort of study is not what is meant here, or in political science generally, by the comparative study of politics, though it could in the proper circumstances become a useful part of it.

There were two other undoubted weaknesses of the study: uncertainties about whether the responses were frank, for example in Mexico, where suspicion of strangers was strong; and the fact that it was 'second-order' research, based on the assumption that already enough was known about the different societies to be sure that they had enough in common to be comparable. Some of this criticism was addressed by Almond and Verba themselves in their *The Civic Culture Revisited* (1989). However, from a purely technical point of view it would always be possible to cross-check and refine the results by the use of other forms of evidence. Among these could be:

- single-country surveys separately designed and commissioned but covering some or all of the common areas of interest in a different context;
- a word-association exercise, embedding key terms such as 'capitalism';

- a free-writing exercise, involving detailed textual analysis of individual essays;
- content analysis of media output standardised by time or place.

The dominant political culture is in part the product of the dominant ideology of the rulers of the society – and of their predecessors, if, as is usually the case, they derive their legitimacy from them and want to make use of the cultural inheritance of the society for their own purposes. However, it is transmitted and shaped by many means. The family, the peer group, religious institutions, education, the mass media, etc., all play their part.

The fact that we can speak of one culture being 'dominant', however, necessarily implies that there can be other cultures (or subcultures) that are subordinate. These cultures reflect lines of cleavage in society. Society is not a homogeneous whole and social cleavages typically indicate divisions between subcultures, whether those subcultures are based on ethnicity, language, religion or class. The key question is just how deep these cleavages are – if they all tend to act together to create major fault-lines in society, its very survival as a unified society must be questionable.

The ability to understand the rules of a culture and to make use of these effectively is as useful in the social field as capital is in the economic. Individuals may, therefore, be regarded as having a store of **social capital** of which they can make use in their social interactions (Newton 1997). Hence the greater the investment in the skills and practices of democracy, the greater the chance that it will survive (see also Przeworski 1992).

Ideology

Ideology is a term which has caused much argument in political science. Karl Mannheim (1946, p. 15) defined it as 'a pattern of beliefs that justifies a social order and which explains to man his historical and social setting'. A more comprehensive definition is 'a set of closely related beliefs or ideas, or even attitudes, characteristic of a group or community' which is both 'descriptive and persuasive' (Plamenatz 1970, p. 15).

The word was originally invented by a late-eighteenth-century French thinker, Count Antoine Destutt de Tracy (1754–1836), to designate the science or study of ideas which he had invented and which he was anxious to popularise. It was – surprisingly enough – Napoleon who first used it as a critical term to disparage as false systems of ideas held by his political opponents. In this respect he was followed by Marx, who used it to refer to the notions of his German rivals, which prevented them from seeing as he did the logically compelling nature of the real truths of politics (Marx and Engels 1940). The irony is that it is Marxism which today is generally regarded by adherents of other ideologies as being the classic example, being a closed system of ideas in which all conclusions follow from certain basic assumptions which are not universally accepted as true.

Marx and Engels regarded logic and mathematics as being universally true. Law and morality, on the other hand, were determined by ideology. The remedy for this was to apply scientific standards of criticism to law and morality and to make the result, termed Marxism, scientific and therefore true. Marx never referred to his own system of thought as an 'ideology', but instead emphasised what he believed to be its unique status as truth by the phrase 'scientific socialism'. What distinguished scientific thought from ideology, for Marx, was that it could be and should be used as the basis for action (praxis). For him, ideology was 'false consciousness', an incorrect view of the world.

In this sense Marx was a positivist thinker, and those of his followers who believe political systems to be determined by their economic base have continued this tradition. More specifically, Marx and his followers see ideological thought as the product of a particular social structure, the dominance of a class. The dominant ideology of capitalist societies today is established by the ruling class, the bourgeoisie, and will be superseded only with the fall of the bourgeoisie following a socialist revolution which will bring an end to the class struggle and result in the abolition of all classes.

For a variety of reasons modern writers would no longer feel able, as Marx did, to draw a hard-and-fast line between 'scientific' and 'ideological' thought. Doubts first surfaced with Freud, who demonstrated that action could be, and frequently was, 'irrational'. Hence 'rational' explanations would give at best an incomplete and at worst a wholly misleading account of the reasons for a social action. Social 'reality', in the traditional sense, does not exist. Instead what is accepted as social reality is itself a social construct (Berger and Luckmann 1972). Other writers have suggested that 'science' itself is an ideological construct, and that the traditional picture of science as an orderly process of research should be replaced by a series of abrupt leaps when the existing paradigm which determines what is considered to be scientific thought becomes outmoded and is replaced by another (Kuhn 1970).

Meanwhile, with familiarity, the word 'ideology' came gradually to lose its critical connotations and to be widely used simply as a handy term for designating different systems of ideas, including Marxism itself. The proponents of ideologies still tend to regard the term as pejorative when applied to their own system of beliefs, which, in general, they prefer to term philosophies. No such imputation is here intended. The term is used simply to refer to the fact that different political systems, and within those systems different political structures (especially political parties), can be grouped according to the ideology within which they operate.

This broader view of ideology derives from the work of the Italian Marxist Antonio Gramsci, who while imprisoned by Mussolini left a record of his views in his *Prison Notebooks* (1973). Gramsci had no doubt that ideology was the main means by which governments exercised political control, and that the use of force, which he termed domination, was an inadequate substitute, only to be used as a last resort. People, he observed, yielded freely to the appeal of ideology, especially in the form of religion or nationalism. From this he deduced that the ability (as he saw it) of a class to control a society came from the acceptance of its system of ideas as the ideas of the whole society, a situation which he termed **hegemony**. Alternatively, with Weber and Easton, it could be said that its system of values was seen as authoritative.

Gramsci, however, distinguishes between two different types of ideologies. Historical organic ideologies he sees as rooted in society and necessary to its structure at a given time. Arbitrary or willed ideologies are not. In other words, an old system of ideas can lose hegemony, or a new one achieve it, before the political changes consequent on the change take place. And at any one time, there will be competition between different systems of ideas for hegemony, the outcome of which has yet to be determined. The distinction between organic and arbitrary ideologies goes further, however, by indicating that certain combinations of ideas are more likely to gain favour than others. Writers who prefer to use the term political culture would agree with this view, and say that those sets of ideas that are more likely to be accepted are those that are congruent with the prevailing political culture (Eckstein 1960).

Case Study | Why Blair Deserves to Have Thatcher's Hair

Why isn't Tony Blair's Labour party more popular? This may seem a strange question given that it has just won another parliamentary landslide: 413 seats against 166 for the Tories and 52 for the Liberal Democrats.

Yet the seat distribution, as so often in the past, reflects not the balance of public opinion but the arbitrary injustice of the first-past-the-post voting system. Labour ended up with nearly twice as many seats as the Conservatives and Liberal Democrats combined. Yet these two parties attracted substantially more votes than Labour – more than 50 per cent of those cast, against more than 40 per cent for Labour.

In a fair system, the anti-Labour forces would have a commanding majority of parliamentary seats, and Blair would be able to form a government only by co-operating with another party.

If you take into account the sharp drop in voter turnout, Labour's lack of popularity is even more striking. One gullible editorial writer claimed that Blair had 'fused social democracy with market forces in a way that middle Britain finds irresistible'. In fact, voters found it eminently resistible: only one in four turned out for Labour. Blair's 25 per cent of the electorate is well down on the 32 per cent that Margaret Thatcher won in 1983 (which was itself anything but a decisive mandate). Even Harold Wilson managed to inspire more voters: in 1974 he received 29 per cent of the eligible vote.

Labour conceives of itself as a progressive party that synthesises previously opposed positions. It claims to join compassion with efficiency, or heart with head, and says it stands by the ideals of its working-class founders because its goal is to extend to all the opportunities that elites used to reserve for themselves. So why did so few voters turn out for it? The politics of spin did more damage than Blair's cynical kitchen cabinet ever thought possible. The doctrine that what matters is not what actually happens but what people think is happening is

deeply corrosive. Taken to the limit, it is the policy of O'Brien in George Orwell's *Nineteen Eighty-Four*. What people resent most is the insult to their intelligence. They see, for instance, a teacher shortage so acute that schools are scouring the developed world for staff, yet the education secretary tells them things are getting better. Spin causes the political equivalent of what psychologists call 'cognitive dissonance', and it kills trust in politicians, as Blair has now discovered.

But for a deeper explanation of Labour's unpopularity, consider the dispute over the rightful place of Thatcher's hair. Labour had an aggressive campaign poster featuring William Hague, the Conservative leader, with Thatcher's hair and earrings.

'Don't let them in again' was its message. *The Economist* magazine responded by putting a laughing Blair on its cover, also with Thatcher's hair and earrings. The caption read 'Vote Conservative'.

The Economist, I suggest, was making the more salient point. Labour claims not to be Thatcherite, but in its philosophical outlook it undoubtedly is Thatcherite. How can this be? Isn't Labour planning a most unThatcherite increase in public spending?

There are two answers to this. First, this spending still remains mostly aspiration. To date, Labour has been aggressively Thatcherite in its approach to the public sector. The biggest reason for the continuing deterioration in many services – one that the spin doctors will never admit – is that Labour spent too little: under Gordon Brown public spending grew at a miserable 1.3 per cent a year, compared with 1.7 per cent under Conservative predecessors. Neither the need for 'economic stability' nor his desire to appease financial markets justified such a squeeze.

Looking forward, Labour wants to keep the ratio of public spending to national income at about the level Nigel Lawson, a decidedly Thatcherite chancellor, deemed

Case Study Continued

appropriate in the 1980s, and far below that of most of the UK's European neighbours.

But Blair deserves Thatcher's hair for a deeper reason, and one that has nothing to do with statistical ratios. What was unnerving about Thatcherism was its insistence on viewing all of life through the narrow visor of market economics. Whether they looked at schools, the BBC or the health service, the Thatcherites were guided by only one set of principles, those that you will find in any classic microeconomics textbook – Milton Friedman's Price Theory would be a good example. Blair and Brown, in their desperate bid to make Labour re-electable, became Thatcherites because they chose to embrace this same, dismal world view.

Indeed, Labour in some respects is even more rigorous than the Conservatives in regarding market economics as a total philosophy of life. You can see this, for instance, in the Treasury's pathological desire to dismember and privatise the London Underground, and in its insistence on private finance, even when far more costly than normal public provision.

Labour is unpopular, I suggest, because most normal people never signed on to Thatcherism. They were never convinced that the market should be the measure of all things. They do not regard the mantra 'compete, ceaselessly compete' as a prescription for a good society. And they are not inspired by Labour's ultimate goal, which is a ruthlessly meritocratic society in which every individual must constantly look over his shoulder, lest some crazy workaholic usurp his position. Like the French revolutionaries who ushered in modernity, people value liberty. But they also care about equality and fraternity, concepts that now have no place in Labour's political philosophy.

Source: *Financial Times*, 16/17 June 2001

As a Marxist, of course, Gramsci himself believed that Marxism was a historical organic ideology. He believed, further, that it had already in his day achieved hegemony, and that it was only a matter of time, therefore, before its validity would be accepted and a socialist revolution take place in Italy. Meanwhile Mussolini's Fascism, being an arbitrary or willed ideology, would, he believed, fail to take root and ultimately be swept away. In this respect, at least, he was right, though sadly he did not live to be freed, let alone to see Mussolini hanging upside down from a lamp-post outside a filling station in Milan.

The main function of ideology in politics, therefore, is to legitimise the existing order and permit the economy of the use of force. In other words, it enables governments to pursue unpopular policies, and for them to be accepted as authoritative. This it does both in authoritarian states and in liberal democracies, where its influence is the more significant for going largely unnoticed. It is therefore clearly a crucial factor in understanding why liberal democracy, despite its obvious weaknesses, has proved such a successful and adaptable form of government. The means by which this is done is by establishing within the dominant culture certain values (e.g. of class, religion or nation) from which are derived specific norms of behaviour.

The vehicles by which the ruling ideology is transmitted are numerous. They were collectively termed the ideological state apparatus (ISA) by the French Marxist philosopher Louis Althusser (1984), but this suggests that they are more closely related to one another than, at least in some cases, they actually are. They include:

- the Church;
- the education system;
- the structure of politics, including the actions and ritual that surround it;
- political parties and their propaganda;
- the mass media.

Though the function of ideology will be similar, the values which are established and the vehicles by which they are conveyed will vary as between competitive and non-competitive systems.

Competitive systems

In liberal democratic systems the contest for hegemony takes place in public and is reflected in the competition of political parties (see Chapter 6) for public support.

1. Ideology above all establishes the dimensions of party. It determines which members any given party can expect to be able to recruit, and whether it can continue to count on their support in changing political circumstances. A striking example is presented by Northern Ireland, where Catholics are scarcely likely to join either of the two main Unionist parties given their historic association with militant Protestantism, and conversely Protestants see the nationalist Social Democratic and Labour Party (SDLP) as a 'Catholic' party.
2. It channels and restricts the possibilities for coalition between parties. In Italy, for example, the Italian Communist Party (PCI) was excluded from all post-war coalitions on ideological grounds.
3. It limits the range of policies which a party can adopt in any given situation. The German Christian Democrats (CDU/CSU) proved unwilling, despite the potential political risk to their dominance, to 'let sleeping dogs lie' and allow the Eastern German *Länder* to retain the right to abortion on demand, for example.
4. By closing off options in this way it limits or deflects criticism and at the same time facilitates the co-optation of young politicians who see no possibility for their future advancement except within the system as already established. Closing off criticism in this way has undoubtedly been a strong factor in the growth in modern liberal democracies of the 'administrative state' (Marx 1967).

Non-competitive systems

Each of these aspects is even more clearly to be found in non-competitive states, but with certain crucial differences.

1. The justification for the single-party state is invariably ideological. Nationalism is most likely to be, as in post-colonial Africa, a justification where the state has been formed as a result of a successful struggle for independence. In some states (Angola, Congo, Guinea, Mozambique, Somalia, etc.) the rulers, either before or after independence, aligned themselves with the former Soviet Union and adopted a form of Marxist ideology, and this remains the basis of legitimacy for the government of Cuba today (2001).
2. In a true single-party state the possibility of coalition does not exist, of course. But in both Poland and the former East Germany the basis of the governing 'coalition' was

exclusionary. In other words, its purpose was to suggest a wider basis of public support than actually existed, while excluding the possibility of the emergence of a true opposition. Significantly the basis for the emergence of overt opposition in Poland was not a party but a trade union, for which Marxist theory offered no clear blueprint.

3. In both single-party states and military dictatorships a simplified, usually nationalist, ideology is used to underpin the *de facto* control of the public by force. Significantly, nationalism has emerged as the main organising principle in the former Soviet Union and Eastern Europe since the collapse of communism there.

4. In consequence co-optation becomes the main (possibly the only) way in which the personnel of government can be renewed, and legitimacy becomes attached more closely than is safe to the survival in office of a specific individual or ruling group.

Classification of ideologies

Students of comparative politics will almost invariably be laying their foundations for the study of the area while at the same time studying political thought in some depth. This section, therefore, is in no way intended to substitute for that detailed knowledge. Its purpose is simply to summarise some key points about our present knowledge of how and where ideology determines political outcomes. Indeed the problem begins with the nature of ideology itself. Largely for ideological reasons, no satisfactory classification of ideologies has ever been achieved, and it is highly unlikely that one will be (see also Vincent 1991; A. Heywood 1992).

There is, however, one with which most people in Europe are familiar: the division of political parties into parties of the left and parties of the right. This is so well established, in fact, that it is commonly used by people who have very little idea what they mean by it.

This is not surprising, since the distinction between 'left' and 'right' is a historic one which need not necessarily have any current meaning. Appropriately it dates from the time of the French Revolution, when those deputies who believed in change symbolised their allegiances by sitting on the left of the semicircular chamber of the French Assembly, leaving those who had more doubts about the wisdom of change to sit on the right. This distinction spread in due course from France to other European countries and from there to the rest of the world. The symbolism of the left as the seat of true progressive thinking, assiduously propagated in Europe in the inter-war period, dies hard, even in an age when the future of communism is very uncertain. Yet only three decades ago the Gaullists in France strove hard to avoid being seated on the right because of the unfavourable image it held even for them. Today it is perhaps best regarded as representing a progressive–conservative axis of classification.

But on the other hand the attempt to use other axes of classification for ideologies and their supporters is fraught with difficulties. Some stem from the indefinite nature of the enterprise since, in the nature of ideas, ideologies cannot be weighed and measured scientifically. Others stem from the uncertain agreement between observers, as has been seen. But most stem from the determination of the participants themselves not to be labelled. A term such as populism, for example, which is very useful in studying political parties in Latin America, is bitterly resented by members of populist parties themselves (Canovan 1981).

Blondel suggests that the use of three axes should be sufficient to represent the principal distinctions between European parties and their ideologies (Blondel 1973). In addition to a progressive/conservative dimension, he identifies a monarchical/republican dimension and a tough-minded/tender-minded dimension, the last named deriving from the psychological distinction popularised by Hans Eysenck (1964). Such distinctions are helpful. They enable observers to identify, for example, within the stream of thought loosely termed 'Thatcherism' in the UK in the 1980s, and 'Reaganism' in the United States, two distinct but overlapping tendencies, which have been termed 'libertarian conservatism' and 'authoritarian conservatism' (Hoover and Plant 1989). They also disclosed streams of thought in the former USSR comparable to the 'New Right' in Western Europe or the United States (Yanov 1978) which were to surface in Russian politics after 1991.

However, perhaps significantly, these dimensions do not include any qualities specific to either religious or nationalist ideologies. Yet even in Western Europe, the major cleavage between political parties has for many years been not between 'left' and 'right', but between different religious groupings.

In *The End of Ideology*, Daniel Bell (1961) argued that ideological divisions were slowly disappearing in modern capitalist societies through the exhaustion of the ideas that had created them in the first place. Though his work dealt specifically with the United States, the decline of ideology was seen by him as the direct consequence of economic development leading to the creation of a mass society. Others, notably Herbert Marcuse (1972), lamented the loss of significance that this represented. Still others suggested that since technological imperatives could be expected to be the same for all societies at a similar stage of economic development, a degree of convergence could be expected between the ideological presuppositions even of the two superpowers, the United States and the USSR (Brzezinski and Huntington 1964; cf. Hollander 1973). Similar conclusions were arrived at independently in Eastern Europe itself (Bahro 1978).

The collapse of communism in Eastern Europe in 1989 would seem, at first sight, to have justified the predictions of the convergence theorists. However, much of their argument was based on the assumption that state intervention in Western economies, far from decreasing, was likely to increase, and certainly they did not predict (nor were they likely to have foreseen) the wholesale abandonment of communist planning in favour of the principles of the so-called 'free market'. At the same time it is clearly of more than passing significance that the sudden void of ideology in Eastern Europe has been filled by two tendencies: religion and nationalism. Where these coincided, notably in Lithuania, Latvia, Estonia and Slovenia, and other conditions were favourable, a unified national movement was able to emerge and in favourable conditions to secure its objectives. Where they were in conflict, as in Armenia, Azerbaijan, Georgia, Croatia and Bosnia-Herzegovina, the consequences have been at best serious and at worst disastrous (Agh 1998).

Liberalism, socialism, social reformism

Liberalism is a political ideology primarily concerned with freedom for the individual. 'Liberals' was a term originally given in Spain to supporters of the ideals of the French Revolution: representative government, freedom from oppressive laws and opposition to clerical domination of thought. Liberals of the Manchester School in England retained these ideas, but added to them the idea that the state should not interfere in economic matters ('*laissez-faire*'). Fortunately older ideas of social responsibility were to prevail and by imposing limits on working hours for women and children and establishing government regulation of dangerous industries a long process of social reform began, which under the conservative Bismarck in Germany led to the first steps towards social security and the welfare state.

Modern writers have sought to distinguish between liberalism and social reformism, but in practice most modern liberals would regard themselves first and foremost as social reformers, and those who (like Ronald Reagan and George Bush) favoured the ideas of the Manchester School would not regard themselves as liberals – indeed in his 1988 campaign Bush habitually referred to 'the l-word' as if it were an obscenity. For this reason, the term 'neoliberalism' is often preferred for the views of who those who like Bush and Thatcher emerged in the 1980s to oppose state intervention in the economy, and to favour deregulated markets, low taxes on the wealthy (all taxes are high to the poor) and the privatisation of state-owned industries. Hence that is the term that will be used here.

The term *socialism* also emerged at the beginning of the nineteenth century. It gained currency as the process of industrialisation spread across Europe and the United States, creating a new class of workers who lacked access to political power. Socialists believed that by organising themselves workers could get access to political power, but they were divided between a minority who, like Karl Marx, believed this could only come about by revolution, and a majority who favoured non-violent action backed up by strikes. They had in common a belief in the principles of equality and fraternity, the need to attack class divisions, and state action as a means of achieving the ideal society. By the end of the nineteenth century the German Social Democrats were a formidable political force and in France the SFIO (1905) and in Britain the Labour Party (1906) gave social democrats a voice of their own.

With the victory of the Bolsheviks in the Russian Revolution of 1917, however, for the first time a socialist government emerged that both claimed to be socialist and to offer the only correct road to socialism. Marxism-Leninism – as it came to be known – differed radically from democratic socialism, or, as it is often termed, social democracy. By 1945, however, democratic socialist parties had gained power thoughout Europe, implementing where they were able economic planning, the nationalisation of key industries and comprehensive welfare state provision. Following the successful onslaught of the neoliberals in the 1980s, however, there has been a general retreat towards social reformism. *Social reformism* differs from both socialism and liberalism in that neither individuals not political parties use it of themselves. Instead it is used by others to define the ideological position of other groups and parties, such as 'New Labour' in Britain, the Democrats in the United States or the Spanish socialists (PSOE).

Anarchism, communism, fascism

Opposition to the growth in the power of the state in the nineteenth century often took the form of *anarchism*. Anarchists see the power of the state as the source of all the ills of society; to solve them it is first necessary to remove the state. Towards the end of the century some of the more extreme anarchists sought to use violence and political assassination to destabilise the state and bring about its fall – this resulted in the deaths of, among others, the Empress Elizabeth of Austria, President McKinley of the United States and King Alexander II of Yugoslavia. Others, the anarchosyndicalists, rejected the rule of the state but were prepared to accept self-organisation in workers' movements; movements influenced by these ideas included the International Workers of the World (IWW) in the USA and the Argentine Radical Civic Union (UCR).

The basic principle of *communism* is the idea of the common ownership of property. Marx believed that classes were the fundamental units of society and predicted that the rule of the capitalist class, the bourgeoisie, would in time be overthrown by the labouring class, the proletariat. In 1917, however, it was a small group who seized power in Russia in the name of the proletariat, and within months Lenin's elite party had displaced the workers' councils, the soviets, in the name of the 'dictatorship of the proletariat'. Thereafter Marxism-Leninism claimed to be building socialism. The new state that emerged after 1922 was called the Union of Soviet Socialist Republics and it and the other communist states established after 1945 referred to themselves as the socialist countries. However, elsewhere political parties loyal to Moscow normally adopted the term communist to distinguish themselves from democratic socialists, a distinction which it was often convenient for their political opponents to ignore.

Under Marxism-Leninism communism was interpreted as state ownership of industry, direction of labour, collectivisation of agriculture and a total ban on private employment of any kind. The Communist Party assumed a 'leading role' and under '**democratic centralism**' its central bodies were able not only to enforce the party line on regional and local committees but also effectively to displace the state as the government of the Union.

'*Fascism*' referred initially to the regime established by Mussolini in Italy after 1922. It was later used to describe Hitler's regime in Germany. As we have already seen, the term 'totalitarianism' has since been used to refer to both. By totalitarianism Mussolini asserted the right of the state to mobilise all its resources, human and material, toward ends that he would set. Other characteristics shared by the two regimes were the leadership principle which gave all power to the leader, a party structured like a militia designed to fight enemies and form a ruling elite, the rejection of reason and democracy, and an aggressive nationalism. In the fascist state there would therefore be no room for the distinction between the public and private spheres (De Grand 1995, p. 2).

In practice, however, fascism in Italy fell well short of its ambitions. Fascism was a form of rule rather than a coherent ideology. The one constant was the role of the leader, and as the years passed Mussolini became increasingly lazy – his failure even to read international treaties was to involve him in the embarrassment of explaining to Hitler in 1939 that he could not afford to go to war. A second theme was the blurring of the boundaries between state and party and a shifting relationship between the two. A third was the belief in the survival of the fittest. In the political sphere agencies were multiplied and allowed to compete with one another for influence and in the economic sphere big corporations were given every encouragement to fulfil the ambitions of the leader to make war on other states, preferably small and defenceless ones. Lastly, Mussolini did not share Hitler's obsessive hatred of the Jews, though he did allow them to be persecuted under the anti-Jewish laws of 1938, and in the last few years evidence has finally emerged about the extent of Italian atrocities in the Second World War.

Class, Status and Party

The notion of ideology is inseparable from the concept of **class**. By class is generally meant a large group of people with a relationship to political power determined by their economic position. Though people today associate the economic basis of class with

Marx, it was in fact an association which was originally made by eighteenth-century economists (Calvert 1982).

Marx saw the concentration of economic power in the hands of a few as leading ultimately to the impoverishment of the majority of the economically productive, leading to violent conflict and the displacement of class by class. By 'class' he meant a group of people with a common relationship to the factors of production, and for him classes, not individuals, were the major 'actors' in the process of social development.

> What I did was to prove 1) that the existence of classes is only bound up with particular historical phases in the development of production; 2) that the class struggle necessarily leads to the dictatorship of the proletariat; that this dictatorship itself only constitutes the transition to the abolition of all classes and to a classless society. (Marx 1962 [1852])

Since the collapse of the Soviet Union it has been widely assumed that this is no longer the case. However, few things in politics are obvious and the empirical study of comparative politics should be able to ascertain exactly where and how far this process has advanced, if it has done so. In practice, however, it cannot. Again there are several reasons.

To begin with, Marx never actually defined class (he died leaving his definition incomplete) and though he frequently refers to classes he is inconsistent in his usage of the term. In some places in his work he writes of two classes, in others of three. It seems he was saying that though there were three classes that mattered, only two of them would eventually be left to come into confrontation, the owners of the factors of production, whom he termed the bourgeoisie, and those who had nothing to sell but their labour power, the proletariat. Ultimately the proletariat would rise and overthrow their masters, the bourgeoisie, in a social revolution. The moment at which the triumph of the proletariat was at hand, however, would be heralded by the point at which a fourth stratum (i.e. not a class), that of the intelligentsia (namely the politically aware section of the intellectuals), would throw their lot in with the ultimately dominant proletariat. This last point has led to considerable uncertainty as to whether those movements led by the intelligentsia that claim to be acting in the name of the proletariat are actually representative of them or not.

Secondly his use of the term 'class', though widely accepted by intellectuals, superseded an earlier popular definition of class as being what today, with Weber, writers would more accurately term **status** (Gerth and Mills 1946, pp. 186–7). By status is meant a perception of relative social standing, which may of course be due to hereditary factors or education, and so largely independent of economic factors. So when people are asked what class they consider themselves to be, in practice they answer in terms of status. Again we may attempt to combine empirical observation (judging for ourselves where a person stands in the status hierarchy) with questioning (asking them where they would situate themselves in the same hierarchy), and this is in fact done in some social research. However, even then the meaning of our answers is very uncertain owing to the size of the social categories involved and the uncertainties of defining their boundaries accurately. What is clear is all societies of any degree of complexity are socially stratified; that is to say, they seem to be arranged in horizontal layers.

Societies may be stratified in a large number of ways. Gender, as noted above, forms the most basic distinction, but one which is always found in conjunction with others. Ethnicity has acted to stratify both traditional and modern societies. But in modern societies class, status and political power, though distinct from one another, are the main ways in which people determine their own social position and that of others, and each can be traded off against the other (Bendix and Lipset 1967). And in both nineteenth-century Europe and the twentieth-century Soviet Union, party, also, formed a basis for the organisation of political power.

Social class

Certainly in the United States, Western Europe and Japan, self-ascribed social position, which can be termed social class, is a major factor in determining individual political attitudes, though it is not the only one. Social position is always defined as relative to that of others and hence is crucially dependent on economic considerations (Parkin 1971). In both the UK and the USA, where religion is not at issue, the main factor determining the way in which people vote is their perception of the economic success or otherwise of the incumbent government. As Bill Clinton told his election team in 1992: 'It's the economy, stupid!'

However, if social class is a key determinant of political behaviour in individual countries, the student of comparative politics is still going to encounter problems in looking at any two or more countries. The problem is a simple one, that government statistical services in different countries categorise their social structures differently. Thus in the United States social class is determined above all by income and conceived of as a sequence of bands ranging from lower lower class to upper upper class. In Britain, where it is extremely difficult to get people to answer questions about their income, the Registrar General's Classification (RGC) established in 1911 consisted of a set of status categories based on the occupation of the male head of household. These categories did roughly correspond to income bands, but in no systematic way, and there was a significant division between 'non-manual' and 'manual' occupations, that did not correspond to any difference in wealth and/or income. In France, categories again follow occupational criteria. However, there are two additional bands. All agricultural occupations are separately listed, and they, like all urban occupations, distinguish further between employers and employees.

Hence together wealth and occupation interact in a complex pattern which bears little or no resemblance to Marx's predicted antithesis between bourgeoisie and proletariat. The most striking difference between the three countries is the way in which education acts in each very differently to form the 'leading strata' of society, being apparently of greatest importance in France and of least in the United States. But in each case the significance of education is not so much that it does not help the rise of the 'lower classes' but that it helps to conserve the position of those already at the top (Calvert 1982, pp. 166–201).

Turning to the position in the former Soviet Union and Eastern Europe, the situation is different again, but not as much so as might have been expected. The society of the former USSR was in communist theory free from antagonistic class divisions, though the 1936 Constitution of the USSR recognised the continuing existence of two classes, workers and workers on collective farms ('peasants'), and one stratum, the intelligentsia.

But Soviet sociologists themselves regarded four forms of inequality within Soviet society as resulting in 'contradictions': 'inequalities between the collective-farm peasantry and the working class, between town and country, between manual and non-manual labour, and finally those arising from the division of labour which transcends the groups of worker, intelligentsia and peasant' (Lane 1971, p. 39).

In addition Soviet society, although technically free from inequalities of wealth, was characterised by very sharp distinctions of inequality of income (Lane 1971; M. Matthews 1978). Cross-national studies showed that the inequalities of esteem that existed between occupations (status) were in fact very similar to those in Western Europe and the United States (Inkeles 1968). Although there were also important differences, manual workers remained grouped firmly at the bottom of the status hierarchy (Lane 1976, p. 182).

Most importantly Soviet society was characterised by the dominance of an elite, which Djilas (1957) did not hesitate to characterise, in Marx's terms, as a 'class'. Though there was no private ownership of property, and it was impossible to employ and so exploit others, this special elite, the Communist Party, gained its power and status from the fact that it managed and so controlled state property. Significantly the existence of special privileges for the elite of the party was identified as a major factor in undermining support for the regime well before the ultimate collapse of the system in 1991 (Zaslavsky 1980). Among these privileges, it was apparent, was the ability to pass on status to their children through special access to educational privileges, so that although in the past it had been possible for people of poor origins (Khrushchev, Chernenko) to reach the very highest position in the Soviet political system, it was not clear that this exceptionally high range of social mobility would, in fact, continue (Parkin 1971).

Civil Society

In 1690, John Locke defined **civil society** as follows: 'Those who are united into one body, and have a common establish'd law and judicature to appeal to, with authority to decide controversies between them, and punish offenders, are in *civil society* one with another' (*Second Treatise of Government* (1690), par. 87, in Locke 1956). Civil society, for Locke, was created by a voluntary act, and an absolute monarchy, therefore, cannot constitute civil society: 'where-ever therefore any number of Men are so united into one Society, as to quit every one his Executive Power of the State of Nature, and to resign it to the publick, there and there only is a *political, or civil society*' (par. 89). However, once put under the law, no one can withdraw from the obligation to obey it: '*No Man in Civil Society can be exempted from the Laws of it*' (par. 94 – all italics in original).

Today civil society, as defined by Rueschmeyer *et al.*, excludes government, the law and the judicature. For them it is 'the totality of social institutions and associations, both formal and informal, that are not strictly production-related nor governmental nor familial in character' (1992, p. 6). The problem both with this, and with Miller and Walzer's limited definition of civil society as 'the space of uncoerced human association and also the set of relational networks – formed for the sake of family, faith, interests and ideology – that fill this space' (1995, p. 000), is the way in which they seem to overlook the economic basis of political interest. However, there are two things that all definitions have in common. Membership of civil society gives civil rights.

And the existence of civil society is characterised by associational autonomy – where civil society exists people are free to organise themselves in a variety of ways away from the watchful eye of the state. The more they do so, the more 'vibrant' civil society becomes.

Modernisation and transition theorists alike argue that a 'vibrant' civil society is a good thing, for three reasons:

1. It is an essential bulwark against the power of the state, concentrating people into groups and increasing interaction between them so that a protest against authoritarian rule is more likely (Diamond 1992). For Diamond, therefore, the existence of civil society is a precondition for democratisation and not something created by it.
2. Its existence changes the balance of classes by mobilising previously excluded classes (Rueschmeyer *et al.* 1992).
3. It is vital to the consolidation of liberal democracy. Drawing on the pluralist theories associated particularly with the name of Robert Dahl, the argument is that democracy is more likely to take root where the *political culture* favours it.

However, the notion of political culture raises problems of its own. Controversial and awkward to define, the notion of political culture easily becomes part of a circular argument: people behave the way they do because of the political culture in which they live; and we know what the political culture is like by the way people behave.

As we have already seen, Almond and Verba (1963) argued that what they termed the **civic culture** of Britain and the United States – a sense of general responsibility for others – facilitated the emergence and maintenance of democracy. This issue is still an open one. However, the emphasis in both countries in the 1980s on 'possessive individualism' was accompanied by a breakdown of this sense of civic responsibility and a steep increase in crime. These features were already characteristic of Italy or Mexico, two countries where Almond and Verba found the 'civic culture' lacking. Conversely in the 1990s crime rates fell as efforts have been made in both Britain and the USA to strengthen the sense of civic responsibility.

Summary

Communication is both the means by which politics operates and the way in which it can be understood. Political socialisation enables members of a given society to understand the messages reaching them. In skilled hands, however, both formal and informal socialisation processes can be manipulated. One of the most important consequences of socialisation processes is the stratification of society, whether by class, status or party. However, society is also held together by communication, and particularly by the transmission to all citizens of the ideas and values of the dominant ideology.

An inportant issue in the theory of democratisation is the importance of the growth of civil society, the area of free, unconstrained social relationships, and the civic culture which some writers argue results from it. The issue remains unresolved, partly because of its complexity and partly because of the technical problems involved in finding evidence about the nature of political culture which is independent of the variables which it seeks to explain.

Key Concepts

civic culture, that part of the dominant culture of society which establishes the values and norms of political debate and decision-making

civil society, 'the space of uncoerced human association and also the set of relational networks – formed for the sake of family, faith, interests and ideology – that fill this space' (Miller and Walzer 1995)

class, a large group of people with a relationship to political power determined by their economic position

code, an economical statement conveying meaning

communication, the transmission of a signal through a channel from a transmitter to a receiver

culture, the entire pattern of behaviour of a given society

democratic centralism, the principle of government in the former Soviet Union by which

decisions of the highest level of the party, once made, were binding on all lower levels

hegemony, for Gramsci, the acceptance of the system of ideas specific to a class as the ideas of the whole society

ideology, a set of closely related beliefs or ideas, or even attitudes, characteristic of a group or community, which is both descriptive and persuasive

metacommunication, information conveyed unintentionally through signs

social capital, for Putnam, a culture of trust which enables a community to solve collective problems through freely operating political institutions

social closure, for Parkin, the power of one group to deny access to reward, or positive life-chances, to another group on the basis which the former seek to justify

status, perception of relative social standing

Sample Questions

Unless the syllabus specifically requires it, the general subject of communication is an unlikely subject for a question. However, understanding the basic principles of communication is absolutely vital in enabling students to interpret political information and to help them distinguish between evidence and opinion, especially in a cross-national context. A possible topic is: 'How far has the growth of the mass media changed the fundamental postulates of liberal democratic politics?'

Political culture and behaviour forms a central theme of the study of individual states and an awareness of the role of social stratification, and social class in particular, is of fundamental relevance to the structure of political parties and a basic requirement

for questions on electoral systems. Possible themes are:

- How far can the notion of the civic culture be applied to countries other than the United States?

- What criteria are used in different societies to determine social class? How far can these criteria be used to make comparisons between different societies?

- 'Political power, properly so called, is merely the organised power of one class for oppressing another' (Karl Marx and Frederick Engels, *The Communist Manifesto*). Discuss.

- Have we finally reached 'the end of ideology' in modern politics?

Further Reading

Almond and Verba (1963) has been much criticised, but remains an interesting starting point for the attempt to apply the notion of 'political culture' in a comparative context. It should be read in conjunction with their own retrospective on the study in Almond and Verba (1989). A modern treatment of the notion of 'political culture' can be found in Rush (1992).

For an overview of the problems of ideology and a survey of current ideologies see Vincent (1991) and A. Heywood (1992). Mannheim (1946) is classic. The social construction of reality is discussed by Berger and Luckmann (1972). On populism see Canovan (1981). Brzezinski and Huntington (1964) came in for sharp criticism when first published, but merits re-reading in the light of the events of 1989 and 1991.

Calvert (1982) is a useful introduction to the concept of class. The concept of social class most widely used (though one based essentially on Western Europe and the United States) is set in perspective by Bendix and Lipset (1967). Inkeles (1968) and M. Matthews (1978) discuss stratification in the former Soviet Union in a comparative context.

The Economic Sources of Power

CHAPTER FIVE

Learning Objectives

By the end of this chapter, the reader will be able:

- to establish the relationship between money and politics;

- to evaluate the economic sources of political power;

- to determine how power resources are obtained and how they are used.

Money and Politics

Power resources are required to reach political power and they are even more important in maintaining it. Money, the currency of economics, can be turned into votes, the currency of politics, though even in 2001 this is far from being an exact science. To gain power in the first place in liberal democracies requires funds to support an election campaign. To keep power involves rewarding followers – either individually or in groups. Politics decides who gets what, when, how (Lasswell 1936).

The ability to use political power depends largely (though not exclusively) on the ability to obtain and use economic resources. Governments need to raise taxes and to borrow money in order to fund political outcomes, and this includes measures to keep themselves in power as well as other outcomes. In the course of the twentieth century expectations of what government could achieve increased remarkably. Before 1945 governments were only expected to conduct foreign affairs, defend the national territory, maintain law and order, and provide some very basic social services. However, a combination of guilt at the impact of the Great Depression and the wish to reward the public who had fought in the Second World War changed this. Since 1945 it has been generally believed in liberal democracies that the state has a duty to maintain the conditions which encourage economic growth. Economic growth enables governments to fulfil enhanced expectations. No less importantly, it enables them also to avoid difficult allocation choices, distributing the surplus for maximum electoral advantage instead of having to reward one group at the expense of another and lose votes in the process (Crosland 1956).

Governments gain their power to tax in the first instance from a *social contract*. This is not, alas, the idealised philosophical bargain between ruler and ruled envisaged by Locke or Rousseau. It is an implicit bargain with the representatives of the people (themselves) by which in return governments provide security both from crime and attack from other countries. They may also provide other things, such as a range of material benefits, such as postal services, roads, schools and hospitals, which it is in the interests of government to ensure are available to all citizens (e.g. to ensure that the country is not devastated by epidemics) or are too expensive for private enterprise to provide (such as a good road and rail network) or both.

States and Money

One of the ways in which people know they are crossing a border from one state to another these days is that they have to change **money**. This is a major block to the effects of globalisation and the emergence of a true world economy. It is a measure of the strength of nationalism that it has taken so long in modern times to try to create a true international currency since the Ancient Greeks not only recognised the value of an international standard of value, they actually established common standards which were accepted by the majority of states.

The Greeks did not invent money, however, which first appeared in a recognisable form in Lydia seven centuries BCE. What made money recognisable as such was the stamp of the authority that issued it. People accepted the stamp as the guarantee that the piece of money was worth a certain amount in terms of goods. The more important the authority the greater the use of the currency in international trade. Originally the material itself was regarded as having value and the stamp was merely to prove that it had been tested and was reliable. But for cheapness and convenience modern money has little or no intrinsic worth: it is easy to carry quite large sums in the form of paper and the metal used in modern coins is chosen for hardness rather than value, as it will spend a great deal of its life being pushed into automatic machines. Hence the value of modern money comes only from the legal authority of the issuer, the state. Issuing money, therefore, ranks with administering justice as one of the two principal signs that a state claims to have 'sovereignty'. Modern banknotes carry a variety of anti-forgery devices as well as national symbols emphasising the power and stability of the state.

The fact that money is easily recognisable is important, since transactions must be able to take place in a wide variety of conditions. Before 1996 US dollar bills had not changed in outward appearance for nearly a century. But continuity brings the risk of forgery – making copies with the intention of passing them off as the real thing. In Europe in the Middle Ages the penalties for forgery included castration, mutilation and execution. Even today some of the most severe penalties inflicted by the state protect the integrity of its currency.

However, to have value, money does not have to circulate. The stone 'money' of the island of Yap was so big that it could not be moved and modern gold reserves stay in the same vaults even when their ownership changes. In fact, it is not even necessary to know where it is or for it to have an actual existence – a dollar bill is a promise to pay a dollar but take it to the bank and all you get is another dollar bill. The important thing is the guarantee that the sum involved will be paid to the person who is entitled to it. From this has evolved the notion of **credit** (see below).

There are more than 180 currencies in the world today (2001). Examples show how much a currency's value depends on the authority and power of the state that issued them and carry a series of political messages for those who use them:

- **USA**. The dollar is the standard by which all other currencies are valued, although like all other currencies its purchasing power has been diminished by steady inflation. Used widely abroad, it is believed that twice as many dollars circulate outside the USA as within it. Many other countries try to peg their currencies to it; some, e.g. Ecuador, have actually gone so far as to adopt it as their monetary unit and Argentina has 'dollarised' the peso by both pegging it to the dollar at par and requiring the National Bank to hold sufficient dollars to maintain parity. National symbols on a one-dollar bill include the head of George Washington and the signature of the current Secretary of the Treasury; on the reverse is the Great Seal of the USA.
- **Spain**. The peseta was the Spanish monetary unit from decimalisation in 1878 until the end of 2001. In recent years it was freely convertible, and its exchange rate has been fixed within the European Monetary System to other EU currencies. It was to be replaced by the first international currency, the euro, on 1 January 2002. Spanish banknotes bore portraits of famous Spaniards of the past; euro notes had to have abstract designs to avoid raising nationalist passions.
- **Brazil**. National symbols on Brazilian currency include the head of Liberty and a vignette of the proclamation of the Republic in 1889. Brazil has suffered from very high inflation for decades and introducing a new currency has been an ineffective way of trying to check it. The old cruzeiro was replaced in the 'heterodox shock' of 1986 by the cruzado; in 1990 the cruzado was replaced by the new cruzeiro and in

1994 the new cruzeiro was replaced in turn by the real. Initially pegged to the US dollar at the rate of 2:1, the real had later to be devalued although inflation had in the meanwhile been substantially reduced.

- **Sri Lanka**. The value of the Sri Lankan rupee is fairly stable. The currency is not convertible and you cannot buy it abroad. Controls ensure that the rupee has high purchasing power in Sri Lanka but the exchange rate is poor in purchasing power terms. The wording on a one hundred rupee note is in English as well as Sinhalese and Tamil. It also bears a mask design which is both traditional and symbolic of good fortune.
- **FYR Macedonia**. A newly independent state, the Former Yugoslav Republic of Macedonia lacks established national symbols. Even the name of the country is disputed (by Greece) and its authority abroad is minimal. Its new currency bore a harvest design showing workers in traditional peasant costume, which could be taken as emblematic of the ultimate source of wealth, the land. But curiously there was no indication on the same side of what the currency unit was and hence what the note was worth.

Money and credit

The purpose of money is to enable people to exchange goods and services. Markets can operate on a barter basis, without a fixed standard of value, but they would be too slow and cumbersome to meet the needs of a modern society. Money should therefore have a fixed value over time, and have a fixed value over as wide an area as possible.

In economic theory money supply should be constant to ensure constant value. In practice, money supply is not constant and governments have given up many of their traditional controls on the movement of funds in order to enable their currency to be **convertible**. Convertibility is supposed to help international trade and is encouraged by the IMF; however, in a global economy money can flow in and out of a country within minutes for reasons that have nothing to do with the ordinary everyday life of the people of that country. Speculation on the currency markets caused the economic crises of the UK and Italy in 1992 – 'Black Wednesday'.

One currency, the US dollar, is in practice the standard by which all others are set. Until 1971 the dollar was linked to gold by the guarantee of the USA to buy and sell gold at $35 an ounce; the devaluation of the dollar by Richard Nixon set the world adrift on a regime of floating exchange rates which other states cannot control effectively. Yet this was a domestic decision in which the interests of other states played no part and this was in fact to trigger the first moves towards European monetary union (Burk 1990, pp. 17–18). Much later, in what were to prove Nixon's last days in office, H.R. Haldeman ventured to ask him what he was going to do about Italian monetary problems but he only replied: 'I don't give a shit about the lira!' (Woodward and Bernstein 1977, p. 295).

States have even less control over the creation of credit. Not only have they abandoned any formal means of control, in favour of the manipulation of interest rates, but they have increasingly regarded even this as a task for a technical agency made up of bankers. However, there are two problems about interest rates. When interest rates are raised to reduce demand they do not just check frivolous expenditure, they also choke off capital investment in industry. And changes in interest rates are extremely slow to act if indeed they act at all. This is because it takes anything up to a year before they significantly affect the biggest of our decisions, what house we are going to buy. When the Irish government locked their currency, the punt, to the euro, they also had to cut their interest rates from 6 per cent to 3 per cent. In theory, this should have fuelled a borrowing boom and sent inflation soaring – in practice inflation in Ireland began steadily to decline, though house prices, for example, continued to rise steeply.

All states maintain the illusion of national control of their economy. However, uniquely, the lead economy, the USA, critically affects all others. Only the USA is unaffected by the relative standing of its currency to the dollar, as for obvious reasons this cannot change. However, only in its case do internal political decisions which affect the dollar directly also affect all other currencies indirectly – after 1979 the steep rise in oil prices led to accelerating inflation in the USA. But when the Federal Reserve raised US interest rates to check inflation it also raised the price of loans valued in dollars on the world market. The result was the 'debt crisis' of the 1980s. In January 2001, after the longest sustained period of economic growth in US history, the Federal Reserve reduced interest rates by 0.25 per cent in order to head off the possibility of a recession. In theory this should have sent foreign investors off elsewhere looking for better rates. Instead the US currency rose against both the euro and the pound sterling because of the expectation of continued growth in the USA itself.

If a government is either unable or unwilling to raise taxes, it will have to borrow money to fund its continuing operations. When President George W. Bush appeared before Congress on 27 February 2001, the USA had since 1986 been by far the world's biggest borrower. Its accumulated public debt was currently standing at 3.4 trillion dollars ($3,400,000,000,000) (*Daily Telegraph*, 1 March 2001). Servicing this immense **debt** (paying interest to creditors) accounted for some 14 per cent of the annual federal government revenue but instead of keeping to existing plans to pay it all off the president proposed only to 'retire' some $2 trillion over the next ten years and spend the balance of $5.6 trillion giving a massive tax cut to the wealthy. It was true that by world standards the US debt is not particularly high, given the huge size of the US economy. However, when other countries go beyond this point they speedily find their freedom to spend money on other things becoming increasingly constrained. It was also true, however, that no more than $1.6 trillion of the sum predicted would become available before 2005, the year after President Bush's term was due to end, and that in the event of an economic recession the US government, far from retiring the debt, therefore, might have again to resort to borrowing. Borrowing is politically attractive in the short term as it is another way of avoiding having to ask the electorate to pay higher taxes immediately before an election.

Ecuador is an oil-exporting country and on the face of it should have no difficulty maintaining a stable economy. However, Ecuadorian governments are very vulnerable to popular pressure and in 1999 servicing the country's US$16,000 million debt required no less than 41 per cent of the annual budget. In fact the country began that year in economic crisis exacerbated by losses sustained in floods resulting from the 1998 'El Niño' weather phenomenon. In early March anxiety about low world prices for oil precipitated a 38 per cent fall in the exchange rate of the sucre and a run on the banks, which were soon closed. Faced in addition with a general strike by trade unions, indigenous organisations and grassroots activists of the political opposition, President Jamil Mahuad Witt proclaimed a state of emergency on 11 March, a partial freeze on bank withdrawals and a tough austerity programme which passed Congress only with a bare majority and in revised form. New proposals by the president then triggered a strike by taxi and truck drivers and public transport workers. Unrest continued to spread following his proclamation of a state of emergency. Forced to cancel proposed fuel increases and make other concessions, he lifted the state of emergency and his finance minister resigned. On 28 September Ecuador defaulted on US$44 million in interest payments due on its dollar-backed 'Brady bonds', bonds issued in the early 1990s with the backing of the US Treasury to enable countries to repay part of their outstanding debts. Ecuador therefore became the first country to default in this way.

This automatically triggered a demand by its creditors for accelerated repayment of capital. The government responded with a letter of intent to the IMF requesting a stand-by loan of US$400 million to enable restructuring of the whole outstanding debt of US$16,000 million representing 110 per cent of GDP. The result was that no less than 54 per cent of the 2000 budget approved by Congress on 25 November was earmarked for debt service. In desperation the president made a highly controversial project to adopt the US dollar as the country's currency, which when announced on 9 January 2000 instantly led to price rises of between 50 and 300 per cent. Following the largest demonstration to date against the government and its economic policies, entirely correct though they were on the assumptions of neoliberal economics, a military uprising on 21 January 2000 led to the flight of the president and his eventual deposition by Congress.

Case Study   Crisis in Turkey

The crisis began when President Ahmet Necdet Sezer, a former constitutional court judge, convened what was supposed to be a routine monthly meeting of the powerful National Security Council. Before the scheduled discussion got under way, President Sezer had something to say. Why, he asked, reading from a prepared statement, had Bulent Ecevit, prime minister, challenged his decision further to investigate state-owned banks suspected of corruption? According to widely published accounts in the Turkish press, the president accused Mr Ecevit of 'humiliating me in the eyes of the public' and asked why the prime minister was reluctant to pursue corruption.

Warming to his theme, he held up a copy of the constitution for the prime minister to see. 'You don't know the constitution', he charged. 'Let's see this constitution', snapped Husamettin Ozkan, a deputy prime minister who is Mr Ecevit's closest aide. Whereupon the president tossed the book in their direction. A shocked Mr Ecevit, who has a reputation for personal integrity, stood up in a mute rage and made for the door. After conferring with his colleagues, Mr Ecevit emerged to deliver the following statement:

'The president has directed a serious allegation at me and acted with a disrespect that has never been seen in the history of this state. Of course this is a serious crisis, but we will have to find a solution to it. We will provide a more detailed statement to the public later.'

There was to be no 'later' for Turkey's financial markets, still fragile after a severe liquidity crisis at the end of the previous year. Within minutes, the Istanbul stock exchange sank 10 per cent, and overnight interest rates soared to 100 per cent from 40 per cent.

It was at that moment that Turkey's banks saw the writing on the wall for the exchange rate regime. Having stayed in Turkish lira after a $7.5bn IMF bailout last December, they rushed to buy dollars. A record $7.7bn left the country that day.

'If there was one day not to have made that statement it was today', said one trader in Istanbul.

Source: Leyla Boulton, 'The political spat that brought economic policy to a halt', *Financial Times*, Weekend 24–25 February 2001

This is an area in which the impact of both globalisation and economic liberalisation is particularly marked. Before 1945 governments were free to borrow money abroad from anyone who was willing to lend. Where globalisation has had a strong effect on national economies lies in the fact that it is no longer possible for a country to shop around in the markets for a loan. Since 1946 the IMF has been responsible for maintaining international exchange stability and today no one will lend to a country that does not have the approval of the IMF, while the IMF can and does insist on a country conforming to its requirements before it will give that approval ('conditionality'). However, currency markets are so volatile that a crisis can arise with alarming speed, as the story of the 2001 crisis that devalued the Turkish lira overnight by 28 per cent shows (see Case Study).

States and Markets

Neoliberals often talk about 'the **market**' as if a) there was only one market and b) it was an entity which had an independent existence of its own and c) governments had no 'right' to 'interfere' with it. This is wrong on all three counts. There are lots of markets, organised according to different laws, though they can and do interact with one another. And markets do not exist independently of the exercise of political power and under the protection of law. Modern states have simply assumed this role, formerly exercised also by big landowners, religious leaders, etc. After all, the sole right to make laws, including laws governing contract terms and payment, is now regarded as one of the distinguishing features of a state.

There is a lot of mysticism talked about complex markets such as the London Stock Exchange or the German Börse. However, all markets operate in the same way as the simple markets for agricultural produce which set the pattern, whether they trade in goods or services and whether or not they have an actual physical location or are merely conceptual.

Modern states play three essential roles in establishing and maintaining all kinds of markets:

- **chartering markets** – they permit markets of all kinds to be held under certain terms;
- **regulating markets** – they impose restrictions on what can be traded and how; they enforce standards (e.g. of currency and weights and measures), ensure the safety of traders and customers (peace is maintained in the vicinity of markets so that it is safe to come and go – the City of London has its own police force), and provide a framework of law for the settlement of disputes;
- **taxing markets** – they raise a steady revenue from fees and charges on trading and on economic activity in general.

Most modern states operate within a **market economy**. This has been defined as:

> An economy based upon the free exchange of commodities under conditions of competition, together with the minimum necessary institutional framework to make exchange possible over time – a predictable system of law guaranteeing property rights and the security of contract. (Beetham 1997, p. 79)

The market economy is currently widely regarded as the most efficient way of allocating economic outcomes. However, this does not mean that this is how it actually works in practice. In more technical language, these outcomes should be 'Pareto-optimal.' An outcome is Pareto-optimal or efficient if and only if it is impossible to make an improvement for one player without at the same time making things worse for the other players. Such outcomes however can only result from a perfectly competitive market, where the players make deals which are kept later on. In principle, therefore, handing social decisions over to the market should result in outcomes which are both stable and Pareto-optimal. However, where there are economies of scale, a Pareto-optimal solution is not possible unless the state intervenes either directly by public resource allocation or regulation, **or** indirectly by creating institutions which promote optimal solutions.

As we have already seen, the fact that there are some things that the state can provide better than private enterprise was recognised in the eighteenth century, in fact by Adam Smith himself. In practice, therefore, most modern economies are not even in theory market economies but 'mixed economies'. However, even if governments had not become involved in providing a range of essential services there is no way of preventing governments from using their political power to ensure that they make as much money as possible from the markets they charter.

Nor can it be assumed that key interests within society really want free competition. Time and again businessmen clamour to be set free from government 'interference', the process known as economic liberalisation. However, closer examination soon shows that what they really want is for the market to be stacked in their favour. The 'level playing-field' is one where your rivals have to run uphill. Much of the frustration shown by the New Right in the USA is caused by the contradiction between their ideals (a free market) and a reality which requires them to operate within a system which in practice is tightly structured by **regulation** having the force of law. Regulation is necessary because unregulated markets soon develop serious problems and the regulations themselves are designed to address each of the obvious weaknesses of markets as a means of allocating value:

- Markets are subject to cycles – governments cannot afford for reasons of social equity to allow people to starve, or at least not where they will become a nuisance.
- Markets have no moral principle – the price of everything from medicines to guns is determined solely by the demand for them. Hence some of the highest prices are paid for narcotic drugs.
- Uncontrolled markets produce waste and pollution as well as goods and from the middle of the nineteenth century governments have found it necessary to step in to prevent damage to public health.

Managing the economy

The powers available to government to manage the economy include:

- the power to create money;
- the power to raise taxes and hence to borrow with very long-term credit because they have the guarantee that they will be able to raise money;
- the power to spend money;
- the power to make and to enforce laws, including laws to regulate the market.

Policy is made in different ways in different countries. Among liberal democracies the main distinction is between parliamentary and presidential systems. In parliamentary systems ministers are accountable to parliaments but provided they command a majority (or in France's semi-presidential system have the confidence of the president) they know that in the end they will be able to enact their budget. In the USA, however, Congress has complete control over appropriations – the president proposes but Congress disposes.

The first task of government is to raise money. There are four ways in which this can be done: taxation, borrowing (which carries costs and is simply deferred taxation), fees and fines (fees for permission to do things and fines for not having done them), and profits on state-owned enterprises. The most important by far is taxation. However, although in principle it is accepted that governments have the right to levy taxes, they are always backed by severe penalties under law and it is illegal to evade taxes – even the most enthusiastic neoliberal economist has not suggested that taxes should be voluntary. Despite this there are still many ways to avoid paying tax and the power to enforce taxation is limited by convertibility; the rich have considerable scope to avoid taxes, if necessary by simply moving their money abroad. Clearly tax rates cannot be zero, or governments would not be able to exist and so to create money. Nor can they be 100 per cent, or the taxpayers would be left with nothing to live on. In between, however, there is a lot of scope for creative accounting.

Much depends on what sort of taxes are being levied. Taxes on goods (sales taxes) are easier to enforce than taxes on income. However, a uniform sales tax would bear proportionately much more on the poor than on the rich, since necessities form a much larger part of their expenditure, so in practice it becomes necessary to exempt certain classes of essential expenditure, such as food or fuel. In post-war Europe a graduated income tax was seen as the fairest way of redistributing wealth. However, in practice this tends to bear most heavily on the middle classes, especially those on salaries, and cuts in income tax are enormously beneficial to the rich without doing any significant good to the poor, who do not earn enough to come up to the threshold for tax. Taxes on capital gains are levied to prevent people evading income tax by trading in income for capital gain; in addition taxes on income alone have a relatively limited redistributive effect. Taxes on business are easy to levy, but business is always a powerful lobby and if the level of taxation rises too high businesses will simply relocate elsewhere. Taxes can also be levied on specific activities which are considered to be either environmentally undesirable (e.g. petrol and diesel) or socially harmful (e.g. tobacco, alcohol). Excise taxes have both the advantage and disadvantage that people are very conscious of paying them.

Finally a major problem for all finance ministers is that tax policy is not simply about raising money. By raising or lowering taxes their decisions also have an effect on the overall level of demand. In strict economic theory taxes should be used purely to raise money and for no other purpose. In practice they are an important instrument in the regulation of an economy and were much used for this purpose in European states in the first thirty years after 1945 (just when European states were enjoying their most rapid rates of economic growth). Although purists still hold that taxes should not be used for this purpose, in practice they are.

In sharp contrast, **command economies** have no need to levy taxation. In the 1930s Stalin's government in the former Soviet Union took pride in announcing the total abolition of income tax. Citizens of the former German Democratic Republic (GDR) paid neither income tax nor sales taxes and only very low social security contributions. Consequently at the reunification of Germany their initial enthusiasm about being able to convert salaries as well as savings into hard currency at par was somewhat tempered by discovering that income tax and social security payments would take a substantial proportion of their gross income:

> After the excitement subsided, many East Germans felt worse off than before. . . . Not only apparatchiks who lost their privileges, but also ordinary people began to grumble about the effect of the currency union. When travel and luxuries were finally within reach, money dried up. Half of the savings beyond the minimum were lost, decreasing average wealth by about 3,500 DM per capita. When they received their first paycheck, workers experienced a take-home shock. With new income taxes, insurance and retirement contributions, Western deductions were almost twice the customary amount. As a result, net income actually declined by 15 percent. (Jarausch 1994, p. 149)

The 'creative destruction' of the abrupt transition to the market economy was alarming. Eastern industry, based on the old Soviet model, proved quite unable to compete with the West, and even those basic products it made which were both cheap and good were spurned in favour of glamorous Western rivals. Unable in many cases to tell whether or not a business was profitable, investors refused to come forward and many factories went bankrupt, some quite unnecessarily. By August 1991 the Treuhandanstalt, the public agency established to oversee the **privatisation** of the command economy in the former GDR, had privatised 3,378 of 10,334 companies but almost two million jobs had been lost and the optimism of the neoliberals turned out to be false: it proved much harder to create new economic life than to destroy the old (Jarausch 1994, pp. 148–56). Despite Kohl's promise at the 1989 elections that 'no one would be worse off because of unification', citizens of the Western *Länder* soon faced a stiff unification tax, a surcharge of 7.5 per cent on income tax from 1991, and further tax increases agreed in a 'solidarity pact' with the other political parties in March 1993.

Central banks. Central Banks exist in the first instance to issue money and maintain state control of money and credit through setting interest rates. This they do by establishing a base rate at which they are prepared to act as bankers to other banks in the system. The model is the Bank of England, the oldest of all central banks, founded in 1694, and nationalised in 1946. However, since 1997 it has been given the power to set UK base rates with reference only to a target for inflation set by government, though on at least one occasion the chancellor, Gordon Brown, has indicated in a public speech what he thought the decision of the Bank should be.

Most other of the world's states have central banks of a similar kind. But in the United States there has been no central bank as such, since Andrew Jackson put an end to the second Bank of the United States. As a result, under the impact of the Great Depression of 1929, the entire US banking system eventually collapsed, throwing millions out of work and into misery. The Federal Reserve System was established as a US government regulatory agency in 1933. To avoid undue party political influence it is headed by a board of three members who must be bipartisan, and organised in twelve regions. It issues paper currency and sets interest rates.

The powers of finance ministers over central banks in parliamentary states vary considerably. The German Bundesbank is constitutionally independent of the federal government and charged under the Basic Law with maintaining a stable currency for Germany. Its decisions on interest rates however have historically had an important effect on other European currencies. However, even the Bundesbank was subject to repeated pressure from Chancellor Kohl. He placed close associates on its governing board, took major steps on both German and European monetary union without consulting it, and tried, though unsuccessfully, to influence its decisions on interest rates and the revaluation of its gold reserves. At unification, 'Kohl's decision on the currency union between the two Germanies, operative in July 1990, was imposed upon a hostile Bundesbank, causing the resignation of its president, [Otto] Pöhl, shortly afterwards' (Cole 1998, p. 125).

Ministers of finance (economy). In parliamentary systems finance ministers are accountable to parliament and will usually be professional politicians, though on appointment to ministerial office many, as in France, have to give up their seats in parliament. Frequently finance ministers have a background in banking rather than economics. In the UK John Major had taken a banking diploma over ten years at night school (Major 2000, p. 52); however, of his immediate predecessors Sir Geoffrey Howe was a lawyer and Nigel Lawson a financial journalist (see also Lawson 1993). Their main task, apart from maintaining day-to-day control of government finances, authorising expenditure and presenting accounts to parliament, is the preparation of the annual budget.

In France, as will be discussed later in Chapter 8, the system of the Grandes Ecoles should ensure that presidents, premiers and finance ministers receive excellent professional training and so they do – but in administration rather than in economics. Laurent Fabius, finance minister under premier Lionel Jospin, studied administration at 'Sciences Po' and graduated from the elite Ecole Nationale d'Administration (ENA) before going on to work for the Conseil d'Etat, the administrative court which is responsible for resolving disputes within the bureaucracy and gives advisory opinions on proposed legislation (Safran 1995, pp. 250–2). President Jacques Chirac, who comes from a very similar background and shares many of the same assumptions, also studied administration at 'Sciences Po', graduated from ENA and worked in the Cour des Comptes, the prestigious French audit office, before entering politics.

Finance ministers can enjoy considerable autonomy if the economy is performing well but they are vulnerable to any economic downturn. In the UK Denis Healey (1974–79) reined in the inflation generated by the 'Barber boom' and the first oil shock and enjoyed a considerable degree of autonomy (see Case Study). Nigel Lawson (1983–89), who had a good command of his subject and initially enjoyed the full confidence of Margaret Thatcher until the general election of 1987, became increasingly irritated at the influence on the prime minister, Margaret Thatcher, of a personal adviser, the economist Sir Alan Walters. Walters, who spent much of his time in the United States, did not seem to feel that this should inhibit his public criticisms of the European Monetary System (EMS), and when he published an article describing it (and so by implication the economic policy for which Lawson was constitutionally responsible) as 'half-baked' Lawson was forced into resignation (October 1989). In the aftermath of 'Black Wednesday' in September 1992, when the UK was forced out of the Exchange Rate Mechanism (ERM) of the EMS, John Major tried to transfer Chancellor Norman Lamont (1990–92) to a lesser post; he refused to accept it and chose to resign instead. In Germany such a confrontation would be much less likely to happen since the requirements of coalition formation would mean that each post had been filled as part of the pay-off for one or other of the interests represented in the coalition.

> ### Case Study   Denis Healey on his Responsibilities
>
> I often envied my foreign colleagues the comparative lightness of their load. Many of them had no constituency duties. In several countries an MP had to give up his seat when he became a minister; in the United States the Treasury Secretary, like most members of the administration, was usually drawn from outside the Congress altogether. No other finance minister carried so wide a range of responsibilities as the British Chancellor of the Exchequer. In most governments, economic policy was under a different minister from financial policy, as it had been in Britain when George Brown ran the Department of Economic Affairs. In the United States the secretary of finance was not responsible for government spending, which came under a separate Bureau of the Budget. But my responsibilities gave me powers which the American Finance Secretary could only envy. Moreover, my decisions were nearly always certain to be endorsed by parliament, since in Britain the Government can normally count on a majority.
>
> In Washington the Congress invariably changes the Administration's proposals for tax and spending, even when the ruling Party has a majority there. Congress is under no obligation to ensure that its decisions are compatible with one another, or meet the needs of the nation as a whole. The only public authority in the United States economy, which can normally rely on its decisions being carried out, is the Federal Reserve Board, which is independent of both the Administration and the Congress. But practically the only decision it can take is on the level of interest rates. Paul Volcker used to complain bitterly as Chairman of the Fed that he was expected to drive the economic automobile with no instrument except the throttle – the steering wheel and the brakes were in other, less responsible hands. In Germany too, the central bank in Frankfurt is constitutionally independent of the government in Bonn. Even the head of the Government has to ask for special permission to address it – a privilege only once requested in my lifetime.
>
> Source: Denis Healey 1989, pp. 384–5

In the USA the Secretary of the Treasury usually has a business background; as Calvin Coolidge said, 'the business of America is business'. George W. Bush's nominee for the post, Paul O'Neill, was president of the Aluminum Corporation of America (Alcoa). In the USA it is quite normal for key officials to move into the private sector and vice versa, and Mr O'Neill had previously served in the Office of Management and Budget (OMB) under Gerald Ford.

The budget process

In parliamentary systems parliament approves the budget, authorises tax changes and acts as a forum for the desires and complaints of the public. In the UK parliamentary majority ensures that a government can always pass its budget; if not it would fall. To avoid this, the French semi-presidential system since 1958 gives the government the power to pass the budget without parliamentary approval if it is not given within seventy days and limits the number of times a government can be forced to undergo a vote of confidence.

The OMB – formerly the Bureau of the Budget – has been responsible since the 1970s for preparing the US budget for presentation to Congress, which has set up its own separate agency, the Congressional Budget Office (CBO), to check its figures and advise on alternative policies. Powerful committees in each House operate independently to produce revised versions of the original proposals. Though constitutionally financial proposals have to originate in the House of Representatives, the Senate has full powers to amend proposals brought before it and seldom resists the temptation to do so. In addition individual members of both Houses are free to come forward with substantial proposals for new expenditure, which cannot happen, for example, in the British House of Commons. It is the budget that is finally agreed in a Conference Committee of the two Houses and ratified by both that will eventually become law. Under the US system if Congress does not vote appropriations the money stops and the activity has to come to an end. Hence the Iran–Contra scandal of 1986, when Congress tried to cut off funding to the Contras in Nicaragua and the Reagan administration kept it going by selling arms to Iran.

Throughout the Reagan years the Democratic-controlled Congress voted budgets of much the same size as the administration had requested. The US two-party system simplifies bargaining. The problem was that Reagan's first budget proposed huge across-the-board tax cuts at the same time as defence spending was drastically increased. The deficit was to be covered by the 'magic asterisk', or the 'mysterious and never-to-be-realized spending economies that Reagan's man, David Stockman, employed to conceal the consequences of that 1981 budget' (Broder 2001; Stockman 1987). The result was some fifteen years of fiscal deficits which left the United States with the largest debt in its history.

The situation in other presidential systems varies considerably, but with multi-party systems budgetary paralysis is much more common and in extreme cases has in the past led to the breakdown of government and to military intervention. In Brazil, with a multi-party system, President Fernando Henrique Cardoso (1995–) has had continually to negotiate for each item of budgetary expenditure. In Argentina, on the other hand, President Carlos Menem (1989–99) could, and repeatedly did, use the previously relatively sparingly-used power to make decree powers to bypass resistance and enact a budget that the Congress would have been unlikely to approve, but the fiscal deficit had returned by the end of his term in 1999. However, both countries have in the past been plagued by the inability of government to drive through spending cuts in the face of well-entrenched resistance from powerful interest groups. When the new Alliance administration in Argentina published an austerity budget in December 1999 the new Congress approved plans to cut public expenditure by $1,400 million, a major tax reform programme and a federal revenue-sharing scheme. A year later, in September 2000, the administration was back with proposals to cut the fiscal deficit in 2001 from US$5,300 million to $4,100 million, with a cut in government expenditure of $700 million. Though Congress declared an economic emergency and passed an anti-evasion law and a law to reduce corporate taxes by November, in a televised address the president had to announce that the country faced 'a veritable catastrophe'. Although the IMF agreed to give emergency help estimated at US$12,000 million, it was on the severest conditions, including abolition of the existing state pension scheme and the freezing of federal transfers to the provinces, and a 36-hour strike brought the capital and other major cities to a halt.

The budget process is largely responsible for the characteristic of government decision-making which Braybrooke and Lindblom termed 'disjointed incrementalism'. This they describe as decision-making through small or incremental moves on particular problems rather than through a comprehensive reform programme (Braybrooke and Lindblom 1963, p. 71). There are three reasons for this. First of all, a governmental budget is compiled from bids from a large number of different departments, and it begins with the assumption that all the existing operations of that department need to be maintained at their current level. The Carter administration in the USA (1977–81) tried to introduce 'zero-base budgeting' – to start from the assumption that no activity whatever had taken place in the previous year – but soon found that the task was impossible. Secondly, none of these estimates take much account of the overall amount of money actually likely to be available. Thirdly, therefore, all departments inflate their estimates for the coming year knowing that in the process of reconciling their bids they are likely to be trimmed. Fourthly, there is little incentive in public service to save money, since if money is not spent the budget for the coming year will be reduced on the assumption that the need to spend the money has not been proved.

It is very difficult therefore to make radical changes in public expenditure without incurring unacceptable costs in terms of political support. Radical innovation in policy tends to happen, therefore, only when there is a major crisis and/or when, as rarely happens, a new area of policy is opened up. The classic example was the US reaction to the Soviet launching of Sputnik–1 in 1957, which led to the creation of the Space Agency and the dramatic acceleration of the US space programme.

It was President Dwight D. Eisenhower (1953–61) who first drew attention to the increasing dominance over US policy processes of what he termed 'the military-industrial complex' (Eisenhower 1963). The basic cause was the onset of the Cold War which established an arms race between the United States and its would-be rival, the Soviet Union. The close relationship soon established between the Department of Defense (the Pentagon), Congressional Defense committees and the arms industry to promote the procurement of new weapons systems and maximised defence expenditure, however, was much stronger than other of the 'iron triangles' that characterise US policy-making. There were three reasons. Technological developments had replaced weapons, as such, with complete weapons systems of considerable complexity. These had (by definition) to work perfectly, yet because of their nature could not be tested under the actual conditions in which they were likely to be used. The cry of national security was therefore easily used to inhibit effective scrutiny of expenditure. Periodic scandals erupted when it was discovered that (for example) the Airforce was spending $5,000 for an ashtray or $7,000 for a toilet seat, examples of everyday items for which even congressmen could recognise the US public was being overcharged. But the real scandal continued into the post-Cold War era of massive and essentially unchecked expenditure on the 'stealth' bomber, which when finally used in Iraq turned out to be detectable by Iraqi radar, or Reagan's 'star wars' project to intercept intercontinental nuclear missiles, which could be easily calculated to be technically impossible.

The market economy

There is a wide range of opinions on how and when governments should intervene in the market but less difference in practice than is often believed. Most Western countries have experienced a wide range of management styles over the past fifty years, varying according to currently fashionable economic prescriptions: for example the classical liberal view, the Marxist model, the social market economy, and the neoliberal view.

1. The **classical liberal view** is that the market is the best mechanism for allocating value. Therefore the correct policy for the state is to leave it alone. The state should play no part in the economy – this should be left to the market. Many people believe that this

is in fact the state of affairs in the United States, the exemplar of free-market capitalism. Of course they are wrong. The fact is that the market can only operate properly in a state of perfect competition and economists generally recognise that in the real world this cannot exist. Among the reasons are that:

- Individuals lack full knowledge of the effect of their decisions and unless every decision is fully rational the behaviour of the market as a whole cannot be rational (the Arrow Impossibility Theorem – Arrow 1963). Hence, for example, UK legislation prohibits 'insider trading' in shares, because if some people have fuller knowledge than others they will have an unfair advantage. However, even if it was effective, which is doubtful, this prohibition would simply mean that no one's decisions would be 'rational', not that everyone's would be. The past performance of shares is no guide to the future.

- Individuals do not start from an equal base. Hence monopoly tends to emerge because the best strategy for the most powerful actor is to try to create one. From the beginning of the twentieth century anti-trust legislation in the United States has sought to check the growth of monopolies and if necessary to break them up, beginning in 1911 with Standard Oil. In 1999 Microsoft was ordered to split itself into two separate companies, though it is resisting this and may well yet succeed. European states, on the other hand, have been less enthusiastic about enforcing anti-trust provisions, believing that only by maintaining the largest possible units can they compete internationally with the USA, and they have increasingly looked to international consortia to maintain their capacity in strategic industries such as aerospace (Airbus, the Eurofighter).

- Governments have a strong incentive to legislate to alter the system in favour of their friends when political circumstances leave them free to do so. The massive vote in favour of the Fifth Republic in France in 1958 left de Gaulle free to impose the Rueff–Pinay reforms, restoring the power of capital over labour by ending wage indexation, reducing public sector wages, devaluing the franc and making it convertible (Lynch 1990, p. 67). With an increased majority following the 1983 election in the UK, the Thatcher government was able to take on the miners at a time of its own choosing and was prepared to deploy enough force to ensure that it won.

- People can benefit from the existence of the system without having to put anything in themselves (the 'free rider' problem). They can do this in many ways but the most important is by using politics to tweak the system to their own advantage. The aviation industry in the United States (Boeing, McDonnell-Douglas) has been able to achieve near-monopoly status world-wide by being subsidised by US defence spending.

- There is no agreement on how to measure and hence to account for certain costs (e.g. unemployment, pollution) and benefits (e.g. open countryside, clean air, silence). Hence these values have simply been ignored, or, at worst, wrongly included, as for example when the costs of cleaning up pollution are regarded as economic activity and hence as a gain not a loss.

2. The **Marxist** model holds that capitalism is fundamentally unsound. Allocation should be carried out by state planning systems acting on rational criteria according to full information. In theory this was applied in the former Soviet Union (from 1930), and later other communist countries. Indeed one of the distinctive features of Marxism-Leninism in the Soviet Union was the Five Year Plan. In practice Soviet state capitalism resulted in:

- An overcentralised state, massive bureaucracy, planning system overloaded, inability to supply consumer goods to the masses despite the promises of the Khrushchev period (1955–64).
- Constant pressure to 'overfulfil' the plan, resulting in very low productivity, unrealistic targets and in the end wholly imaginary statistics. It was this that lay behind Gorbachev's advocacy of *perestroika* and *glasnost*, the process by which the free exchange of information would enable failings in the system to be disclosed and structural reforms carried out (Gorbachev 1996). Instead the whole system collapsed.
- A workforce which lacked motivation and required non-economic incentives to work hard (under Stalin building communism, in the Great Patriotic War resisting foreign attack). Hence in the Stalinist phase there was extensive resort to forced labour under brutal conditions. After the death of Stalin in 1953 forced labour was ended. Then the positive side was that state direction of labour meant that everyone had a job of some kind. With the fall of communism in Eastern Europe this security disappeared.
- The subordination of all else to the development of heavy industry and the supposed needs of economic development. Results included the pollution of the waters of Lake Baikal, the world's deepest freshwater lake, the contamination of the Danube by heavy metal residues, and the drying up of the Aral Sea.

3. The **social market economy** is based on Keynesian principles of demand management. This view acknowledges a world of imperfect knowledge. Decisions on investment and decisions on savings are in real life done by different groups of people. Unemployment is not only unjust but a waste of resources. It is the job of government, therefore, to expand demand to enable output to expand and so maintain full employment. Moreover economic growth enables the state to provide social services as well as social security for the old and the unemployed. In the years after 1945 a wide variety of instruments were used to promote economic growth, including physical controls on the market in the UK, but it was in West Germany that the term *soziale Marktwirtschaft* was coined and German policy has shown a striking level of consistency: moderate taxes, municipal or regional rather than national ownership of gas, water and electricity, reliance on subsidised non-state institutions to provide housing and health services, and an efficient state education system which renders private education virtually superfluous (Hallett 1990, p. 80).

The experience of wartime had shown the advantages of a centrally directed economy. In the immediate aftermath of the Second World War, the US government through the Marshall Plan helped fund the state-led rebuilding of the devastated economies of Germany and France. In France the Ecole Nationale d'Administration (ENA) expounded the new ideology of growth and converted the Finance Ministry, the Bank of France and French business interests to the merits of 'indicative planning' (Lynch 1990, p. 66). Coal and steel, electricity, railways and telecommunications were all in state hands. At the same time in France as elsewhere in Europe social security systems were developed to prevent a repetition of the miseries of the Great Depression of the 1930s which had led to the rise of fascism. In addition governments with no particular ideological enthusiasm for the idea had **nationalised** other key industries to keep them going, such as the post-war de Gaulle government with Renault in France, and the Heath government with Rolls Royce in the UK. This model became general in Europe in the thirty years between 1945 and 1975. Again in practice states encountered a number of problems, which included:

- The tendency of the economy to oscillate between boom and bust, leading to sudden switches of demand management between 'stop' and 'go' which made individual economic planning difficult. Once political scientists showed that the health of the economy was the major factor when voters came to decide whether or not to support the incumbent government, 'stop–go' was made worse by attempts to use demand management to engineer a boom at politically strategic intervals.

- The apparent choice posed between a steadily rising level of taxation or a rising level of debt which in the weaker economies reached crisis levels after the 'second oil shock' of 1979 and was to result in the 'debt crisis' in Latin America (Mexico, Brazil, Argentina, Venezuela) and other Third World countries.

As early as the 1970s there was considerable discussion as to whether various competitive states had lost the ability to process demands effectively and were becoming 'ungovernable'. As late as 1976 the British economist Samuel Brittan predicted that 'liberal representative democracy suffers from internal contradictions that are likely to increase in time, and that, on present indications, the system is likely to pass away within the life-time of people now adult' (Brittan 1976, p. 96). The 'ungovernability' thesis was supported by both left and right, though for very different reasons.

The first was the emergence of anti-system violence. In many competitive states, despite their apparently open societies, the 1960s saw the emergence of violent movements dedicated to overthrowing the system: in West Germany the Baader-Meinhof gang, in Japan the Japanese Red Army, in Britain the Provisional IRA. To the left this represented 'the intensification of contradictions' which, they believed, would eventually lead to the break-up of capitalist states.

At the same time, the extension of the 'welfare state' was consuming an increasing share of resources. The growth of taxation relative to GNP rose generally in the advanced industrial countries. In the UK it rose from 35.3 per cent in 1966 to 47.2 per cent in 1985; in West Germany the comparable figures were 36.7 per cent and 47.2 per cent. In theory progressive systems of taxation were leading to a transfer of wealth from the richest to the poorest members of society. In practice, research showed that the redistributive effect of taxation was generally rather limited, and that both the contributors to and the beneficiaries of welfare-state systems were in the main the articulate middle classes. As states were apparently running out of resources, they decided to call upon their citizens to tighten their belts, and the citizens did not like this (Hood and Wright 1981). 'New Right' theorists like Brittan in the UK and Milton Friedman in the USA argued forcefully that the limits of the system had already been reached. Hence not only would the state have to give up some of its responsibilities, but it was actually counterproductive for it not to do so.

The third was 'the presumption of impotence in the face of external pressures' (Cairncross 1990, p. 49). Though the term 'globalisation' was yet to be coined, the close interaction between the major economies and the crucial role played in the system by the USA was obvious to all. In 1981 Reagan was elected president of the United States and the Republicans gained control of Congress. US interest rates went up to check rising inflation and a new economic strategy was introduced that was to be touted as a model for the rest of the world.

The 'Lafer curve', named after the distinguished economist who suggested that a reduction in tax level would actually lead to an increase in tax revenues, formed the basis for the economic strategy of President Reagan in the United States. However, the strategy of massive tax cuts went badly wrong from the beginning, when the administration decided simultaneously to increase spending on the armed forces (Stockman 1987). For most of the next two decades the national debt of the United States climbed

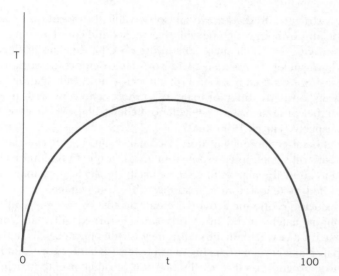

T = Tax revenue, t = tax rate
As the tax rate increases, the Tax revenue rises to a peak and then
falls off sharply

Source: http://www.eco.utexas.edu/faculty/Norman/Class.Notes/Fiscal.Policy/FiscalPolicy.html

Figure 5.1 The Lafer curve

remorselessly, while Congress and president argued about who was responsible for it (Koven 1991). It reached $5 trillion by 1998.

'Thatcherism' in Britain tried to reduce government spending, but signally failed to do so. This was despite the fact that after 1983 it embarked on a far-reaching programme of 'privatisation' of state-owned industries and utilities, while at the same time cutting back the powers of trade unions and increasing the freedom of employers to resist wage demands. In the later 1980s privatisation came to be seen by the governments of many other countries as a method of escaping from the limitations of the 'weak state'. It was also a quick way of raising funds which all too often were spent on bribing the electorate instead of paying off the national debt.

4. **Neoliberal** economists blamed the crisis of the 1970s on the failure of Keynesianism. The real cause was of course the ill-advised attempt of wealthy elites in the oil-producing states to exploit their dominant position by sharply increasing the price of crude oil. The problem was that this caused accelerated inflation in the advanced industrialised countries (AICs). The only way that their governments knew how to check inflation was to check spending, in the case of public spending by cutting budgets and in the case of private spending by raising interest rates. The problem was that cutting budgets meant cutting back on social security spending and measures to maintain employment, and these policies were both unpopular and unjust.

Neoliberals such as Schumpeter (1943) do not therefore justify their views on economic grounds alone. Instead they argue that economic freedom is a necessary condition for political freedom, which is itself a good thing. Hayek took the position that the sole duty of the government was to provide those services which cannot be provided by competition and to ensure 'security against severe physical privations'. Like Marx, Hayek did not confine his strictures to the known and observable, but went on to assert propositions about the future about which he had no evidence and could have had no evidence. Like the McCarthyites and their successors in the USA, he drew no distinction between fascism, communism or democratic socialism. 'That democratic socialism, the great utopia of the last few generations, is not only unachievable, but that to strive for it produces something so utterly different that few of those who now wish it would be prepared to accept the consequences, many will not believe till the connection has been laid bare in all its aspects' (Hayek 1976, p. 23).

Among neoliberal economists Milton Friedman (1962) went even further, arguing that government's only economic responsibility was simply to maintain a steady supply of money and to allow the market to regulate itself. Hence, for example, inflation could only be controlled by reducing money supply. This, if it worked, would have the consequence of reducing economic activity even at the cost of rising unemployment. Fortunately or unfortunately, it did not work, since it turned out that economists were unable to agree on just what constituted money for this purpose. Since the neoliberals were not prepared to countenance using their powers (as earlier governments had done) to reduce private expenditure directly, by taxation or otherwise, they helpfully ensured that the whole cost fell on the public sector. In 1977 Friedman visited London and recommended that one-sixth of all civil servants be sacked (Friedman 1977). Cutting public expenditure regardless of the social cost became the strategy pursued by the Thatcher government in Britain after 1979 and was subsequently recommended as a standard prescription to Third World countries by the IMF. But it was not until 1985 that the fact that there was no agreement on what constituted money became so blatant that monetarist theory was quietly dropped from government speeches.

It was only after 1983 that the idea of privatisation – selling off state industries – really took off, to begin with in the UK and subsequently in other parts of the world. This not only brought in large sums of money which could be used to subsidise tax cuts for electoral purposes, at the same time it reduced public expenditure both directly and indirectly (since the workers in these industries were no longer formally state employees).

The United States under Ronald Reagan is also claimed to be a test case which shows that non-interference with the economy is the secret of economic growth. However, though the Reaganites cut taxes and talked about cutting expenditure, the administration drastically increased defence spending and Congress continued to be dominated by 'pork-barrel' politics, concerned only with the share-out of public resources among voters. The massive increase that took place in defence expenditure pumped billions of dollars into the economy, mostly funded by borrowing.

The neoliberals were, however, let loose to experiment freely on Eastern Europe after 1989. They were also able under the Bush administration to block any notion of a 'Marshall Plan' for Eastern Europe. The result, as we have already noted (Chapter 4), was that Russia developed so-called 'nomenklatura capitalism' – an economy dominated by members of the former Communist elite who were able to convert public resources to their private benefit.

Limits on government power

Limits on government power to intervene in the economy are of three kinds: globalisation, constitutional restraints and ungovernability, and the hidden economy.

1. **Globalization**. We have already noted the reassertiveness of the world capitalist system after the fall of communism in 1989. The Bretton Woods institutions already had the power to control national spending by setting terms for treasuries and central banks ('conditionality'). But as a result few national governments try to challenge them and in Gramscian terms the 'Washington consensus' has achieved *hegemony*, unchallenged acceptance on all sides.

The most visible signs of this are the regular conferences of the so-called 'Group of Seven (Eight)' or G7 (G8) nations. The first of these conferences was called by President Giscard d'Estaing of France in the 1970s to cope with the major international economic crisis brought about by the first 'oil shock'. They became a regular feature of the landscape and since 1991 have been increasingly a forum for political as well as economic decisions.

Meanwhile in the new world order transnational corporations have become major economic actors, operating across fading national boundaries. They cannot be easily controlled except by their home governments, which have little interest in restraining their urge to make money. They can shift production from one part of the world to another if they dislike the actions or distrust the intentions of the local government.

Setting up the World Trade Organisation (WTO) has enormously strengthened the power of the United States to dictate terms. However, to some extent economic power has been diffused by the emergence of multiple centres of power. New regional economic groupings are being formed which strengthen regional economic hegemons such as South Africa, India or Brazil. Finally, as noted above (Chapter 3), three areas have become differentiated in ways that are politically interesting:

- The oil-rich Middle Eastern states. Possession of great wealth based on the exploitation of this essential resource enables these states to maintain traditional styles of government. States in the Gulf region are generally less democratic than France was before 1789.
- The 'Asian tigers' (Singapore, Malaysia, South Korea, Taiwan, etc.) until 1997 were seen as a model for other states to follow, actual proof that even in a globalised world it was possible for a country to become a major economic player. They all began with a low level of economic development, and have experienced an authoritarian phase (in some cases still continuing), low wages, and relatively equal distribution of wealth.
- Small island developing states. These are the most vulnerable states in a globalised economy.

Two examples will demonstrate the vulnerability of the small island developing states. Bananas produced in the former British territories in the Caribbean have traditionally enjoyed preferential access to the EU. In recent years the EU has faced pressure to end quotas on the import of so-called 'dollar bananas'. The consequences for the smaller Caribbean island-states are potentially catastrophic, since although many are not particularly suitable for banana cultivation, they lack alternative cash crops. The new WTO had hardly been established when agitation began for the US government to use it to end the preferential quotas. This was resisted fiercely by the leaders of the smaller island states, and in a meeting in Washington on 13 September 1995 the prime minister of Jamaica, Percival J. Patterson, sought and received assurances that the US government would not pursue its case. Despite this, two weeks later the US government went ahead and filed a complaint against the EU's banana regime on behalf of Chiquita Brands, the US transnational corporation, which coincidentally had just made a large donation to President Clinton's campaign fund. The US government claimed that the EU system favoured imports from African, Caribbean and Pacific states over those from Central America; its argument that in consequence Central American exports had suffered was however hard to sustain, given the very small production of the islands. Despite all attempts to resolve the dispute amicably, the US government persisted and was authorised by the WTO to levy sanctions in return. The sanctions, curiously, were levied against British industries because Britain had supported the islands' position, and the US was autho- rised to choose which industries to punish – a flagrantly unjust abuse of power.

The Caribbean state of St Lucia has long complained about the high tariffs charged by Cable and Wireless. For historical reasons C&W had a monopoly of telecommunica- tions in eight English-speaking Caribbean countries and the St Lucian government even- tually opened negotiations with the company to end its exclusive licences. When the company threatened to pull out of St Lucia altogether if agreement was not reached before its existing licences expired, however, the other regional governments made it clear that if it did so, 'the issue of withdrawal' would arise in their countries also. On this occasion, ironically, the regional governments were arguing that the company's exclusive licences were not only 'hindering economic development' but also 'inconsistent with agreements with the World Trade Organization' (*Financial Times*, 17/18 February 2001).

2. **Ungovernability**. There is great uncertainty about the actual performance of mixed market economies. Back in the early 1970s the government of Salvador Allende in Chile bought a computer which was supposed to tell them daily how the economy was doing. However, since the statistics on which its model was based were collected only once a month, once a quarter or even once a year, the model could not possibly have done what it was supposed to do.

Governments have only a limited number of instruments to control an economy. Moreover some of these instruments either cannot easily be used or carry unacceptable risks for politicians who try to use them. Raising taxes is an option which is either not used or when used is carefully disguised, since it is very unpopular with the electorate. George Bush promised 'No new taxes' in his election campaign in 1988 (Hill and Williams 1994); his failure to keep his promise was later blamed for his failure to win re-election in 1992. Weak corporate regulatory regimes have little effect. In Britain they have been positively harmful. The idea that you can get better performance out of a privatised company by fining it for failing to deliver on targets specified by government or regulator is so obviously counter-productive that it is amazing that any government should have been so silly as to suppose it would work. For most of 2000, following the Southall and Hatfield train crashes, the British rail network was in a state of chaos. Driven by the need to save money at all costs, Railtrack, the company responsible for maintaining the track, had contracted the work out to outside contractors, and inevit- ably failed to exercise adequate supervision over so many different activities. The need to repair the track played havoc with the timetables of the train operating companies, who not only faced hefty fines from the regulator for failing to keep to time but were also required to pay compensation to passengers who were delayed or unable to travel.

3. **The hidden economy**. The complexity of an economy means that there is always a certain amount of economic activity that can avoid scrutiny. Statistics on world trade and world financial movements do not add up. The abolition of exchange controls has made it much easier than before to move money around. Donors can take advantage of this to ensure that their donations to political campaigns are not traced to them; this practice, known as 'money laundering', was, for example, used by supporters of the Guatemalan dictatorship to enable them fund Ronald Reagan's presidential campaign in 1980. US legislation on campaign funding prohibits foreigners to fund American

political parties. However, it is known that very large sums of money were paid by the US Central Intelligence Agency (CIA) to the Italian Christian Democrats (DC) from the 1940s onwards to enable them to compete successfully against the electoral challenge of the Italian Communist Party (PCI).

The neoliberal ideology favours what has been termed '**possessive individualism**' (Macpherson 1977). People who are encouraged to believe that they have a right to do what they want are not likely to be easily constrained by laws intended to protect the public interest. The silencing of the opposition in single-party states, claimed by its proponents to be enhancing efficiency, allowed corruption to become rampant. In elaborate and inefficient bureaucratic systems it becomes commonplace to pay inducements to officials to obtain something that one is entitled to. The boundary line between this, and the practice of paying to obtain something one is not entitled to, is very easily crossed, and so quite properly both practices are regarded as corrupt. Even in colonial times the practice of paying a 'dash' to get something done in Nigeria was established practice. However, corruption is not confined to post-colonial states and allegations of corruption have helped bring down governments in France and Britain, while Congress is currently probing (2001) the decision of Bill Clinton to issue in the last hours of his presidency presidential pardons for various offences to people believed to have given substantial sums to fund the building of his Presidential Library and other worthy causes.

Estimates of the size of the '**black economy**' in Europe vary from around 7 per cent in the UK to over 15 per cent in Italy. In Third World states, however, corruption is a major problem. Surveys in 2000 showed that Finland is regarded as the least corrupt of the world's states, Nigeria the most (2000 Corruption Perceptions Index, http://www.gwdg.de/~uwvw/2000Data.html) (see Table 5.1).

Table 5.1 Perception of corruption, selected countries, 2000

Rank	Country	Score	Amount	SD
1	Finland	10.0	8	0.6
10	UK	8.7	9	0.6
11	Switzerland	8.6	8	0.3
13	Australia	8.3	10	1.0
14	USA	7.8	10	0.8
17	Germany	7.6	8	0.8
18	Chile	7.4	8	0.9
19	Ireland	7.2	8	1.9
21	France	6.7	9	1.0
24	South Africa	5.0	10	0.9
39	Italy	4.6	8	0.6

Source: The 2000 Corruption Perceptions Index, http://www.gwdg.de/~uwvw/2000Data.html

Summary

A major task of all government is to establish and maintain the standard of value of a currency. The purpose of this is to enable goods to be traded in an internal market, which is created, regulated and taxed by government. Taxes provide the resources not only for the operations of government but for the exercise of political power. Funding is also essential for a successful campaign to gain power through elections.

Since 1945 ideas of how far government should intervene in the market have changed according to changes in the prevailing ideology. These changes have been accompanied by the strengthening of international forces operating to constrain governmental decisions. Limits on government power therefore are of three kinds, globalisation, constitutional restraints and ungovernability, and the hidden economy and corruption.

Key Concepts

black economy, that part of an economy generated by illegal activities, e.g. drug smuggling

command economy, economic system in which economic resources are allocated by the state rather than by the free operation of the market

convertibility, the ability to trade a currency freely on the world markets

credit, the power to obtain goods and service before payment is made based on trust in the ability of the creditor to pay

debt, for government, money borrowed against a promise of later repayment from taxation or other income

market, an arena established by government in which goods and/or services can be exchanged

market economy, an economy based upon the free exchange of commodities under conditions of competition, together with the minimum necessary institutional framework to make exchange possible over time – a

predictable system of law guaranteeing property rights and the security of contract (Beetham 1997)

money, a uniform standard of value established by governments to facilitate exchange

nationalisation, the process of transferring privately owned resources to state ownership, by international convention, in exchange for full and fair compensation

neoliberalism, uncritical belief in the efficacy of the 'free market'; its general acceptance by policy-makers after 1989 is often termed the 'Washington consensus'

possessive individualism, characteristic of neoliberalism to ignore the need for social awareness in pursuit of wealth (Macpherson 1977)

privatisation, the process of transferring state-owned assets to private ownership

regulation, the process of making or applying rules having the force of law to correct the weaknesses of unregulated markets

Sample Questions

This is an area in which much of the everyday debate is characterised by more heat than light. However, the ability (or otherwise) of governments to manage economies is so central that many other questions involve some consider-

ation of the fundamental issues. Again, any answer should show awareness of empirical evidence for the argument that is being put forward. Questions specifically directed at the material in this chapter might include:

Sample Questions continued

- Where are we now on 'the road to serfdom'?
- What is the role of government in a globalised economy?
- What tools for economic management are available to a modern government?
- What relationship, if any, is there between economic prosperity and democratisation?

Further Reading

The theoretical argument for neoliberalism was set out in (among others) Hayek (1976) and Friedman (1962). Hoover and Plant (1989) discuss its relevance to the modern politics of the UK and the USA. The relationship between the market economy and democracy initiated by Schumpeter (1943) is discussed from differing angles by Brittan (1976) and by Beetham (1997). The edited collection by Graham and Seldon (1990) is an attempt to review how European governments actually performed post-1945. Carsten's 1967 study of the rise of fascism in the 1930s reminds us of the real reasons why the control of the economy was seen as central by post-war governments. Hirsch (1977) was an early, but so far unheeded, warning about the limits to economic growth. Krugman (1994) was a timely warning that the neoliberal interpretation for the rise of the Asian tigers had to be taken with a pinch of salt.

The best statement of the view that politics is primarily about the allocation of material resources is still Lasswell (1936).

PART THREE   **Demands, Support and Decision-Making**

How Demands are Presented

CHAPTER SIX

Learning Objectives

By the end of this chapter, the reader will be able:

- to understand how demands are made on government, how they are made known in the first instance and how they are aggregated so that meaningful policy choices become possible;

- to identify types of interest groups and political parties, and how the nature of political parties is affected by the party systems within which they have to act;

- to evaluate different models of the relationship between interests and government in a specific context.

How Demands Originate

Demands on the political system originate in the minds of individual citizens, often in a quite unformed state. They may well not be immediately recognised as political, and whether they are seen to be or not will depend on the nature of the society concerned. In almost all societies the citizen has the right of petition. That is, they may express demands as an individual by speaking or writing to a recognised outlet at some level of government. Historically this right of petition applied in the Soviet Union as well as in non-communist countries (Lane 1978) and is still of great importance in the traditional autocracies of the Middle East.

However, except in a very local sense, the voice of one individual in a modern society will normally carry little weight. There is an exception. If the individual in question is a member of the central elite and, even better, its decision-making body, his or her inputs – what Easton (1957, 1965) calls 'withinputs' or 'intraputs' – are very much more likely to be taken seriously. If not, the best strategy is to get together with others who share a common interest and aggregate all the demands made by the group into a programme for action.

In liberal democracies typically demands are *articulated* by interest groups and *aggregated* by political parties. But the interest group differs from the political party, to which it is closely related, by not seeking political power for itself. It merely seeks, when it acts at all, to influence decisions taken by others. However, this model is by no means always applicable elsewhere and a great deal of research still needs to be done on how interests are translated into public policy.

Interest Groups

It is now recognised that **interest groups** – people sharing a common interest – exist in all societies. Some hold that these groups exist in a latent rather than an active state, waiting to be activated by a relevant issue. If so they would cover the entire field of political interest articulation other than that of the individual, for the family itself can be regarded as an interest group. Once activated, with the added strength that comes from formal organisation, they can aggregate interests also into a common action programme, as in the case of the Countryside Alliance in the UK, and then they are often referred to as **pressure groups**. For the purpose of comparative politics, the most useful system of classification of interest groups is still that of Almond, who divides interest groups into four categories (Almond and Coleman 1960, pp. 33ff.). These categories are non-associational, institutional, associational and anomic.

1. **Non-associational**. People do not join non-associational groups; they are born into them, and therefore as far as politics is concerned the groups may remain latent rather than active, often for many years. They include family and kin groups (clans in Scotland or Pakistan), castes (or non-caste members, e.g. the Dalits in India), classes (such as workers or peasants collectively), religions or sects (such as the Muslims of Bosnia-Herzegovina), and ethnic groups (such as the Serbs and Croats). Membership of such groups is, at least at the beginning of their politically interested life, a given in their environment. They are defined as non-associational, therefore, indicating that

they have not joined together in the specific way, they just happen to have a common bond of interest.

2. **Institutional**. Institutional interest groups include all groupings to which one belongs by virtue of economic necessity – the need to earn one's living. They include bodies like the armed forces, police, civil servants, teachers, professional groupings generally, and other occupational groups. However, although physicians (medical practitioners or physicians), for example, form an institutional interest grouping, bound together by their common profession, in practice they can only practise medicine if they are members of a formal organization, in the USA the American Medical Association (AMA) or in the UK the British Medical Association (BMA). Each of these organisations speaks for the views of physicians because to practice as a physician membership is a legal requirement. So institutional interest groups have a formal structure and engage in overt, participatory politics.

3. **Associational**. As the name suggests, membership of an associational interest group is a matter of choice. Straddling the boundary-line between institutional and associated groups are the trade unions. It is necessary for many purposes in many countries to belong to a trade union in order to earn one's living, but in Britain they are, at least, still considered to be in some sense voluntary bodies, as in the United States. They are therefore regarded, for most purposes, as being an associational interest group. The associational category also includes most of the various forms of pressure groups. Pressure groups can in turn be subdivided into two categories: those that are designed to defend interests on the one hand, and those that are formed to promote interests on the other. *Protectional groups*, such as the National Farmers Union in Britain or the French Wine Growers Association, consist of people who are actively engaged in a trade or profession whose interests they seek to defend. *Promotional groups*, on the other hand, do not necessarily consist of the people whose interests they seek to promote, and in the case of the British National Association for the Prevention of Cruelty to Children, or the international pressure group Greenpeace, they could not in fact do so.

4. **Anomic**. 'Anomic' refers to a state of alienation from the normal processes of society, such as was originally described by Emile Durkheim in 1893 (Durkheim 1964, p. ix). However, Almond does not define the word anomic in this sense, which is extremely confusing. Anomic groups, to Almond, have only a temporary existence and no formal organisation. They are 'spontaneous irruptions from the society into the polity' (Almond and Coleman 1960, p. 34). Riots, demonstrations, strikes, walk-outs and sit-ins form anomic interest groupings in this sense and the 'People's Fuel Lobby' in the UK (2000), a temporary alliance of truckers and farmers prompted by the sudden rise in oil prices, was a good example.

Table 6.1 Institutionalised and anomic interest groups

	Latent	Institution	Anomic
Non-associational	Sect	Church	Religious riot
Institutional	Occupation	Trade union	Strike
Associational		Pressure group	Demonstration

For the purposes of comparative politics, therefore, what is interesting is not whether or not there are interest groups – because there are going to be interest groups, if only latent, in any given society selected for study – but the preponderance of one type rather than another. However, there is an implicit suggestion in Almond that the sophistication of the society is measured by the extent to which it manages to separate off political processes from the general social world. In other words the more complex the society, the more advanced it will be. And thus, for example, India is characterised as having 'poor boundary maintenance between the polity and the society'. That is to say that the kind of social organisations which exist within Indian society also perform political purposes, and Almond considers this to be a sign of inadequate differentiation and therefore not sufficiently 'modern' (Almond and Coleman 1960, p. 45).

Such a view reflected the contemporary obsession with 'modernisation', which viewed political development as closely analogous to economic development. Since economic development can be measured and recorded in terms of simple indices of wealth and production, it was easily believed that the same must be true of political development. The same notion of 'efficiency' would then give rise to more, and more diverse, interest groups – specifically to a shift from non-associational or institutional interest groupings towards institutional and associational interest groupings. So non-associational survivals, such as the religious base of Northern Ireland politics for example, struck Almond and Coleman as being archaic. This view is certainly correct, but it does not explain why one gets this apparent obsession with religion, of all things, in the more economically developed and industrialised end of Ireland. This suggests that political and economic development are certainly not following parallel courses.

Pluralism

The pluralists see the ability to form groups as *the* necessary condition for a democratic society. However, Dahl goes much further than this. He recognises a flaw in what he terms 'Madisonian' democracy: democracy based on the notion of one person one vote, with the emphasis on the role of the individual. That flaw is that in modern society there are so many individuals that any given one will carry little or no weight as such. The only way that the individual can successfully articulate interests, therefore, is in conjunction with others.

However, the existence of interest groups does not itself restore the capacity of the individual to affect policy. Indeed the existence very close to government of powerful interest groups is all too likely to have just the reverse effect. Dahl argues, therefore, that the only way individual interests can make themselves felt, and the balance of democracy restored, is by multiplying the number of groups indefinitely, so that all possible interests are again represented (Dahl 1964b). Pluralism, therefore, is not concerned merely with observing how things are; it is prescriptive, an argument in favour of liberal democracy.

However, there are others who argue that group action is not a substitute for individual action. Kornhauser, for example, agreed that the more associational interest grouping occurred, the more it downgraded individual action, and the less weight, therefore, the individual had within society. But he did not see the remedy for this as lying in the further multiplication of groups. In 'mass society' the individual could no longer hope to exert any real influence (Kornhauser 1959, pp. 92–3). Although the pluralist thesis cannot be wholly sustained from a conventional perspective, therefore, its testing undoubtedly remains one of the key tasks of present-day comparative politics.

Its main weaknesses are two. On the one hand, it is plain that major power centres now lie in many cases outside the boundaries of the state. Where that is the case, the ideal pluralist balance cannot be achieved. On the other hand, in modern capitalist societies one set of organisations clearly outstrips all others in power, namely large corporations, and under the influence of neoliberalism the powers of the only organisations able to counter-balance them, the trade unions, have been systematically weakened in the Anglo-American model (though not in the French or German). Again this runs contrary to the basic assumptions of pluralism.

Corporatism

Corporatism is a system of demand management involving a co-operative relationship or 'social contract' between the state, employers' associations and trade unions. Representatives of these corporate bodies (hence the name) are appointed to policy-making bodies. In exchange for being given some opportunity to have a say in the making of policy, they are expected in return to support the government and to implement government policy. The classic instance is to be found in Austria (Gowland, O'Neill and Dunphy 2000, p. 65). The basic principle has a variety of policy outcomes. In the first phase of the New Deal in the United States under the National Industrial Recovery Act (NIRA) corporations were empowered to write and operate under codes which had the force of law. Unions retained the right to organise under the Wagner Act (1935) but since 1980 their power has significantly declined. In post-war Germany and Sweden workers sit of right on the boards of large companies and annual negotiations establish what wage levels the companies can afford to pay. The Spanish Economic and Social Council was intended by the present Constitution to 'assist the government in economic planning, in collaboration with the unions and business and professional organisations' (Newton and Donaghy 1997, p. 87). However, owing to the determination of the government to make it purely advisory it was not formed until 1991 and then given very limited powers. In Britain workers and management were represented on the National Economic Development Council (NEDC) and attempts to control wages through the so-called Social Contract in the 1970s marked the high-water mark both of corporatism and of the open state intervention in the economy which had begun in wartime. Then in a time of high inflation trade unions refused to be bound by successive attempts to persuade them to rein in wage demands, and a series of strikes destroyed the credibility of the Callaghan government which fell in 1979. The Thatcher government refused to consult the unions at all and disbanded the NEDC. It then curbed the powers of the unions by a series of laws, ending 'contracting out' for union dues, requiring them to ballot their members before a strike, forbidding secondary picketing and imposing legal liability for the consequences of strike action. It did not tighten up the regulation of company management so effectively.

The idea of an essential harmony of the interests of workers and management is at least as logical as the Marxist view that they must be irreconcilably opposed, though this does not, of course, mean that either view is correct – their interests might coincide on some things (high sales) and not on others (low wages). The continued success of corporatism in Austria and Germany stems partly from the emphasis on harmony in Catholic social thought and partly from the decision of the Western Allies to limit the number of trades unions in the former West Germany to eighteen, which facilitates bargaining. However, a valid critique of corporatist institutions is that the general public (as opposed to the members of the corporations involved) have no say in the decisions made by the institutions which negotiate on their behalf, and unlike those members, if they do not like the outcome they cannot vote them out.

In this respect, certainly, corporatism is totally different from **corporativism**, the view that all of society should be organised in and governed by corporations of employers

---

Case Study   Change of mood paves way for reforms

Austria has set a new course. After three decades of Social Democrat-led administrations, a new right-of-centre government is intent on shaking up the politics and the economy of a country that has been dominated for more than half a century by corporatism and consensus.

The new government of Chancellor Wolfgang Schussel's conservative People's party (OVP), and Jorg Haider's right-wing populist Freedom party (FPO), has weathered months of domestic protests and foreign sanctions without cracking. It was put together in a hurry, without much understanding of the consequences. But it has triggered a change of mood in Austria that is far from all bad.

In areas such as pensions and budget policy, the new government has begun reforms which would have been unthinkable under the old coalitions led by the Social Democrats (SPO). It has also been more aggressive in facing up to the dark side of Austria's past – agreeing on payments to slave labourers and negotiating a settlement of the even more vexed question of restitution for the properties and businesses seized from Austria's 185,000 Jews at the time of the second world war.

In purely economic terms its scorecard is less impressive. The tax burden has gone up, not down, and outside observers – such as the IMF and the OECD – are concerned that the government will put more weight on raising taxes than cutting spending – a problem that dogged previous administrations – as it struggles to achieve its target of reducing its budget deficit to zero by 2002.

Nevertheless, there is a new spirit abroad in Austria. One of the most visible symbols

of change is the board of OIAG, which owns the government's stakes in a variety of industries. Professional businessmen, such as Allianz's Paul Achleitner and DaimlerChrysler's Jurgen Hubbert, have replaced party hacks on the supervisory board. They do not share their predecessors' belief in the overpowering need for the state to be a long-term shareholder when the market can provide a better discipline.

The sale of Bank Austria, the country's biggest bank, to Germany's HypoVereinsbank, indicates that a more open mood is also permeating the private sector. The idea that Austria has to have an Austrian-owned banking flagship – the rationale for Bank Austria's 1997 acquisition of Creditanstalt – is no longer paramount.

It is too early to tell whether the stultifying proporz system, under which appointments were handed out on political party lines, really has been abolished, especially in the provinces. But certainly the government is challenging other taboos, such as the social partnership, a talking shop for industry, unions and other vested interests.

The social partners have helped maintain Austria's impressive strike-free record. But they have also blocked needed reforms in areas such as taxation and competition policy. Consultation continues, but the power of the social partners is receding. 'The difference is that this government is governing, the other was just administering,' says Christoph Leitl, president of the Austria Federal Economic Chamber.

Source: *Financial Times*, 7 December 2000

and employed in which the employers speak for the employed, in the fashion of the medieval guilds. Under Italian Fascism it was hoped for a time that corporations of this kind would not only organise production and working conditions in each industry but even form the basis for a new kind of parliament made up only of corporate represent-atives. In practice however the workers were given no say in management decisions, the conflict between management and workers was suppressed and not superseded, and the Chamber of Corporations did not work. And the betrayal of workers' interests in this way powerfully aided the resurgence of the Italian Communist Party after the Second World War. But in post-war Italy the industrial and financial elite continued to enjoy near-ministerial status until 1994, when their dominance was threatened by both the collapse of the Christian Democrats and the rise of Silvio Berlusconi and the Northern Leagues. Both developments had been unintentionally facilitated by the change of the electoral system in 1993 (Gundle and Parker 1996, pp. 263–6; Chapter 7 this volume).

Interest groups and policy-making

All interest groups are only significant in so far as they can be related to the political pro-cess through a strategy of *intermediation* (see e.g. Schmitter 1981). There has, in short, to be some kind of linkage and that linkage will be in some degree a reciprocal one: sup-port will have to be offered in return for demands. In theory at least, groups have a choice both of the level at which they exert their influence and the manner in which they do so.

Though the number of levels available will vary from one society to another, possible categories will include:

- the chief executive (whether president, prime minister, chancellor or chairman);
- the cabinet;
- the bureaucracy;
- legislators;
- political parties;
- the general public.

The tactics to be used will obviously depend to a considerable extent on which of these levels is available for the exercise of influence. A private word with a member of the cabinet can obviously be very effective, but only if the government is receptive to the ideas being put forward. If the government is unreceptive, it may be necessary to apply indirect pressure and appeal directly to public opinion. In this case possible means will include petitions and demonstrations to obtain publicity through the media and a lobby of political organisations to use their influence on behalf of the cause.

For some groups, their influence begins at election time, when they try to secure the return of legislators favourable to their cause. In Britain a substantial group of Labour MPs are sponsored by trade unions – a custom which dates back to the days before MPs were paid. In the United States candidates of either party may be endorsed by unions and receive financial support for their campaigns. In both countries, and in other liberal democracies, many legislators are effectively privileged lobbyists for special interests, while since the rest are not specialists on matters outside their own specialities, informa-tion from pressure groups has become an important part of the way in which they make up their minds.

There is therefore a general relationship between the nature of the pressure group and the tactics employed, even though in practice there may be quite a lot of variation from one time and place to another. There are at least three different ways in which people have sought to categorise the possibilities.

1. We can first look at the kinds of aims the group has and the degree of acceptability of those aims to those involved in the decision-making process. This gives us three categories:

- **Clandestine/illegal**. Some groups, such as ETA in Spain, the Provisional IRA in Britain or the Tamil Tigers in Sri Lanka, have aims which directly challenge the basis of the existing order and therefore operate largely in secret.
- **Ideological/open market**. Other groups are entirely legal but challenge political norms as defined by government. Examples have been the Campaign for Nuclear Disarmament in Britain, various 'Black Power' movements in the United States, and the African National Congress (ANC) in South Africa during the transition to democracy. Governments may, therefore, refuse to deal with them, and in extremes regard them as subversive and so to be excluded from decision-making. Hence they tend to use 'open market' tactics such as marches, lobbies of legislators, demonstrations, posters, etc.
- **Pragmatic/'insider'**. Others, especially protectional groups, have information and co-operation to offer government. They tend to have pragmatic approaches to their aims and are often given limited access to the decision-making process.

2. If we stick to groups which are legally accepted, and categorise them on the one hand by their aims (protectional and promotional) and on the other by tactics (ideological, radical, mass or pragmatic, piecemeal, elitist), we can sort any number of examples from different countries, as in Figure 6.1.

3. If we follow Lijphart in looking at the extent to which groups are integrated into the decision-making process we can develop a typology based on the degree of fragmentation or integration of the behaviour of the groups and of the decision-making system respectively (Lijphart 1969). An integrated system like Sweden is more likely to result in central planning and redistributive policies. What Lijphart termed 'consociational' democracies like the Netherlands have the power to integrate fragmented demands

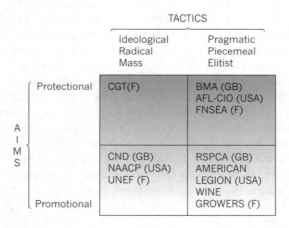

Figure 6.1 How interest groups act to affect policy

Stages of policy-making

Interest aggregation
{ Executive   Departments
  Assembly   Committees

Can act on:
① personnel
② admin structure
③ admin procedures

Interest articulation
{ Party   Policy groups
  Electorate   Meetings, Press, TV etc.

Figure 6.2 Input behaviour and decisional systems

and are likely to be highly regulated. Conversely, integrated groups facing a fragmented decisional system like the UK are more likely to be left to self-regulation. Where both input behaviour and the decisional system are fragmented, as in the USA, the result is 'disjointed incrementalism' and logrolling. By *disjointed incrementalism* we mean the tendency in a complex bureaucratic organisation for decisions to be taken at different times and in different places without much in the way of effective co-ordination ('co-ordinating committees', the standard remedy for this, have a tendency to make matters worse). By *logrolling* we mean the practice, institutionalised in the US Congress, by which two politicians agree to vote for one another's proposals, to their mutual benefit. Although it is unlikely that either will actually detest the other's proposal, it may well be that they would not have supported it had they not needed the political support for their own idea.

We can identify therefore at least three rather different models of the relationship between interest groups and government: a pluralist model, a modified pluralist model and a corporatist model.

1. The **pluralist model** sees a variety of groups competing freely for attention. If one group becomes too powerful (e.g. business), a countervailing power (e.g. labour) arises to contest it.

> Pluralism can be defined as a system of interest representation in which the constituent units are organised into an unspecified number of multiple, voluntary, competitive, non-hierarchically ordered and self-determined (as to type or scope of interest) categories which are not specially licensed, recognised, subsidised, created or otherwise controlled in leadership selection or interest articulation by the state and which do not exercise a monopoly of representational activity within their respective categories. (Schmitter 1970, pp. 85–6)

This is the pattern assumed by James Madison and the framers of the US Constitution and it is still widely believed to be the system that operates in the United States. Would that things were so simple!

First, to make the task of government easier, ministers often recognise the value of consulting with representatives of interests before formulating policy or embarking on legislation. They are not always pleased to be told that their ideas will not work or are unpopular, but in the event they may be glad they took the advice given them, even if they seldom have the grace to say so.

Secondly, in European states generally many government committees contain representatives of interest groups as a matter of course. This situation appears to support the pluralist model of politics and to be desirable, in that a multiplicity of interests are being represented. But the process is highly selective and international comparisons make clear just how careful one has to be about accepting the pluralist position uncritically. In the words of Schattschneider (1961, p. 35), 'the flaw in the pluralist heaven is that probably 90% of the people cannot even get into the system'.

2. A **modified pluralist model** focuses on the notion of *subgovernments*, as they are termed in the USA. For Heclo (1977), loose 'issue networks' exist in the USA to communicate ideas between those interested in a specific policy area. For Richardson and Jordan (1970) policy-making in the UK takes place within subsystems which they term 'policy communities' in which government agencies and pressure groups negotiate with one another. Each segment is separate and distinct and impenetrable by outsiders. Marsh and Rhodes (1992) see what they term 'policy networks' as lying somewhere between these two extremes. They are composed of organisations and not of individuals as such, but though there is a different policy network for each issue area, they are less rigid than the policy community.

3. The **corporatist model** takes account of certain practices which the pluralist model does not.

> Corporatism can be defined as a system of interest representation in which the constituent elements are organised into a limited number of singular, compulsory, non-competitive, hierarchically ordered and functionally differentiated categories, recognised or licensed (if not created) by the state and granted a deliberate representational monopoly within their respective categories in exchange for observing certain controls on their selection of leaders and articulation of demands and supports. (Schmitter 1970, pp. 93–4)

In Britain government has long since found it convenient to offload some of its responsibilities onto semi-public bodies. Hence, as in the case of the British Medical Association and the Department of Health, some interest groups have not only won a legal right to be consulted but are actually expected to undertake tasks which the government does not wish to undertake, so when they are consulted they expect to have their views taken into account. The BMA is a particularly useful group to the British government for two reasons. On the one hand medicine is a highly emotive subject which arouses strong feelings in the electorate and the co-operation of Britain's physicians is essential. On the other hand it is an area in which 'expert' opinion is especially strongly valued. Hence the BMA, which was closely involved in the setting-up of the National Health Service, but nonetheless opposed it, has hitherto invariably been consulted over any changes involving it.

Its American equivalent, the American Medical Association (AMA), has long been one of the most formidably effective pressure groups in the United States, ensuring that any discussion of what it pejoratively terms 'socialised medicine' has no chance of getting to first base. The reason is that it utilises the most characteristic feature of US government, the separation of powers. While in parliamentary states such as the UK government and interest groups deal directly with one another, in the United States policy-making involves three elements: the executive bureau, the congressional committee and the interest group, arranged in what felicitously has become known as an 'iron triangle' (Lowi 1969).

> Each actor in the iron triangle needs the other two to succeed and the style that develops is symbiotic. The pressure group needs the agency to deliver services to its members and to provide a friendly point of access to government, while the agency needs the pressure group to mobilize political support for its programs among the affected clientele. (G. Peters 1986, p. 24)

So powerful did special interest groups become in the United States in the 1980s that concern arose at the effect of their negative impact on the process of choice. They may not have been able to secure victory for their chosen candidates, but they were able to destroy the chances of their opponents. The systematic destruction of the Democratic candidate for the presidency in 1988, Michael Dukakis, by a combination of invective and innuendo, merely repeated what had already become the norm at state and local level.

Political Parties in Liberal Democracies

Party and faction

Today the almost universally recognised mechanism for the articulation of interests, for the communication of articulate interests to the aggregative process, and indeed for the partial or general aggregation of interests, is the **political party**.

Parties do not exist in a vacuum. They are defined by their relationship to other parts of the political system. This means, firstly, whether there are other political parties, since, if there are, they collectively form a **competitive party system**, which is a subset of the political system as a whole. (Non-competitive systems and semi-competitive systems will be discussed below.)

Marxists used to distinguish between 'bourgeois' and 'proletarian' political parties, and this terminology is still used (by the Swedes) to classify the multi-party system of Sweden. However, this does not appear to accord with any well-defined differences in the origins of their members. When new systems came under scrutiny after decolonisation, the structural-functionalists distinguished 'western' political parties which competed with other political parties, and so-called 'non-western' political parties that did not (Almond and Coleman 1960, pp. 9–10, 17). They correctly recognised that both performed the function of interest articulation as well as to a greater or lesser extent that of interest aggregation. But it is of course the differences that are significant, and this requires a much more rigorous reason for classification than mere geographical location. In any case there are instances in which it would be positively misleading to do so – in Japan, for example. Hence here they will be termed 'competitive' and 'non-competitive' parties, in keeping with whether the system as a whole is competitive or non-competitive.

A 'non-competitive' party is in a sense a contradiction in terms, since the origin of party lies in competition. In the life of any community, at some stage, there emerges a dispute which causes people to take sides and form **factions**. A faction is an informal group of people seeking a common policy within a political party, or where there are no political parties. The key difference between factions and political parties is that factions have no permanent organisation or membership.

The reasons for factions to emerge are obvious enough and they have recurred again and again in the history of new nations from the American Revolution down to the present day. For almost every practical task, and that includes *a fortiori* (more conclusively) the task of government, there are a multitude of possible ways of doing it. And faction, therefore, is almost inevitable in political discussion. It is not wholly inevitable. It is possible for everyone to agree, at least for a time, on most things. But, generally speaking, the possibilities of disagreement increase rapidly in direct proportion to the number of people actually engaged in the political process.

The first political parties emerged in a number of European countries out of existing political factions in the late eighteenth and early nineteenth centuries, and spread rapidly, coming to be recognised not only as existing but as having a right to exist (Sartori 1976, pp. 3–13). It is interesting to note that in the periods when political parties were still forming, in Sweden with the Hats and Caps, or in Britain with the Whigs and Tories, in each case the parties' name was derived from disparaging epithets attached to them by their opponents. For example, though the etymology is disputed, 'Tory' means 'an Irish robber' and 'Whig' seems to mean 'someone who drives a horse to look for corn' – presumably someone else's!

Parties and civil society

In Europe, however, and even in the United States though there for a much shorter period, 'competitive' political parties were shaped by the expansion of the **franchise**, that is, the extension to new social groups of the right to vote in elections. They came into existence as relatively small groupings aggregating common interests in parliament or congress. Parties with this sort of basis we now term *caucus parties*. They expanded outwards from this limited basis into mass organisations over a set of stages which gave them a particular kind of historical relationship to their societies.

Not surprisingly, where in the rest of the world the twentieth century has seen the emergence of political parties in the pursuit of independence from colonial rule, they have emerged with the assumption of competitiveness already established. However, twentieth-century political parties were created as mass organisations all in one go, and this gives these parties a very much more diffuse and less separable relationship to the interests. It means that whereas, on the one hand, the competitive political party in its traditional guise is much more intimately related to the interests that it is supposed to be articulating and therefore a better interest articulator on the whole, conversely it is, of course, also much more under the domination of those interests.

Parties, in the true sense of the word therefore, are distinguished by permanence of structure, a deliberate attempt to win membership, and orderly procedures for recruitment of leaders at higher levels. Parties grew up in Western Europe in the nineteenth century, and to this day there, and in other parts of the world where similar views prevail, the ideal form of politics is seen as involving *universal mass participation in universal militant parties free to operate in a highly aware population* (Duverger 1959). General participation in universal militant parties is, in fact, to the people who live in these areas, the distinguishing feature of democracy, and the parties they have, therefore, are direct in structure, mass in membership, with institutionalised recruitment patterns, and non-ideological in their appeal for votes.

For much of this period political scientists have therefore tended to focus on the study of the relationship between political parties and civil society. Certainly the evolution of mass parties reflected widespread dissatisfaction at the failure of caucus parties to articulate the interests of new social groups. The first problem was who was entitled to vote. The expansion of the franchise involved three main issues: age (traditional societies varying in their concepts of physical maturity); social responsibility (the necessity or otherwise for some kind of qualification, e.g. property, to be entrusted with the responsibility of voting); and gender (whether women could vote as well as men and if so on what terms).

1. **Age.** In most of Western Europe, all adults of sound mind over the age of 18 have the right to vote, except in Switzerland and Liechtenstein. In other parts of the world, the position varies more than is often realised. In the United States the minimum age of 18 was established by the XXVI Amendment (1967), during the heady days of militant youth.

2. **Social responsibility**. However, in Northern Ireland as late as the 1970s only those who owned property were allowed to vote in local government elections, a relic of a view once widespread in Europe that voters should have 'a stake in the community'.

In parts of Latin America as late as the 1960s a married man was allowed to vote at the age of 18, but an unmarried man (obviously not being a responsible member of society) could not vote until he was 21. Women, married or unmarried, could not vote until 25 or in extreme cases 30 (Pierson and Gil 1967, pp. 340ff.).

Another argument was that a vote, being a legally significant act, should only be entrusted to those who could read and write. Between 1860 and 1979 no one in Peru who was illiterate could vote at all. However, reading is by no means the same thing as understanding, and in any case the spread of radio and television has done much to combat the lack of literacy.

3. **Gender.** Universal male suffrage as a principle was established in the United States by 1830. Women were first accorded the vote in Wyoming in 1893 but had to wait until after the First World War (XIX Amendment, 1920) for this to become universal. The first country in the world to allow women to vote was New Zealand, also in 1893. In the UK women were allowed to vote in local elections from 1893 but not for parliamentary elections until 1918. The first country outside Europe to hold an election on a full adult franchise was Ceylon (now Sri Lanka) in 1929, and the first country in Latin America to accord women the vote was Ecuador in 1931. But because republicans considered women to be conservative and unduly influenced by the Church, in France they were not conceded the vote until 1945 and in Mexico not until 1952.

Organisation of political parties

'Who says organisation says oligarchy', wrote Robert Michels in 1911, and his observations on the the German Social Democratic Party are equally applicable both to political parties today and to other bureaucratic organisations. Michels's thesis (the 'iron law of oligarchy') was that in any organisation the minority will come to dominate the majority. 'It is organisation which gives birth to the domination of the elected over the electors, of the mandataries over the mandators, of the delegates over the delegators' (Michels 1969, p. 5).

There are three main reasons for this: the size of the organisation, the value of specialist information and the distance between the leaders and the led. Once an organisation has grown beyond a certain size, a division of labour becomes necessary. This leads in turn to the delegation of power to specialists. As a result, these specialists take on the status of experts. Concentration of expertise leads to the concentration of both power and influence in their hands. The rank-and-file have not had the necessary training, are not specialists and therefore cannot participate. The size of the organisation also means that participation is limited by the sheer physical distance between the top and the rank-and-file.

Provisions for the leaders to remain in power include:

- Superior knowledge because of specialisms, access to files, just being there when decisions are made. Knowledge gives the power to manipulate the organisation and win any debate.
- Control of the organisational media (journals, etc.). Views approved by the top are transmitted; others not.
- Time, which, as highly paid, full-time organisational workers, the leaders have (together with the incentive) to prepare debates, accumulate knowledge, etc.
- Political skill, needed by full-time organisational workers in order to attain power; once in power they develop this skill further and become full-time politicians (cf. Panebianco 1988).

There are also factors external to the organisation which contribute to oligarchy:

- The general illegitimacy of opposition. Criticism is viewed as subversion.
- The economic and social gap between leaders and followers. Leaders start developing a set of interests peculiar to their own group. These conflict with the interests of the organisation.
- The need for leadership, the political gratitude of the masses and the cult of veneration among the masses. The masses are politically incompetent and apathetic. They are collectively grateful for having the chores of administration lifted from them.

Implicit in the distinction between caucus and mass parties is that they can be organised internally according to one of two structural types – direct and indirect (Duverger 1959, p. 1).

Direct parties are those mass parties in which there are direct channels of communication from bottom to top; indirect parties are those which allow the members at large only a limited say in the choice of leaders. They can be based on either of two kinds of unit – the branch and the caucus. The caucus is a small group of people who meet for a common political purpose. In Britain the origins of Liberal and Conservative political organisation stem from such groups, both at the centre and at the periphery, which, with the expansion of the franchise, found that they had a common cause to work for. Organisation at the local level was necessary because parties at the centre were dependent on it for their survival.

The branch is much more common today – political parties are formed in new states as centralist organisations which try to set up branches (like Abbey National in English high streets, or Household Finance Corporation in every American main street), so that they can tap sources of interest articulation and, more importantly, finance (see also Randall 1988). This for them means primarily support rather than demands, although they will then receive the demands from these various areas and will deal with them accordingly. The distinction between the caucus and the branch is quite noticeable; the caucus has some kind of independent possibilities of survival. Caucuses can and do regroup themselves into new parties, as in Northern Ireland with the many offshoots of the former Ulster Unionist Party. Branches have no independent existence. The branch of the Labour Party in Britain which attempted to do the same kind of thing would be disowned, and a new branch formed with party approval. The indirect political party, of course, may also have branches. If so, the branch will be under tight hierarchical control.

But the caucus and branch are not the only possible forms of organisation. It is also possible to organise political parties on a cell or militia basis. The cell, numbering between three and five members, is used by terrorist organisations and insurgent movements to limit the dangers of betrayal. In each cell only one member is known to the next cell above. It is also the basic unit of clandestine political parties in countries where either all parties are banned or an authoritarian government backed by a secret police makes open organised opposition impossible.

If the central government is weak, and unable or unwilling to exercise effective central control over the means of force, the other possibility is to organise like a militia, that is, along military lines. This form has historically been favoured by the extreme right. The AWB in South Africa in this respect resembles the Fascist parties of the 1930s. In a militia-based party everyone is subject to central control through a pyramid of officers and NCOs whose duty it is to carry out the orders of the leader of leaders. The idea of organising a political party on a kind of quasi-military basis is very attractive to people of certain political persuasions, and it is also very effective for limited purposes. As Duverger points out, however, these two extreme forms, the cell and the militia, are related and tend to occur together (Duverger 1959, pp. 36–40).

This leads to the criterion of membership. In a competitive liberal democracy, *mass parties* seek to recruit all the members they can and there are no theoretical reasons why they should not do so. However, even in liberal democracies, there are (or may be) also *cadre parties*. Cadre is a military term, orignally French, for specialised units made up of specially trained personnel. Cadre parties are therefore not the same thing as caucus parties, with which they are often confused, for in single-party states such parties have a special significance.

For the objective of cadre parties is to bring about far-reaching social change. This needs a membership which is dedicated to a specific cause, so the party is not open to all, but is limited to those cadres who have passed through a process of training and initiation. The existence of such tests is certainly not a sophisticated, modern idea; they are, it seems, one of the most primitive social rituals marking the stage of transition to full adult citizenship rights. The existence of tests of membership – other than the formal paying of dues – has significant implications for the nature of the political party. It cannot therefore be an associational body open to all, but must be more narrowly defined in terms of non-associational or institutional membership.

The best studied example of a cadre party was the Communist Party of the Soviet Union (CPSU). Members had to be nominated by two existing members, fulfil certain conditions, be accepted as members, and then undergo a period of candidate membership. In 1973 5.8 per cent of the Soviet population were members, which sounds rather restrictive. However, Hough points out that this figure represents 8.9 per cent of the eligible adult population (Hough 1977, p. 126). Hence though party membership fell far short of that found in Austria, where a third of voters belong to a political party (Gerlich 1987, p. 82), it compared favourably with Ireland's 7 per cent (Mair 1987, pp. 103–5), the United Kingdom's 5 per cent (Byrd 1987, p. 210) or Spain's 2 per cent (del Castillo 1989, p. 187).

Ferdinand Tönnies, whose distinction between community (*Gemeinschaft*) and company (*Gesellschaft*) is fundamentally the same as that between cadre and mass parties, wrote of a third type of organisation distinct from either. This was the Order (*Bund*), a cadre organisation which unlike them does not serve a single purpose, but caters for all the needs of its members through a range of services which lock them firmly into membership. Before the First World War, membership of a political party such as the German Social Democratic Party did have something of this significance, in that membership of it became a complete way of life, with its own health insurance plan, journal, and recreational and social facilities. However, the fascist period in Europe tended to discredit the idea of total commitment to a party, regardless of its actual ideological affiliation, and though more recently the Greens (Grünen) in Germany have tried to develop a similar model, the evidence is that a great many of the members remain inactive between elections (Kolinsky and Paterson 1976, p. 174; Scharf 1994). Today among the few survivals of this pattern are, in Europe, the Austrian Socialist Party, and, outside Europe, the Israeli Labour Party.

Political parties also differ by the criterion of recruitment – namely, how are their leaders chosen? There are some well-known cases in which the leader chose the party, and not the other way round: Hitler held party card no. 7 in the National Socialist German Workers Party (NSDAP). Yet the position he held as Führer ('Leader') was unique. There could never have been, and could not be in logic, a training-school for Führers. Even a man who rises to unusual eminence in an established party, such as Roosevelt, Stalin or Churchill, takes care not to provide for the succession of a man who could challenge him while he still holds power. Of their three successors, Truman, Malenkov and Eden, only Truman, a man with the strongest institutional base and an independent fount of power in the American political system, managed to survive to become a political power in his own right.

It is, of course, the hallmark of a well-institutionalised party that it does not matter whether it has a good leader or not; the system survives despite the leader. Some leaders, such as Truman himself, or Attlee in the United Kingdom, seem to lack charisma, yet they grow in office and develop their own personalities in their years of power. But not all politicians do grow in office: some even shrink – Eden in Britain, Erhard in West Germany, more recently Cresson in France and George Bush in the United States. In a stable party with a strong organisational base continuity will be maintained until public support returns.

The question here is: do the leaders of political parties in a given country become leaders because they start their own parties? If so, one would expect to see a very large number of parties of very short life with little or no institutional continuity, and might well feel, with Sartori, that such bodies do not really deserve the name of party at all (Sartori 1976, pp. 254–5). Such parties do exist, and many have actually taken the name of their leaders for their designation, but have scarcely survived the death of their founders before either losing political support, as with APRA in Peru in the 1980s, breaking up into factions, as with the MNR in Bolivia, or, as with the Justicialist Party in Argentina under Carlos Menem, changing their whole basis of appeal radically (Calvert 1990b).

Lastly, a party may be limited in its possibilities on either of these counts by the nature of its ideology (see Chapter 4). Political parties thrive on ideas – within reason, and only so long as they remain or can be represented to be logically consistent with one another and with the traditional clientele of the party and their interests. Ideology thus limits the positions which a party can adopt in any given situation. At the same time it enables us to classify political parties into 'families' according to their intellectual ancestry. As discussed below, however, there have been clear tendencies in recent years for political parties to lose ideological definition.

Parties and the state

As long ago as the 1950s, Duverger recognised that parties are shaped by their articulation, as he somewhat awkwardly terms it (Duverger 1959, p. 64). They follow the configuration of the country in which they operate – physical, economic and demographic. They are shaped, above all, by its political structure, and in particular by the nature of the electoral system as a system of choice. Whether the tangible prizes are to be won locally or nationally – or, in a few federal states, regionally – determines the nature of the contest for which they gear themselves.

Even more important is the effect on a political party of actually winning and exercising political power. Increasing dissatisfaction with the mass party model has led political scientists to question the widespread assumption that it represents the ultimate form of political organisation.

The interesting thing is that despite the ideal of competitive political parties, in a number of 'Western' states there are one-party systems to which no effective opposition is manifest, but where there do not appear to be any very good reasons why such an opposition might not develop.

Sartori classifies party systems in liberal democracies according to two dimensions: the number of parties and the ideological distance between them. This produces five types of party system: predominant party systems, two-party systems, modified pluralism, polarised pluralism and atomised pluralism (Sartori 1976).

It cannot of course be assumed that all one-party states enjoy the support of all the people who live in them, but predominant party systems arise because some hegemonic parties (Sartori 1976, p. 230) have been able to convince the electorate of their merits and opposition parties enjoy some freedom to organise in a sufficiently aware population. A clear distinction has to be drawn, therefore, between single-party systems, which are non-competitive, and one-party or predominant-party systems, where competition is possible if not very effective.

Related to this was the emergence of a new form of party in liberal democracies. Leaders of mass parties, and particularly of those right-wing caucus parties that had adopted mass features, disliked the idea that once in power they should continue to be dominated by the extra-parliamentary organisation. They wanted to maintain the independence of the parliamentary group and soon found that they could use the resources of the state to enable them to do so. The new parties still looked like mass parties but there was a fundamental difference. For them the mass organisation was merely a form of supporters' organisation and in practice their appeal was directed outwards, beyond their supporters, at all social classes, although obviously with markedly different results in different social classes. This form of party is what Kirchheimer termed the *catch-all party* (Kirchheimer 1966).

For Kirchheimer the 'classical example of an all-pervasive catch-all party system' was, of course, the United States with its two-party system, but in 1966 he already saw 'acceptance of the law of the political market' as 'inevitable' in the major Western European countries (Kirchheimer 1966, p. 185) and singled out the Gaullist UNR, created from scratch in 1958, as an example of a successful 'catch-all' party. Though ideology still formed a barrier to the expansion of Italian Christian Democracy (DC), the de-ideologisation of the German and Austrian Social Democrats already suggested that they were heading in the same direction, and by the 1990s we could include under this category the German CDU, the British Conservative and Labour parties and (to a lesser extent) the French Socialists.

As Katz and Mair put it, in Kirchheimer's model, 'parties are less the agents of civil society acting on and penetrating the state, and are rather more like brokers between civil society and the state, with the party in government . . . leading an essentially Janus-like existence. On the one hand, parties aggregate and present demands from civil society to the state bureaucracy, while on the other they are the agents of that bureaucracy in defending policies to the public' (Katz and Mair 1994, p. 103). This suggested to Katz and Mair that the catch-all party was not the end product of this process but represented only a further state in the evolution of political parties. And for them the next form was already emerging: what they term the *cartel party* (Katz and Mair 1995).

The most important change in the last two decades of the twentieth century was the increasing tendency of parties to rely on the state for their funding. This process brings both risks and opportunities. On the one hand it strengthens parties; state funding and privileged access to the electronic media (i.e. radio and television) helps maintain existing parties while denying access to new parties. On the other hand it could bring disaster if they lost an election and with it political power. Parties therefore have insured against this risk by allowing funding to favoured rivals, a process already highly institutionalised in the United States, but also seen in the support for the 'official opposition' in Ireland and the UK.

The cartel party is therefore characterised by both interpenetration of party and state and inter-party collusion to maintain the existing order, and Table 6.2 summarises the

Table 6.2 Katz and Mair's models of political parties

Characteristics	Caucus party	Mass party	Catch-all party	Cartel party
Time period	19th century	1880–1960	1945–	1970–
Basis of party competition	Ascribed status	Representative capacity	Policy effectiveness	Managerial skills, efficiency
Pattern of electoral competition	Managed	Mobilisation	Competitive	Contained
Principal source of party resources	Personal contacts	Members' fees and contributions	Contributions from many sources	State subventions
Relations between elite and members	Elite are members	Elite accountable to members	Members are cheerleaders for elite	Stratarchy; mutual autonomy
Relations between party and civil society	Unclear boundary	Party belongs to civil society	Parties as brokers between civil society and state	
Relations between party and state	Unclear boundary	Party tries to gain control of state		Party becomes part of state

Source: adapted from Katz and Mair 1994, Table 5.1, pp. 110–1 main features of the four varieties. Cartel parties therefore do not come singly, but as part of a cartel, and the most dramatic support for the thesis has been the behaviour of the British Labour Party since regaining power in 1997. Dumping its earlier enthusiasm for proportional voting over the side, together with anything resembling ideological commitment, it has already legislated to restrict private funding for political parties and hence by implication increase all established parties' dependence on public goods and has enormously increased the use of patronage to consolidate its position. Given its past history, however, the UK is still at the beginning of the evolution from catch-all to cartel; the process is most developed in 'countries such as Austria, Denmark, Germany, Finland, Norway and Sweden, where a tradition of interparty cooperation combines with a contemporary abundance of state support for parties, and with a privileging of party in relation to patronage appointments, offices, and so on' (Katz and Mair 1994, p. 108).

Other Party Systems

Non-competitive systems

Non-competitive party systems are of two kinds. First of all, there are those states in which, often as a result of military intervention, all political activity has been prohibited and political parties are not allowed to operate at all. Secondly, there are those states in which only one political party is permitted.

In countries where the inhabitants perceive a constant external threat the compulsion to form or to maintain a single party (even if originally formed for other purposes) is overwhelming. In the belief that the bourgeois world would stop at nothing to destroy it, the former Soviet Union experienced this compulsion, sustained by four historical experiences: the invasion of Russia by the allies in 1919, the continued refusal of Western powers to recognise the Soviet government, the unprovoked attack by its German ally which led to the Great Patriotic War (1941–45) and the onset of the Cold War in 1945–47 which led the Soviet Union to create a *cordon sanitaire* of like-minded states to protect it from the West. But in other European communist states this mindset rested more on the fear that without the Soviet Union their regime could not long survive, and as events since 1989 have shown, in this assumption they were correct.

It was however in the first instance for ideological reasons that the non-competitive, single-party states were created (Neumann 1965, p. 158). Their rulers believed that their formula was the sole one for future success. They were future-directed in that they believed that their role was to modify society in a very specific way. Hence the party as a vehicle for what people want had to give way to an instrument for compelling people to accept what they are supposed to need (Hill and Frank 1983; see also Gehlen 1969; Schapiro 1970).

A number of countries in Asia and Africa adopted the single-party model after decolonisation, although many of them (Kenya, for example) are now returning to (or adopting for the first time) the multi-party model. Zimbabwe, where President Mugabe had repeatedly professed his enthusiasm for the one-party state, thought better of it. Certainly the nature and structure of the party system in these single-party states cannot be explained by internal factors alone, but must be sought in the wider context of world politics. For the argument often advanced in defence of these systems was that in the aftermath of colonisation the emerging state simply could not 'afford' the 'luxury' of competitive politics. Hence in these cases, too, the ideological justification of the monopoly of power by the single party was that total control of the economic system was essential for the planning of future development. The trouble was, as events showed, that the silencing of criticism by opposition, far from enhancing efficiency, allowed corruption to become rampant, and in an extreme case, Sierra Leone, the existing economic base of the country was virtually destroyed without any compensating advantage for the bulk of the population.

In Eastern Europe corruption came more slowly, and the system was tolerated for longer, mainly because of the rigidity introduced by superpower rivalry, which meant that in Hungary in 1956 and in Czechoslovakia in 1968 military intervention by the Soviet Union pre-empted possible change. However, Sartori's warning that no country had yet passed from a one-party to a multi-party system, or vice versa, without a fundamental discontinuity in its political process, namely, the use of force (Sartori 1976, pp. 280–2), proved excessively pessimistic. Since this prediction was made not only Spain, but more recently Poland, Czechoslovakia and other East European states have made the transition from a single-party state to a pluralist one without the use of force. However, in the East European states a common feature is that the 'catch-all' opposition groups originally formed to oppose communism, which formed the first non-communist government, disintegrated by the second post-communist election. Croatia under Tudjman was an exception, and in 2001 had an eccentric arrangement in which the ruling party, with a minority in parliament, had the support of the opposition Conservative Liberals. With four or five parties the norm, and the ideological distance low, most East European states had developed modified pluralism with coalition government the norm.

A complicating factor was that in some cases (Romania, Moldova, etc.) the process has liberated ethnic conflicts which have involved significant levels of violence and have yet to be clearly resolved (Kitschelt 1999). Furthermore, in the Caucasus and Central Asia the former communist parties, having made sure to retain control of the resources they managed before the transition, were able to restructure themselves into powerful competitive parties and either to hold on to or to regain power (Ishiyama 1999; see also Rose 1996). The term 'nomenklatura democracies' is now often applied to these systems, the 'nomenklatura' being the term used for the Soviet-era elite. Hence in the year 2001 there were still some non-competitive party states, as Table 6.3 shows.

Was Michels right, therefore? Is it impossible to democratise parties? Clearly Ware was right to argue that establishing procedures which formally cede power to members is insufficient to guarantee that members will be able to influence the selection of leaders and policies (Ware 1987a, pp. 173–4). The McGovern–Fraser proposals for the reform of the Democratic Party in the United States were soon copied by the Republicans and

Table 6.3 Non-competitive party systems

No. of parties	Country	
None	Kuwait, Myanmar (Burma), Saudi Arabia	
Single	Armenia, China, Cuba, Laos, Vietnam	

led to a dramatic increase in the number of states where presidential candidates were chosen in primary elections. Primaries, previously almost unknown outside the United States, have also spread to Argentina and Mexico. But though in the United States the effect seems to have been to make it easier for 'outsiders' like Jimmy Carter (1976) and Bill Clinton (1992) to be nominated, it does not of course follow that they will find it easier to win. As for the choice of policies, the Greens in Germany have tried a variety of devices: mandating their representatives, rotating them every two years, forbidding multiple office-holding, encouraging the nomination of women and requiring all elected representatives to pay a proportion of their salary to the party (Ware 1987a, pp. 179–82). But rotating representatives and forbidding multiple representation prevented candidates building up a reputation and though they gave democratic control to members it was at the cost of making it harder for the party to compete successfully in elections.

Semi-competitive systems

All other systems are notionally competitive. However, as noted above, there are a significant number of countries in which opposition parties stand little or no chance of gaining power (**semi-competitive party systems**).

Though its hegemony has been broken following the breach in its dynastic leadership by the assassination of Rajiv Gandhi, the example of the Congress Party in India seems to illustrate both the reasons for this situation, and the limitations on it. There the party of Nehru enjoyed its initial hegemony as the combined effect of its leadership of the struggle for Indian independence coupled with the presence of Pakistan as a target for organisational and individual hostility. Nehru himself strengthened this position through the international goodwill and attention India obtained as the result of advocating, on behalf of smaller and less influential countries, a theory of their place in the world which they found congenial. But basically the supremacy of the Congress Party was maintained as the result of its success in monopolising patronage and being able to 'deliver' on its political promises.

The importance of these rewards was such that, regardless of the intentions of the national leaders, local political activists had no reason whatsoever to see the monopoly challenged. As Turkey found previously, and Mexico found between 1985 and 1995, it is extremely difficult to develop a second competing party so long as a single ruling party controls national political life and with it the national economy. Effectively, the only real possibility of such rivalry developing will come from competition within the ruling party, which is most likely to occur as the result of changes within the social order precipitated by a crisis. Yet when such a major crisis did occur in Mexico in 1987–88, the ruling Revolutionary Institutional Party (PRI) was successful in retaining sufficient of its support, even in face of a major secession led by a charismatic personality, to make a convincing case for having won the elections of 1988. It was only after a second major crisis in 1994 and the rise of a charismatic opposition candidate with a credible record as a state governor, that a challenge from an opposition candidate in the presidential election of 2000 became possible and, in the event, successful.

If, as often happens, the crisis arises from without, as when the Portuguese revolution of 1974 led South African-backed forces to attack the Marxist government of Angola (1975), the effect may be the exact reverse – to unite rather than to divide the political community, in this case the limited electorate of apartheid South Africa.

Table 6.4 Two-party and multi-party systems

No. of parties	Country	
One	Bulgaria, Georgia, Japan, Kenya, Lithuania, Malaysia, Mozambique, Paraguay, Romania, Singapore, South Africa, Venezuela, Zimbabwe	
Two	Australia, Austria, Barbados, Canada, Colombia, France, Jamaica, Mexico, New Zealand, Nicaragua, Nigeria, Portugal, Spain, Sri Lanka, United Kingdom, United States, Uruguay	
Two and a half	Argentina, Chile, Germany, Ireland	
Multi	Belgium, Brazil, Belarus, Denmark, India, Italy, Luxembourg, Netherlands, Norway, Poland, Russia, Sweden, Switzerland, Ukraine	

Is there then a similar explanation for two-party and multi-party systems? As regards two-party states, it may be significant that they grew up in the period before the control of the economy became an accepted part of the burdens of government. This being the case, the government of the day did not enjoy the ability to use these constraints to cut off opposition. It is the very sophistication of modern governmental control over banking, imports and economic production that enables it to discriminate against its political opponents in a way so subtle that the necessary resources for opposition are hard to accumulate unless a base for them can be found on foreign territory. Two-party systems, also, seem to be associated most effectively with regional strongholds or bases as in Britain, the United States or Colombia, and most often rooted in a conflict between centre and periphery as in Australia, or between two co-equal regional centres with pretensions to national leadership, as with the Liberals and Conservatives in Nicaragua (Table 6.4). In such regional strongholds, economic resources and political strength go hand in hand. However, as Ware warns us, all may not be as it seems: even two-party competition can involve collusive strategies designed to maintain the dominant position of both parties (Ware 1979). The electoral registration laws in many US states make it difficult for third parties to register.

All political parties, whatever the nature of their system, operate in a process of ultimate choice, which either directs their decisions or enforces them. Fundamental to this process of choice is the electoral system, which is capable of considerable elaboration, but may equally be very simple indeed. It is at this point of choice that the party changes from a body intended to present demands into one which is designed to mobilise support. This is done by permitting the public at large a carefully graded share of participation in the formal process of choosing representatives, provided that share is compatible with the continued maintenance of the governmental system. If that is not possible other parts of the system come into play and the elections are nullified or re-run under conditions which will give the 'right' answer.

The ability of pressure groups and political parties to transform their demands into action depends in addition to a large extent on the 'transformativeness' of the legislature, which depends in turn on the degree of its independence from the executive. The nature and working of executives and legislatures will be discussed further in Chapter 8.

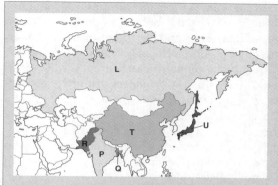

The Former Soviet Union

RUSSIA

Official name: The Russian Federation
Type of government: Federal presidential republic
Area: 17,075,000 sq km
Population (2000): 146,000,000
GNP per capita (2000): $2,300 (PPP $3,950)

Evolution of government: Under absolute rule of tsars until February 1917. In October 1917 power seized by small group (Chapter 11) led by Vladimir Il'ych Lenin. 'War Communism' established, and power extended to rest of former Russian Empire by 1922 when the Union of Soviet Socialist Republics (Soviet Union) was formed; the Russian Federated Soviet Socialist Republic was by far the largest part of the Union but was not a true federal state (Chapter 2). However, under J.V. Stalin (1924–52) the Leninist theory of 'democratic centralism' and the use of communist ideology (Chapter 4) was used to centralise power in Communist Party cadres (Chapter 6). The Soviet Union became a personalist dictatorship cited as a type example of totalitarianism (Chapter 2). Between 1945 and 1947 it emerged as one of two world superpowers. After 1952 party rule was restored under the leadership of a series of general secretaries and a 'new class' (Chapter 4) of the party elite but the central control of the economic system proved highly inefficient. Efforts to reform the system under Mikhail Gorbachev led to the collapse of the Soviet empire in Eastern Europe in 1989 and the disintegration of the Soviet Union itself in 1991, whereupon Russia seceded from its own empire. Democratisation and liberalisation of economic system followed (Chapter 1).

Main features of government: Presidential federal republic. Directly elected president has considerable powers including power to legislate by decree. Highly fragmented party structure in State Duma (lower house) elected by list system. Economic power in the hands of members of the former Communist Party elite ('nomenklatura capitalism') resulting in clientelism and corruption.

The former communist states

A distinctive feature of the former communist states was that power did not lie with the constitutional authorities. Instead it was concentrated in the hands of the party **apparat**. Ghita Ionescu defines the apparat not just as a network of power which controls the formal structure of power, since this is true of most if not all states, but more precisely as 'any centralistic organisation which in an oppositionless state holds, in proportion to its share of responsibility in the running of the state, a smaller or larger part of the power of the state' (Ionescu 1967, pp. 16, 20). In communist states this means the Communist Party and its appendages. Why did this happen? First, it is because of the contradiction in communist theory between the theory of democracy and the commitment to change. In such circumstances there was a substantial number of people who did not like the idea of too much change. To achieve it required a centralistic organisation which used part of the coercive power of the state to control the rest. What was distinctive about it was that its professed purpose was changing society. It is, thus, the exact opposite of a structure such as the army, whose task it is to preserve the status quo. A second reason, as Milovan Djilas argued in 1957, is the petrifaction of the ruling party, which came to be composed of a 'new class' of officials, commonly known as the *nomenklatura*, who exercise their collective power to impede, and perhaps even reverse, the possibility of movement towards a more egalitarian state (Djilas 1957).

Certainly one-party rule was not expressly stated in the 1936 Soviet Constitution; it was merely assumed to follow from the claim made in Article 126 that the party was the sole organisation representing the working people there (Hazard 1964, p. 245). However, in the 1977 Constitution the absolute position of the party was made explicit. Whichever way one looks at it, therefore, the formal structures of communist states cannot simply be ignored (Fejtö 1974). Provided it is remembered that behind them the effective control of politics has for many years been in the hands of the party, it becomes clearer why such a wide range of variance was in fact permitted.

The Soviet Union, Poland, Hungary, Romania, Bulgaria and Outer Mongolia had convention theory-style governments, at least on paper. In theory the system of government was based on a pyramid of soviets or some similar form of committee. In it responsibility ran from the bottom to the top of the society. Each level of the hierarchy elected delegates to the next highest level, with supreme control in theory vested in the vast assembly, supposed to be fully representative of the entire nation. However, in practice the decisions of the party Politburo and its Central Committee were binding on all lower levels of the party membership. Since the formal structures of government at Union republic level and below were dominated by party members, this meant that orders travelled downwards, a practice rather misleadingly termed 'democratic centralism'.

Before leaving the Soviet Constitution of 1936 we should note other signs of the influence of convention theory. Under it the Soviet Union did not have a designated head of government – Stalin was only chairman of a committee, as was Mao Zedong in China. The executive was, again in theory, only a committee of that assembly. Even more surprisingly, until 1977 there was not in the Soviet Union even a formally designated head of state, only a chairman of the executive committee of the Supreme Soviet (Hazard 1964, p. 221). It is by no means the same thing to be a chairman as a president. A president has, or may have, executive power of his own; a chairman, notionally, only acts as a voice for the committee which he heads. It is hardly surprising that Leonid Brezhnev, as chairman of the Praesidium of the Supreme Soviet, preferred not to be thought of as a chairman, though strictly speaking he was not quite a president. His real power, like that of all Soviet leaders from Stalin to Gorbachev, came from the combination of a formal office in the state apparatus with the real position of power held in the party (Calvert 1987, pp. 250–3).

Secondly, a very characteristic feature of the Soviet system which was maintained almost to the last was the idea of the collective responsibility of everyone, at any given level, for whatever others around them may be thinking or doing (Barghoorn 1972,

p. 148). Everybody was responsible for the deviation of a single individual; collective responsibility did not stop at the executive as against the legislature, or the legislature as against the executive, as in the parliamentary or true presidential systems. Collective responsibility ran throughout the society and involved collective responsibility of every group for every member of it. This again is no new phenomenon; it was no less characteristic of Spain in the time of the Inquisition or Geneva under the rule of the Saints, but it is no less coercive in its effect on the individual, since its corollary is that no deviation can be countenanced without endangering the logic of the entire structure.

What was new about the Soviet system was, thirdly, the fact that the basis of control of the state was vested in a single party, and that this party claimed to have a special and unique ability to decide what was in the best interests of the community as a whole. This special knowledge is not an original idea; what is original is the fact that it is regarded as being vested in a political party, and not in a priesthood, as in the Islamic Republic of Iran. Political parties were, of course, well established features of politics in Europe when in 1902 Lenin first enunciated in *What is to be done?*, his view of the political party in its special role as a vehicle of continued agitation for revolutionary change (Lenin 1967, pp. 97ff.). It is from this role, and from the fact of his seizure of power in the name of the party in 1917, that the characteristic notion of the party as a permanent directing feature of government, carrying out a specific plan for change, is derived. This role, moreover, was specifically written into the Soviet Constitution of 1977 (Finer 1979), only to collapse in 1991 in face of the clear evidence that it was unable to use it effectively.

This leads, fourthly, to that distinguishing feature of communist systems which made 1917 a second key turning-point in modern political development, comparable only with 1789 and the emergence of the assembly. This is the assumption by the state of complete responsibility for economic matters. As it states in the 4th Article of the 1936 Constitution of the USSR:

> The economic foundation of the USSR is the socialist system of economy and the socialist ownership of the instruments and means of production, firmly established as a result of the liquidation of the capitalist system of economy, the abolition of private ownership of the instruments and means of production, and the elimination of the exploitation of man by man.

Aspirational as this inevitably is, it should be read in conjuction with Article 11:

> The economic life of the USSR is determined and directed by the state national economic plan, with the aim of increasing the public wealth, of steadily raising the material and cultural standards of the working people, of consolidating the independence of the USSR and strengthening its defensive capacity.
> (Hazard 1964, pp. 221–2, 223)

Since the control of the state was in fact vested in the party, it followed that, even though the USSR itself had chosen to demonstrate its democratic credentials by setting up political forms with a strongly convention theory tinge, there was no reason why actual control by the party elite could not be combined with any other system of government generally regarded as democratic. This is, in fact, what did happen elsewhere in Eastern Europe.

Czechoslovakia after 1948 and the German Democratic Republic after 1949 continued to have formal parliamentary governments. In fact the GDR adopted a Constitution surprisingly similar to the old Weimar Constitution. It has often been alleged that the Weimar Constitution made stable government impossible in pre-war Germany. But it worked well enough if all political parties were abolished except one. At the top, moreover, after an experiment with 'collective leadership' in the early 1950s, power and the title of head of state were combined in the GDR in one man long before this idea had been accepted in the Soviet Union itself (Heidenheimer 1971, pp. 265ff.). In 1974 an executive presidency was created for Ceaușescu in Romania.

Yugoslavia had a more complicated history. Under Tito, it was a presidential state with an executive nominated by the assembly. It was also nominally a federal state, divided into six states according to old divisions between Serbs, Croats and Slovenes. Socially it was a state which provided for a high degree of workers' democracy, with characteristic structures of intensive participation in committees. But the control of the party, the Yugoslav League of Communists, underneath the formal structures of the presidential state, was all-pervasive (Rubenstein 1965, pp. 202–3).

When Tito, who was a Croat, died in 1980, he left his successors a deliberately weakened state structure. Its formal head was not one person, but an executive council, originally created to help the executive function, and to prepare for the transition when Tito died. It survived until 1991, though only at the cost of failing to make many crucial decisions which helped accelerate the drift towards regional nationalism. What destroyed it in the end was the collapse of the Soviet Union, fear of which had helped hold it together, and the belief of the Serbs who controlled the Yugoslav National Army that their only remaining way of safeguarding Serbian interests was to resort to force.

The People's Republic of China was originally constituted on the Soviet model after the communist seizure of power in 1949. In the 1960s it passed through the spectacular period of the Great Proletarian Cultural Revolution, when Chairman Mao attempted to renew the state by direct participation and self-criticism. During this period the formal institutions of government were not only disused but actually in disfavour, with the sole exception of the People's Liberation Army which came to hold much of the effective power (Robinson 1969, pp. 32ff., 122–3). Then came a slow return towards constitutional order, culminating in the writing of the 1975 State Constitution. Even this retained many of the revolutionary committees of the 1960s, a large number of which were eventually abolished and the authority of the Communist Party restored at the meeting of the fifth National People's Congress in February 1978 (*Sunday Times*, 19 February 1978). Despite this, the structure of Chinese government resembles the 1936 Soviet version rather than the 1977 one, except that the central organ is the Executive Committee of the Politburo, the body of which Chairman Mao was chairman.

Cuba, on the other hand, remained quite different from other communist states until 1975, when, under pressure from the Soviet Union, it established a series of formal state structures culminating in a National People's Power Assembly chosen by regular elections, which had, in common with the 1940 Constitution, been suspended since 1959 (González 1976). During this very long period Cuba resembled what in any other state in Latin America would be called 'democratic Caesarism' in that Fidel Castro, then nominally only prime minister, effectively controlled the government of his relatively small country by direct communication – radio and television. Even the formal structure of the Communist Party, though older than the state structure, came into existence relatively late to conform with the doctrine of Marxism-Leninism that a true proletarian revolution could only be led by one (Goldenberg 1965, pp. 267–8). Here, too, military influence grew until in 1975 Cuba embarked on overseas ventures in Angola, Ethiopia and Somalia in Africa which had interesting implications for the future role of smaller states.

Nationalism

The collapse of the former Soviet empire in Eastern Europe, and of the Soviet Union itself, was closely tied up with the spread of *nationalism*, defined above in Chapter 1 as the belief that the only appropriate basis for a state is the nation.

The concept of nation is in turn closely bound up with the notion of *ethnicity*. A nation is a group of people who claim to be bound together by common descent, a common language or a common culture. However, the first of these, descent, is largely if not wholly fictitious. Since time immemorial marriage has taken place across supposedly 'ethnic' lines and DNA analysis has shown that there is more variance in the DNA of the population of individual countries than there is between the populations of different countries. And language and culture are both cultural, i.e. learned attributes. However, people continue to think of nations in terms of ethnicity, and where nationalism arises it can do so either amongst a primary ethnic community, which regards itself as living in its 'own' homeland, and among one or more secondary ethnic groups, which do not. Hence groups claiming an ethnic identity characteristically seek to reinforce their claim to be the 'original inhabitants' of the country, the classic case being the Jews in Israel, who use historical documents (the Bible), backed up by archaeology, to reinforce a claim which in secular terms rests solely on the resolutions of the United Nations in 1948.

Karl Marx himself regarded nationalism as irrelevant. It was class and not nationality that for him was the major line of fracture in society. His cry 'Proletarians of all lands unite!' became a slogan of the Russian Bolsheviks and the problem of the nationalities in the former Russian Empire was supposed to have been solved by Josef Stalin when the Soviet Union was created in 1922. Over the next sixty years under 'democratic centralism' the Soviet Union was treated as a single unit and centrally-directed labour policy ensured that there was a considerable movement of peoples between Union republics. The problem was that what the government in Moscow saw as the rational use of labour was seen in the outlying republics as Great Russian chauvinism.

The problem was particularly acute in the three Baltic republics, Latvia, Lithuania and Estonia, which had been annexed by the Soviet Union against their will in 1940. Nativist nationalists not only resented domination by Russia, but they identified it with Russian migration – a classic example of 'native' bonding against the non-native. The result in Lithuania was a series of measures designed to discriminate against Russian immigrants, and there, as in Poland, religion formed an important element in cementing the sense of national separateness. In Moldova, annexed from Romania in 1940, people hoped to be united again with their fellow Romanians, but as they surveyed the state of Romania after Ceauşescu's rule their enthusiasm cooled and caution prevented this ambition being realised. However, in 2000 veterans groups supported the creation of a new political party pledged to seek compensation for the damage allegedly done to Moldova during the Soviet period.

Once the first signs had appeared secessionist nationalism spread rapidly throughout the Soviet Union. After the abortive coup of 1991, awakened by Boris Yeltsin and others it had also spread to the Russians themselves, and the Russian Federation which had so long dominated the rest completed the destruction of the Union by seceding from it (McCauley 1993, p. 364; Solovyov and Klepikova 1992). Meanwhile the recognition by Chancellor Kohl of the independence of Slovenia triggered the collapse of former Yugoslavia. First Serbs and Croats fought one another, popularising the sinister phrase 'ethnic cleansing' to describe their efforts to maximise their territorial holdings and knit together in strategically defensible units territories which had previously been home to a patchwork of both groups. Then both rounded on Bosnia-Herzegovina, carving off slices for themselves where they could. Though the majority of Bosnians were indeed Muslims, the fact that they were referred to constantly by both Serbs and Croats, and indeed most outsiders, as Muslims, not Bosnians, was the clearest sign of how both parties saw them as aliens who had no right to be where they were. The Serbs deliberately destroyed historic monuments such as mosques and the Turkish bridge at Mostar in order to deny Bosnians their Muslim national identity.

Despite attempts after 1918 to redraw boundaries in Europe on ethnic lines, secessionist nationalism in Western Europe is not dead, either. Basque separatists have for years waged war on the government of Spain and the Provisional IRA on the people of the United Kingdom. Though in Italy the granting of autonomy to the Alto Adige seems to have reduced the claims of Austrian separatists, UK governments have followed the reverse strategy, imposing direct rule and focusing nationalist resentments against themselves.

Summary

We can conclude, therefore, that interest groups are to be found in all societies, though possibly only in latent form. The number of active interest groups increases rapidly with the mobilisation of a politically aware population. However, this does not mean that traditional forms of interest group, such as clans or religious bodies, lose any of their power to influence events.

The pluralist ideal is that many interest groups will compete in an open arena for the attention of several political parties free to compete with one another in a well-educated society. Once the general principle of representation is conceded, the emergence of competitive parties is very hard to resist. But it can be hindered by many factors, including in some cases the emergence of a strong hegemonic party backed by powerful interests.

The fact is that the formal structure of all states embodies the real feelings of their governments towards the participation of others, in that the most common reason that they do not work the way they are apparently supposed to do, is that they have been carefully designed not to do so. Two alternative models of policy-making, the corporatist model and the modified pluralist model, both take account of the fact that government agencies can and do co-opt interest groups with which they share a common interest.

Some variation, fortunately, occurs as the art of designing political institutions is as yet by no means perfect, and so governments cannot always stop their people having an effective say. Liberal democracies, therefore, can be divided into two categories according to how the notion of participation is itself divided. As they exist to do at least two things – satisfy demands and generate supports – which are not compatible with one another, they all depend on some sort of compromise. However, the nature of these compromises and the way in which the constitutional order actually operates is continuously tested by the struggle for power.

Key Concepts

apparat, a centralistic organisation which uses part of the coercive power of the state to control the rest

competitive party systems, systems in which political parties are free to organise and to contest for power

corporatism, the tendency of modern societies to be dominated by large corporations

corporativism, the view that society should be organised in and governed by corporations of employers and employed in which the employers speak for the employed

faction, an informal group of people seeking a common policy within a political party, or where there are no political parties

franchise, the right to vote in elections

interest group, a group of people joined together by a common interest; can be either latent or active (see pressure group)

non-competitive party systems, systems where competition between political parties either does not exist or is not allowed

political party, a formal organisation of people seeking to achieve or to retain political power

pressure group, a formal organisation of people seeking to exercise influence over governmental decision-making

semi-competitive party systems, systems where competition between political parties is formally permitted but in practice is severely constrained

Sample Questions

Questions in this area focus on the themes of representation and the way in which governments can be held accountable for their actions. They can be more specifically directed to one of the specific themes of public opinion, interest groups and political parties.

- Do interests in society need to be represented by formally constituted groups or organisations?

- Which categories of interests are most likely to gain representation in liberal-democratic states?

- 'The flaw in the pluralist heaven is that probably 90 % of the people cannot even get into the system' (Schattschneider 1961). Discuss.

- Can we arrive at a universal definition of a political party? How can we differentiate parties from other groupings?

- Can we construct a useful typology of political systems based on differences in political parties?

- Is political protest an inevitable and healthy feature of modern liberal democracies?

- What devices help to ensure the political accountability of governments?

Further Reading

The 'mass society' thesis is presented by Kornhauser (1959) and Lipset (1960). Michels (1959) contains the full statement of his 'iron law of oligarchy' and the reasons for it.

On social movements see Tarrow (1994) and Jenkins and Klandemans (1995). Wilson (1990) is an interesting study of interest groups, while Ball and Millard (1986) deal comparatively with pressure groups in industrial societies.

On political parties generally see especially Duverger (1959) and Sartori (1976). Political parties in competitive states are comparatively treated in von Beyme (1985), and Scarrow (1996) draws specific comparisons between parties in Britain and Germany. Lijphart (1995) deals with the relationship between party systems and electoral systems. For the former Soviet model see Hill and Frank (1983) and Lovenduski and Woodall (1987), and for post-communist parties Kitschelt (1999). Randall (1988) and Cammack, Pool and Tordoff (1993) are both interesting for what they have to say about parties in the 'Third World'.

How Voters are Made to Choose

CHAPTER SEVEN

Learning Objectives

At the end of this chapter, the reader will be able:

- to identify the main features of electoral systems;

- to determine what conditions have to be fulfilled for an election to be 'free and fair'.

Elections

How support is shown varies considerably from one society to another. In Saudi Arabia the successor to the king is chosen by family conclave. In the Vatican, cardinals have a choice of three methods: divine inspiration, selection by committee, or ballot (the only method normally used and probably the oldest still in use). A whole variety of means have been used as substitutes for election: ratification by a nominated Council of State, acclamation by crowds, nomination from among the combined Chiefs of Staff, choice by a group of senior military officers or approval of a *fait accompli* by plebiscite. But today most states either choose or ratify the choice of leader by elections.

There is nothing like taking part in elections to show the possibilities they offer for enjoyment, and otherwise. On the other hand, many people who do take part in elections become so keen on them that they come to believe that they are what politics is all about. That is not true, as is easily shown by the fact that some political systems have little or no place for them. And although at first sight the literature on elections looks very complicated to the uninitiated, it merely reflects the fact that no electoral system will please everyone (see *inter alia* Carstairs 1980; Grofman and Lijphart 1986; Mackie and Rose 1991).

Elections are a process of choice. But they are not necessarily a choice between alternatives, and, if they are, they are seldom if ever a simple process of choice. Most electoral systems, in fact, are required to enable the electorate to do at least two different things at the same time. One is to choose candidates, the other is to register the approval of certain policies (Milnor 1969, pp. 3–4).

Now, it is not wholly possible to register approval or disapproval of any specific policy by the choice of candidate, because candidates do not necessarily agree with one another on specific policies, even where they regard themselves as being of the same party or holding very similar views. There are, moreover, numerous policies to be accounted for, many of which may seem relevant neither to an individual candidate, nor to the voters. All elections, therefore, involve some compromise between things as they ought to be and things as they are.

Consensus and Choice

The nature and importance of elections within any given society depends in the first instance on its concept of agreement, or *consensus* as it is often termed.

The *unanimity theory* holds that society must express Rousseau's *volonté générale* or general will of its inhabitants (Rousseau 1958, p. 23; Partridge 1971, p. 36). This will particularly be the case where elections are seen as the ratification of policies, since agreement on policies naturally involves the reaching of a common view by all concerned.

If agreement on policies is not essential, and the most important thing is to choose who is going to have to carry them out, then the *majority theory* will serve. It will be sufficient to count heads and give the decision to those who have the greater numbers. Indeed, to them may well be delegated all those day-to-day tasks with which the rest of society does not wish to be concerned.

Both assume that the question of choice is relevant. However, if one believes, as the Athenians did, that all citizens are equally well fitted to hold any office of state, then one might as well do as they did, and choose candidates by lot (Bury 1956, p. 349). Arguably this is the most democratic way, and certainly it is the only way which is at least as fair as holding a vote.

In 1983 the present writer suggested (Calvert 1983) that if the British House of Lords were ever to be properly reformed (which seems increasingly unlikely), it would be an excellent idea to replace it with a Chamber selected by lot, by electronic means, from all adult citizens, to serve for a year at a time. Such a Chamber could be a really effective

Case Study	Market Slump Greets Koizumi Election Triumph

Japan's stock market fell to a new 16 year low on Monday and industrial production tumbled providing a sobering reminder of the challenges facing prime minister Junichiro Koizumi just one day after his party triumphed in upper house elections.

This grim economic news came in the wake of a stronger than expected showing for Mr Koizumi's Liberal Democratic Party which campaigned on a reformist platform.

The LDP, and its coalition partners, won 78 of 121 seats being contested – leaving them in control of the Upper House.

Mr Koizumi on Monday declared the election result had given him a strong mandate to press ahead with structural reform in Japan, and said that this would start later this month. 'I have been given a foundation to implement reform. I will release reform schedules in three steps. First in the summer, the next one in the fall, and the last by the year-end,' he said.

Mr Koizumi also appeared to be trying to strengthen his power base within the LDP, where he faces many conservative opponents. His close ally Taku Yamasaki, LDP secretary general, suggested that the LDP might hold an internal vote within two weeks to confirm Mr Koizumi as party secretary. If this occurs, it means that the prime minister could avoid the disruption of fighting LDP elections this autumn – and would effectively give the prime minister a powerful longer mandate.

The prospect of political stability would be welcomed by foreign investors, given the instability seen in Japan's leadership in recent years. However, many investors remain doubtful about whether Mr Koizumi can implement the type of reforms that he has promised, since these could be very painful for the economy.

Planned reforms include public spending cuts, deregulation, privatisations, and measures to clean up the banks' bad loans.

Unease about Mr Koizumi's policy plans contributed to Monday's drop in share prices: the Nikkei 225, the key stock market indicator, closed at 11,579.29, its lowest level since 1985. This is 20 per cent below the level that the stock market touched in May, or shortly after Mr Koizumi swept to power.

Sentiment was further hurt by unexpectedly weak industrial production data. 'The deflationary undertow is worse than policy makers realise and reforms would worsen deflation,' warned Jeffrey Young, economist at Nikko Salomon Smith Barney. 'These numbers point to a very big decline in GDP in the second quarter.'

The share price falls on Monday weakened the yen against the dollar, pulling it down near Y125 to the dollar, prompting Masajuro Shiokawa, finance minister, to deny that he wanted to deliberately drive the currency lower. 'Business leaders may be interested in a natural fall in the yen but I will remain silent.'. . .

Source: *Financial Times* (FT.com), 30 July 2001

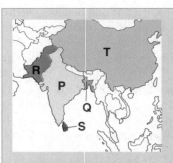

South Asia

INDIA

Official name: Republic of India
Type of government: Federal parliamentary republic
Capital: New Delhi
Area: 3,387,000 sq km
Population (2000): 980,000,000
GNP per capita (2000): $430 (PPP $1,700)

Evolution of government: Northern India unified in fifteenth century by the Mughals, a Central Asian dynasty, but rule disintegrated after the efforts of Aurangzeb (1658–1707) to convert his Hindu subjects to Islam had led to war with the Marathas backed by Britain. British and French rivalry to control India, decisively settled in favour of Britain by 1763, followed by expansion of British East India Company. Following the 'Indian Mutiny' (now known as the First War of Independence, 1857) the Mughals were deposed and British India placed under direct rule from London. Some 500 princely states under varying degrees of control incorporated in Indian Empire 1877 with Queen Victoria as empress. Limited self-government introduced by the Montagu–Chelmsford reforms 1919, but increasing pressure and resistance led by Mahatma Gandhi and the Congress Party led to promise of independence. Independent as Dominion in 1947 and became Republic within the Commonwealth in 1950.

Main features of government: Presidential functions largely ceremonial. Parliamentary government interrupted only briefly by state of emergency under Indira Gandhi 1975–77. Subsequently voted out of office, she was re-elected in 1980 but her assault on the Golden Temple and her assassination by her Sikh bodyguard 1984 ended the unquestioned dominance of Congress Party. In recent years rise of Hindu nationalism provides main unifying factor in fragmented multi-party system. In 1966 states consolidated on linguistic lines and vestiges of old princely states swept away; now 25 states under appointed governor-general and elected legislature. Central government has frequently used its power to place recalcitrant states under 'president's rule', but states still retain a substantial degree of autonomy. Owing to linguistic diversity, English remains a working language of government.

check on the House of Commons, which would in itself probably be a very good thing. No doubt its members would not have the specialist knowledge of a professional body of representatives, but they would not share their prejudices, and in any case election is not a good way of choosing people with specialist knowledge, as those Greeks discovered who tried to choose their military commanders that way. It may or may not be a good idea to have a large number of lawyers in parliament, since parliament's job is to make laws, but if it is, then a better way of ensuring that members had the necessary legal knowledge would be to set them a competitive examination. Unfortunately the

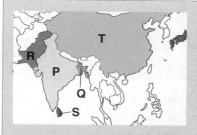

BANGLADESH

Official name: People's Republic of Free Bengal
(Gana Prajatantri Bangladesh)
Type of government: Parliamentary republic
Capital: Dhaka
Area: 144,000 sq km
Population (2000): 126,000,000
GNP per capita (2000): $350 (PPP $1,100)

Evolution of government: As East Bengal, part of British India till 1947. Aided by India, the former East Pakistan rebelled against Pakistani rule and gained its independence in 1971. Political unrest and the assassination of its first president, Sheikh Mujibur Rahman, inaugurated a period of military intervention until civilian rule was restored in 1986. The country consists of the greater part of the delta of the Ganges and Brahmaputra so uniquely 97 per cent of the country is liable to flooding and damage from cyclones in the Bay of Bengal.

Main features of government: Presidential power reduced in 1991 following unrest the previous year. Two-party system, involving persistent and at times violent confrontation between Awami League (in power from 1996) and Bangladesh National Party, both (2001) led by women. The single-chamber parliament has 30 reserved seats for women.

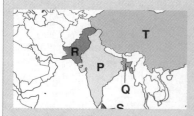

PAKISTAN

Official name: Islamic Republic of Pakistan
Type of government: Provisional military rule
Capital: Islamabad
Area: 804,000 sq km
Population (2000): 130,600,000
GNP per capita (2000): $480 (PPP $1,560)

Evolution of government: As India till 1947. The Muslim desire for separate state led to simultaneous independence of India and Pakistan in 1947, whereupon the princely states were constrained to accede to one or the other. Pakistan (including East Pakistan, later Bangladesh) initially a parliamentary republic led by Jinnah, whose early death left his Islamic League leaderless. Patrimonial rule by large landowners terminated by military intervention, so-called 'tutelary democracy' (Chapter 2) and the overthrow and subsequent execution of the charismatic Bhutto by General Zia. Under Zia's military dictatorship 1977–88 new capital built at Islamabad and Islamic Law adopted. When Zia was killed in an air crash civilian government was restored but the vendetta of Prime Minister Nawaz Sharif against his chief rival, Benazir Bhutto, whom he forced into exile, led to unstable and unpopular government. His government's attempt to oust India from disputed territory in Kashmir, however, failed and in October 1999 General Pervez Musharraf assumed power. He proclaimed himself president in 2001, apparently as a first step towards restoration of representative government.

Main features of government: Federal state of four provinces and federally administered tribal areas. Military dominance (Chapter 10). Bitterly divided two-party system. Importance of patrimonialism in electoral politics; accusations of corruption standard charges against politicians.

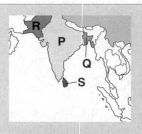

SRI LANKA

Official name: Democratic Socialist Republic of Sri Lanka
Aka: Ceylon
Type of government: Presidential republic
Area: 64,500 sq km
Population (2000): 19,000,000
GNP per capita (2000): $820 (PPP $3,230)

Evolution of government: Unified state under Sinhalese leadership emerged c. 200 BCE. Island was part conquered in turn by Portugal (1505), Netherlands (1658) and Britain (1796), but the Kingdom of Kandy remained independent until its voluntary cession to Britain 1825. Ceylon (as then known) was the second territory in former British Empire to hold election under full adult franchise 1929. Independent as Dominion 1948. Sirimavo Bandaranaike was world's first woman prime minister (1960–65, 1970–77) and name Sri Lanka restored for parliamentary republic 1972. Transformed into presidential republic 1982–83 under personalist leadership of Julius Jayawardene 1977–87. However, since 1983 unitary state and Sinhalese dominance has been challenged by civil war in North and East led by Tamil secessionist movement the Liberation Tigers of Tamil Eelam (LTTE).

Main features of government: Presidential government but with strong two-party system and active parliament. President Chandrika Kumaratunga, who was elected president 1995, re-appointed her mother, Mrs Bandaranaike, prime minister (1995–2000). She survived a suicide bomber's assassination attempt in 1999, but has failed either to defeat insurgency or reach agreement with Tamils, who form approximately 20 per cent of the population.

Blair government opted instead simply to abolish the rights of hereditary peers, leaving the House essentially a nominated body where the prime minister of the day tries to seat as many of his or her friends as possible ('Tony's cronies').

The question of choice can also be irrelevant because the office is powerless, and then the methods by which it is filled become quite meaningless. Heredity, for example, has in the past been an essentially random process, and it may do as well for selecting a formal head of state as any other. The Greeks themselves long retained it in the selection of priests, when secular offices had long since been made the subject of popular choice. But notwithstanding the aspirations of Jean-Bedel Bokassa, who created the short-lived Central African Empire (1976–78), few people would be prepared to introduce heredity as a constitutional device today.

Perhaps it is not necessary, since hereditary succession is no stranger to republics: in the United States George W. Bush has succeeded his father, as has Bashar al-Assad in Syria. For the moment the Nehru–Gandhi dynasty is out of power in India, as are the Bhuttos in Pakistan. Haiti under the Duvaliers, Nicaragua under the Somozas and Equatorial Guinea under Macías Nguema and his nephew Teodoro Obiang Nguema are examples which hardly inspire enthusiasm.

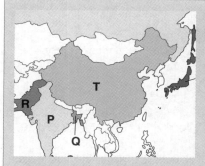

East Asia

CHINA

Official name: People's Republic of China
(Chi Zhonghua Renmin Gonghe Guo)
Type of government: Unitary people's republic
Capital: Beijing
Area: 9,600,000 sq km
Population (2000): 1,248,100,000
GNP per capita (2000): $750 (PPP $3,220)

Evolution of government: In the nineteenth century China subject increasingly to pressure for concessions from Europe and the USA. In 1911 the Nationalists under Dr Sun Yat-sen overthrew the monarchy but were unable to establish a working republic; with much of the country under the rule of local war-lords, in 1931 the Japanese invaded Manchuria. War resumed in 1937 and merged with the Second World War. Weakened by the war effort, the Nationalists were overthrown by the Communists under Mao Zedong in 1949, who established a Soviet-style regime which shed its dependence on Moscow after the death of Stalin and was increasingly characterised by a 'cult of personality' (Chapter 9). After the failure of the Great Leap Forward (1958–59) Mao launched the Great Proletarian Cultural Revolution in 1966 to destroy all vestiges of the old order but the movement got out of control and the army was called in to restore order (Chapter 3). Since Mao's death in 1976 a gerontocracy.

Main features of government: Leadership in general secretary of Communist Party (see Chapter 6); administration in prime minister and 45-member State Council. 'Leading role' for Communist Party. Elected National People's Congress of 3,000 deputies rubberstamps decrees. Harsh legal system with death penalty for numerous offences. Substantial economic liberalisation in 1990s and creation of economic development areas in e.g. Guanzhou. Hong Kong since 1997 a Special Administrative Region.

Electoral Systems

Elections offer choice between both *candidates* and *policies*. There is a wide range of outcomes possible, however, according to the method chosen, the main division being between unanimity systems, plurality systems and majority systems (see Table 7.1).

Unanimity systems

Unanimity systems claim attention first for three reasons. First, they are the ideal of political philosophers. Obviously, in an ideal world, nothing would be done except by universal agreement. Secondly, they appear to have come first in historical time, and to

JAPAN
Official name: Nippon
Type of government: Unitary parliamentary
constitutional monarchy
Capital: Tokyo
Area: 378,000 sq km
Population (2000): 126,000,000
GNP per capita (2000): $32,380 (PPP $23,180)

Evolution of government: Imperial house since 660 BCE; rule by Tokugawa Shogunate (1603–1868) until arrival of US ships broke isolation from outside world. After Meiji Restoration developed representative government which fell under military dominance in the 1930s leading to war with the United States in 1941. After 1945 emperor retained as formal head of state and democratic government restored, strengthened by long period of economic growth in which Japan became the world's second-largest economy.

Main features of government: Dominance of Liberal Democratic Party (LDP) 1945–96; has yet to fulfil the 'two-turnover test' (Chapter 3). Elections to Diet by single non-transferable vote (now replaced – Chapter 7). Executive power in prime minister and Cabinet, but recent prime ministers have been weak and constantly changing. Dominance of economic system by big industrial conglomerates has resulted in bankruptcy of banking system and economic slowdown accompanied by deflation throughout the 1990s (Chapter 6).

Table 7.1 Classification of electoral systems

Unanimity systems
1. Committees: 'the sense of the meeting'
2. 'Method of marks': the problem of cyclical majorities
3. Random choice
4. Single party and candidato unico

Plurality systems
1. Single-member single-ballot

Majority systems	
Not proportional	Proportional

1. Single-member second-ballot
2. Primary elections
3. Alternative vote (AV)
	1. List systems
	  • Largest remainder
	  • Largest average
	2. Mixed systems
	3. Single transferable vote (STV)

have formed the basis upon which all other systems of choice have been erected. And thirdly, unanimity remains the basic daily principle of everyday choice in small communities everywhere, even where more complex systems have been developed for making choices of representatives or policies on regional or national level.

Examples are all around us. Many forms of committee, from church organisations to university senates, will go to enormous lengths to avoid the divisive consequences of taking a vote, and will deliberate at enormous length in the hope that general agreement will be reached. Often there will be an expression, usually by the chairperson, of what the Quakers call 'the sense of the meeting': that is to say, the policy which no one person has actually advocated but which combines the salient features of all those principal policies which have been advocated. Similar behaviour has been noticed in many other societies, whether it be the former Soviet Politburo, Indian panchayats or the *cofradías* or fraternities of Central American villages. Wherever it occurs, it is another example of the belief that reasonable people, discussing a range of policies, ought to be able to arrive at a just and fitting solution which is not necessarily likely to result from the mere counting of heads.

Indeed it is possible, as Duncan Black has shown, to prove mathematically that in many kinds of issue the mere counting of heads will not produce the answer that most people want. It can, and often does, produce a solution that is wanted by almost nobody (Black 1958, pp. 69–72, 218–19). The mathematical proof, moreover, is quite independent of the fact that the rationality of group decisions, however small the group, is limited by human nature. Discussion can be terminated by irrelevant factors long before the point of rational agreement is reached; such factors include the fatigue of the participants, their desire to get up and move around, to have a cup of tea, to go home and have dinner, or the fact that the bar opened ten minutes earlier. And with larger groups the problems are considerably worse, and no one can pretend that a hundred people sitting in a hot, overcrowded room for several hours of discussion really reach the most rational possible conclusion, unless it is to postpone the whole debate to a later and more suitable time.

At this point, too, come into play the many tricks by which individuals seek to steer the course of the decision in the direction they favour. And it was the observation of them by Charles L. Dodgson (Lewis Carroll) which set that mathematician and logician to devise a system of choice by which policies could be selected by small groups on the basis of a mathematical procedure. This system, a modification of what Dodgson termed the 'Method of Marks' and which is more generally known as the **Borda count**, involved each member listing the policy options available, including that of not doing anything; if a vote on the agreed list failed to produce a majority for any single proposal, then each issue would be voted on in turn against every other, and if this produced a cyclical majority (A beat B, B beat C, C beat A) there should be no decision, this evidently being the favoured option. Significantly enough, on the most important occasion on which this method is known to have been used, the choice of a design for a new belfry, the Fellows of Christ Church agreed to combine two proposed designs, rather than to accept any one of them (Black 1958, pp. 206–7).

Obviously this is not something that can be done when choosing candidates, rather than policies. It is impossible to combine two or more candidates. A candidate who is not on the original list can, of course, be chosen by way of compromise (a **'dark horse'**), but by definition such candidates are seldom the first choice of anyone. How then, otherwise, to choose candidates who command the unanimous consent of the electors?

The obvious way is the simplest, to offer them a single **slate** of candidates which they have only to ratify or to reject. The classic instance of this practice was the former Soviet Union, where the elector could either drop an unmarked ballot paper into the box, thus voting automatically for the single name on it, or enter a polling booth and cross the name off. Consequently, to avoid the imputation of disloyalty it was, well into the 1980s, 'not done' for anyone other than a very high party dignitary to vote in secret. Hence the 'right' to cross names off was a dead letter, at least as far as elections to the Supreme Soviets of the Union republics and of the USSR itself was concerned.

If the right was exercised at city or province level, then it was ineffective. At elections to village, settlement or district soviets, however, the right was exercised and a limited number of candidates did fail to get majorities: in June 1973 eighty candidates were rejected in this way. A second election was then held with a fresh official candidate, nominated, as before, by a section of the Soviet Communist Party (CPSU) or of a recognised social organisation, such as a trade union, factory or farmers' collective, Komsomol or cultural society, often one recognised as having the right to nominate to that particular seat. Candidates, even for the Supreme Soviet of the USSR, did not have to be members of the CPSU, with the curious result that in the 1970–74 Supreme Soviet, for example, 421 of the 1,517 deputies (27.8 per cent) were non-party members, a situation most unlikely to occur in a competitive liberal democracy (Churchward 1975, pp. 103ff.)

In Poland under Communist rule the Sejm officially contained a coalition of parties, and elections were held by a **party list system**. Only one list, however, was nominated for the seats to be filled, though as in the USSR this allowed for the possibility of crossing off some names rather than others. As early as 1958 this facility was used, though not to any great extent, and certainly not to the extent that any one candidate was actually defeated. It has been suggested, nevertheless, that the ruling party was keenly alert to any evidence from the electors that particular candidates were unpopular. They might then take care to see that such candidates were given a less prominent task to do in the future, thus preserving the principle of unanimity, but at least taking note of the electorate's views (Butler 1959, pp. 170–1).

There are other parts of the world in which the fact that only one candidate is presented for election is not regarded by many people, and particularly perhaps not by Russians or Poles, as a sign of unanimity. The single candidate election (*candidato unico*) which was rediscovered in Eastern Europe after the Second World War and more recently was adopted by many African states had in fact been a feature of Latin American systems since the early years of the last century (Stokes 1959, pp. 344–6). As noted above (Chapter 6), the tendentious argument that political competition was 'wasteful' of energies that otherwise should have been used in national development has long since been discredited by the examples of states such as Ghana and Nigeria. Kenya has recently returned to multi-party competition and Zimbabwe has reluctantly thought better of eliminating opposition. There are varying degrees of subtlety possible. Sometimes the candidate himself does not allow anyone else to stand, but perhaps more frequently no one else seriously thinks there is much point in trying.

Two other possibilities exist. The plebiscite involves inviting a mass electorate to vote yes or no to a predetermined proposition. It can therefore be used to confirm the self-choice of a ruler, and has been much copied since Louis Napoleon seized power in France in 1851. He ratified his *coup d'état* by a plebiscite that year and in 1852 confirmed his self-appointment as emperor by a second plebiscite.

Finally, occasionally even in more open systems opposition parties fail to agree on a candidate. This happened in Mexico in 1976, when the official candidate for the presidency, Gustavo López Portillo, was unopposed. The Mexican presidency is not a meaningless office. In presidential elections, where one person, however chosen, will in the end represent an entire nation with all its cross-currents of opinion, it is an impossible task to give free rein to all shades of opinion. We can scarcely be surprised therefore that it is seldom well performed, but that is hardly a good reason for not contesting the office. However, legislative seats may be keenly contested in the very states where the president holds absolute power, as in Brazil under a succession of military governments after 1968.

Plurality systems

Next to the principle of unanimity, in order of age, comes the idea of a **plurality**, as it is termed in the United States, or, as it is known in Britain, a simple majority. In the United States a majority means one more than 50 per cent of all the votes cast, and so the American terminology offers less possibility of confusion.

The first attempts to reach a mathematical approximation to the views of the people in a given area were certainly not devised by political scientists, and they were not devised by people of much mathematical skill, so the concept of a plurality, being the simplest, was easily adopted. The fact is, it did not really matter that such a simple method was used until political parties came to be accepted features of the political landscape, since the majority of elections went uncontested. It was only towards the end of the eighteenth century that the French Encyclopaedists, and in particular the scholar and mathematician Condorcet, began first to study possible alternatives which gave less peculiar results (Black 1958, pp. 156–85). It was Condorcet who laid down the principle that an electoral system must lead to the election of the candidate who has the support of a majority of the voters, a principle known since as 'the **Condorcet criterion**'.

The only plurality system still used is the '**first past the post**' system: more correctly, the **single-member single-ballot system** (*scrutin unique a un tour*), used in the United Kingdom, the United States, Canada, New Zealand and South Africa. Under it the country is divided into geographical constituencies each of which will return one representative. On the appointed day the electors vote for one candidate by marking a cross on a ballot paper; the candidate who has a plurality of the votes, even if he or she lacks a majority, is declared elected. If a tie occurs, as it frequently has done at British municipal elections, and recounts fail to disclose an error of counting, the tie is broken by the drawing of lots.

The system, then, is exceptionally simple, but it does have disadvantages. Locally these are well illustrated by the example of the constituency of Caithness and Sutherland in Scotland in 1945, where in a three-way contest only some sixty votes separated the winner from the bottom of the poll. The subsequent history of the constituency, one of the few in Britain whose boundaries remained unaltered during that time, shows an even more remarkable sequence of anomalies (Table 7.2 below). Nationally the system merely generalises such anomalies, so that in the general election in Britain in February 1974 the Conservatives obtained the most votes, but the Labour Party got the most seats. Hence Labour formed the new government despite the fact that in a three-party election the overwhelming majority of the electorate had voted against them (*The Times* 1974, p. 266). This position was reversed for the four elections between 1979 and 1992, in which the Conservative vote remained remarkably constant at some 42 per cent.

Table 7.2 'First past the post' – Caithness and Sutherland, UK, 1945–70

Party	1945	1950	1951	1955	1959	1964	1966	1970
Conservative	5,564	6,969	9,418	10,453		4,662	4,662	5,334
Labour	5,558	5,767	6,799	5,364	6,438	6,619	8,308	8,768
Liberal	5,503	6,700	3,299	2,674		7,894	8,244	6,603
Independent Conservative					12,163	2,795		
Scottish Nationalist Party								3,690
Majority	6	269	3,015	5,089	5,725	1,275	64	2,705
Result	C gain	C	C	C	Ind C gain	Lib gain	Lab gain	Lab

In fact at no election in the United Kingdom since 1935 has the winning party obtained an overall majority of the votes cast. The same was true of the American presidential elections of 1960, 1968 and 1976 (Pulzer 1975, pp. 4, 97, 98), while in the election of 2000, the winning candidate, George W. Bush, not only failed to gain a majority but actually obtained fewer votes than his rival Al Gore. Hence there is always a risk that under this system a minority may obtain a spurious victory and then entrench itself in power. Apartheid became possible in South Africa only with the election of 1948 when under the single-member single-ballot system the Nationalists obtained 51.6 per cent of the seats, with only 40 per cent of the votes cast. Then, having once obtained power, they proceeded to disfranchise voters of non-European descent and to impose punitive laws on the majority of their society so that they could not be deprived of power by legal means (Butler 1959, pp. 232–4; Carter 1958, ch. 5). If that is not alarming enough, consider the thought that if the same system had been used in Weimar Germany, the Nazis, with only 37.4 per cent of the votes cast in July 1932, would have won 60 per cent of the seats and so found themselves in power a year early (Pulzer 1975).

This is the necessary consequence of two effects of plurality systems that are usually praised by their supporters. First, they produce a majority government. This is true in one sense: in very few countries (not even the United States) does one party actually command a majority of the votes, but a plurality system will give one party a majority of the seats if it commands a majority in at least 50 per cent of the electoral districts. But it does not give them a real majority; it only makes it look as if they had a majority. Worse still, particularly in small countries with only a few seats at stake, it tends to give governments a clean sweep, as Table 7.3 shows.

Secondly, as a result, plurality systems do, as their advocates suggest, lead to a sort of stability. Since the winning party does not have to fulfil the onerous condition of achieving a genuine majority, it is able to push through its legislative programme despite the fact that most of the electorate voted against it. With all the advantages of incumbency, it can then go on to ensure its own re-election.

Table 7.3 Caribbean elections, 1999

Barbados General Election, 20 January 1999		
Party	Percentage votes	Seats 28
Barbados Labour Party	65.4	26
Democratic Labour Party	34.6	2

Grenada General Election, 18 January 1999		
Party	Percentage votes	Seats 15
New National Party	62	15
Democratic Labour Party	38	0

Antigua General Election, 9 March 1999		
Party	Percentage votes	Seats 18
Antigua Labour Party	52.9	12
United Progressive Party	44.9	4
Barbuda People's Movement	1.3	1

British Virgin Islands General Election, 17 May 1999		
Party	Percentage votes	Seats 13
Virgin Islands Party	38	7
National Democratic Party	36.9	5
Concerned Citizens Movement	4	1

Turks and Caicos Islands General Election, 4 March 1999		
Party	Percentage votes	Seats 18*
People's Democratic Movement	52.8	10
Progressive National Party	40.3	3

* Plus 2 ex-officio, 2 nominated members. Speaker not contested.

Milnor moreover points out that the use of the single-member single-ballot system results in 'the blatant punishment of parties of limited appeal and the reward of pragmatic competitors' (Milnor 1969, p. 43). In the United Kingdom this means that in February 1974 the Liberal Party got six million votes but only a handful of seats. On the other hand, Nationalist parties, hitherto even more unfairly treated, were suddenly given a quite disproportionate importance in the balance of seats in Parliament (*The Times* 1974, p. 266), which they subsequently lost.

Of course, the fact that the British Liberal Party survived so long and the Liberal Democrats were able to increase their share of seats proves that 'first past the post' does not eliminate all variety of opinion. It would hardly have been acceptable for so long if it did. Even in South Africa under apartheid a small though almost wholly powerless opposition was able to survive. Nor did the system prevent the rise of the British Labour Party as a third party at the beginning of the twentieth century. What it did do was to accelerate its arrival as the second party, just as it did with the Republicans in the United States between 1854 and 1860. Since then no third party has gained more than ephemeral success in the United States. Anderson's vote in 1980 was barely sufficient to qualify for federal funding and in 1992, though Ross Perot won some 20 per cent of the popular vote for president (despite having at one stage withdrawn from the contest), no new party emerged with him and the ultimate beneficiaries were the Democrats.

The fact is that under the single-member single-ballot system the big rewards are allocated as the result of the capture of a small group of so-called 'floating voters', whose votes in relatively few constituencies determine the outcome. In 1945 these key constituencies in the UK numbered approximately eighty, or some 12.5 per cent of the total (Milnor 1969, pp. 41–2), but with continued population movement the number has been declining steeply since 1979. For rather similar reasons relating to the movement of population out of the big cities and into the suburbs, and southwards to the 'Sun Belt', in the United States some two-thirds of the states are dominated by a single party for all or most of the time and the big Northern industrialised states (with the idiosyncratic exception of California) have been slowly losing their key balancing role in the maintenance of the two-party system.

Hence if there is a really serious criticism of the 'first past the post' system it is not so much that minorities have very little say, but that the vast majority have very little either. Their massive votes, piled up in so-called 'safe seats' for one or another party, contribute very little to the result, and so can virtually be taken for granted by the party managers in determining party policy and strategy. Moreover, though nationally the balance in both Britain and the United States may come out about 'right' in terms of the two main parties, it is the result of good luck, not good management. The argument that the anomalies of the system can therefore be disregarded is specious.

For the problem with good luck is that it is always liable to run out when most needed. Composing a legislature, such as the British House of Commons or the American Congress, is not in itself critical; the real problem is to choose a government. Under the parliamentary system this is done indirectly by the choice of individual members of parliament of the majority party or parties, and they have to live with the result, which makes them appropriately cautious. It is not surprising, therefore, that when drafters of Constitutions have sought to impose some check on the choice of an executive president (or governor of a state, or mayor of a city), they have usually chosen to have the selection of the people ratified by the legislature. This, it should be emphasised, does not make the plurality system a majority one, but in theory it should make the final choice more generally acceptable.

In practice, however, it merely introduces new complications. Thus in 1970 in Chile, Salvador Allende, candidate of the Popular Unity (UP) coalition, secured 35 per cent of the popular vote between three candidates and so a narrow plurality. Congress had therefore to ratify the election, but the majority of his opponents, being committed to the principle of popular choice, felt impelled to accept the plurality as the expression of the popular will (Feinberg 1972, pp. 162–3). Instead, however, of accepting the limitations of his position, Allende then proceeded to carry out a very far-reaching programme of social change, culminating in the formation of large-scale armed movements forcibly seizing and redistributing land without any form of legal sanction, and ultimately the army stepped in, deposed Allende, seized power, and having once seized it refused to give it up, leaving Chile with a totally unconstitutional regime.

Majority systems

Leaving aside the question of the numerous other factors that contributed to this unhappy result, what could the Chileans have done to their Constitution which might have helped to ensure a presidential majority? They could have adopted a majority system, as indeed their neighbours the Argentines had done on the other side of the Andes. There they have a second ballot, or 'run off' election as it is known in the American states, between the leading contestants (**single-member second-ballot system**). A number of countries use the same system in the choice of their legislatures.

As applied to presidential systems, the second ballot merely means that the top two candidates have to fight it out at a second round, thus ensuring that one must have a majority of the votes cast. This certainly does not guarantee that there will be no argument, and the history of Argentina since 1955 demonstrates that even the best constitutional arrangements are useless if key people are determined to disregard them. But given goodwill it is a simple and effective device.

In France since 1958 (except in 1986) elections to the National Assembly have been conducted on the same system (*scrutin unique a deux tours*) (Butler 1959, pp. 33ff.). The country is currently divided into 555 constituencies, each returning one deputy (an additional 22 members are elected by the overseas departments. Two ballots are held on successive Sundays. On the first ballot only those candidates who achieve a majority of the votes cast in the constituency are elected, provided also that they are the choice of at least 25 per cent of the registered electors. In the remaining constituencies all candidates who have achieved in the first ballot at least 12.5 per cent of the votes enter the second ballot, in which a simple plurality suffices to elect. In 1978 only 68 of 491 metropolitan seats were filled on the first ballot (*The Times*, 13 March 1978).

Though this is a proper majority system it still has its faults. As applied to a single constituency, it gives a reasonably fair result; but applied to France as a whole the result is by no means proportional. In 1978 the parties of the left, for example, obtained 49 per cent of the votes on the second ballot but still received only 40 per cent of the seats (182). This is because the population size of the constituencies varies very considerably, and this variation in size leads in France, as in Britain, to the piling up of useless majorities in many seats which happen not to return members which support the government (*The Times*, 20 March 1978). The same phenomenon used also to be true of the United States, but as the result of a Supreme Court decision there the 1960s saw a thorough reapportionment of the congressional districts and other electoral districts in the search for more exact proportionality (Baker 1966). In the United Kingdom, the advantage to the Conservative Party was estimated in 1991 to be in the order of 3 per cent, but boundary changes implemented in the 1990s gave a slight advantage to the Labour Party. In Brazil the over-representation of the rural north-east gives an even greater advantage to right-wing parties.

A second type of majority system involves holding the second ballot before the main election. This is the system, invented in the United States, of the **'primary election'**. Electors who register as members of one or another political party may take part in an official ballot to select the candidates of that party in their area or district. Where there is not more than one party likely, in normal circumstances, to win, and that means in about two-thirds of the United States, this system will not guarantee a majority, but it will at least ensure there is some kind of election. This situation, from the region with which it is most often associated, is often termed 'the southern primary', and in states such as Florida, where a large number of party factions might otherwise result in the election of a candidate with very little popular support, a second primary election is required if a majority is not achieved on the first round (Milnor 1969, pp. 49–52).

The third type of majority system is the most logical of the three, since there is no second ballot at all, the process of forming a majority being combined in one act of choice. This is the **alternative vote** (AV), as used in Australia for elections to the Federal House of Representatives. Here the country is divided into single-member constituencies as before, but the voters, instead of making a single mark on their ballot paper, number their candidates in order of preference. If no one candidate secures a majority on first preferences, the second preferences of the bottom candidate are added to them, and so on until a majority is achieved.

Unhappily, though the alternative vote looks an attractive idea, and works very well in the choice of officers for small organisations such as student unions, it is disproportional and it does not even seem to be very effective at reconciling choices. Between 1900 and 1951 some 77 per cent of successful candidates for the Australian House of Representatives achieved a majority without it, and in only a handful of cases, it seems, would the result have been different under the 'first past the post' system (Rydon 1956).

It is not necessary to stop either at two ballots or at a simple majority. In papal elections there is an indefinite number of ballots, though the fact that the cardinals are walled up with no access to the outside world is designed to hasten the process of agreement. The winner is the first candidate to secure two-thirds of the votes cast.

Proportional systems

Before truly proportional electoral systems became generally known, there was a number of attempts to improve older systems. A few of these semi-proportional systems are still used. The limited vote, by which the elector has fewer votes than there are seats to be filled, was used for a few constituencies in Britain between 1867 and 1885, and ensures at least some representation of minorities. It is still used in Gibraltar. The extreme form of this system, the single non-transferable vote in a multi-member constituency, has been used in Japan in election to the Diet since 1900. Another variant, the cumulative vote, where the elector has as many votes as seats but can give any or all of them to any candidate, was used in Cape Colony from 1850 to 1909, and after 1870 in school board elections in the United Kingdom. In the United States it was still in use in the State of Illinois in 1976 (Hansard Society 1976).

Each of these systems in different ways lessens to some extent the importance of party membership to the candidate. It is, accordingly, ironic that the first truly proportional systems to be devised, and those still most widely used, not only in Europe but in the Middle East (Israel, Lebanon), Latin America (Argentina, Bolivia, Guatemala, etc.) and the Caribbean (Guyana, Suriname), are the **list systems** (*scrutin de liste*), which have exactly the opposite effect.

Under list systems optimum proportionality would be secured by treating the country as one vast constituency, as in Israel or the Netherlands. In Israel there are two problems which arise as a result. One is that there is a very large number of very small parties represented in the Knesset, and this has given them disproportionate influence in the choice of a government. The other is a certain isolation of the elector from the representative, made evident by the fact that in 1967 over half the members of the Knesset lived in Tel Aviv (Milnor 1969, p. 85).

Normally a country is divided into multi-member constituencies, which may be simply the existing departments, provinces or regions. The elector casts a vote not for an individual candidate, but for the party list of his or her choice. The votes are then counted and seats allocated to each party in proportion to their respective totals. In the simplest form of the system the candidates are chosen in the order simply in which their names appear on the list. Under this system, used for example in France in 1945 and 1946, great power is given to the parties and within them to the local general secretaries, who tend to put their own names at the top of the lists.

There are two ways of making the allocation. The simpler is also the earlier: the largest remainder system (*le plus fort reste*). Here the number of votes cast is divided by the number of seats to be filled to give a quota. Seats are then allocated to parties for each complete quota they have received, and the one not allocated by this method goes to the party with the largest remainder – hence the name. As in other list systems, the remainders may alternatively be credited to a national pool, from which additional seats may be allocated. Unhappily this system, which favours small parties and for just this reason was retained in Paris in the 1951 and 1956 Assembly elections, is also open to manipulation by any large party that has the ingenuity or courage to divide itself into two or more parts. In Europe it was used in Italy down to 1992. It is still used in Denmark and Greece, as well as for the allocation of additional seats in Germany.

Under the Imperiali system formerly used in Italy, the country was divided into electoral regions. Within each region, a quota was obtained by dividing the total number of votes cast by two less than the number of seats to be filled. Seats were then assigned to each party according to the number of quotas obtained. Remainders were then carried over to a national pool, from which additional seats could be assigned to a district on the basis of that district's quota (see Table 7.4). Any further remainders were then disregarded. Until its replacement in 1993, the system enabled the Christian Democrats to maintain their position as the dominant party, governing in alliance with a number of smaller allies, while apart from the Communist Party, the opposition was so fragmented that no serious threat to the system arose.

Elsewhere the largest remainder system has long since been superseded by one or another version of the largest average system (*la plus forte moyenne* – Lakeman 1970, pp. 90ff.) The principle is the same in each case, that seats should be allocated to each party in such a way that each party has as near as possible the same average number of votes per seat. There are two main variants of the formula by which this is done: the d'Hondt system, which tends to favour large parties, and the Saint-Laguë system, which favours small ones, though not as much as the largest remainder system.

The arithmetic in each case is quite simple if on the face of it the reasoning behind it is inscrutable. Under the d'Hondt system the totals cast for each party are set out in order of magnitude, and below them the results of successive divisions by whole integers

Table 7.4 Italy, the Imperiali largest remainder formula, Como-Sondrio-Varese, 1976 Chamber of Deputies election: Italy, district (Quota = 54,073)

Party	Popular vote	Seats at district	Remainders to national pool	Pool seats	Total seats
Christian Democrats	516,128	9	29,471	0	9
Communists	308,661	5	38,296	0	5
Socialists	134,574	2	26,428	0	2
Social Democrats	42,563	0	42,563	0	0
Republicans	37,860	0	37,860	1	1
Liberals	20,040	0	20,040	0	0
Italian Social Movement	41,237	0	41,237	1	1
Proletarian Democracy	23,138	0	23,138	1	1
Radicals	11,398	0	11,398	0	0

(2, 3, 4, . . . etc.), of each of the larger values to the last value before that achieved by the smallest party. The figures thus produced are then arranged in rank order, and that one corresponding to the number of seats to be filled, the 'electoral quotient', is used in the same fashion as the quota in the largest remainder system to determine the allocation of seats. Any remainders are then either disregarded (Lakeman 1970, pp. 93–7; see also Rae 1967, pp. 31–4) or, alternatively, for greater proportionality, assigned to a national pool. The Saint-Laguë system, used in Sweden and Norway since 1952, is similar, but uses the divisors 1.4, 3, 5, 7 . . . etc.

The d'Hondt system is used unmodified with closed party lists in Israel, Spain and Turkey. It was chosen by the British Labour Party for elections to the Scottish Parliament and the Welsh Assembly, and it is also to be found in most countries outside Europe which use proportional systems. Since it favours large rather than small parties, it was used in France in 1951 and 1956 for all constituencies outside Paris. But it was not intended to have its usual effect, which in this case would have been the over-representation of the extremes of the Communists on the left, as well as the Gaullist RPF on the right. It was therefore used only with the ingenious addition of the *apparentement*, a provision that any party or coalition obtaining a majority of the votes in a *département* would receive all the seats of that *département*. This blatantly disproportional feature of an otherwise apparently proportional system did not work perfectly, but it worked well enough in 1951 for the centre parties to get 60 per cent of the seats in the Assembly for only 51 per cent of the votes, and for the Communists to get only 16 per cent of the seats for 24.8 per cent of the votes (Campbell 1951; Cole and Campbell 1989). When the Socialist government re-introduced the system for the 1986 elections, the *apparentement* was not used, but the relatively small size of the constituencies used gave a markedly disproportionate result.

In Spain the constituencies *on average* are very small, 6.73 seats – close to the minimum for proportionality. But since the 52 provinces are used as the basic units for the choice of the 350-member Chamber, the smaller ones only return 2 deputies each (P. Heywood 1999, pp. 71–2). As a result, party representation in the Cortés is almost as disproportionate as it is in the British Parliament under the British system and Spain's politics has tended to consolidate around two large and a number of very small parties (Montero 1999). More proportional results are obtained in Portugal, where districts average some 12 members.

Other modifications of list systems have generally been made to give the voter greater choice of individual representatives, the 'open list' system. The elector can choose one candidate within one list in Belgium, the Netherlands and Denmark; more than one candidate within one list in Italy, Norway, Sweden and Greece; and candidates from more than one list in Finland and Luxembourg and elections for the Swiss National Council. In Finland and Luxembourg, with large electoral districts, the system is highly proportional and affords the voter a fair range of choice.

At first sight the system devised by the allies for West Germany, and retained since reunification for the whole country, looks very different. It combines territorial representation by single-member constituencies with a party list system to give a proportional result overall. It is therefore often called a 'mixed' system, and in the UK the Hansard Society's term, the **'additional member' system**, has gained general acceptance (Hansard Society 1976). However, it is in fact a fully proportional system utilising a single national pool.

In Germany since December 1990 the country has been divided into 328 single-member constituencies for elections to the Bundestag. There are an equal number of seats allocated by region (*Land*) to the political parties to make the overall balance of parties in that *Land* proportional. Hence the voter has two votes, one for a candidate and one for a party.

Counting begins by totalling all second (party) votes on a national basis. Then all parties that have achieved at least 5 per cent of the national vote, or three elected seats, are allocated a total number of seats in proportion to their national vote. These seats are then divided by *Länder*. Meanwhile, as will already be evident, the first (candidate) votes will have been counted by constituency and the results declared. The number of directly elected seats achieved by each party in each *Land* is then deducted from their proportional total, and the balance made up by allocating additional seats to additional members from the party list of that *Land* according to the largest remainder system. In the rather rare eventuality that a party has won more directly elected seats in any given *Land* than its national share would give it, it is allowed to keep them, and the overall number of seats in the Bundestag is increased by that number. In the first all-German elections of 1990 there were 6 of these *Überhangsmandaten*, making a total of 662 members in all (*Keesing's* 37904–5). Hence as used in Germany the system is not perfectly proportional. A by-product of the system is that, as is usual with list systems, there are no by-elections; in the event of a vacancy occurring, the next name is selected from the regional list (Hansard Society 1976, pp. 49–51, appendix 1).

The German system was originally the product of a compromise between the three rather different electoral traditions of the allies, and was designed to avoid the multi-partyism of the pre-war Weimar Republic (1919–33), which had used the unmodified d'Hondt system. (Unusually, though, the Weimar Constitution fixed the number of voters per seat and not the total number of deputies in the Reichstag, so the number of deputies increased with the population.) As Lakeman points out, the same number of parties had in fact existed under the single-member second-ballot system used before 1918. Hence it is reasonable to believe that the causes for their number lay in the nature and complexity of German society and not in the electoral system (Lakeman 1970, p. 196).

In Mexico in 1963 the basic single-member single-ballot system was modified by the addition of extra members to increase opposition representation, which was embarrassingly low. In 1977 this was extended to make a fully proportional result possible. At first the ruling Institutional Revolutionary Party (PRI) continued to gain almost all the directly elected seats, and in 1988 the result of the presidential election was so close that accusations of fraud were widely believed. But in 1994, for the first time since it was founded in 1929, the governing party found itself in a minority in the Chamber and in 2000 it finally lost the presidency also.

One of the two favourite arguments against proportional systems is that they will act to create a multiplicity of small parties. The other is that this will give rise to political instability, caused by a succession of weak coalition governments unable to take decisive action. The French political scientist Maurice Duverger is credited with what is often termed 'Duverger's Law': that single-member systems tend to lead to two-party systems and proportional systems to multi-party ones. What he admits, however, is that, though proportional systems tend to preserve a multi-party system, they do not appear to act very strongly to create one (Duverger 1959, pp. 245–52). The facts seem to bear this more cautious view out. On the one hand, in the UK since 1951, the number of political parties represented in the assembly has increased in number even under the 'first past the post' system. And under the German system the exact opposite has happened. The number of parties represented in West Germany dropped sharply during the 1950s and in 1961 only 'two-and-a-half' parties were left, creating a stable system giving an overall majority in the Bundestag regardless of which party or combination of parties was in power. Despite this, the results, considered nationally, have continued to be strikingly proportional, while to date the ability of the parties to manipulate the lists has been used with reasonable restraint (Lakeman 1970, pp. 103, 265; Hansard Society 1976; see Table 7.5).

The example of Italy since 1992 is even more instructive. By 1990 the old system of dominance by the Christian Democrats and their allies through what Sartori called 'polarised pluralism' (Sartori 1976) had become so unpopular that in 1991 Mario Segni called for a referendum on the abolition of the multiple preference vote. The Christian Democrats did not oppose the idea, hoping that their supporters would simply not vote and the proposition fail to get a sufficient proportion of the electorate. They were wrong, and in the last election held under the old system in 1992 the four parties of the ruling coalition for the first time failed to gain a majority of the votes cast, while the two parties into which the old Communist Party had split both lost ground also (see also Putnam 1993).

The new electoral system adopted in 1993 was a compromise and the result was something which broadly resembled the German system. For the Chamber each voter would cast two votes. Three-quarters of the seats in both the Chamber and the Senate were to be allocated on a single-member simple-majority system. The remaining quarter would be allocated proportionally from a national pool, the optimum condition for proportionality, though not at the national level, but at that of the twenty-seven *circunscrizione*. A refinement was the 'proportional recuperation quotient' (*scorporo*) designed to compensate the losing parties in the constituency contests. The result in 1994, however, was not to save the Christian Democrats; instead an alliance between Forza Italia and the Northern Leagues emerged as the strongest force in no less than six regional groupings (Parker 1996, pp. 46–52).

Table 7.5 Constitutency and list seats in the West German Bundestag, 1949–87

	CDU const	CDU list	CDU total	SPD const	SPD list	SPD total	FDP const	FDP list	FDP total	Other const	Other list	Other total	Surplus*
1949	115	24	139	96	35	131	12	40	52	19	42	61	CDU1 SPD1
1953	172	71	243	45	106	151	14	34	48	11	23	34	CDU2 DP1
1957	194	76	270	46	123	169	1	40	41	6	5	11	CDU3
1961	158	86	244	91	99	190		67	67				
1965	154	91	245	94	108	202		49	49				
1969	121	121	242	127	97	224		30	30				
1972	96	129	225	152	78	230		41	41				
1976	134	109	243	114	100	214		39	39				
1980	121	105	226	127	91	218		53	53				SPD1
1983			244			193			34				G27
1987			223			186			46				G42

Under the third proportional system, however, party influence is reduced to a minimum, for the simple reason that it is the only system which enables the individual elector to choose between individual candidates regardless of party which still gives an accurate overall balance of party representation. This is the system known in the United Kingdom as the **single transferable vote** (STV) and in the United States and Australia as the Hare System. Thomas Hare is credited with inventing it in 1857, but it had in fact been devised independently two years earlier by C.C.G. Andrae in Denmark. It is used in Australia for the Federal Senate, for the Upper House in New South Wales and the Lower House in Tasmania, for the Senate in South Africa, and in Ireland and Malta for both Houses. In Britain it was used from 1917 to 1949 for the election of university representatives, in Northern Ireland from 1920 to 1929 for Stormont and more recently for the Northern Ireland Assembly. It seems that in London proportionality is considered best for the Scots, Welsh and Irish, but not for the English, or at least not for those who have not had a university education (Lakeman 1970, pp. 105ff.).

It is not necessary to have a university education to understand STV, however, and one need not be more than literate to use it. All the elector has to do is to mark on the ballot paper an order of preference (1, 2, 3, 4, etc.) for the listed candidates, and drop the paper into a box. Such arithmetical problems as then arise are handled entirely by the returning officer and staff.

Under STV the country (or area) concerned is divided into multi-member constituencies which should ideally, for the maximum degree of proportionality, be as large as possible. In a multi-party system the minimum requirement, broadly speaking, is that each return five or more representatives. In Ireland between 1935 and 1980 a large proportion of the constituencies returned only three members of the Dáil, the balance of which was in consequence distorted markedly in favour of the dominant Fianna Fáil party. In 1947 and again in 1969 the proportion of small constitutencies was increased, while in 1959 and 1968 constitutional amendments proposed by Fianna Fáil to replace it by the British system (and so entrench themselves in power) were rejected by the voters. The official reason, the desire to keep constituencies as small as possible in a predominantly rural country, points to the only theoretical disadvantage of STV. It is very well adapted to a heavily urbanised area, like England, though in a multi-party situation it would probably be difficult for voters to exercise effective choice for more than about ten seats.

In each constituency counting begins by ascertaining the total number of votes cast. This determines the quota, which in this case is called the **Droop Quota**, after H.R. Droop who proposed it in 1869. The Droop Quota is the minimum number of votes a candidate must have to be certain of being elected, that is the total number of votes divided by one more than the number of seats to be filled, plus one, or:

$$\frac{\text{votes}}{\text{seats} + 1} + 1$$

While the quota is being determined, the first preference votes (1s) for each candidate are being added up, and any candidate who has achieved or exceeded the quota is declared elected.

If a candidate has got more votes than the quota, however, his or her surplus votes are 'wasted', and it is one of the basic principles of STV that no one's votes can be wasted. The second count, therefore, involves the distribution of any surpluses from the first count, in order of magnitude if there is more than one. Now, obviously, the surplus votes are not just taken off the top of the pile – that would be ridiculous. What happens is that all the fortunate candidate's ballot papers are counted a second time, this time by the second preferences (2s). Then the number of each, reduced to a proportion corresponding to the size of the surplus, is credited to the account of each remaining candidate. Any candidate who has now received the quota is elected.

The next step is to eliminate the bottom candidate. None of this unfortunate's votes has yet had a chance to elect anybody, so they are all redistributed to the second preference candidates at full value. If the eliminated candidate has received any second preferences from the candidates who have already achieved the quota, they are transferred on to the next (3rd) preference candidate marked on them, if any, but only at the reduced value at which they were received.

If at the conclusion of this second count there remain any further seats to be filled, the process will be repeated until the final result is achieved, which occurs either when the necessary number of candidates has reached the quota, or when the number of candidates left in the running is equal to the number of remaining seats, or when only one seat remains to be filled, and one candidate has a majority over all the other candidates left in the race, whichever is the sooner.

The following example from the 1992 Irish general election illustrates the process (see Table 7.6). Two candidates, David Andrews (Fianna Fáil) and Niamh Bhreathnach (Labour), reached the quota and were elected on the first count, though in the latter case with such a small surplus that it was not distributed until count 7, when 4 minor candidates had already been eliminated without much effect on the totals. Sean Barrett (Fine Gael) was elected on count 11 and Liz Keogh (Progressive Democrat) and Eamonn Gilmore (Democratic Left) on count 12, the latter without achieving the quota, when only one other candidate remained in the race.

Of course it is quite a valid criticism of STV that even if its mathematics is not particularly obscure, the fact that it does involve a greater need to trust the returning officer and staff makes it unsuitable for general use. However, the interim report of the Labour Party Commission on Electoral Systems, which considered this argument, did recommend the adoption of the system for the Scottish Assembly they had planned to set up after the British general election of 1992 (Plant 1991b), though the system actually chosen was a combination of single-member single-ballot and the closed list on the German model (Hassan 1999). The reason was that any other than a proportional system applied to Scotland was likely to give rise to a permanent one-party dominance, which, as the example of the Stormont period in Northern Ireland demonstrates, is unhealthy for the continued survival of liberal democracy.

Certainly proportional systems do not tend to favour one-party dominance. But do they lead to unstable government? In one sense, of course, it does not matter if they do. If that is what the people want, they should be allowed to have it. The mathematicians give an awkward answer from the point of view of the practical politician. Their models of electoral behaviour suggest that electoral choice should be much less stable than it actually seems to be in practice (Riker 1982). Further research has tended to confirm that electoral choice is unstable but that this does not matter since no one actually knows what is happening (Nurmi 1987, p. 220).

As we have now seen, there is much truth in the view that for any given desired result, an electoral system can be devised. And in consequence, proportional systems, paradoxically, occur in two quite different situations: one where this condition of general trust manifestly exists, as in the countries of Europe, and one where the condition manifestly

Table 7.6 Dun Laoghaire, Irish general election, November 1992

Electorate: 87,495 Total Poll: 60,049 68.6% Valid Poll: 59,370 Quota: 9,896
Elected: *D Andrews (FF) N Breathnach (Lab) *S Barrett (FG) H Keogh (PD) *E Gilmore (DL)

Surplus/Votes of Votes distributed	Count 1	Count 2 Surplus Andrews	Count 3 Votes McAneny (49)	Count 4 Votes Murdock (115)	Count 5 Votes F'Ptrk (849)	Count 6 Votes Quinn (1,823)	Count 7 Surplus Brat. (178)	Count 8 Votes McDowell (2,337)	Count 9 Votes Coffey (3,688)	Count 10 Votes Cosgrave (4,422)	Count 11 Votes Barnes (6,068)	Count 12 Surplus Barrett (1,694)
*D Andrews	13,418											
N Breathnach	10,074											
*E Gilmore (DL)	7,045	+218 7,263	+6 7,269	+35 7,304	+254 7,558	+173 7,731	+68 7,799	+681 8,480	+281 8,761	+251 9,012	+417 9,429	+359 9,788
H Keogh (PD)	6,497	+211 6,708	+1 6,709	+10 6,719	+16 6,735	+93 6,828	+28 6,856	+379 7,235	+181 7,416	+344 7,760	+1,096 8,856	+1,182 10,038
*S Barrett (FG)	4,852	+243 5,095	+2 5,097	+5 5,102	+36 5,138	+101 5,239	+17 5,256	+120 5,376	+147 5,523	+2,044 7,567	+4,023 11,590	
*M Barnes (FG)	4,261	+195 4,456	+5 4,461	+4 4,465	+14 4,479	+35 4,514	+31 4,545	+234 4,779	+192 4,971	+1,097 6,068		
L Cosgrave (FG)	3,683	+119 3,802	+1 3,803	+1 3,804	+15 3,819	+377 4,196	+11 4,207	+109 4,316	+106 4,422			

Table 7.6 (cont.)

Candidate	1st											
*B Hillery (FF)	2,973	+1,173 / 4,146	+5 / 4,151	+2 / 4,153	+84 / 4,237	+388 / 4,625	+4 / 4,629	+143 / 4,772	+2,482 / 7,254	+348 / 7,602	+155 / 7,757	+153 / 7,910
B Coffey (FF)	2,119	+1,227 / 3,346	+4 / 3,350	+5 / 3,355	+91 / 3,446	+87 / 3,533	+5 / 3,538	+150 / 3,688				
V McDowell (G)	1,784	+65 / 1,849	+14 / 1,863	+19 / 1,882	+153 / 2,035	+288 / 2,323	+14 / 2,337					
M Quinn (Ind)	1,705	+35 / 1,740	+9 / 1,749	+7 / 1,756	+67 / 1,823							
K Fitzpatrick (SF)	801	+30 / 831	+1 / 832	+17 / 849								
E Murdock (WP)	110	+5 / 115										
M McAneny (Ind)	48	+1 / 49										
Non-transferable			1	10	119	281		521	299	338	377	

does not, as in Latin America, where one is forced to the regrettable conclusion that it does not matter anyway, since the vote is free in inverse proportion to the importance of the result. Electoral systems are determined by governments and not governments by electoral systems. It is therefore governments that have both the inclination and the opportunity to interfere with freedom of choice. Democratization, therefore, is not just about ensuring that elections are held. The conditions under which they are held determine whether or not they can be taken seriously.

The Election Campaign

The requirements for an election to be both free and fair are summarised in Table 7.7. The key point is that the freedom and fairness of elections does not depend just on what happens on polling day. What happens before and after polling day is just as important.

Above all candidates must be able to campaign freely for the post they seek, to put their case and to answer criticism. Interestingly, the techniques of election campaigning are a good example of the impact of globalisation on national systems. The Clinton campaign in the United States in 1992 borrowed from British practice and in 2001 the Labour Party campaign for re-election in Britain showed significant US influences. This is not altogether a new phenomenon; the first 'whistle-stop' campaign, for example, was that of Gladstone in the UK in 1880 and the idea of campaigning from a train was only later taken up in the USA.

Table 7.7 Requirements for free and fair elections

	Free	Fair
Before polling day	Freedom of speech etc. Freedom of movement No impediments on or intimidation of candidates Universal suffrage	Fair electoral law Independent electoral commission Open registration Orderly campaign Equal access to media No favours to government
On polling day	Freedom to vote No intimidation of voters	Secret ballot Vote only once Clear ballot papers Party observers permitted Help to aged etc. Rules for void papers
After polling day	Legal possibilities of complaints Mechanism to resolve contested decisions	Proper counting and reporting Care of ballot papers etc. Impartial reports on results Impartial treatment of complaints Acceptance of results by all involved

Source: after Eklit and Svensson 1997

Campaigning serves a number of different purposes. The main ones are: to ensure as far as possible that existing supporters cast their votes; to win over uncommitted voters; and, if possible, to discourage voters from voting for political opponents. How this is done is a much more complicated problem, given that opinion polls show that many people's minds are made up before the campaign even begins. Democratic theory assumes that parties and candidates put alternative programmes before the electorate, who then make a rational choice. Would that this were true! Even in ancient Greece philosophers deplored the fact that candidates appealed to the voters with rhetoric designed less to illuminate the issues than to stir up emotional feeings. Moreover even when voters make a rational choice based on their own self-interest there is no logical reason to expect this to be the choice that would best benefit the country as a whole.

The large size of modern electorates limits campaigning possibilities. In theory the personal appeal of the candidate to the elector is the most powerful influence, but with today's populations in all but the smallest states electoral districts are simply too large for direct personal contact to operate. Instead candidates reserve direct personal contact for those 'opinion formers' within the community who can influence others, while staging 'media events' such as 'walkabouts' to enliven a national campaign strategy. Throughout Western Europe, following the example of the United States, television has become the main, and indeed almost the only means by which parties appeal to the electorate. Of course, the more 'real' the image presented by television, the more effective it is likely to be.

It has long been known that the main influence on voting choice in the United States is the voters' perception of their own economic position. If they feel well off they are not likely to vote for change (Campbell *et al.* 1960). Hence the 'surprise' victory in 1948 for Harry Truman, whom the voters saw as the heir of Roosevelt and the New Deal. In 1992 Clinton ensured that in every precinct Democratic party activists remembered: 'It's the economy, stupid!'

In 1992 the Bush campaign had relied heavily on the president's reputation for leadership during the Gulf War. On the day, this did not offset the feeling that the Republicans were not managing the economy well. It is a truism in most countries that the voters do not see foreign policy issues as very important, and the United States is no exception. However, in Europe, with increasing economic integration, what was previously 'foreign' is increasingly seen as 'domestic'. Voters show strong suspicion of the integration process, as the defeats for the government in the referenda in Denmark in 1992 and Ireland in 2001 show. If it seems to affect their prosperity they react even more strongly. Having successfully been re-elected in 1992, Britain's precipitous exit from the ERM fatally undermined the British Conservatives' reputation for sound economic management, leaving many of those who had benefited from the 'right to buy' mired in 'negative equity', and the Major government never recovered its former support.

Hence the significance of social class as a predictor of the way people will vote. Globalisation, however (as noted in Chapter 1), has been felt not only in the way in which computer programs can now identify the social composition of relatively small areas and how their electorate is likely to vote. The information gathered from these programs can and does enable parties to direct their appeals to specific target groups, and these appeals may well be to emotion rather than to reason. One of the first examples of this management occurred in the US presidential election of 1980, when Republican strategists were sensitive to Reagan's 'mad bomber' image. They countered it by inserting the word 'peace' as many times as possible into their candidate's next speech and were rewarded by an immediate swing in his favour.

Election Rigging

If a government feels that, for the sake of its national and international reputation, it must hold elections, but wishes to guarantee that it does not lose power as a result, it frequently happens that it arranges for the elections to be 'rigged'. In fact **election rigging** is a widespread practice in ostensibly 'democratic' countries with allegedly 'free' elections, and governments in those countries are frequently charged with it in the speeches of their political opponents. Unfortunately, riggng is also found locally in elections in countries where the government does not exercise any direct control of them, so individual cases are often very difficult to judge. The reason is quite simple. Although a government may be quite confident that a free election will return it to power, or accept an arrangement by which its tenure of power is shared from time to time with its political opposition, local officials with their political careers at stake may not take the possibility of personal defeat so calmly. Hence, unless central control is strong, paradoxically elections may be marred by a greater or lesser degree of interference in the freedom of choice.

The weakest point in any electoral system is the candidate. If candidates are unwilling or afraid to present themselves for election then no free choice can take place.

In all countries, candidates for election have to fulfil certain basic legal requirements. They must be citizens of the country, of full age and of sound mind, and not have a criminal record. In Côte d'Ivoire in 2000, however, the government of Gen. Robert Guëi, who had seized power in December 1999, first changed the Constitution to disqualify non-Ivorians from the presidency and then claimed that the main civilian candidate, Alassane Ouattara, had been born in Burkina Faso (*Keesing's* 43661).

'Frivolous' candidates are discouraged by a formal process of nomination and in the United States candidates may be required to secure a substantial number of signatures in a number of different areas to demonstrate that they have sufficient support to warrant a contest. The requirement that a very large number of signatures be secured on a nomination paper can of course be used to discourage competition, particularly when, as often happens, some of the signatures are subsequently 'found' to be fraudulent.

Candidature may be discouraged simply by social pressures. Would-be candidates may discover that their position at work is threatened either by their colleagues or by their employers. If they are professionals or self-employed they may find that their livelihood is threatened by the refusal of others to supply them, to work with them, or to consult them. Where membership of a trade organisation or of a trade union is obligatory in order to work in a particular occupation, fear of having this membership withdrawn may be more than enough to discourage political activism. Then it is possible to construe the basic criteria of fitness more or less strictly, applying a legal prohibition to candidature. In the USSR political opponents of the regime have been certified as mentally ill, and detained as such; in Brazil and Uruguay they have been deprived of their political rights, but allowed to retain their liberty; while in South Africa under the apartheid regime restrictions could be and were placed on their freedom of movement, speech and assembly by the minister of justice (*sic*).

In many countries, people are imprisoned for their political views, sometimes, as in Cuba and Paraguay, for very long periods of years, sometimes, as in Argentina, Chile or Iran, in response to specific challenges, though it is impossible to draw a hard-and-fast line between these. The political nature of the imprisonment, too, is normally disguised by presenting charges of involvement in conspiracy – charges which, by the nature of the secrecy surrounding state security, are usually very difficult to refute altogether.

In extreme cases, political figures who presented a threat have been murdered. The instigators of the death of Jorge Eliecer Gaitán in Colombia in 1948 are still unknown, but the belief that his assassination was intended to preclude political reform was sufficient to touch off a major civil war, which, sadly, in the end resulted in the imposition of a dictatorship (Fluharty 1957, pp. 99–101). Assassination has been an increasingly prominent feature of Colombian politics since the rise of the drug cartels and in the run-up to the election campaign of 1990 the leading candidate, Dr Luís Carlos Galán Sarmiento, and another presidential candidate who had also promised to tackle the problem were both murdered. Assassination is less commonly used by governments, though the assassination of Pedro Joaquín Chamorro in Nicaragua in 1978 is generally regarded as having been the work of agents of President Anastasio Somoza (who was himself in turn assassinated in Paraguay in 1980 by an Argentine group).

Fortunately such tactics sometimes provoke a public reaction. In Guatemala in 1966 the assassination of Mario Méndez Montenegro, the principal opposition presidential candidate, created such anger that his brother stepped into his place and was carried into office on a tide of public sympathy which neither the government nor the army could resist (Gott 1970, p. 67; Melville and Melville 1971, pp. 204–6). In the Philippines the opposition leader Ninoy (Benigno) Aquino was shot in the back in August 1983 at Manila on the steps of an aircraft closely guarded by the security forces of the dictator Ferdinand Marcos. Deprived of electoral victory in 1986 by a blatantly rigged election, his widow, Cory (Corazón) Aquino, was instead swept into power by a popular insurrection.

Restraint on candidature is imposed less dramatically but more effectively by institutional means, by restraining the freedom and scope of action of political parties, which in many countries serve as the sole legal vehicle for nomination. Parties may be dissolved altogether, as in Chile in 1973 or in Peru after 1968. Only official parties may be recognised as having legal status, as in Syria or Egypt. Or 'extremist' political parties may be singled out for special treatment, as with the banning of the German Communist Party (KPD) in the former West Germany, where the rise of Fascist parties has been similarly precluded.

Even where candidature and political organisation are both officially free, the electoral process itself may be subject to several kinds of manipulation. In the United Kingdom party nomination is not required but independent candidates are discouraged by the requirement that the candidate must lodge a deposit, which is only returned if he or she secures more than 5 per cent of the votes cast. Fortunately, as a result of inflation rather than of any sudden act of government liberality, the deposit, currently £500, is sufficiently small not to act as much of a restraint, bearing in mind that it represents the equivalent of about £10 in 1918, when the deposit was originally introduced at £150 and the candidate had to get 12.5 per cent of the votes cast.

Electoral districting is subject to two sorts of manipulation. Varying the number of electors per constituency can bias the results in favour of one party rather than another. However, given the propensity of human beings to group together in certain areas rather than another, it may be necessary to tolerate a degree of variation rather than have some constituencies unreasonably large in geographical terms, and in the UK for this reason Scottish constituencies have fewer voters on average than English ones. Varying the boundaries of electoral districts can also alter outcomes. To draw a complex shape in order to secure a desired result is at least as old as Governor Elbridge Gerry of Massachusetts, who in 1820 devised an electoral district shaped like a salamander – or 'gerrymander'.

In Britain voting in public, ended by the Ballot Act of 1870, displayed evident abuses in the form of intimidation of electors, which led to its abolition. But there are two ways in which the same effect can be achieved by different means. In the USSR and other communist countries, as noted above, it was simply socially 'not done' to make use of the secret voting facilities which are available. To do so was to attract unfavourable attention. Where voting machines are used in the United States, the voter has first to pull a handle which ensures that curtains are drawn tightly round the booth, ensuring complete privacy.

However, facilities may be provided that are not in fact secret although they profess to be so. For obvious reasons, ballot slips in the UK bear serial numbers and when issued to a voter the voter's registration number is written on to the counterfoil. Hence in principle it would be possible to trace how any individual had voted. In practice, it cannot be done because at the conclusion of the count the boxes are resealed until it is clear that the result is not going to be challenged and then the contents are destroyed.

Secrecy was not maintained in the French referendum in Algeria in 1958 on the adoption of the Constitution of the Fifth Republic. For the convenience of the largely illiterate population, the authorities had thoughtfully provided them with two voting slips: one white which said 'Oui', and one purple which said 'Non'. It was, of course, the aim of the exercise to secure the largest possible number of votes that said 'Oui', and the colour purple for the 'Non' slips was deliberately chosen because it was regarded as being unlucky. However, this was not all. When Muslim voters, clad in long flowing robes with no pockets in them, went into the booths to vote and went to fold up their slips and put them into the box, they discovered that no repository had been provided for the slip they did *not* use. They could either drop it on the floor, in full view of the soldier stationed outside, or they could walk out holding it in full view. Neither seemed a very attractive idea.

In the same election other artistic touches included the careful distribution of polling stations so as to keep them well away from centres of opposition – one was even stationed on an island in the middle of a river, where the only boat was operated by the army. Where all else failed, the army supplied the necessary number of voting papers to make up the balance.

'Ballot stuffing' is perhaps the most common, and almost certainly the tidiest way of rigging elections, but it has to be carefully done. In the Bolivian elections of 1978 votes cast were found to exceed the number of live electors by an astonishing amount. And in Northern Ireland personation (voting dishonestly on behalf of others) continues to be a problem, symbolised by the well-known slogan 'vote early and vote often!'

Even in the United States, where the control of elections is in the hands of the state governments and local interests, maladministration still occurs and may indeed have important consequences. In the presidential election of 1960, the very narrow margin in favour of President Kennedy could be accounted for by rather dubious totals from Cook County, Illinois, and from Texas, both areas notorious for electoral malpractice. However, despite subsequent claims that Richard M. Nixon had been magnanimous in defeat, there was no real doubt that Kennedy had won both the popular vote and the Electoral College.

In the disputed presidential election of 2000, on the other hand, with one state unde-cided, Gore led Bush both in the popular vote and the Electoral College. But the result was decided in Florida, where at the least the procedures were irresponsibly lax. The State Secretary of State, who hastened to certify the result for George W. Bush, was a keen partisan and had actively campaigned for him. Republican workers were allowed to fill in certificates for absentee ballots which had not been correctly certificated. Different counties used different counting systems and no unified procedure existed for seeing that these were adequate. Machine counts failed to record presidential choices on some 10,000 ballots in Miami-Dade County. However, the Bush camp used the legal process to stop them being checked by hand and in the end their successful efforts to block hand recounts were upheld by a partisan majority in the US Supreme Court. Last but not least, the National Association for the Advancement of Colored People (NAACP) presented evidence of intimidation of black voters by the use of road blocks, recalling the widespread use of the same technique throughout the American South before the Civil Rights Act of 1965.

US legislators had since the 1980s presumed to require other countries' elections to be certified as 'clean' before they could qualify for US aid. They had certainly not been consistent: in El Salvador in 1982 US observers accepted the elections as free and fair when more impartial witnesses thought there had been extensive malpractice and the reverse happened in Nicaragua in 1985. The 2000 election confirmed that both American legislators and American judges themselves had a lot to learn about the proper conduct of elections in a free society.

Case Study	Yucatán's Poll Dinosaurs are Threatened with Extinction

A few calcified bones, preserved under glass, are all that remain of the great tusked mastodons that roamed the Yucatan pen-insula before being wiped out by climate change thousands of years ago.

These days, prehistoric animals of a different, political stripe still dominate the oppressively hot landscape. But elections in Yucatan tomorrow are threatening the state's last remaining species with extinction.

Victor Cervera is considered the king of the 'dinosaurs', the name given to traditional hardliners of the Institutional Revolutionary party (PRI).

The governor of Yucatan, he has ruled the state with an iron fist for the past 20 years, say critics, through a mix of intimida-tion and corporatism.

Mr Cervera first rose to prominence when he was accused of stealing ballot boxes as a student leader. Now 65, he was widely reported to have given away tens of thousands of bicycles and washing ma-chines in return for PRI votes during pres-idential elections last July.

Although he is stepping down at this election, his political longevity has helped turn southern Mexico into the PRI's chief power base. That is why a loss in the state elections could deal a fatal blow to the party still recovering from its first presidential defeat in 71 years, when it was routed last year by President Vicente Fox and his National Action party (PAN).

Pollsters are giving Patricio Patron, gubernatorial candidate for a coalition of four opposition parties including PAN, a lead of between 11 and 16 points over the PRI's Orlando Paredes, Mr Cervera's suc-cessor as candidate for governor. The expected defeat would be the latest in a string of setbacks for the party in its southern stronghold.

Case Study continued

In a sign of the new openness that has begun to trickle south, an opposition coalition won Chiapas state elections in August.

Four months later, federal electoral authorities revoked a narrow PRI victory in neighbouring Tabasco on charges of fraud. A new election has been set for November.

'The election in Yucatan is crucial,' says Mr Patron. 'If the PRI loses Yucatan it will lose its bastion of power. It will have a domino effect throughout the south.'

More than half of Mexico's 31 states are still ruled by PRI governors, and the party is the largest bloc in Congress. Nevertheless, it is finding its movements severely restricted in the first state election since President Fox took office in December.

To begin with, the money has dried up.

Under Mr Fox, federal funding for social programmes – once the traditional source of pork barrel politics – is being delivered directly to recipients instead of being channelled through the state. More important, say observers, poor farmers and indigenous communities, who rely on such funding and are the PRI's main electoral base, are realising the money does not depend on the PRI being in power.

'With Mr Fox's victory, the farmers have lost their fear,' said Felix Ucan, a journalist with the local *Diario de Yucatan*. 'They now know that all the things the PRI has been telling them – that the money will disappear, that they will be forced back into slavery – are not true.'

The political pluralism has also bolstered the confidence of local business people, many of whom have come out publicly to support the opposition for the first time.

The opportunity has not been lost on Mr Patron, who at 1.94 metres is the same height as Mr Fox and shares his rugged good looks. Mr Patron has used the campaign slogans coined by Mr Fox, and his promises of rule of law, transparency and strengthened institutions mirror those of the president.

But while Mr Patron admits an unpopular proposal by Mr Fox to tax food and medicine has hurt his campaign, his real concern is electoral fraud.

Mr Cervera, he says, already tried once to manipulate the election by openly defying the federal electoral tribunal's authority in the designation of a state electoral council. PRI supporters occupied the electoral institute for nearly two months and members of the state council had to be given police protection.

The showdown ended in April when the Supreme Court ruled in favour of the federal tribunal, giving the state electoral council less than six weeks to prepare the election.

Electoral authorities say fraud will be limited but the opposition calculates it needs to win by a margin of 7 per cent to overcome vote tampering. To monitor the state's 1,865 polling booths, the coalition has recruited thousands of volunteers, each equipped with candles and a flashlight in case of a sudden power cut – a favourite tactic in past elections.

Source: *Financial Times*, 26/27 May 2001

Democratisation is normally seen as consisting of three stages. The first is a period of liberalisation, in which an authoritarian regime relaxes its control to some extent, and political parties are allowed to organise openly. Then either the government simply collapses in face of opposition power or, quite commonly, it seeks to strike a bargain with the opposition for an orderly transfer of power to a provisional government. Elections

Oceania

AUSTRALIA

Official name: The Commonwealth of Australia
Type of government: Federal parliamentary
constitutional monarchy
Capital: Canberra, ACT
Area: 7,687,000 sq km
Population (2000): 19,000,000
GNP per capita (2000): $20,300 (PPP $20,130)

Evolution of government: British settlement of Australia began with the 'First Fleet' of 1788; the legal fiction that it was previously unoccupied has now been abandoned (Chapter 1) and the welfare of the indigenous inhabitants has become a major political issue. Rapid growth in numbers followed the discovery of gold in Western Australia in 1840s. In 1901 the five mainland colonies and Tasmania agreed to create a federal union with full internal self-government (Dominion status) but retained some direct links with Britain. Independent since 1931.

Main features of government: Effective head of state is Australian-born governor-general representing the queen of Australia; strong but divided republican sentiment. Triennial elections for Federal House of Representatives under alternative vote (Chapter 7) give two-party system; long periods of single-party dominance at state level. Executive Council headed by prime minister responsible to parliament. As an advanced industrial country, Australia's economic record contrasts strikingly with that of Argentina (q.v.). Recent immigration from southern Europe and from Asia (since 1974) has changed social composition and raised some local ethnic tension. Exceptionally unequal distribution of landownership remains (Chapter 3).

are held and a new government takes office. In a third stage, under the new regime constitutional order is restored, elections become habitual and power passes in an exclusively peaceful manner. Following the inauguration of the new government there follows a long period of consolidation.

Unlike the other two stages consolidation has no definite limit, and in recent years the 'consolidologists' have tried with some difficulty to define it more closely. It is during this stage that there emerges a new sense of civil society and even of a civic culture which supports a democratic government. There will be general acceptance of new order and regular elections will become normal.

Summary

To sum up, therefore, there is a wide variety of electoral systems in use. Unanimity is the ideal but in practice impossible to secure in modern states. Majority systems are a minimal requirement for major offices such as an executive presidency. Fully proportional systems have a well-established track record in some of the world's most stable liberal democracies and are necessary to guarantee fair representation in a parliament. Plurality systems present the illusion of agreement rather than the reality. However, the problem of securing a genuinely free electoral choice is not an easy one. Even in the advanced industrial countries full freedom of choice is not necessarily guaranteed and for an election to be 'free and fair' essential conditions have to prevail before, during and even after the act of choice.

Fortunately, even where there is extensive local or national interference in the outcome of elections, they continue to give observers much evidence of the real balance of political power within the society.

Key Concepts

additional member system, or mixed system, a list system (q.v.) with single national pool

alternative vote, system of election in which voters number candidates in order of preference, the least successful candidates being eliminated and their votes redistributed until one candidate achieves a majority

Borda count, choice of policies by a group assigning marks to each and then totalling the results

Condorcet criterion, the choice of a candidate who is preferred by the most voters

dark horse, a candidate not on the original list who is chosen by way of compromise

Droop Quota, the minimum number of votes that a candidate must have to be elected

election rigging, illegitimate interference with the freedom of electoral choice

'first past the post', in Britain, common, if incorrect, nickname for the single-member single-ballot system

gerrymander, the drawing of electoral boundaries in such a way as to give an advantage to one party rather than another

list system, fully proportional electoral system assigning seats in proportion to voters' choices between rival party lists in a multi-member constitutency

majority systems, electoral systems in which a candidate does have to achieve an overall majority

plurality systems, electoral systems in which a candidate does not have to achieve an overall majority

primary election, a formal election held amongst the registered members of a political party to select their party's candidate(s)

proportional systems, electoral systems which give a distribution of seats in proportion to the number of votes cast for each party

single-member second-ballot system, system of election in which if no candidate receives a majority (overall majority) of the votes cast in the first ballot, a second ballot is held among the leading candidates

single-member single-ballot system, known familiarly in the UK as 'first past the post', system of election in which voters vote for one candidate to represent the area in which they live, the winner being the one who obtains a plurality of the votes cast

single transferable vote, fully proportional electoral system utilising voters' rank order of preferences for individual candidates in multi-member constitutencies

slate, list of candidates for various offices

unanimity systems, systems of election requiring the unanimous consent of the electorate

Sample Questions

The main concern of this area of the syllabus is with electoral systems and their effects, with reference to the choice both of leaders and of assemblies. Understanding of these processes is essential information for a question on a recent election in a specific country (e.g. France, Germany), while electoral reform is a traditional topic and remains a strong possibility on a paper on British government.

- Does it matter which political leader is chosen and which is not?

- What are the minimum requirements that must be fulfilled for an election to be fair?

- If a 'free' election were held in Eastern Europe, how could we tell?

- How far is it possible to devise an electoral system that gives an accurate representation of popular preferences?

Further Reading

On elections generally see Carstairs (1980), Grofman and Lijphart (1986), Mackie and Rose (1991). Since Black (1958) there has been an extensive debate on the mathematical foundations of choice. On the consequences of electoral laws Rae (1967) and Bogdanor (1983) are indispensable. For British readers, the Hansard Society (1976) summed up the advantages and disadvantages of the different systems. Lakeman (1970) argues the particular merits of proportionality, but Plant (1991b)

argues a wide range of other factors need also to be taken into account.

Ware (1987b) is useful on the effects of electoral changes on party systems, and Western European party systems are discussed in a fully comparative way in Mair (1990). On the specific effects of the changes in Italy in the 1990s see Parker (1996).

Research on the impact of corruption and electoral malpractice has until recently been relatively neglected, and there is as yet no accessible introduction to the subject.

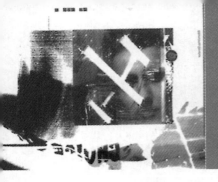

Inside the Black Box

CHAPTER EIGHT

Learning Objectives

By the end of this chapter, the reader will be able:

- to assess the role of political leadership in arriving at decisions;

- to assess the role of bureaucracy in making decisions, to clarify how the administrative staff are chosen and what influence they have on outcomes;

- to compare and contrast the alternative models that have been proposed of the policy-making process;

- to evaluate the concept of a political elite.

Decision-Makers

At the centre of government, where the ultimate decisions are taken and inputs converted into outputs, sit the *decision-makers*. It is here, inside what has been playfully termed the 'black box', that the popular imagination places unimaginable mysteries. It does so, moreover, despite the many memoirs by leading politicians and statesmen, which tend on the whole to show that the business of government is very much like any other managerial job, the main difference being the scope of the decisions taken. As a result it is possible to interpret the way in which decisions are made according to a number of different interpretations or models.

The fact is that people in all countries look to their political leaders for something called leadership. They do this whether or not they have chosen them to do the job, and the surest sign of the legitimacy they attach to their leaders is the ease with which they accept their right to lead, even if they do not agree with what they are doing. Generally, however, they set some distance between themselves and their leaders, indicating that they belong to a distinct political group. Such groups, forming a relatively small part of a society as a whole, are often termed **elites** – a term invented by the Italian sociologist Vilfredo Pareto (1965). Traditionally, the ability to lead, and hence the right to membership of a ruling elite, has been attributed to the outstanding qualities of the individual or individuals concerned. Weber, as noted above, regarded this kind of claim to political authority, which he termed 'charismatic' authority, as being the earliest or original form of authority. For him, it was 'routinised' in modern societies, where by developing the idea of 'legal-rational' authority – authority based on formal legal processes – dependence on personalities could be reduced and political stability strengthened.

Leadership

Quite a lot of work on leadership has been done in laboratory conditions by psychologists. They work with small groups, but this in itself presents students of politics with no problem, because most councils, cabinets, committees, boards and the like, are rather small. True, such groups certainly cannot be studied under clinical conditions, and in the absence of the responsibilities they have their reactions to stress can only be partially simulated. What can and should be done, however, is to use all available information to deduce the way in which such groups should behave, checking these deductions against the information about their actual behaviour which subsequently becomes public.

Such deductions are much more likely to be accurate if it is remembered that psychologists now regard *individual personality* as only one of four factors of leadership (Stodgill 1948, p. 45; Gibb 1969). The other factors are the nature of the *group*, the *situation* with which it is confronted and the *task* to be performed. Hence different personalities will be effective leaders in different situations or when confronted with different tasks.

The political leader plays a crucial role in keeping the ruling elite or party together, by maintaining what is termed group **syntality**, that is to say, the will to work together to perform the task in hand. And in open-ended experiments with small groups, usually of soldiers or student volunteers, where leadership is not necessarily predetermined, it appears that there are four main ways in which leaders may emerge (Cattell and Stice 1954, p. 493):

- The **problem-solving leader** is the person who knows how to deal with the problem in hand, and shows the others how to do so.
- The **salient leader** assumes leadership in all situations by a combination of the inadequacy of the others or the adequacy of the leader himself.
- The **sociometric leader** is the one whom the others say they would choose to lead them if they were given a chance to do so.
- The **elected leader** is the person whom they actually do choose. S/he may not be the same person as the 'sociometric' leader, the person who is most popular; and, indeed, given the characteristics of most electoral systems, there are structural reasons why s/he will often not be.

These then are the four types of leadership that have been identified in small group situations. Clearly, these findings must in some way be relevant to the problem of leadership in politics, and in comparing aspects of leadership between different countries, it will be useful to use these categories. First, however, some general principles have to be identified which explain how the differences between leaders can be expected to vary.

A key to this can be found in the psychologists' overall conclusion that, in any given situation, it is easier to suit the task to the leader, than to find a leader to undertake the task. It is the understanding – or misunderstanding – of this principle that determines the development of structures of government, for the two problems cannot in fact be separated from one another. A particular leader long in office alters the job to suit his or her approach to it. The initial response of a successor is usually, but not always, to try to continue with the same methods, in which in any case they have a vested interest. But when they find that they cannot effectively operate within the same structures, they set to work to alter them. Hence over a period of time leaders change the nature of the offices they hold, downgrading some which have previously been powerful and increasing the strength of others (Calvert 1987). This is why, generally, rapid periods of institutional change follow long periods of stable succession. The prediction of such periods of rapid change, and determining whether or not they are likely to follow a given course, is one of the fundamental questions of political science (see Chapter 11).

Executives

The executive is that part of government that is concerned with the taking of day-to-day decisions.

Although in early societies monarchy did not always emerge, nevertheless it was widespread, and historically its patriarchial and patrimonial characteristics shaped the formation of most modern states (Chapter 1). Monarchy, replicating the primitive structure of the extended family, in small societies where the monarch was approachable and so to a considerable extent accountable, was effective because efficient. The president of the United States is in many ways a republican monarch, entrusted with a large array of powers to exercise for a limited period.

As states grew, the monarch was no longer able to oversee all the business of government. Simply ordering individuals to carry out tasks *ad hoc* without any long-term responsibility for them lightened the load only slightly. The remedy was delegation. The most frequent form seems to have been the delegation of all the tasks of government by a hereditary leader to a single figure, the vizier responsible for all the tasks of government, but this form positively encourages the palace coup (replacement of the leader at the hands of the strongest subordinate). Hence though such first ministers can give strong and capable rule, the first strong ruler that emerges will wish to curtail their powers. In 1660 Louis XIV recovered the power exercised in France under the reign of Louis XIII (Cardinal Richelieu) and his own minority (Cardinal Mazarin). The Japanese Shogunate ruled for three centuries until ended at the Meiji Restoration (1867).

Delegation of the powers of government to those territorial magnates who wanted it, on a geographical basis, similarly proved to have its weakness. In this case the great danger was that the state would be split up altogether, as nearly happened to France with the rise of late medieval Burgundy, temporarily happened in China under the 'warlords' of the 1920s and 1930s, and actually did happen in former Yugoslavia and the former Soviet Union in 1991. In each case the danger to centralised control was the alienation of the balance of military power. Once lost, it could seldom be recovered, and then only by good fortune coupled, perhaps, with external aid, as in China during the Second World War. Afghanistan and Somalia both form examples where in the 1990s central government effectively ceased to exist as a result of the multiplication of regional armed forces.

The solution to this long-standing problem was found centuries ago by developing the structures, not of the family itself, but of the household in the wider sense. The separation of functions already familiar from the organisation of large bodies of servants in a great house, was modified to make use of its distinctive feature, the division of responsibilities among a large number of people by the subject, and not the geographical area, of their responsibility. Out of this developed, ultimately, the concept first of a **council** of the principal officers responsible for carrying out the orders of the monarch, which forms the apex of a staff for maintaining them.

Councils differs from assemblies in being composed of people chosen by the ruler, each of whom will have a specific task. Collectively they were not specialists; yet because of the need for the ruler to authorise all decisions, they had to discuss and resolve all matters brought before them, regardless of subject. The process was thus tedious, time-wasting and highly inefficient. A viceroy of New Spain in the eighteenth century is said to have said of the Council of the Indies at Seville: 'If death came from Spain we should all be immortal'.

Conciliar government has, however, been retained at the highest level, the **Cabinet**, in the British parliamentary system, and copied by many other countries. There too, however, its inefficiencies have had noticeable effects: in time of war the Cabinet has had to give way to an Inner Cabinet, a War Cabinet, or a system of 'overlords' (Jennings 1951, pp. 297, 306), while other key officials play a major role in the decision-making process. Hence modern writers talk of Britain being administered by the 'core executive' of which Cabinet ministers form only part.

Despite the inefficiencies of the Cabinet system, however, it supplies something that nothing else can do, a forum in which decisions can be taken that affect the work of several or of all departments. As noted above, however absolute a ruler, or however feared a modern dictator, neither would have any power were it not for the existence of people prepared to carry out their orders and to act on their behalf. The same is true of Cabinet ministers, and, among them, of the prime minister. Ironically, as we shall see, it is only the concurrent growth of the civil service that has enabled the Cabinet as such to survive at all, since it provides the individual ministers with the capacity to do their jobs, and keeps the lesser decisions off their desks (Cohen 1941, p. 37). Even then it has been calculated that the average British Cabinet member spends only about half an hour per week actually running his or her department. Not surprisingly the majority of them speedily become 'house trained', acting as mere spokespersons for the departmental point of view rather than agents of government bringing about change.

Bureaucracy

The permanent staff of government are known as civil servants, or, less happily, as bureaucrats, and the administration of states and other bodies by a corps of salaried officials is known as **bureaucracy**. 'Bureaucracy' is used even more loosely to designate decisions which the speaker regards as unsatisfactory, and this in turn reflects the fact that most ordinary citizens do not understand just how complex the network of governmental decision-making really is. Hence, if they do not get what they want from it they attack 'bureaucracy', in the same way that if their television set does not work they give it a good thump.

This is unfortunate, because one of the major characteristics of the modern state is the fact that it possesses a permanent bureaucratic structure. In fact the word 'bureaucracy' (a hybrid word, from French *bureau*, a desk, and Greek *kratein*, to rule) was coined in the mid-eighteenth century in France by Vicomte de Gournay to designate a new and he believed previously unknown type of state, one in which power itself had passed into the hands of salaried officials (Albrow 1970).

In fact, historically, he was wrong; bureaucratic systems had been devised independently in several of the historical bureaucratic states, for example Egypt and the Byzantine Empire. Indeed the Chinese, who developed in the mandarinate the foundation for a remarkably stable social as well as administrative structure, were in due course, through the Northcote–Trevelyan reforms, to influence the formalisation of bureaucracy in the British Empire (Bridges 1956, p. 25).

But de Gournay lived at a time when in Europe there was much concern about an individual's right of recourse against the state. There were, then, three possibilities. In the *Rechtstaat* a clearly formulated system of administrative law set out precisely what the citizen's rights were, and provided a remedy through special administrative courts. (This is the position today in France and other countries of the Code Napoléon.) In the *Justizstaat* there was no separate system of law or courts, but the citizen had recourse through the ordinary courts to the remedies afforded by common law. (This is the case today in Britain, the United States, Ireland and most Commonwealth countries.) In the *Polizeistaat* the state assumed the right to 'police' every citizen for the common good, and there was no recourse. The general power, found also in other states, is still known rather misleadingly as the 'police power' in the United States (Chapman 1970, p. 16). The bureaucratic state differed from all three types. There, though the formal recourse through law existed in theory, in practice it was denied by the secrecy attached to the bureaucratic process. This is a complaint which has had new life in the twentieth century. What then is bureaucracy, and why has it spread so widely?

Bureaucracy can be most simply defined as *a system of administration by paid, appointed officials arranged in a disciplined career hierarchy*. Weber, analysing the characteristics of bureaucracy, found ten aspects that he considered of particular importance, in defining the position of the bureaucratic staff in its purest form:

1. They are personally free and subject to authority only with respect to their impersonal official obligations.
2. They are organised in a clearly defined hierarchy of offices.
3. Each office has a clearly defined sphere of competence in the legal sense.
4. The office is filled by a free contractual relationship. Thus, in principle, there is free selection.
5. Candidates are selected on the basis of technical qualifications. In the most rational case, this is tested by examination or guaranteed by diplomas certifying technical training, or both. They are appointed, not elected.
6. They are remunerated by fixed salaries in money, for the most part with a right to pensions, and primarily graded according to rank.
7. The office is treated as the sole, or at least the primary, occupation of the incumbent.
8. It constitutes a career. There is a system of 'promotion' according to seniority or to achievement, or both. Promotion is dependent on the judgement of superiors.
9. The officials work entirely separated from ownership of the means of administration and without appropriation of their position.
10. They are subject to strict and systematic discipline and control in the conduct of their office. (Weber 1965, pp. 333–4)

We can summarise his position, however, by saying that for Weber bureaucracy is a system of administration by paid officials chosen by merit and arranged in a hierarchy by which the higher officials supervise the work of the lower ones.

Three themes run through the distinguishing characteristics of the Weberian model. The first is the importance of strict legal criteria delimiting the sphere within which the official operates, which in turn depends on a strong accepted concept of legality. Second is the clear separation of the private from the public aspect of the official's life; s/he is fully accountable to superiors, but only for the job s/he is paid to do, and s/he is not accountable in any way to the general public. Third is the way in which rational criteria determine both the nature of the job and the official's fitness to perform it.

As an 'ideal type' the picture of the legal, rational and accountable bureaucrat is obviously attractive to those who wish to see such principles operate in government. The creation of a civil service therefore appealed both to governments, as in Europe, and to their citizens, as in the United States, as a systematic solution to the problem of reconciling their divergent interests more closely. In France, Prussia and the former Austro-Hungarian Empire its origins go back to the eighteenth century. The UK followed suit in the 1850s and the first Civil Service Act in the USA was passed under President Chester A. Arthur in 1882. The continued extension of bureaucracy in the twentieth century is the clearest proof that this reconciliation has been seen as a success, even if it is at the same time attended by steady criticism.

The most substantial criticisms of civil servants focus on the secrecy that surrounds government decisions, the ability of senior officials to control information and their responsiveness (or otherwise) to political direction. To understand why this is the case it is first necessary to examine how civil servants are recruited and trained, since this determines the nature of their relationship with the politicians to whom they are nominally responsible.

In the USA recruitment is typically on the basis of training and educational qual-ifications in the specialist area covered by the department concerned. More than a third of all higher civil servants in the US federal government have scientific or professional qualifications. Though the Ethics in Government Act does act to some extent to restrain both practices, many top administrators are seconded from business and industry and conversely many career civil servants are eventually hired by private industry. One of the problems of this is to create a 'government of strangers' made up of people who have no long-term commitment to public service (Heclo 1977). A particularly sensitive area is the close relationship built up between the Department of Defense (the Pentagon) and the defence industries, which underpins one of the most powerful 'iron triangles' that characterise US administration.

In the UK recruitment is through formal tests and interview on graduation from university and placement is centralised. Most higher civil servants have arts and human-ities degrees but there is no formal requirement for any particular choice. The Civil Service College acts as a staff college for higher civil servants. In the UK the civil service is strictly non-partisan; civil servants are discouraged from participating in any way in politics, even at local level. It is seen as a career to be followed till retirement, followed by receipt of an inflation-proofed pension. Pay is generally good, with due allowance for London prices, and senior civil service salaries compare very favourably with min-isterial ones. However, they now fall far short of the grossly inflated pay packages obtainable since the 1980s in private industry, at least partly because of a systematic policy of 'deprivileging' senior civil servants practiced by the Thatcher government (Hood 1995).

A similar structure is found in India (the reformed government of which was a major objective of the Northcote–Trevelyan reforms), Australia, Canada, New Zealand, South Africa and other Commonwealth countries. However, in India civil servants are propor-tionately much better paid and as in Sri Lanka the civil service is regarded as a high-status occupation and is correspondingly sought-after (Kearney and Harris 1964, pp. 254–5). In each case a great deal of power is vested in the top civil servant in each ministry, the permanent secretary.

In Germany (and Switzerland) entrants to the civil service typically take a law degree: 66 per cent of German higher civil servants have legal qualifications. The civil service at federal level is relatively small, reflecting its limited powers. In many areas it is divided: the upper level consisting of federal employees and the lower level ones being employed by the *Land* government. So recruitment takes place at both levels. However, the merit system is rigorously enforced and post-entry training is an essential requirement for the appointment to be made permanent. A post as *Beamte* is expected to be a career appoint-ment and is rewarded as such. More surprisingly, it is not considered incompatible with political partisanship. Indeed not only are German civil servants free to take leave to contest elections but at any one time over half of the members of the Bundestag are civil servants who have taken leave to pursue their political ambitions (B.G. Peters 1989, p. 87).

In France higher civil servants (*foncionnaires*) have high status, excellent salaries and strict security of tenure. However, their position is very different from that of British civil servants in three respects: they can be detached to other state organs (e.g. nationalised industries), they staff ministerial *cabinets* and therefore play a political role, and they practice *pantouflage* (literally 'putting on their slippers') – the practice of leaving state service after a period of time to work in private industry.

Case Study   The French Civil Service

Entry to the French civil service is by gaining high grades in (typically a prestigious Parisian) Lycée and succeeding in the *concours* (competitive examination) for entry to one of the Grandes Ecoles. The importance of the *fonction publique* cannot however be fully understood without some reference to the distinctive structure of French government ministries. Only the Ministry of Foreign Affairs (Quai d'Orsay) has a secretary-general; otherwise there is no equivalent in France of the British permanent secretary, and the staff of ministries are divided vertically into some 1,200 different corps, in some ways analogous to the regiments in the army on which they were originally modelled. Hence only the minister links the 5–6 Directions Générales, the several autonomous Directions, and the many bureaux which make up a French ministry. To do his job the minister has the backing and assistance of his *cabinet ministériel* which follows him from post to post. In it the directeur de cabinet organises the work of up to twelve attachés, while the chef de cabinet (who is also a *fonctionnaire*) undertakes the minister's political work. 'Ministerial structures are always in turmoil and constitute a bewildering world for any observer. Each year, managers have to scrutinize new directories to find where some of their former colleagues have gone' (Rouban 1995, p. 45).

Entry to the leading corps, the Grands Corps, is through one of the Grandes Ecoles – France is unique in that universities do not form the highest rank in the French educational system. The leading Grande Ecole is the Ecole Polytechnique, founded in 1795 and reorganised by Napoleon on military lines. Exceptional intelligence and skill above all in mathematics and physics is required to gain one of the 300 places annually offered by *concours* (competitive examination) for admission to the ranks of 'Les X', as these highly qualified technical experts are known. They wear a smart military uniform and carry ceremonial swords on formal occasions and will go on to serve the state in the oldest and most prestigious of the Grands Corps: Ponts et Chaussées (1747) or the Corps de Mines (1786).

The Ecole Nationale d'Administration (ENA – from which the joking term *énarques* for its graduates) was founded only in 1946 but now commands the leading places in French administration. It was created to widen admission to the higher ranks of the French public service, previously dominated by the upper middle class and Paris. It has had little success in doing so, though it did successfully broaden the formerly law-dominated curriculum to include economics and business studies. Entry is by a diploma from the prestigious private IEP ('Sciences Po') or five years' service in an administrative post and only 100 a year are admitted. One tenth of *énarques* also go to industry; more significant still, already by 1972 they held 30 of 44 key posts in the 20 largest public enterprises in France. The leading Grands Corps to which they gain access include L'Inspection des Finances, the Cour des Comptes, the Conseil d'Etat and the Corps Diplomatique. Lower ranks of the civil service are trained in the Instituts Regionaux d'Administration (IRA).

The skill and power of French administration is shown by 'les trente glorieuses', the thirty years of rapid, state-led economic growth from 1945 to c. 1975, which enabled France to retain its status as a leading power. Under the Fourth Republic administrators provided the continuity that rapidly changing politicians did not, but with the advent of the Fifth Republic in 1958 their position was reinforced, until by the 1970s the political and administrative elites were regarded as effectively one. 'A specific equilibrium appeared during the first years of the Fifth Republic that overrode the political market as regards any serious attempt to set some pluralistic policy evaluation process. For twenty years, technocratic politics and majoritarian party rule dominated the policy-making process' (Rouban 1995, pp. 49–50). Then with the advent of the Socialists in 1981 there were major changes. The system became increasingly politicised and after 1986 'modernisation' has meant that civil servants are much less well paid and the service has become much more middle class.

In Spain, northern Europe and Latin America centralised placement is not used. Instead each agency is responsible for recruiting and hiring its own staff, applicants being judged in the first instance on the basis of specified minimum qualifications for the job but susbsequently on other grounds, which may, and often do, include other criteria. 'It is a simple matter to hire partisans when there are no formal restrictions to prevent it, and the parties in power would be extremely foolish if they did not try to provide employment for their own supporters and employ administrators likely to be favorably disposed towards the programs they will be administering' (B.G. Peters 1989, p. 84).

The common feature of all these systems is their tendency to create an elite, a select group which exercises disproportionate influence and even power in the making of decisions. Two concrete examples illustrate how elite attitudes structure the decision-making process through a combination of secrecy and the control of information. In 1946 both Britain and France were deprived of access to information on nuclear technology by US legislation. In Britain the prime minister, Clement Attlee, took the decision to go ahead with Britain's own nuclear programme, without consulting the Cabinet. At the same time, under the Fourth Republic, with its bewildering kaleidoscope of government changes, the foundations were laid for the *force de frappe* which was later to bolster the status of General de Gaulle in international relations. It was the French bureaucracy that provided the necessary continuity of decision-making to make the French programme a reality and it was bureacratic control of information that enabled them to disguise for many years that they did in fact get help from the United States.

Secondly, the outstanding success of the Concorde project in engineering terms owed much to the close working relationship between government and business in France. British attitudes towards the project were always ambiguous and the project only survived the change of government in Britain in 1964 because the French negotiators had had the forethought to ensure that the contract between the two countries was unbreakable. Once this was realised, the politician responsible hastened to put a favourable 'spin' on the decision. Who now remembers that it was Tony Benn, a future British Labour Eurosceptic, who as Secretary of State for Transport announced with apparent enthusiasm that in future Britain too would spell Concorde with an 'e' – e for enterprise and E for Europe!

The economic failure of Concorde, on the other hand, had its roots in another power of bureaucracy, the power to delay. The phenomenon of the 'sonic boom' gave the US government the pretext to use its administrative powers to deny Concorde landing rights while US companies explored the possibility of building their own supersonic passenger aircraft. Once it was clear US manufacturers were not going to go ahead with their own project the rights were granted, but by that time the chance to manufacture enough of the aircraft to make a profit had already been lost.

The critique of bureaucracy

Bureaucracy has been criticised on four main grounds.

1. **The civil service is too impersonal**. This, the greatest attraction of bureaucracy as a system of administration, is also one of its most frequent grounds for criticism by citizens in all countries. If it works as it is intended to, it operates, as Weber noted, by implementing common instructions impersonally without regard to the power or position of the individual suppliant (Gerth and Mills 1946, pp. 198, 215). If efficiently maintained (but cf. Blau and Duncan 1967), this can be an admirable feature (LaPalombara 1963; Marx 1967), and it is certainly much preferable to any older system where the will of the prince is law.

The impersonality of bureaucracy was challenged from the 1960s onwards. The division between politics and administration which it assumed, it was said, was false and if the problems of society were to be tackled successfully administrators had to take account of values, ethics and morals in their decision-making (Heady 1991, p. 3). In the 1980s this was to have an important influence on views of developing countries from abroad. Increasingly the governments of advanced industrialised countries were to require developing countries to meet a certain standard of 'governance' before granting them aid. On the face of it this was a reasonable requirement in view of the need for audit and accountability in spending public money, but 'political conditionality', as it became known, was much resented.

Even before the rise of this, the 'new public administration', however, it had been found necessary to mitigate the apparently harsh effects of impersonal decision-making by strengthening the process of appeal against administrative decisions. Britain, France (Ridley and Blondel 1964, pp. 24–7, 31) and Germany have each found very different solutions to this problem, but the fact that so much has been done in each country since 1950 indicates the felt need for change. A major problem is that administrative tribunals too are part of the bureaucratic structure and appeals from them can be difficult (Allen 1947, pp. 76ff.; Keeton 1960). Hence the Scandinavian countries were the first to appoint an independent officer, the *ombudsman*, to review administrative decisions with the power to quash or vary them, and in Britain the parliamentary commissioner for administration and in France (where of course there already were administrative courts) the *médiateur* have been given a similar brief though with lesser powers (Stacey 1978).

2. **The civil service is too big**. In the 1990s there were some 3.1 million civil employees of the US federal government, 90 per cent of whom worked outside Washington. But the positive image that they had of themselves as a well-trained and highly professional force with a strong sense of duty was not shared by the public at large. Not only have presidential candidates for decades campaigned against big government and against bureaucracy, but the Oklahoma bomber Timothy McVeigh represented in an extreme form the hostility towards the federal government that these populist appeals have helped generate. It comes as something of a surprise to learn that staff costs account for less that 10 per cent of total federal government spending.

3. **The civil service is too expensive**. Bureaucracy is criticised for what in another context might be regarded as a success, the increase in public expenditure brought about by rising government employment (Parkinson 1958, pp. 5–14). In an influential pamphlet published in London in 1973 Niskanen used a 'rational choice' argument to claim that bureaucracy had an inevitable tendency to maximise budgets. Hence, he argued: 'All

bureaus are too large. For given demand and cost conditions, both the budget and output of a monopoly bureau may be up to twice that of a competitive industry facing the same conditions' (Niskanen 1973, p. 33). The remedy for this was to hive off as many functions of government as possible to competitive private agencies, and this was the remedy later to be adopted by the neoliberal Thatcherites in Britain and copied in other parts of the world.

How well did this work in practice? The Thatcher government inherited in 1979 an administrative ('white-collar') payroll of some 540,000 staff. By 1990 one in six public employees had gone. Most of them however were 'industrial' staff and the 'white-collar' payroll still remained at just over 500,000. The costs of government, needless to say, did not fall by the same amount and staff cuts were accompanied by a 'retrenchment bonus' for those who remained, who were disproportionately the most senior. Justice and law and order gained while the Ministry of Defence, which lost half its staff, increased its budget in real terms by one-fifth. The big losers among the major departments were those concerned with industry, employment, trade and agriculture. Furthermore many of those who did 'go', at least 40 per cent of the whole, had simply ceased to be regarded as public employees as a result of privatisation and 'contracting out' of services (Hood 1995). Subsequently the contracting-out of various services (social security, the Passport Office, even prisons) to independent agencies or contractors has brought in its train a new set of problems. Once contracted-out, ministers can no longer be held accountable for or even questioned in parliament about the workings of these agencies.

4. **Bureaucracy is unfair to women**. Women, especially in the United States, have appealed to government to integrate women into the public sphere. But 'the bureaucratic organisation of public life directly controls the work of most women who hold jobs outside the home and affects the entire society in a way that is antithetical to the goals of feminist theory and practice' (Ferguson 1984, p. 4). This criticism is based on the belief that the principle of hierarchy which is fundamental to the operation of bureaucratic managment must, as things stand, reflect existing male structures of dominance and subordination.

Privatisation

'Privatisation' is the term now generally used to refer to a process by which state assets are transferred to private ownership. In this sense it is a new term, originally popularised in Britain when, following its successful re-election in 1983, the Thatcher government embarked on a crusade to divest the state of its ownership of profit-making enterprises. The first official statement of the objectives of privatisation was that made in November of that year by John Moore, then financial secretary to the Treasury (Veljanovski 1987, p. 8). However, there is nothing new about privatisation itself, and even the term, invented by David Howell, owes its origin to ideas put forward by Peter Drucker in 1970 (Drucker 1970) and was only slowly accepted by the Conservative Party. In Britain the original term used was 'de-nationalisation', as when the bulk of steel industry nationalised by the 1945–51 Labour government was sold off again by the Conservatives after 1951, only to be re-nationalised in 1967. But though as early as 1970–74 a Conservative government was committed to wholesale de-nationalisation in principle, in practice the largest state-owned company they sold was the travel agent Thomas Cook and they actually increased the state's holdings by nationalising both Rolls Royce and British Leyland. After the further nationalisation of companies in aerospace and shipbuilding the public sector in Britain accounted for 12.7 per cent of GDP and 9.4 per cent of employment in 1977 (Pryke 1981, p. 2).

The sale of public enterprises has however gone on for many years – as long, perhaps, as public enterprises have existed. In Argentina, for example, a report by Raúl Prebisch for the interim military government of 1955–58 recommended the sale of all state enterprises except the railways and the oil industry, but no action was taken (di Tella and Braun 1990, p. 7). Under President Frondizi, however, in order to reduce public expenditure the government sold off forty companies previously German-owned which had been expropriated at the end of the Second World War and privatised the urban bus transport network in Buenos Aires, with, the then minister of economy claims, 'excellent results' (Roberto T. Alemann, in di Tella and Braun 1990, p. 69). At the same time, private participation was invited both by Argentina's state oil corporation YPF and by PEMEX in Mexico. Despite the strong encouragement throughout by the United States for private enterprise solutions, the real shift towards privatisation in Latin America did not get under way until the 1970s, when it was associated with the policies of the 'Chicago boys' in Chile, and it is only since the early 1980s that it has become a major theme both of European and Latin American economic policies (Glade 1991, p. 2), spreading after 1989 to the countries of Eastern Europe.

One of the attractions of privatisation was that it promises to replace whole squadrons of civil servants by taking away their functions and giving them over to external contractors. Probably because the process has to be organised by civil servants, however, this does not happen and in fact a new set of powerful and largely unaccountable 'regulators' backed by substantial offices have been appointed to 'regulate' the new privatised industries so that they do not charge their customers too much and cause political embarrassment.

Administration in developing countries

Administration in many developing countries faces much more trying problems. The initial problem there was that the bureaucracy was seen as having been invented not for the sake of the local inhabitants (although their interests have not necessarily been infringed), but for the sake of the colonising power. Civil servants in post at independence were regarded as collaborationists, and their great powers made them an easy target for nationalist criticism.

However, the problem is not necessarily bureaucracy as such, but the purposes it is supposed to serve. The *instrumental* model does still work for many purposes and might do so for all if politicians would only allow it. The politicians however distrusted the administrative machine they inherited at independence and wanted to replace it with a *politicised* model in which administrators would simply do as they were told. And organisational theorists argued that the need for development called for an *entrepreneurial* model which would incorporate and organise change (Burns and Stalker 1962).

Riggs's (1964) classification of bureaucratic systems was designed to reflect this developmental perspective and in 1991 Heady described Riggs's *Administration in Developing Countries: The Theory of Prismatic Society* (1964) as continuing to be 'probably the most notable single contribution in comparative public administration' (Heady 1991, p. 16). Riggs seeks to distinguish between three stages in the development of postcolonial states, using an analogy drawn from optics, namely the passage of light through a prism.

- Traditionally, in the conciliar state, decision-making was 'fused', the decisions in different areas being incorporated in the same body in the way that white light contains all the colours.
- In a modern government, on the other hand, the area of competence of government is split into functional areas, each the responsibility of a different government department. Decision-making, therefore, is 'refracted', just as white light leaving the prism is refracted into different colours.
- However, most developing countries have mixed institutions in which functions are incompletely separated. The analogy is with light actually passing through a prism; hence Riggs's term, 'prismatic' society. Riggs later refined his model and restyled this type of administration 'orthoprismatic' (Riggs 1973). The important thing about it is that it is both differentiated and malintegrated.

Prismatic society, Riggs suggests, is characterised by what he terms the Sala system of administration: namely an over-centralised system in which every decision has to be taken several times over, and people still hanker after the multi-functional model. They speak to a friend of a friend, they write to the president of the Republic, or they take his private secretary to lunch, trying to find a single point at which all decisions that interest them can be decided.

There are four consequences (see also Hyden 1995):

1. Decision-making became, or remained, over-centralised. The president's will was law, so every decision was taken several levels higher up than is really necessary, and the top level in particular was both over-worked and over-powerful. An excellent example is Nigeria, where a combination of weak civilian government and military intervention has created a stratum of 'perm. secs.' with hugely inflated salaries, and lesser bureaucratic offices multiply at great cost to the public purse.
2. Policy-makers were discouraged from using the past as a guide for the future (Dror 1968). Nor were they encouraged to take enough time to explore all the possible alternatives. This gave rise to the practice known as **'satisficing'**, which means simply adopting the first solution that comes to mind which appears more or less to fit.
3. There was serious waste. This arose because of what Hirschman has termed 'motivation-outruns-understanding' (Hirschman 1975). The urge being to do everything at once, money got spent two or three times over and no one knew exactly how much was being spent. In Sierra Leone the money given by the IMF to build a bridge connecting the capital to Lungi Airport mysteriously disappeared. Two new ferries were purchased from Japan to operate a service instead. One soon broke down and was abandoned for want of spare parts to replace it. Of course such failures are not unknown in developed countries also; as the French political scientist Michel Crozier pointed out, inadequacies or 'dysfunctions' are bound to develop in all human organisations (Crozier 1964).
4. The prime task of the civil service was not seen as making policy but as providing patronage for key groups in society (Joseph 1987). Hence government offices were not recruited on any consideration of merit but distributed clandestinely as private property and inevitably they were treated as such by some recipients who enjoyed the status but had no intention of doing the work. The extent of public employment however was found in 1980–81 to be actually much higher on average in developed countries than in developing ones. Britain employed in 'general government' (a category which includes, where applicable, state and local government) 9.57 per cent

of its population. The USA employed 7.77 per cent, West Germany 6.06 per cent, France 5.73 per cent, Italy 5.34 per cent and Spain 4.00 per cent. Argentina employed 4.77 per cent, but most of the 36 developing countries surveyed failed even to equal the 3.75 per cent in Japan: e.g. Sri Lanka 3.02 per cent, India 1.81 per cent and South Africa 0.94 per cent (Heady 1991, pp. 80–3).

Corruption

Unfortunately in the uncertain atmosphere of developing countries administrative and political corruption flourishes (Wraith and Simkins 1965). Many of the military coups that have deposed governments in Africa (e.g. those that brought to power Ibrahim Babangida in Nigeria, Jerry Rawlings in Ghana and Valentine Strasser in Sierra Leone) have had as one of their two or three principal avowed aims the ending of corruption. The bitter irony is that within months the new military regimes are usually at least as corrupt as the civilian governments they replaced or supplanted – and often much more so.

The belief that political office brings with it the duty, as well as the opportunity, to use patronage on behalf of one's family is often found in connection with the illegal making of personal gain out of one's office (Clapham 1982). This is often seen as being the distinctive feature of Third World politics and the Riggs model helps explain the mechanism by which it becomes 'necessary'.

Certainly it is inevitable that under a clientelistic system there will be no hard-and-fast distinction between public and private and corruption will be endemic. What seems clear is that the effects of clientelism are much more serious in authoritarian or one-party states than they are in competitive systems. Though it is probably impossible to eliminate corruption entirely, the threat of public scrutiny forms an effective brake on the more outrageous forms of corruption, and may well be more significant than the possibility of legal charges, which are themselves subject to the influence of patronage.

Even the definition of corruption is problematic. However, the boundary is crossed when payment or reward is made directly to government officials to secure a service of some kind. A distinction can be made between payment to expedite a service to which one is entitled anyway, and payment to secure a service to which one is not entitled. But in practice both are properly regarded as corrupt.

The dangers are highest where the divisions between public and private are blurred. The persistence of traditional culture, where the structure of government is based on reciprocal gift-giving, may contribute to a culture of corruption. Similarly nepotism, the employment of or granting of favours to relatives, is often the logical extension of extended kinship networks. The low salaries paid to all but a few in the bloated bureaucracies of states such as India and Nigeria and the fact that in all societies status is measured by the conspicuous display of wealth may contribute too.

Typologies of bureaucracies

Looking at the long history of bureaucratic systems of administration, Fritz Morstein Marx proposed to classify them into four categories: guardian, caste, patronage and merit. Since in modern times only the last two survive, and there are many other variants to be taken into consideration, Fainsod (1963) categorises only modern systems. He also offers a convincing explanation of their characteristics by relating them to the locus of authority as follows:

1. **Ruler-dominated bureaucracies**. These are characteristic of traditional regimes where the ruler remains the traditional source of authority, such as Morocco, Nepal or Saudi Arabia.
2. **Military-dominated bureaucracies**. These are subordinate to the will of the military elite, which may be either conservative or 'modernising'. However, the military elite is itself part of the bureaucracy so that it is in effect the bureacracy that rules.
3. **Ruling bureaucracies**. In these senior civil servants make political as well as administrative decisions, regardless of their constitutional position. Heady terms these 'bureaucratic elite' systems.
4. **Representative bureaucracies**. In these countries – including the United States, Western Europe and Japan – political parties deriving their authority from competitive elections control the political process and set limits on the power of the bureaucracy. There is sufficient political control of the bureaucracy to ensure that it is in some degree accountable to the public at large.
5. **Party-state bureaucracies**. Formerly the norm in Eastern Europe, these organisations lacked accountability but were subject to party control. They can be expected to change substantially as the process of liberalisation and democratisation continues, though with a variety of possible outcomes. The emergence of 'nomenlaktura capitalism' and the continuing role of state intelligence in the former Soviet Union suggest, however, that one of the possible outcomes might be a ruling bureaucracy.

Heady also suggested a new category of 'pendulum' systems: systems in which since independence political control had swung back and forth between bureaucratic elite (often military) dominance and elected representative government. In these, he believed, the tendency will be for the bureaucracy to become more prominent (Heady 1991, p. 450). However, like other modifications that have been proposed, this one seems to reflect relatively transient distinctions.

Decision-Making

When one has identified the leaders and their **staff**, however, one has done no more than lay the essential foundation for assessing how they actually make decisions. It is easy to assume that those taking the decisions are rational persons freely operating in conditions of full information and unlimited time. Yet such is certainly not the case.

Policy can be defined as a consistent set of views on the correct action to be taken about a problem or set of problems. Policy, in short, is 'what to do'; decision-making is 'how to do it'.

The first step in the making of policy is to get an issue on the agenda. As Bachrach and Baratz pointed out (1962), some actors have the power to keep political issues off the agenda so that no decisions are made:

> Non decision-making is a means by which demands for change in the existing allocation of benefits and privileges in the community can be suffocated before they are even voiced; or kept covert; or killed before they gain access to the relevant decision-making arena; or, failing all of these things, maimed or destroyed in the decision-implementing stage of the policy process. (Bachrach and Baratz 1971, p. 44)

Assuming that the issue does reach the decision-making stage, the traditional assumption is that any decision made will be rational. It was dissatisfaction with the obvious weaknesses of what he terms the **'rational actor' model** of decision-making, particularly in foreign affairs, that led Graham Allison critically to compare it with two rival models of the decision-making process, using the Cuban missile crisis of 1962 as the subject of analysis (Allison 1971).

The 'rational actor' model assumes the rationality of the decision-making process as a whole: it will have clearly formulated goals, and make decisions so as to maximise its objectives in attaining those goals. In doing so it chooses among a range of rational alternative policies so that, by examining the action taken, the observer can deduce the reasons that led to the adoption of that policy option. Such a model is inherently satisfying on logical grounds, but it leaves much unexplained. It conspicuously fails to account for decisions which later proved disastrous, such as the Anglo-French attack on Suez in 1956, the Bay of Pigs expedition in 1961 or the introduction of the community charge ('poll tax') by the Thatcher government in 1990.

The two alternative models which Allison offers, however, seek not only to explain what the first model does not, but to do so in a way which is itself coherent and meaningful.

The **'organisational process' model** sees government as a constellation of organisations grouped in parallel and in hierarchy, each with different tasks and different procedures (Allison 1971, pp. 78–95; drawing *inter alia* on Barnard 1938; March and Simon 1958). There is no one set of goals, but, for each level of disaggregation, the goals are the maintenance of the organisation itself in terms of budget, manpower, job satisfaction and esteem. All problems therefore are 'factored', different parts of the problem being handled by different organisations in terms of their perceived goals. Such is the volume of routine work, moreover, that each organisation develops routines, or standard operating procedures, by which the majority of its work is handled. The 'answer' to a new problem, therefore, involves, not a complete search through all possible policy alternatives, but what has been termed satisficing, the acceptance of the first routine that comes to hand that will handle the task in terms of the organisation's perceived goals at that moment. Such routines, and even more the complex programmes of routines of large, complex organisations, are inflexible and unlikely ever to be wholly appropriate to any specific task. Moreover there is a general tendency to avoid uncertainty about the future by constructing responses to likely scenarios which are thought particularly likely to happen, though such long-term plans are likely to be ignored thereafter in the construction of lesser plans and routines used also for day-to-day action. Change therefore proceeds incrementally, and major changes in policy within the organisation can only proceed from deliberate intervention from a higher level aimed in such a way as to prevent the attempts to circumvent or forestall it by standard operating procedures. As we have already noted above, the tendency towards decision-making by 'disjointed incrementalism' is strongly encouraged by the nature of the budgetary process.

Such processes, however, are no less characteristic of the highest level of decision-making than of its subordinate organisations, and there, in Cabinet or Politburo, where disagreements from time to time come into the open, it becomes clear that policy outcomes are themselves the product of the competing individuals of which the organisation as a whole is composed. Allison therefore offers us what he terms a **'governmental politics' model** (Allison 1971, pp. 162–80; see also Neustadt 1964). Others have preferred to call it the 'bureaucratic politics' model, though its usefulness is not limited to examination of the workings of the bureaucracy.

The 'governmental politics' model sees individuals as players in a game, whose output is the sum total of all their decisions. The player's power to influence decisions depends on his or her job; possession of that job in turn determines how s/he will look at every issue ('Where you stand depends on where you sit', Allison 1971, p. 176, quoting Don K. Price). The game proceeds along action channels structured by rules and deadlines that have to be met, by a process of bargaining in which action on one issue is traded off against action or inaction on another, and this bargaining is vertical as well as horizontal in its implications, as between those who have much power ('Chiefs') and those who have little ('Indians'). Since the noise level is high and time short, decisions taken to meet deadlines tend to be based on the minimum of evidence and defended much more strongly than a rational examination might suggest desirable, and decisions are both misperceived by the participants and miscommunicated to others. But because of the importance of hierarchy to each individual, gains may be maximised by reticence such that major objections are not voiced despite being seen or felt.

Table 8.1 illustrates the main points of comparison between these three models. Though the 'governmental politics' model comes closest to the position adopted in the organisation of this book, it is, as will be seen, not in any way an exclusive explanation of the way in which government works. The fact is that the 'governmental politics' game is 'played' by members of organisations, who as part of their working beliefs about the game as a whole hold that their actions, in some not wholly clear way, contribute to the making of policy which is in the 'national interest' and must therefore be 'rational' in overall terms. Yet in the United States it is clear that the division of powers between executive and legislature, and the power of large corporations in the US economy, combine to ensure that the policy process is disproportionately influenced by 'iron triangles' linking outside lobbyists, executive bureaux and congressional committees.

Table 8.1 Models of decision-making

Rational actor	Organisational process	Governmental politics
One organisation	Constellation of organisations	Individuals players in a game
Hierarchy of goals	Goal is maintenance of organisation	Job determines issue
Goals clearly formulated	Problems 'factored'	Rules and deadlines channel action
Problems analysed	Standard operating procedures	Bargaining
Search of all alternatives	Programmes of routines	Chiefs and Indians
Rational choice of best alternative	Satisficing	Win some lose some

Source: after Allison 1971

Case Study An Early Victory

... While there have been mis-steps in specific areas of policy, Mr Bush has achieved success where it really matters in these difficult early days – in overcoming many of the broader political challenges that faced him when he took office on January 20. The controversial circumstances of his election made Mr Bush's early task more difficult than most other presidents. But in the three months he has already passed at least four crucial political tests.

First, he needed to put at rest lingering doubts about his legitimacy as president. His defeat in the popular vote and his contested victory in the Florida courts threatened to leave an indelible suspicion among a large proportion of the population and the political class that he was an illegitimate chief executive. Three months later, the legitimacy question seems as remote as the images of dimpled chads and late-night court decisions. His decision to press ahead with a firmly conservative line rather than attempt to govern from the centre in a nod to the fragility of his mandate has, in fact, contributed to the popular perception that this is a fully legitimate government. Of course, it is also true that Mr Bush's case was assisted at the outset by the month-long furore over his predecessors's last days in office, including pardons for fleeing tax dodgers and convicted drug pushers.

Mr Bush's second main challenge was to gain an early political victory on his chief legislative goal, the tax cut. Although the Senate trimmed it, something very close to the Bush plan seems almost certain to be passed by the whole Congress.

The scale of this victory should not be underestimated. Few gave Mr Bush much of a chance of getting any sizeable tax reduction through a sceptical and split Congress. And yet, by recasting the plan as a fiscal stimulus, the president has succeeded in getting Congress to pass a cut of about $1,400bn.

Third, Mr Bush needed to allay widespread concerns that he would not be up to handling an international crisis. In spite of the reassuring way Mr Bush has surrounded himself with able foreign policy staff – 'just as the hole surrounds itself with the doughnut', as one late-night comedian put it – doubts remained about whether the man in the Oval Office would fumble an important challenge.

Yet with the EP-3 surveillance plane incident, Mr Bush has had an early chance to dispel many of these doubts. Although a few critics (in his own party) felt he gave away too much in return for the 24 crew members, most members of Congress, and an overwhelming majority of the public, seemed to find his handling nearly flawless.

Fourth, and perhaps most important, the president needed to demonstrate that his constantly repeated promise in the campaign – that he would represent a change of style in office – was a serious one. In the end, it was this promise – of an end to the bitter partisanship of the Clinton years and a restoration of 'honour and integrity' to the White House – more than any specific campaign proposal, that lay behind Mr Bush's electoral victory in November.

In office, though he has not deviated from his conservative agenda, he has won high marks from members of Congress for a willingness to listen and a willingness to step out of the limelight. The Bush style – low-key, *primus inter pares* alongside his senior advisers and officials – is in marked contrast to the dominant presence of his predecessor.

Source: *Financial Times*, 28/29 April 2001

Legislatures

Assemblies form the last stage of interest aggregation in both parliamentary and presidential systems. In both, therefore, even where they have little visible effect on policy outcomes, they have a number of very useful functions:

1. They enable issues to be ventilated and act as a conduit for grievances. This helps reduce a sense of injustice and lowers pressure within the system as a whole.
2. They play a vital role in the structure of party rule, pressing the claims of constituents and of special interests, and so form an important part of the structure of patronage by which the government is maintained (see Chapter 9).
3. They consent to the levying of taxes, legitimating the government in extracting power resources.
4. They consent to legislation, arbitrating between interests and enabling those not considered socially desirable to be excluded from legitimate access to power altogether.

Clearly in presidential systems the assembly as a whole is substantially more likely to play a significant role in decision-making, since in parliamentary systems the presence of the executive in parliament, and its ability to control the outcome as long as it can maintain majority support, severely curtails the assembly's independence of action. Thus Mezey's (1979) classification of assemblies according to the degree of their impact on policy is critically dependent on the context in which they have to operate. Only in presidential states, and under unusually favourable conditions, can assemblies be categorised in his terms as active makers of policy. The United States is the only example which has operated in this way consistently over many years, and even there it has been subjected to substantial pressure from the executive in the era of the 'Imperial Presidency'.

Nelson W. Polsby (1975) also classifies legislatures by their impact on policy-making. He uses two broad categories: transformative legislatures, which make policy, and arenas, which are only debating-chambers. In practice, however, both are modified, so that four categories are generated as in Table 8.2.

Few legislatures are highly **transformative** and the Congress of the United States, the most independent of them, is perhaps the only really good example. However, this can change and at the end of the twentieth century the Brazilian Congress, for example, was highly coalitional, very decentralised and characterised by great flexibility in forming policy majorities. Until the advent of 'gridlock' in the 1990s, the two-party system and the need for bipartisanship in foreign policy helped stabilise relations between president and Congress in the USA. In contrast, Brazil's highly fragmented party system bred frustration on both sides and contributed to the successful impeachment of President Collor in 1993.

The sad fact, however, is that presidential states, because of the separation of executive and legislature, are much more commonly prone to intense and debilitating conflicts between the two. Conflict of this kind has frequently in the past in Latin America led to one of two outcomes: either military intervention accompanied by the deposition of the executive and the suspension of the assembly, as in Chile in 1973, or a 'self coup' (*autogolpe*) in which the president uses force to close the assembly and to rule by decree, as in Peru in 1993. Alternatively at the end of the decade the electors of Venezuela rejected both the traditional political parties and elected as president a political novice, General Hugo Chávez, who was committed to a platform of strong executive leadership and immediately amended the Constitution to give himself the necessary powers.

Table 8.2 Polsby's classification of legislatures

Determinants of transformativeness			
Independence of legislature	Parliamentary organising majorities	Parliamentary party management	Successive policy majorities
HIGHLY TRANSFORMATIVE			
United States	Highly coalitional	Very decentralised	Very flexible
MODIFIED TRANSFORMATIVE			
Netherlands	Coalitional	Decentralised	Flexible
Sweden	Moderately coalitional	Moderately decentralised	Moderately flexible
MODIFIED ARENA			
Germany	Coalitional	Moderately decentralised	Moderately flexible
Italy	Coalitional	Moderately decentralised	Moderately flexible
France (IV)	Unstable	Decentralised	Flexible
ARENA			
United Kingdom	Moderately coalitional	Centralised	Fixed
Belgium	Narrowly based	Centralised	Fixed
France (V)	Narrowly based	Centralised	Fixed

Source: after Polsby 1975

In Britain and France parliament as an assembly is dominated by the executive of the day and can be categorised as reactive in Mezey's terms or as an arena in Polsby's. Both influence government policy but seldom control it. There are exceptions. In Britain, the apparently convincing majority achieved by the Major government in 1992 was rapidly eroded by divisions in the ruling Conservative Party, forcing the government into a defensive strategy (Major 2000). Under the Blair government (1997–) a large majority has been challenged only by the insubordination of the (unelected) House of Lords. The French parliament, shackled by the constraints of the 1958 Constitution, is even weaker. Though individual members of the National Assembly may well exercise a greater influence over policy than their British counterparts through the effect of the *cumul des mandats* (the fact that as well as being deputies they normally hold elective office either at local or European level), they have little power to influence legislation and government business takes absolute priority.

At an individual level the Italian deputy has much more power, and collectively can make and unmake governments, but the prolonged dominance of the system by the Christian Democrats made much of this activity rather superficial and it is only in recent years that coalitions have been really meaningful. Germany has also seen important changes during the 1990s though the party structure has remained broadly intact. In 1982 in former West Germany Chancellor Kohl demonstrated the subordination of the Bundestag when he was able to engineer the 'constructive vote of no confidence' by which his government was overturned by its own supporters and so received a new mandate from the electorate. He reached the peak of his power in 1990 with the reunification of Germany but it declined following the outbreak of war in the Balkans, to which he contributed by his hasty recognition of Croatia (Clemens and Paterson 1998). Since his defeat in the general election of September 1998 a series of revelations about the secret funding of his Christian Democrats (CDU) has weakened them as an opposition in the Bundestag and led to their defeat in *Land* elections in Schleswig-Holstein in February 2000.

The most powerful parliamentary assemblies are those of the present or former 'consociational democracies' such as Denmark, Finland, Iceland, Luxembourg and the Netherlands, where multi-party government requires negotiation between coalition partners on a wide range of issues. These are the 'modified transformative' assemblies which collectively exercise a significant influence on policy outcomes. Party management is decentralised and policy majorities are flexible. Ironically, such are also the legislatures in which the individual voter's choice is least likely to make a difference. In Switzerland, which has been governed by a four-party coalition almost continuously since the 1940s, it has no effect at all (Ware 1987a, pp. 72–3).

However, many assemblies cannot even be regarded as arenas owing to the restraints under which they have to operate. The existence of extra-parliamentary controls, whether wielded by the military, a party militia or a 'secret' police, adds an external dimension to one-party dominance or control. In many newly independent countries since the 1960s assemblies have been speedily marginalised. There are exceptions: those of India and Sri Lanka, for example, have retained influence, despite executive dominance in India under Indira Gandhi and in Sri Lanka under J.R. Jayawardene.

In the former communist countries assemblies were minimal, the Supreme Soviet of the USSR meeting for only a handful of days a year to acclaim the reports of government ministers and committees. It is hardly surprising, therefore, that the performance of assemblies in Eastern Europe since the fall of communism has been very varied. In the Czech Republic parliamentary democracy has been successfully restored but in Slovakia following secession in 1993 President Meciar was able to whip up nationalist resentment to override opposition and entrench himself in power. The Baltic States, Poland and Slovenia, like the Czech Republic, have hoped soon to fulfil the requirements for membership of the European Union (the *acquis communautaire*), which include free elections and functioning parliamentary democracy. Russia's State Duma elected in 1999 was highly fragmented; when Vladimir Putin became president he inherited formidable powers and has consolidated his control with extra-parliamentary means. In January 2000 the fragmentation of the Ukrainian State Council culminated in a split, with parallel sessions being held in different buildings and three months later President Kuchma won a referendum to reduce its powers. In Belarus and the Central Asian and Caucasian states of the former Soviet Union authoritarian regimes remain in power. In Mongolia in March 2000 constitutional amendments passed by the Great Hural were first vetoed by the president and then quashed by the Constitutional Court.

Any categorisation of assemblies must allow for the fact that in other regions of the world there is also a significant number of states in which assemblies do not operate at all, or in which, as in Burma, they have been suspended and the country placed under martial law (see Chapter 10). In January 2000 there were no parliaments in the Gulf region with the problematic exception of Kuwait, whose assembly had very limited powers and was in any case elected by only some two-fifths of the country's adult inhabitants. In December 2000 it was announced that the assembly in Bahrain, which had operated briefly until 1975, was to be restored. Unlike their Kuwaiti sisters, moreover, women would be allowed both to vote and to stand for office (*Daily Telegraph*, 20 December 2000) and did vote at a referendum held early in 2001.

Decentralisation and Deconcentration of Power

How far governments have been willing to cede power can be tested, in Dahl's terms, by the degree of subsystem autonomy and the number of subsystems within the political system as a whole (Dahl 1964a, p. 35). It is clearly very relevant to any assessment of the power of central government to determine the extent to which the state is differentiated into subordinate units, or the extent to which it is centralised. The more centralised it is, the fewer opportunities individual citizens have of making their views felt. But simple deconcentration of power – granting power to subordinate governments or agencies – has its limitations since the powers given can always be taken back again. On the other hand few if any central governments are willing to decentralise power once they have discovered the advantages of being able to use it.

Some states, France and Ireland among them, are unitary states with no provision for elected regional government. Spain and Italy, in differing degrees, provide for a considerable degree of regional autonomy. Belgium, uniquely, has evolved into a federal state constructed by devolution. In Switzerland, the powers of central government extend to little more than the conduct of defence and foreign affairs.

The Constitution of Spain recognises 'autonomous communities' within the Spanish 'nation' and affords them three alternative routes to seek self-government (Lawlor and Rigby 1998, p. 33). But for a country created by the unification of a number of very different states in the 1860s, Italian regionalism is surprisingly weak. The Italian Constitution of 1948 provided for regional government but regional government was created in the first instance only for a few peripheral areas. It was only in 1970 that parliament legislated to provide a regional structure for the rest of the country, something that was not always easily accepted. The major split in Italian politics was the split between the developed North and the underdeveloped South and in the 1980s there were times when there was real concern that the unity of the state might break down given the intractability of what was normally regarded as 'the Southern problem'. Only in the 1990s were the Northern Leagues successful, at least for a time, in allying themselves with other right-wing elements and harnessing the widespread frustration at the slowness of Roman decision-making (Levy 1996).

Since 1997, with a perhaps surprising disregard for consistency, Britain has established a Scottish Parliament and a Welsh Assembly, neither of them particularly like the devolved government that has been returned to Northern Ireland. In Germany, on the other hand, the new *Länder* were incorporated in the existing federal structure of the Federal Republic with much less trouble than had been expected, owing to the overwhelming success in the East of Chancellor Kohl and the CDU. Even then some very mundane needs were felt: 'Building state governments from scratch proved difficult. Lack of facilities and equipment hampered decisions: meeting rooms, telephones, and copiers had to be improvised. At the same time, neophyte parliamentarians needed to acquire experience with forming democratic coalitions' (Jarausch 1994, p. 190).

Dahl's interest in this range of possibilities is natural enough, since, being an American, he lives in a federal state – one in which, as we have seen, the balance between central power and regional autonomy is very carefully fixed. However, as we saw in Chapter 2, federalism is the product of a political compromise, and so very unusual – a compromise between centripetal and centrifugal forces, the demands of central power and the demand for independence. Where this does not happen, what are the chances of local or regional government being able to survive for long without having its powers curtailed?

Although at national level the pressures of politics do not always allow for the degree of direct participation that one might perhaps hope for, in many states the conduct of local government is subject to noticeably less rigour and control. It is still possible for many societies, for example India, Tanzania and Brazil, to permit decisions at the local level to be made by the general gathering of citizens or by a locally elected assembly, subject to some kind of overall control from the centre, but with only a very generalised degree of control. In New England in the United States some townships still retain direct government through township meetings. More recently local cable television has enabled Californians to take part personally in the debates of the 'electronic town hall'.

In a British local authority there is an assembly in which, in theory, everybody is equal; again, the control of business is in its own hands, and it controls its own place of meeting. This is a relic of an old freedom which can operate at local level because there is a check in the overriding national interest. The recent history of local government in Britain and France shows just how tenuous that freedom is. In Britain, local authorities have been deprived of all significant autonomy and many are now threatened with individual abolition. They are no longer able to raise what money they like or to spend what money they like, subject only to the will of their electorates. Worse still, they have been ordered to do a great many new tasks for which they have been given no resources.

France is a particularly interesting case. At the French Revolution the old provinces were swept away and the country divided into even-sized units, the 90 (now 96) departments (*départements*) named after innocuous features such as rivers or mountains. These in 1981 were divided into 317 *arrondissements* and those into 36,433 basic units called *communes*. The *commune* could be anything from a remote farming area in the Pyrenees to a large city like Lyon or Lille. The Napoleonic state concentrated power in central government whose delegate, the prefect (*prefet*), administered the department. The establishment of the Third Republic in 1871 brought back elected local government with a legislative council in each department, though the prefect remained the chief executive. The commune was governed after 1882 by an elected *maire* assisted by a council (*conseil municipale*). But both worked under the supervision (*tutelle*) of the departmental prefect.

In 1981 the incoming Socialist government abolished the prefectoral *tutelle* and (until 1988) even the title of 'prefect' itself disappeared. At the departmental level many of the powers of the former prefects were transferred to the elected Conseil Générale. At the communal level the traditional structure remained unaltered, though inducements had already been offered to communes to merge in an effort to reduce their numbers and ensure at least a minimum level of provision of services and this process has continued. Though the central government clearly retains the right to alter or to abolish local government, France still has more local government units at communal level than the whole of the rest of the European Union, over 30,000.

As will be seen later, the concept of total participation voiced at the time of the French Revolution is also embedded in the characteristic political structure of communist states and a handful of other socialist states too, in a special way which varies significantly from the structure of liberal democratic states. Both the parliamentary system and the presidential system as compromises are, moreover, subject to certain types of mutations, and these types of mutation are most inclined to happen when governments fail to resist the pretensions of small groups within the state to assert authority over the majority. There are other circumstances, but these are the ones in which most differentiation in status has occurred.

This can be even more clearly seen in the case of India. As the very successful examples of Australia and Canada show, the parliamentary system is readily adapted to the special conditions of federal government. However, the Indian Constitution of 1949 considerably modifies the traditional assumption of federalism: that both federal and 'state' governments will have clear and distinct areas of authority. It does so by providing for the federal government to impose 'President's Rule' on a state which is regarded (by the federal government!) as being unable to govern itself responsibly. Direct rule from the centre, carried beyond a certain point, would destroy federalism and create a unitary state, though the point at which this might happen could be difficult to determine with certainty. But it is quite compatible with the overall sovereignty implicit in the concept of the parliamentary system. Indira Gandhi's use of force, essentially a coup, did change the form of government radically (*Annual Register* 1975, p. 253), but when submitted to the verdict of the electors they rejected the change.

Elites

Outside the ranks of the political leadership and the bureaucracy in most – if not all – societies a number of people can be identified who, together with the political leaders and the senior bureaucrats, monopolise a disproportionate share of political power. In so far as this forms a self-conscious group of men and women aware of their special position, it is commonly termed an elite (Parry 1969, p. 31). It is a term, however, which defies easy handling in the comparative context because of its indefinability. Although everyone knows what an elite is when they see one, they seem to have a great deal of difficulty deciding what exactly an elite is not.

Pareto's original concept of an elite as a group conscious of its own existence was straightforward enough. But relatively few people have read Pareto, and for most English-speaking readers the concept was fundamentally transformed by C. Wright Mills in his book *The Power Elite* (1956). The '**power elite**' for Mills is not an elite in the older sense, in that the members of the power elite – if there is such an entity – do not necessarily know each other, and indeed they may not be sure that each other exist; in the United States, his argument runs, key people in business, the armed forces and government will act together in a certain kind of way without having common links between them, or indeed without really knowing that they are acting together. The British equivalent is still sometimes referred to as 'the Establishment' (H. Thomas 1959). The power elite seems much too diffuse to be useful in a comparative context, and for that reason is best abandoned.

What then of the elite proper? This is probably best considered as a phenomenon, not of societies, as Pareto originally envisaged it, but of organisations, as Michels suggested in the context of political parties, and the political decision-makers do form such an organisation. As such they can be identified, labelled and studied. When this is done, some trends are immediately obvious. In the small group of key decision-makers women are scarce; minors are excluded altogether. And not all males of adult age can take part, because they lack some or all of the necessary qualifications. Hence though individual members of the elite are not necessarily easily identified by their social characteristics, the elite as a whole has a very different social composition from the social strata from which it is drawn.

So much is obvious enough. What is not so obvious is the astonishing number of these qualifications, and the extent to which the possession of a sufficient number is restricted to a very few. So much is this the case that even in the most 'democratic' state the access to political power is broadened, if at all, not by widening the circle of eligibles, but by limiting the time that any one person can stay in a position of power. This may be done by formal as well as informal limitations on the duration of office. When all the necessary exclusions have been made, there remains a small group of about a hundred people who appear to be the most influential people in the society. But this method pre-determines the result. To say that the country is run by an elite is to accept that these people really run it, and that their identities are known. Neither may in practice be the case.

Elites can be divided into two distinct but overlapping types. Traditional elites are rigid, and the distinctions by which they define themselves are absolute. If to be a member of the elite it is 'necessary' to be male, it is no use being female; if of a majority ethnic group, minorities need not apply.

But how relevant is this today? In Western European states, certainly, there is no formal barrier against any citizen becoming a member of parliament, a minister or even prime minister. But in practically all presidential states there is a constitutional requirement that the president must be a 'natural-born' citizen of the republic. So Madeleine Albright, President Clinton's Secretary of State, was debarred from succeeding him because she was born in Czechoslovakia and emigrated to the United States in 1948.

As this rather special case shows, it is not necessary to be able, even in the United States, to become president in order to be a member of the political elite. But to be a member of a political elite does not imply equal possibilities of access to all levels of it. The close relationship between Nixon and Henry Kissinger stemmed at least in part from the fact that Kissinger, having been born in Germany, could be appointed Secretary of State without danger to Nixon's own political position.

In some other countries the restrictions on access to the highest office are even more constraining. In Mexico, the president must not only be a natural-born citizen, but the offspring of natural-born citizens (Wolf-Philips 1968, p. 153). A similar restriction would have excluded Woodrow Wilson from becoming president of the United States, or Winston Churchill from being prime minister of the United Kingdom. And a whispering campaign in Peru persistently suggested that Alberto Fujimori, president 1990–2000, was in fact ineligible and had been born, not in Peru, as he claimed, but in Japan. Ironically, though this was not true, when he wrote his letter of resignation as president in a Japanese hotel, it turned out that though born in Peru he was registered in Japan as a Japanese citizen and Japan had no extradition treaty with Peru (*Daily Telegraph*, 21 November 2000).

Transitional elites are relatively flexible. These are groups which use acquired characteristics in their strategies of 'social closure' – excluding the non-elite. Such a characteristic *par excellence* is education. In both Britain and France, though in very different ways, the nature of the educational process is crucial to access to the higher reaches of political power. Religion is another characteristic which may be acquired; so too, historically, is ethnicity, for there is no biological basis for racial discrimination, and the interpretation of what constitutes a 'race' has varied historically so much that its role as a strategy of 'social closure' is shown very clearly. Other, perhaps even less definable criteria are often lumped together into a generalised notion of 'social class', based loosely on income, wealth or occupation. Again, there is no way of assuredly separating individuals into distinct groups by such criteria, partly because there is not meant to be. Lastly, occupation itself may serve as a criterion on its own, as in the case of the military profession. Flexibility here is limited to an extent depending on the degree of skill involved. An ancient Spartan would not have got far without being good at the arts of war, whatever the arts of war may be, and Athenian democracy placed a high premium on skill in rhetoric.

Two points about criteria for office in modern states are of particular importance. Many of them are interrelated, or may be interrelated, such that deficiency on one account may be made up for by proficiency on another. All of them tend in practice to be related to wealth, itself a measure of power resources. Wealth, status and political power can be traded off against one another, and inherited wealth, in particular, implies early advantages in education and training which predispose an individual to leadership. And, historically, two types or aspects of training have been of particular importance: military or legal.

At one time soldiers, perhaps, actually were the strongest members of society, though skill must always have been very important too. But the introduction of firearms has been a great leveller in this respect. In liberal democratic states the majority of politicians train as lawyers (Gerth and Mills 1946; Tapper 1976, p. 44). Both the law and teaching, being branches of the performing arts, are a good training for politics. In theory acting should be also, but Ronald Reagan was an exception in this respect. Not surprisingly, successful businessmen seldom want to take the cut in pay to become full-time politicians; hence those that do have often not proved particularly successful.

The views of political thinkers on elites can be categorised according to three criteria: whether they believe that they are inevitable or not; whether they believe they are desirable or not; and whether they think they are part of them themselves or not. Among those who considered they were inevitable were Pareto, who invented the word, and Michels, the sociologist who demonstrated that they were a feature of all types of organisations and not just of government (Michels 1959, p. 390). It was Pareto who regarded the ultimate determinant of political change as being the possibility of the '**circulation of elites**', that is to say, the replacement of a spent elite by a new one (Michels 1959, p. 378). But as we have already seen, this tells us little that we do not know already, particularly since the replacement of members of an elite will happen anyway through the ineluctable processes of mortality. And it is perhaps more rewarding to regard, as Michels does, elites as being in a perpetual state of competition, and to try to identify their characteristics more precisely.

The sort of questions that need to be asked before accepting the assumption of a ruling elite uncritically are as follows. Is there really just one ruling elite, or do different elites control different organs of government? Does the army, for example, come under the same sort of control as civilian organisations? Are there different answers for different regions? What do we mean by ruling elite? How many of the so-called elite actually rule, and how often can they expect to get their own way? These are difficult questions to which we may expect to get different answers from personal observation and from asking others in the society what they think, and we may well agree with Geraint Parry that some combination of the two methods alone can give any satisfactory answer for it is doubtful if the word elite will ever be anything more than a vague collective noun for the government of the day and its friends (Parry 1969, pp. 115, 139).

Summary

Political leadership enhances group syntality, making it easier to arrive at decisions. Individual qualities are only one element, however, the other three being the group, the task and the situation.

A permanent staff or bureaucracy is an essential part of all modern states. Administrative staff ideally are chosen for their special abilities and their collective role and input exercises a strong influence on outcomes. The French civil service offers a particularly cohesive model with a strong track record in guiding France's economic development. The system does however result in the creation of a self-conscious political elite, though the concept of an elite has proved difficult to apply in practice.

The comparative study of public administration has developed dramatically in the past sixty years and offers a wide range of important insights. The 'rational actor' model of the policy-making process is flawed; even if individual actors behave rationally, it does not follow that the process as a whole will be rational. Alternative models such as the 'organisational process' model and the 'governmental politics' model are needed to supplement our understanding of how government actually works, as well as in teasing out the complicated relationships between executive, legislature and interest group.

Legislatures vary a great deal both in their capacity to hold the administration to account and in their independent capacity to make decisions. The administration of developing countries is characterised by a range of problems stemming both from limited resources and from the social structures within which it has to operate.

Key Concepts

bureaucracy, a system of administration by paid officials chosen by merit and arranged in a hierarchy by which the higher officials supervise the work of the lower ones

Cabinet, in the UK a collective body of ministers (secretaries of state) forming the highest executive organ of government

circulation of elites, for Pareto, the replacement of a spent elite by a new one

conciliar system, a system of administration by a ruler in council

council, in a conciliar system, a group of people appointed to advise the chief executive

Key Concepts continued

and to act on his/her behalf in defined areas of responsibility under delegated powers

elite, in any society those who, together with the political leaders and the senior bureaucrats, monopolise a disproportionate share of political power

'governmental politics' model, often termed the 'bureaucratic politics' model, for Allison a model of the political system explaining political outcomes in terms of competition between individual actors in governmental positions following recognised institutional rules

office, each formal position held by a decision-maker, whether elective or appointive

'organisational process' model, for Allison, an interpretation of decision-making based on competing goals of organisations within government

Parkinson's Law, for C. Northcote Parkinson: 'Work expands to fill the time available for its completion'

power elite, for C. Wright Mills, the most powerful and influential people in American society, whether or not they know it or each other

prismatic society, for Riggs, a society characterised by a governmental system with incomplete functional separation of powers

'rational actor' model, for Allison, a pattern of decision-making characterised by total information and a search of all available alternatives

satisficing, the acceptance of the first routine that comes to hand that will handle the task in terms of the organisation's perceived goals at that moment

staff, a group of officials responsible for carrying out the will of a leader

syntality, the will to work together to perform the task in hand

transformativeness, for Polsby, the ability of a legislature to influence decisions and to bring about significant change

Sample Questions

Questions on decision-making will expect some knowledge of administrative theory, the ability to relate some or all of public opinion, interest groups, party interests etc. to a specific decision or set of decisions. In the comparative context, to concentrate on a single issue area where a range of information exists would be helpful. Alternatively, a question may expect the application of a range of theoretical ideas in a single-country context.

- 'Not what is to be done but how it is to be done is the main difficulty facing

politicians and administrators alike.' Comment.

- Why are policy and administration in developing countries frequently criticised as elitist, centralised and remote from people's real needs?

- Outline your preferred model of decision-making within British central government. Give reasons for your choice.

- Using recent examples, show how public opinion has affected a specific governmental decision in a country of your choice.

Further Reading

Beetham (1987) is an interesting and accessible introduction to bureaucracy. B. Guy Peters (1989) is thorough and covers a wide sweep in a genuinely comparative way. Page (1992) contains a well-argued critique of Weber (Gerth and Mills 1946). The relationship between bureaucracy and modernisation is discussed by Fainsod (1963). Other works not mentioned above which are useful include Pierre (1995).

Still an excellent, sound overall introduction to comparative public administration is Heady (1991). The flavour of Riggs (1964) can only really be fully appreciated in the original but the terminology is a bit of an acquired taste.

As a critical treatment of the policy process in general Ham and Hill (1993) is helpful.

Allison (1971) is still interesting both because it systematised concepts of decision-making which had already attained recognition by specialists such as March and Simon (1958) on the 'organisational process' model or Neustadt (1964) on 'governmental politics' and because its case study was controversial. On the concept of the elite see especially Parry (1969).

On political leadership Blondel (1987) and Edinger (1990) are both informative. Pareto's views on the 'circulation of elites' are expounded in Pareto (1965). Calvert (1987) is a comparative study of political succession with a European focus, and heads of government in Western Europe are discussed by G. Jones (1992).

PART FOUR System Maintenance
and Political Change

Maintaining the System

CHAPTER NINE

Learning Objectives

By the end of this chapter, the reader will be able:

- to define political stability;

- to tell how far governments can ensure that it is maintained;

- to identify what means governments use to ensure their own continuance and that of their regime.

Political Stability

Once in power, the major task of any government is to stay in power. At the same time, the maintenance of a stable government is the fundamental assurance of the political control of a ruling elite. Losing control of government means at the least that their power will be severely curtailed, at most that it will be lost for good. But maintenance of a government is only part of political control, since it can only operate effectively if the system of relationships around it is maintained also. For this reason the need of a government or regime to maintain itself is often referred to as '**system maintenance**' and the continuation of the existing state of affairs as '**political stability**'.

There is probably no term in political science that is less clear than 'political stability'. A stable political order should be one which is not easily adjusted, altered or destroyed. The problem begins with the metaphorical use of the term 'stable'. A book resting on a flat table is stable; unless a force acts on it, such as a human hand, it will not move. However, a government is not like a book and when a government has been in power for many years, it may in fact be very unstable. It all depends on whether or not it has been continuing to fulfil the expectations of its supporters. Political stability, therefore, is only the reasonable expectation that the existing order of things will be maintained for the foreseeable future.

Constant adjustment is the key to the survival of governments. In this respect the stability of a government or regime is more like the dynamic stability maintained by a bicycle as long as it continues to move forward. Provided that a government is sensitive to the need to do so, and has the necessary resources at its disposal, it will seek through **adaptive change** to forestall more serious challenges. For a regime, this means accepting changes of government. The experience of Spain, Iran or Paraguay suggests that when one government stays in power for a very long time – in these cases decades – this adaptive change does not take place and the regime itself is liable to collapse without notice.

This problem can also befall democracies, which is why Ben Barber argues so strongly that 'weak democracy' is not good enough; democrats must have the confidence to argue for 'strong democracy'. Strong democracy does not depend just on tacit consent or apathy, but on active commitment (Barber 1984), and in his celebrated metaphor 'bowling alone' Putnam (1995) has drawn attention to what he sees as a steady decline in community involvement which has accompanied a consistent decline in electoral turnout both in Western Europe and the United States and plumbed new depths in the USA in 2000 and the UK in 2001.

The term 'system maintenance' also conjures up a misleading picture of a rigid, static framework, like a historic house preserved from decay, but not capable of adaptation to meet new needs and circumstances. Yet the definition of the ruling elite (Chapter 8) is imprecise and vague simply because it is in a necessary state of constant change. The same is equally true of governments themselves. Certainly there may be few if any differences, as far as most citizens are concerned, between one government and the next, for the administrative structure around it changes more slowly than it does. But on the other hand no government, even a dictatorship, remains the same for very many years at a time. In the case of a very long-lasting regime, such as that of General Franco (1939–75) in Spain, the mere combination of ageing in office with the blockage of promotion for younger elements, may postpone change. However, this is not in itself sufficient to prevent change in the system overall, even during the ruler's lifetime, as has been demonstrated by the wholesale transformation of Spanish politics since 1975. The rapid moves towards a market economy in Eastern Europe since 1989 were preceded by limited reforms under Gorbachev's policy of *perestroika*, allowing the creation of co-operatives and permitting a limited amount of market activity. However, this period was too brief to change basic attitudes. Given that in a closed society with little or no access to outside sources of information three generations of Soviet citizens had been told that capitalists were conspirators who gouged, cheated and swindled everyone they met, it is hardly surprising that as soon as they got the chance to do so they did the same. Certainly the version of capitalism that has emerged in the Russian Federation since 1991 leaves a lot to be desired. It is now often called 'nomenklatura capitalism', from the fact that the big players are the members of the former Communist elite or nomen-klatura and the major player in the Russian economy is Gazprom ('the Gas Board').

Analytically, system maintenance requires four things. Power resource extraction involves a certain proportion of the power resources available to government being used to generate further resources. For this purpose governments maintain a national bank, a finance ministry, and a range of departments concerned with taxation (as noted in Chapter 5). Other resources will be used to control demands on the political system. The maintenance of governments is ensured in this way most easily by a judicious combination of rewards and sanctions, or, as Rosenthal calls them, 'punishments'. The thinking behind this is that 'a person's activity is dependent on the value of the rewards and punishments it is expected to produce and on the estimated probability that the rewards will be received and the punishments avoided' (U. Rosenthal 1978, p. 5). Indeed the absence of punishment may be its own reward: the carrot consists of the absence of the stick. **Input control** is backed in the last instance by the sanction of force (see Chapter 10). Governments try to avoid this by **interest arbitration** – the process by which the balance between different power blocs in society is maintained in such a way that challenges to the regime are minimised. Finally governments fund **political social-isation**, to ensure that as far as possible the citizenry are happy with their lot. Free pub-lic education is a good thing for individuals, but it is also a good thing for governments.

Rewards and Sanctions

Rewards are available both for members and would-be members of the elite, and no less significantly for potentially useful people who might otherwise be political opponents, who may be co-opted into the system. As well as co-option (co-optation), rewards include promotion, pensions and honours. Sanctions include demotion, dismissal, fines, banishment, imprisonment and even execution. There is a significant difference between the two. Rewards are wholly within the control of the government, provided always that they can extract the necessary power resources from the population to pay them. Sanctions, however, can only be freely used where their impact is wholly polit-ical, for the fear of citizens of the arbitrary use of power by a government is such that the use of the more extreme forms of sanction, without clear legal basis, will destabilise the social system.

Use of rewards and sanctions in this way is concerned specifically with the mainten-ance of the political system. The reasoning behind it is, of course, equally applicable to the government's relations with the public at large. System maintenance therefore also involves the use of both positive and negative sanctions on the social system as a whole, which have here been termed positive and negative interest arbitration, and this will be dealt with subsequently.

Maintenance of a government depends in the first instance on rewarding those within it, who form, as Machiavelli pointed out, the most dangerous rival claimants to political power (Machiavelli 1950, pp. 414–15). Making war on another state is a reward to some and a useful opportunity to punish others without fear of retribution. It is therefore useful for the coercion of reluctant supporters, as is the threat of it, as Hitler seems to have understood very well.

Rewards

Anticipation is the key to reward. The reward that one gets is seldom as good as the reward one thinks one is going to get, as every child has speedily found. Hence a well-organised, stable political system places great emphasis on an elaborate system of ranks, and promotion within it. This is not as easy as it sounds, as the higher offices are necessarily fewer in number than the lower ones, and fewest where they become most desirable. Perhaps the most efficient such structure, and certainly the longest lived, was that of the mandarinate in the Chinese Empire. All modern civil services are organised on much the same lines, with fixed rules of retirement and rotation in office (as with ambassadorships) to ensure the constant expectation of vacancies to be filled.

In the United States from the time of President Andrew Jackson (1829–37) civil service positions were filled with political appointees on the 'spoils system', which rewarded the supporters of the victorious political party with jobs. Even today the highest positions in the various departments continue to be filled by political appointees. This calls attention to the value of a career structure in political office, which is very conspicuous in the United States, where experience in a lower elective office is almost indispensable to be taken seriously as a candidate for a higher one. At first sight, this would seem to be quite independent of the wishes or needs of the government. But in practice the administration may also confer a period of appointive office, to make someone a possible candidate for a much higher post (Anderson 1968, pp. 474–5).

In Mexico rotation in elective office is guaranteed by a complete prohibition on re-election. Consequently, candidate office-holders alternate spells of elective and appointive office in a pattern in which, under the rule of the Institutional Revolutionary Party (PRI) from 1929 to 2000, service within the ruling party came to form the main criterion in political advancement (Grindle 1977, pp. 46–7; Needler 1990, pp. 81–2). An awkward by-product was that because all jobs had to be appointed anew with the change of president every six years, the system developed chronic and at times almost acute bureaucratic inertia, since it was much more dangerous to make the wrong decision than to make no decision at all.

The 'party-state' of the former Soviet Union was also characterised by terminal bureaucratic inertia. It was the inertia of the Brezhnev years that Gorbachev's campaign for *glasnost* and *perestroika* was designed to combat (Gorbachev 1996). To the end both formal governmental offices and posts in the party hierarchy were elaborately graded, allowing 'Kremlinologists' and journalists to play the fascinating game of assessing the relative standing of members of the praesidium by the places in which they stood on Lenin's tomb on May Day, and the order in which they were listed on the occasion of state visits (Barghoorn 1972, p. 1977). The corresponding process of assessment in

Washington, London, Brasília or New Delhi could only be a matter of rumour and gossip, though leaked information might well anticipate important changes in the composition of a future government.

Co-option (co-optation)

When a vacancy occurs in an appointive office, that vacancy has to be filled. Apart from promotion, this is also an opportunity for **co-option** (co-optation in the United States) – the bringing of new members into the political elite by appointing them to formal governmental positions. Co-option is the basic mechanism from which all other forms of choice have been derived (Calvert 1987). It serves four principal purposes, apart, of course, from its basic purpose of choosing new members of the elite to undertake specific tasks which need performing.

First, it can be used to reward supporters for their loyalty and so consolidate the power of the ruling group. The British Cabinet in this way habitually includes representatives of all major factions within the ruling party, and in fact it was Margaret Thatcher's policy of excluding those who thought differently from her that was in the end to lead to her downfall. In the United States system it was traditional before 1960 for a successful presidential candidate to appoint his defeated rivals of his own party to Cabinet posts. Though he did not wish to do this, Kennedy appointed Adlai Stevenson as ambassador to the United Nations and gave his job Cabinet status.

Secondly, therefore, co-option may be used to maintain an existing regime in power as far as possible unchanged despite the inevitable processes of ageing and mortality. This has two major disadvantages: any government left to its own devices tends to appoint safe, dull and uninteresting people who will not form a threat to government political control, and no one else can get a chance of access to power. This process is unlikely to be challenged as long as the senior leaders remain capable of discharging their duties, since there are few people who will take the risk of offending them. Those within government have got used to them and refuse to believe that they will ever go. Those outside console themselves with the thought that they cannot last for ever, and this is of course true.

An interesting feature of politics since 1945 has been the number of men who have been able to retain political power to an age far beyond that which would be permitted in most other occupations. Churchill in the UK, Franco in Spain (Matthews 1958), Salazar in Portugal (Figueiredo 1975), Adenauer in West Germany, de Gaulle in France (Werth 1965, p. 9), Tito in Yugoslavia (Auty 1970), Mao in China (Fitzgerald 1976), Brezhnev in the Soviet Union and Reagan in the United States, all remained in office long beyond the normal retiring age. An extreme example is Taiwan, where Chiang Kai-shek remained president until his death in 1975, surrounded by the people who had supported him at the time of his flight in 1949, on the assumption that they formed the legitimate government of something called the Republic of China. Since no by-elections could be held on the mainland, for obvious reasons, vacancies in its parliament as well as its government were filled by co-option (Lumley 1976, p. 63). Long periods of government of this kind are distrusted by many political observers on the grounds that the pressures for change that build up under them may prove when they are released to be uncontrollable.

Thirdly, co-option may, on the other hand, be used much more subtly to bring in and to advance young and active members of society who, from their political connections, charisma or ability, might otherwise come to form dangerous political opponents. Their talents, harnessed to the service of the government, can then be of positive value in ensuring that adaptability which enables a system to survive even serious crises. The example of Mexico has already been mentioned. France is another, where the institution of the *cabinet ministériel*, or small group of personal advisers surrounding a ministerial hopeful, enables young aspirants to gain experience in the inner circles of government before launching out on their own (Marceau 1980, p. 53). In the United States each presidential hopeful carries along a team of advisers. Some, as with the group from Arkansas surrounding President Clinton, will follow on to Washington as the key figures in setting up a new administration; others, as with George W. Bush, will be brought in from other jobs. Some of these 'president's men' have thus begun an independent political career, notably Clark Clifford, who began his career in the White House under Franklin Roosevelt (Anderson 1968, pp. 134ff.) and ended it in disgrace under indictment for involvement in the collapse of the Bank of Credit and Commerce International.

Lastly, subtly used, co-optation can be used to bring rival leaders of other parties into the governing circle. Again Roosevelt is an excellent example of a president who appointed political opponents, valuing the conflict of ideas and advice that they brought him. Other more recent presidents have systematically used the same device to disarm important sections of political opposition. Richard Nixon appointed Governor Connally, a Democrat from Texas, to his Cabinet, and Ronald Reagan appointed Jeane Kirkpatrick, then a Democrat, to the high-profile post of ambassador to the United Nations. The custom in many European states of creating a ruling coalition larger than is actually required to ensure a majority in the assembly, as in Italy under the 'Pentepartito' governments, is only an extension of the same idea (Gundle and Parker 1996).

Case Study | Wanted: Enforcer to Keep fox Cabinet in Line

Mexico's long-deprived political observers are in heaven. After decades of dour federal cabinets packed with straight-laced technocrats and docile yes-men, they at last have something to gossip about.

Seven months after Vicente Fox, Mexico's president, took office, the rumour mill is rife with stories of personality clashes, competing agendas and threatened resignations within the new cabinet.

How much of it is true is hard to say. What cannot be denied is the damage it has done to the credibility of the new president, already under fire for disappointing results after his historic defeat of the Institutional Revolutionary party, which ruled Mexico for 71 years.

'The cabinet is sending a clear message of discord and the only one it is hurting is the president,' says David Najera, political science professor at Mexico City's Universidad Iberoamericana.

In a bid to form a transition government, Mr Fox cobbled together a cabinet from all walks of life. The list includes candidates found by headhunters, party loyalists, hometown buddies and even his girlfriend, who was named presidential spokesperson.

The odd mix is a radical change from the clubby, close-knit cabinets of Mexico's one-party past, when elitist but subservient handpicked groups of pseudo-aristocrats willingly bent to the presidential will.

'Before, the cabinet members were all part of the same social class, went to the same schools together and lived in the same part of town,' says Denise Dresser, political science professor at Mexico's Itam University.

Case Study   Continued

In contrast, the new cabinet is an uneasy combination of frank-talking provincial politicians, upper-crust intellectuals and conservative churchgoers.

There is Carlos Abascal, labour minister and an ultra-right Roman Catholic who was recently upbraided for saying women's rightful place was in the home. Josefina Vazquez Mota, the social development minister, wrote a self-help book for women entitled *For God's Sake, Make Me a Widow*. Jorge Castaneda, minister of foreign affairs and a well-respected leftist academic, has a long list of books to his credit, including a biography of Che Guevara, the Argentine-born guerrilla and one of the leaders of the Cuban revolution.

The divergent backgrounds, particularly in Mexico, where social mixing remains minimal, have led to tensions, say analysts. The problems, in turn, have been aggravated by Mr Fox's seeming unwillingness to intervene and establish a clear set of priorities.

Unlike the previous three administrations, which were defined by economic objectives and led by respected economists, Mr Fox is 'the only president in the last 24 years who is not guided by typical International Monetary Fund policies', says Rogelio Ramirez de la O, economist with Ecanal, a Mexico City consultancy.

Instead, the field is open to a well-intentioned president who 'wants to change everything' and prefers to delegate responsibility, allowing each minister to 'do his own thing'. As a result, his ministers often seem to clash on policy. In the most obvious case, Mr Castaneda and Santiago Creel, the interior minister, publicly disagreed over the establishment of a 'Truth Commission' to review abuses of the former regime.

The two men are also rumoured to be at odds because they both have presidential aspirations. But they are not the only ones filling the gossip columns.

In recent weeks, reports that Francisco Gil, the finance minister, wants to resign have been making the rounds in Mexico and on Wall Street. The rumour, fed by unpopular budget cuts and a heavily criticised tax reform proposal, has put some market analysts on 'alert mode'.

The finance ministry has denied the reports. Some Wall Street analysts attribute the talk to an orchestrated campaign by investment managers to weaken the market and lower asset prices.

'People make a lot of money off these kinds of things,' said one analyst. 'It is kind of sleazy.'

No one, however, seems to question the havoc caused by Martha Sahagun, the former presidential spokesperson who quit her job last week to become the First Lady. After she was criticised for overstepping her bounds, publicly chastising cabinet ministers and issuing erroneous information, many urged the president: 'Marry her or fire her.'

By opting for the former, Mr Fox took an important step toward alleviating tensions and restructuring the cabinet, say analysts (although many are concerned that as the president's wife she will exercise even more power).

There have, however, been widespread calls for Mr Fox to find himself an enforcer to knock heads together. According to Ms Dresser, the dilemma underlines the need for a chief of staff-style leader to command the somewhat rudderless cabinet: 'Fox needs a consigliere, someone behind the scenes with real power to call people into compliance.'

Mr Castaneda is considered the most powerful member of the cabinet, regularly organising private dinners with the president and key people. However, the most widely talked about name for the position is Pedro Cerisola, the transport and communications minister and one of Mr Fox's former campaign managers.

Mr Cerisola's brass-tacks attitude and political neutrality would make him ideal for the post, analysts say. Mr Fox, however, is said to oppose the idea. In the meantime, the rumour mill will continue to grind away.

Source: *Financial Times*, 12 July 2001   **FT**

Sanctions

Down to the time of President Kennedy (1961), the American Eagle, which appears on the Great Seal of the United States holding an olive branch in one claw and a sheaf of arrows in the other, used to face towards the arrows. The president, feeling that this suggested aggressive intentions inappropriate to the modern world, had the eagle reversed to face the olive branch (Sorenson 1965, p. 517) – and the Vietnam War followed.

Obviously, there is no direct connection between these two events, but the story does symbolise the great importance attached in all ages to a government's ability to punish transgressors, in this case from outside. The ability to punish people who break the internal laws of a government is symbolised in the House of Representatives by two great reliefs, one on either side of the Speaker's chair, of the ancient Roman symbol of authority, the fasces, a bunch of sticks bound round an axe. Symbolically the rods are for beating people and the axe for cutting their heads off.

In modern governments the sanctions for internal opposition within the elite are seldom as drastic as this, and the power to punish is, in its more severe manifestation, reserved for criminals (negative interest arbitration). But the government does still use sanctions to retain control of the political process.

The simplest and most effective sanction for prominent figures is dismissal from office. In Britain in 1962 the prime minister, Harold Macmillan, dismissed seven members of his Cabinet in what came to be known as 'The Night of the Long Knives'. One of those dismissed, the foreign secretary, Selwyn Lloyd (later Speaker of the House of Commons), went simply because he seemed to be unpopular (*The Times*, 14 July 1962). In the United States, the Supreme Court has consistently held that though the president cannot appoint to many key posts without the advice and consent of the Senate he has the sole power to dismiss the people he has appointed. Thus President Nixon dismissed his acting attorney-general when he refused to carry out orders to dismiss the special prosecutor appointed to investigate the Watergate affair (*Congressional Quarterly Weekly Report*, 21, 43, 27 October 1973). The orders, which he had believed to be illegal, were carried out by the solicitor-general Robert Bork, who was later nominated for a place on the Supreme Court by Ronald Reagan, happily unsuccessfully. In the former Soviet Union Marshal Zhukov was dismissed from the Politburo in 1957 when it was feared he might be becoming too powerful. In Russia President Yeltsin dismissed a whole succession of prime ministers to demonstrate his power. In France President Mitterrand dismissed prime minister Michel Rocard in 1991 in spite of (or because of?) his apparent success – though by doing so he harmed his own political credibility (Gaffney and Milne 1997, p. 46). There is a great deal of power to sack in most political systems but of course a price may have to be paid.

Demotion, either real or symbolic, may be less severe in its consequences, but it is no less real. It can either take the physical form of transfer to a less significant office, or the symbolic one of exclusion from the centres of power and decision-making. No specific action is needed to qualify for such treatment. The failure to support sufficiently vocally or consistently the power of the decision-makers may in itself qualify for sanctions, though the possession of a strong independent power-base or other useful qualities may protect to some extent. In Britain under Margaret Thatcher Sir Geoffrey Howe was ostracised in this way, before being transferred to a job in which he had little or no interest.

Exclusion from prospective rewards may in itself be sufficient sanction. This is particularly the case where the ruling elite is rigid in its criteria for admission and can control access, as with the Broederbond in the South Africa apartheid state. Failure to be admitted to the 'club' of the powerful is not subject to appeal. But the position in society of a political opponent may be made absolutely untenable by being subject to mass denunciation and abuse, as was the case in China during the Cultural Revolution (Robinson 1969).

The treatment of suspected opponents in communist states was particularly disagreeable since the individuals subjected to such treatment, or, worse, to physical detention or molestation, had to secure permission from the state to leave the country, and such permission was often denied, evidently in the belief that a desire to leave the country would be a bad advertisement for the country they left behind. Fidel Castro, tried for insurrection in 1953, was released under amnesty by Fulgencio Batista in 1955, went into exile, and returned to overthrow the government that had given him clemency. Castro did not repeat his predecessor's mistake. When his old friend Huber Matos was arrested for expressing opposition, he was sentenced to twenty-five years in prison and made to serve every minute of his sentence. The Berlin Wall stood until 1989 as a memorial to the fact that, prosperous as life might have been in East Germany compared to other communist states, politically it was so restrictive that thousands were willing to risk death to escape from it, and 217 were actually killed in the attempt. However, such restrictions are not confined to communist states. In early 2001, Aung San Suu Kyi remained under house arrest in Myanmar (formerly Burma), despite the fact that as leader of the opposition she successfully won a democratic election organised by the military regime which is still holding her captive.

Only towards the end of the Brezhnev period did the leaders of the former Soviet Union show signs of realising that banishment may have its uses. By releasing Alexander Solzhenitsyn from house arrest, allowing him to go into exile in the United States, they succeeded in calming opinion abroad while removing the embarrassment at home. And at the other end of the scale of tolerance, the practice of voluntary or forced exile as a treatment for political opponents is so much part of the Latin American tradition that it has given rise to important initiatives to recognise the right of political asylum in international law. Many Latin American politicians spend a noticeable proportion of their lives in exile. Victor Raúl Haya de la Torre of Peru founded its most important political party, APRA, while in exile in Mexico. Having during one dictatorship spent six years in the Colombian embassy in Lima (Alexander 1973, pp. 13–14), he was elected president in 1962 but a military coup deprived him of victory. He died in 1980 as president of the Constitutional Convention which helped return Peru to democratic government. In a different way, Hugo Banzer of Bolivia, overthrown in a military coup and retired from direct involvement in politics by diplomatic exile as Bolivian ambassador to Argentina (*Annual Register*, 1978, p. 74), later returned to Bolivian politics as a successful leader of a right-wing party and was re-elected president in 1999. The importance of political exiles in other parts of the world, however, is no less. Ex-King Norodom Sihanouk of Cambodia, who gave up his throne to act as prime minister, fled from the Khmers Rouges to exile in China, only to be returned by international agreement to the position of head of state in a coalition government. Even more dramatically, Ayatollah Khomeini returned from exile in France in 1978 to act as focus for the Iranian Revolution of 1979 which overthrew the Shah and led in time to the Islamic Republic of which he became symbolic head.

Case Study   Dissent Grows Within Tokyo Cabinet Team

Dissent within the Japanese cabinet is growing, just three months after Junichiro Koizumi, prime minister, formed his select team and less than a week after a key election victory.

Relations between the prime minister and Makiko Tanaka, the foreign minister, deteriorated sharply yesterday after Mrs Tanaka refused to obey an order from Mr Koizumi to remove a key diplomat.

Mrs Tanaka eventually agreed to the prime minister's orders but only after a day of frantic telephone calls during which Yasuo Fukuda, chief cabinet secretary, said Mrs Tanaka risked being fired if she disobeyed Mr Koizumi.

'This is the first sign of the erosion of the popularity of the cabinet. It is starting to look as if the cabinet is poorly prepared for their task,' said Shigenori Okazaki, political analyst at UBS Warburg.

In addition, Masajuro Shiokawa, the finance minister, and Heizo Takenaka, the economics minister, are having difficulty agreeing over the compilation of next year's budget, which must be set by next week.

Relations between Mr Takenaka and Hakuo Yanagisawa, the financial affairs minister, are also strained following differences of opinion over proposals for the disposal of banks' bad debts.

The most serious rift is between Mr Koizumi and Mrs Tanaka, who was told by the prime minister to remove Shunji Yanai, Japan's ambassador to the US, but refused to obey his order.

Mrs Tanaka said she wanted to keep Mr Yanai in place but Mr Koizumi was concerned that keeping him might indicate his administration was not serious about reforming the foreign ministry.

Relations between the two had already deteriorated after Mrs Tanaka was convinced by Chinese and South Korean diplomats at a recent meeting in Vietnam to ask Mr Koizumi to cancel a visit to a controversial war shrine.

Mr Okazaki pointed out that Mr Koizumi would be playing with fire if he chose to oppose Mrs Tanaka publicly, saying he estimated about half of the prime minister's popularity was attributable to the foreign minister.

Mrs Tanaka has earned high popularity ratings because of her adversarial style and her desire to tackle entrenched interests inside the powerful but scandal-tainted Ministry of Foreign Affairs.

Meanwhile, Mr Shiokawa appears determined to restore the finance ministry's control of the compilation of Japan's budget while Mr Takenaka, economics minister, is seeking to wrest some control away from the ministry.

Source: *Financial Times*, 3 August 2001

Though the arrest, detention and execution of political figures is all too common, the government cannot necessarily act wholly arbitrarily, though it has much more freedom to do so if it has first assumed emergency powers. Arrests in themselves may have no custodial intent, but merely be used to break up foci of political activity. Since, though, they are often used as an opportunity to beat up or torture captives regarded as opponents of the regime, their mere possibility acts as a deterrent to political opposition. Detention of political opponents for longer periods is in any case so commonplace that it was a feature of decolonisation by Britain in places as far apart as India (Nehru), Kenya (Kenyatta) and Cyprus (Makarios). Detention differs from imprisonment in being an arbitrary act of administration rather than a judicial procedure, but the conditions and consequences need not be any different.

Execution of political opponents is seldom practised openly by established governments for fear of international repercussions. Covert and disguised examples are, unhappily, far from rare. Since the restoration of democratic government in Chile the bodies have been located of many of the hundreds killed by military or police after the coup of 1973, as earlier of many of the more than 9,000 killed in the 'dirty war' in Argentina (1976–79). There are many reports of executions from Iran after 1979 following at best only a nominal trial by the religious authorities, though similar reports from Iraq under the dictatorship of Saddam Hussein were long ignored by the Western powers. In Africa thousands died under the dictatorship of Macias Nguema in Equatorial Guinea, while under his first government, Jerry Rawlings of Ghana had three of his predecessors as head of state and head of government shot on the beach as an example to others. In Guatemala and El Salvador in Central America ruling elites have used 'death squads' closely linked to the armed services to assassinate political opponents. A Serbian armed secret society ('the Black Hand') which had killed King Alexander and Queen Draga of Serbia in June 1903 (Goodspeed 1962, pp. 24–5) was responsible for the assassination of the Archduke Franz Ferdinand in Sarajevo which sparked off the First World War. Serbian irregulars throughout the 1990s engaged in 'ethnic cleansing' of Croats and Muslims in the secessionist states of Croatia and Bosnia-Herzegovina as well as of ethnic Hungarians in the Vojvodina. Such activities, however, go well beyond the bounds of morality, to say nothing of the relatively limited needs of system maintenance.

Adaptive Change

Interest arbitration is basically the art of knowing when to engineer or to permit adaptive change. Adaptive change may, and does, occur constitutionally and as a matter of course, through a government responding to the demands made upon it, the administrative apparatus functioning efficiently to meet these demands, and the courts impartially deciding the law, regulating disputes and averting the development of potential trouble in the social system. In practice, the main effect of such institutions is felt indirectly, through the process of political socialisation, which ensures that the great majority of people regard the system as more or less legitimate.

Adaptive change can take the form of major constitutional change. The introduction of devolution in the UK, or of federalism in Belgium, shows that far-reaching change of this kind is possible under favourable circumstances: in Britain because the government had a substantial majority in Parliament and in Belgium because the parties were agreed that all other measures had been tried and had failed. For parliamentary systems, the competition between parties which can prevent constitutional change can bring important lesser changes, such as the reform of local government in France in the early 1980s.

We have already noted that a major problem for governments in seeking adaptive change is the existence of social cleavages (Chapter 2). Bringing different interests into the process of decision-making, as in consociational democratic systems, enables this problem to be minimised, though only as long as everyone gets enough out of the system to wish to maintain it. Underlying social cleavages bring structural problems, in particular a series of weak coalition governments (Chapter 7), which may well have difficulties delivering on any of their promises.

What happens, then, when people become increasingly disillusioned with the system as a whole and there is no obvious way of tackling the problem? There is evidence that this has happened in the last decades of the twentieth century in most liberal democracies and three main explanations have been advanced as to why this should be so.

1. One builds on the Marxist theory of Milovan Djilas to attach disproportionate influence to a 'new class' of 'knowledge workers' who have difficulty reconciling their relative administrative autonomy with their restricted place in the economy. People like doctors, lawyers, teachers and social workers are independent and articulate but with very few exceptions they are no longer well paid.

2. A second sees the wider impact of the trend towards 'post-industrial society' as creating tensions between the goal of affluence and the reality of an economy more than ever dependent on the sale of services. The wealth of the industrial revolution was based on the manufacture of goods. Although insurance policies and mortgages are commonly referred to as 'products', they have in fact no real existence, unlike the articles manufactured by the 'old economy', and as the recent collapse in the shares of the 'dot.com' companies has shown, they have no intrinsic value either. So how will these countries continue to change raw materials into wealth by the application of energy?

3. A third focuses on the resulting political changes: a decline in ideological commitment, party dealignment and the emergence of **neocorporatism**. Neocorporatism is a monopolised and centralised system of interest organisation within liberal democracies, in which the state formally designates and recognises only a limited number of interest groups (Schmitter 1970). Certainly in the past thirty years there has been a striking decline in party membership in most industrialised countries and this has been accompanied by a steady decline in turnout at elections. But there is no evidence that partisan dealignment has in fact increased the potential for protest. The impact of neoliberalism, leading to the liberalisation of economies, the deregulation of business activity and the privatisation of state enterprises, has been accompanied by the exclusion of trade unions from the decision-making process and the increased prominence of a moneyed elite. However, neocorporatism has had a greater effect on the actual expression of protest than the willingness to engage in it (Wallace and Jenkins 1995).

Political Socialisation

In 1969, political socialisation was regarded as a relatively new field of political inquiry (Hyman 1969), but its concerns are central to both disciplines. Since the time of Karl Marx and Alexis de Tocqueville scholars have studied the complex relationship between attitudes to authority and their relationship to class stucture and political institutions. Both the tendency to accept things as they are and the process of control by the state begin with the socialisation of youth. Social stability depends on how far young people are successfully convinced that it is better to keep the existing order of things, either because they do not want change or because they are able to obtain the changes they want within the system as it is.

The family is the earliest vehicle of socialisation, though from an early age the influence of the child's peer group modifies its effects. The family is the most effective agency in transmitting the traditional values of the society embodied in stories, proverbs, legends and nursery rhymes. These can be translated into norms which people expect to obey as a matter of social custom. In turn such norms are often enshrined in specific rules of behaviour. Collectively values, norms and rules form the political culture of a given society and shared value systems are the foundation of social and hence political stability.

It is interesting and significant how far the material for early socialisation differs between states, forming the basis of nationalism and other value systems in the process. As between Britain and the United States, there is a shared basis of language and legend, and many of the basic social virtues are perhaps not so very different. Both societies tend to undervalue intellectual achievement as compared with, for example, French, German or Japanese society. However, the US system tends to place a much higher value on social conformity and 'getting along' than the British. The US self-image of a tough frontier society which has 'made good' has however considerable influence throughout the rest of the world, through the agency of Hollywood, and the American child seems to be exposed to a diet of cartoons and stories in which a high level of personal violence is seen as normal if not indeed amusing. At the same time the police hold a very low esteem in the American community, and there is a high emphasis on force as a means of settling disputes in the folk mythology of its members. Both are replicated in the influence of the peer group.

Political socialisation not only involves the inculcation of certain values, more or less unconsciously, but also the code by which aggressive behaviour is ritualised and sublimated. The more elaborate the ritualisation, the more the members of the society can be incorporated into it, and the less likely force becomes in actual fact. The emphasis placed by neoliberalism on 'possessive individualism' has been accompanied throughout Europe in a rise in crime levels, indicating a degree of breakdown in the authority of the state and society. 'Possessive individualism', by focusing attention on the success of others, also accentuates social cleavages. Stable societies, on the other hand, tend to be those in which social cleavages are either relatively faint or occur at different points in the social fabric (Rae and Taylor 1970).

The educational system is the major vehicle by which the state can influence the socialisation process at a stage early enough to make some difference. It has been understood since ancient times that a democratic society must educate its citizens in the ways of democracy and since the late nineteenth century the state has gradually taken over responsibility for ensuring at least an elementary level of education for all citizens. But even within liberal-democratic states there are considerable differences in emphasis both in the way things are taught and in the unconscious attitudes that accompany them:

> While, for example, Britain is known for deference, Germany for regimentation and authoritarianism, and the United States for the acceptance of self-chosen authority, France is not normally perceived as fitting neatly into any single category of authority relations. To some, the French are individualists opposed to all forms of authority; but to others, the French are seekers of authority and even authoritarianism.
> (Schonfeld 1976, p. 7)

It seems obvious that there must be some linkage between different kinds and levels of authority patterns (Eckstein 1973). In *The bureaucratic phenomenon*, the French sociologist Michel Crozier confirmed this to be true in his study of two government-owned organisations (Crozier 1964). The French school system has long been distinguished both by its uniformity and by the extent of its elitism. French students learn distinct modes of relating to authority and absorb their 'political' content, above all in secondary school where authority relations become dispersed and 'impersonal'. It appears that secondary school experience plays a major role in moulding French citizens' attitudes to authority both in higher education and in national politics, and Schonfeld concludes that France is peopled by fragmented individuals who both need and fear authority and Frenchmen are particularly likely to join occupationally related voluntary associations (Schonfeld 1976, p. 167).

Reforms in the 1980s, however, loosened the control of Paris over the curriculum at just the same time as in Britain increasingly rigorous controls were being introduced by a powerful central government determined to impose standardisation. Since 1871, the British system of education had two aims: to train people for work and to educate citizens so that popular government could work properly. However, the latter aim was never made explicit and the technical schools envisaged by the 1944 Education Act were not built: 'British schools have been noteworthy for both their lack of explicit political training and their failings in the field of technical education' (Tapper 1976, p. 43). The educational 'reforms' of 1987 moreover specifically banned from the curriculum anything in the nature of civic education. And the way in which the curriculum was constructed was by competition between interest groups, with the result that the curriculum was hopelessly overloaded and applied science and 'minority' languages lost out.

Germany, on the other hand, has been noteworthy for its emphasis on technical education and this is invariably cited as an important factor in the country's industrial success (though not, it appears, in the former GDR). However, in the Bundesrepublik, under collaborative federalism, education is primarily a matter for state (*Land*) governments. The *Länder* accordingly compete with one another to offer a high-quality education which lays great emphasis on practical skills. The educational system of Japan, which is modelled on the old Prussian system, is highly elitist and has a strong technical element.

In the United States, control of the curriculum is a matter for the local community and the emphasis is less on education as an instrument of social control and more on its role in widening personal development and promoting social mobility. From a political point of view, the structure of American education is 'universal and unitary' (Tapper 1976, p. 47) since most people complete secondary education within the public school system. Primary education in the USA lays considerable emphasis on awareness of one's democratic rights and obligations. However, in practice civics education has been criticised on the one hand as bland and formalistic and on the other as being on the high end of nationalistic content. At the same time, success and failure are personalised, which deflects attention and therefore criticism away from institutional failings.

A major contrast between Britain on the one hand and the United States and France on the other is in the formal role of religion, though there can be little doubt that in each case religious belief has tended on the whole to be a stabilising and indeed conservative force. In England, with its established (official) Church, religious instruction has for many years been one of the only two subjects required by law to be taught to all children (the other is physical education). But in the United States the Constitution prohibits the teaching of religion in public schools, while in France, as the Republic of 1875 was actively anti-clerical, the law bans even the wearing with school uniform of articles showing one's religious affiliation.

In Ireland the Catholic Church has a special place and the Christian Brothers have been foremost in establishing and maintaining Church schools which perhaps unconsciously have also instilled a sense of super-patriotism. Freedom of religious belief is a constitutional right, however, and the first president of Ireland was a Protestant. In Northern Ireland social cleavages all lie along the fault-line between the two communities and two quite separate systems of schools inculcate sharply different views of what the world is all about. Even then, as the case of Belgium and the Netherlands shows, such societies can develop stable democratic institutions, but in Northern Ireland, with its 'zero-sum' model of society, sadly, this has not been allowed to happen.

New social movements

A key role in maintaining political stability in liberal democracies, therefore, is played by intermediate groups. It is they who form the framework of civil society, the maintenance of which is the assurance of the continuation of the democratic order. The term **'new social movements'** (NSMs) can be conveniently defined as 'protest groups that challenged traditional politics and made identity a key factor in political mobilization' from the 1960s onwards (Woodward 2000, p. 34). The common feature is that although they originated from a sense of oppression, they sought to redefine their own identity in positive terms. Examples include the women's movement, the peace movement and the environmental movement, all of which had a global impact. Giddens (1991) and Beck (1992) have argued that these movements stemmed from changed perceptions of the way in which the world is organised. On the one hand, people had developed a growing sense of insecurity and a consequent desire to avoid risk. On the other, they were less and less willing to trust experts and even to apportion blame and hold them responsible for the world's problems. So they were more inclined than previously to try to work out their own view of the world, a process helped, of course, by the spread of universal primary education and the impact of globalisation as experienced through the transnational media, which transmit and magnify the message of protesters.

Chance events affect outcomes also. The nuclear disasters of Three Mile Island in the USA and Chernobyl in the former Soviet Union (now Ukraine) halted civil nuclear power programmes throughout the world. But they would not have done so had popular unrest not first reached the point that governments considered it a waste of time to try to continue with their nuclear policies.

Some NSMs, such as the civil rights movement for blacks in the USA, or gay and lesbian rights movements, even challenged traditional concepts of identity. However, in these cases their grievance lay specifically with the laws and power structure of the nation-state. Their political action therefore was constrained by state boundaries, even though it might be emulated a long way away. Thus themes of the US civil rights movement were taken up in a very different political context in Northern Ireland. But in Islamic countries gay rights not only failed to gain acceptability but led to a fundamentalist backlash, including the adoption of Shari'a law (the legal precepts of the Koran), under which homosexuality is punishable by death.

NSMs in liberal democracies frequently rejected some if not all of the traditional assumptions of liberal democratic politics. Animal rights activists were prepared to use violence against individual human beings and to bomb institutions even though this might result in injury to humans (who were not classified by them as animals). Anti-abortionists have done the same. Peace activists were prepared to disrupt military manoeuvres and even to sabotage military aircraft. Environmentalists tried to halt environmental destruction by hugging, as in India, or chaining themselves, as in Canada, to trees; their greater awareness of the interconnectedness of the world economic system led to attempts to outflank the power structure by buying up environmentally sensitive sites or organising consumer boycotts. However, at the same time pressure was brought to bear on local authorities to use political power to halt development, reduce waste and encourage individual and group recycling initiatives.

These developments, in short, formed part of globalisation, in that they challenged that traditional division between international relations and comparative politics, which few specialists on either side would now wish to maintain. Environmentalists were urged by the Brundtland Report to 'think globally, act locally' (World Commission on Environment and Development 1987). In Germany, national anxiety was focused by the death of trees as a result of 'acid rain', and gave a strong impetus to moves for recycling. But the smoke and exhaust fumes which were believed to cause the phenomenon started life much further West, in the United Kingdom, and in turn emissions from German industry drifted east over Russia.

It has to be said, however, that the weak point of most new social movements has been securing political action. Getting action means first building a coalition that has an interest in changing the status quo. The defenders of the status quo have a much easier task. They only have to ensure that a successful coalition does not form. This can be done by selective inducements to a small group, by the introduction of additional issues, and, in the case of environmental questions, by arguing that action should wait upon scientific proof, so that nothing gets done. 'Green' movements have secured some electoral success (though not, interestingly enough, in France). However, they got off to a poor start in Germany on account of their suspicion of all forms of leadership, subsequently gaining power only when prepared to accept the rules of German politics and enter into coalition at *Land* level (Scharf 1994, pp. 3–5).

What happens, then, if groups become so alienated that they resort to violence? Anomic interest groups, defined by Almond as 'spontaneous irruptions from the society into the polity' (Almond in Almond and Coleman 1960, p. 34), have already been mentioned in Chapter 6. But anomic interest groupings, considered as politically active entities, are not in fact distinct from non-associational, institutional and associational groups. Some (demonstrations) are only actions performed by established groups and the rest (riots, insurgency) can be regarded as a special type of associational group – a temporary one. There are some that are institutional, and there are some that are non-associational as well, so that it might, for some purposes, be more convenient to think of anomic interest groupings as a completely separate category of political action (Calvert 1967).

Anomic groups, in short, are ones in which protest escapes from the normal channels of discussion because they are not yet institutionalised (see also Chapter 11). Anomic interest group activity is generally regarded as an indicator of widespread alienation from the existing system and so of serious structural problems in a society which could in turn lead to significant political change (see Table 6.1, p. 153). Globalisation, where it reduces the number of options open to a group and threatens its economic existence, creates a focus for hostility and is likely to generate protest. Neocorporatism is a strategy to try to resist this sort of impact from world markets and is reasonably successful in doing so, at least when the economy is not performing well. The rational choice argument that protest is simply a response to short-term economic performance has not been supported by empirical research (Nollert 1995).

Protest and Ungovernability

However complex modern states are, they are made up of very simple assemblages of horizontal and vertical links, replicating the tribe and band of primitive times. It is easy to make fun of this idea, for the notion of modern man as an ape in spaceman's clothing is richly comic. But it is, nonetheless, uncomfortably true.

It follows that a crisis which leads to the replacement or mutation of a relatively small number of links in the system by which interests are balanced, amounts to a fundamental change in the system as a whole. Such crises are, naturally, likely to arise in certain well-defined circumstances. Five such possibilities were identified by Binder *et al.* (1971): identification, legitimation, penetration, distribution and participation. They may, of course, occur in conjunction with one another.

- **Identification:** people may cease to identify themselves with the ruling order and seek a separate identity, as in former Yugoslavia after 1991.
- **Legitimation:** people may come to question whether the government is legitimate and its efforts to relegitimate itself may be unsuccessful, as in the Philippines in 2001, or even counter-productive, as in Iran after 1973. Habermas (1976) argued that a specific form of this problem would afflict 'late capitalism' but so far there is only limited evidence that this is correct.
- **Penetration:** foreign influence, such as the 'Cocacolonisation' of Europe by the USA after 1945, can result in the government being viewed as excessively affected by foreign influences.
- **Distribution:** people may feel excluded from the material rewards distributed by government, as in Nicaragua after the Managua earthquake of 1973.
- **Participation:** people may feel excluded from political power by being denied the right to participate effectively in the political process, as in South Africa after 1948.

Regardless of the means employed for the regulation or suppression of force in general, it is of course inevitable in human societies that there will also be some sort of unregulated or unsuppressed minimum. This minimum is here referred to as 'violence'. The definition of violence as the unregulated use of force is normal, though in popular usage force and violence may be – and often are – considered as interchangeable terms. Behind protest lurks the spectre of ungovernability, the possibility that protest organisations will not only employ violence but that in rejecting the system as a whole they will actually choose this as their preferred strategy.

In liberal democracies, violence in society is controlled through the use of the legal system. But even there behind the legitimate authority of the government lies a very wide range of powers to control and to coerce, all backed by the sanction of force (see *inter alia* Hillyard and Percy-Smith 1988; Hewitt 1982). More or less prominently displayed according to the nature of the system, the resources available to government include as a matter of course a substantial army, an extensive police system, and some kind of paramilitary reserve or militia that can be called upon in emergencies.

The role of these instruments will be discussed in detail in Chapter 10.

The Collapse of Constitutional Government

If, as Diamond (1999) argues, we are already entering upon a third 'reverse wave' of democratisation, a number of existing states can be expected to forsake liberal democracy for some form of authoritarianism. The visible signs of this will be clear enough, but they will not be the same in all cases. The differences between parliamentary and presidential systems extend to the circumstances in which they cease to be accepted as functioning liberal democracies, or are so changed that they are no longer recognisable.

Parliamentary systems fail or mutate when the collective responsibility of the executive collapses. The problem with an executive that sits in parliament and is continuously responsible to parliament is that, whether for psychological, social or political reasons, it finds it difficult to withstand the pretensions of the assembly, which are, after all, embodied in the constitution of the state, unless it can count on the collective loyalty of its members. This is possibly the only good argument against coalition government, namely that if people rush from Cabinet meetings to give press conferences saying they think their colleagues are swine, in a very short space of time the system ceases to work, because everyone is getting so cross with one another. It is necessary, therefore, if the very close and intimate interrelationship of the executive and the assembly is to continue, for the executive to remain collective. If one person becomes paramount, then the hostility of the assembly and of others becomes focused upon that one person, and he or she, in turn, is tempted to assume exceptional powers and even to rule as a dictator.

The tendency for the executive to assume additional powers has been a feature of those governments that have inherited the parliamentary system from a colonial country. States with parliamentary systems such as France and Britain that had colonies early in the nineteenth century have tended to implant parliamentarianism in them, and very successfully so in Australia, the Bahamas, Barbados, Canada, India, Jamaica and New Zealand. In these states there has been relatively little tendency to move away from it, and in Pakistan and Sri Lanka there has recently been a significant desire to move back to the parliamentary system.

But a great many of the French and British colonies were acquired with great haste near the end of the nineteenth century, and the social systems, structures and decision-making processes of those states were subordinated without actually being removed. In other words, there is continuity between pre-colonial and post-colonial times, because the intervening period of colonial organisation has been relatively short. Furthermore, in protectorates such as Malaysia or Morocco, by definition, the existing social structure was left largely untouched and rule was indirect, leaving the existing decision-making mechanism substantially intact (Milne 1967, pp. 14–16). The tendency in many, but not all of these states has been away from parliamentarism, because it has been felt uncongenial in view of the colonial associations it holds. The very natural, if perhaps misplaced, desire to get back to the state of affairs as it was before colonisation began, coupled with the habit of accepting authoritarian decisions engendered by the very nature of colonial rule, make the parliamentary system with its compromises temporarily unattractive. Faced with the burdens of development, the new executive is inclined to envy the apparent freedom of action of the presidential system and to urge its adoption, as in Ghana (Afrifa 1966) and Nigeria, Zaire, Angola and Mozambique.

This is a reasonable, predictable and understandable development. It was to be expected that a new compromise would have to be reached in new states. What is improbable is that the presidential compromise, as at present understood, is going to last for a very long time. It necessarily involves the overt conflict of interests in public, and that seems, on the face of it, very unlikely beyond the next ten or twenty years.

Parliamentary systems cease to exist in any meaningful sense when one of three things happens:

1. When the head of state assumes power. In Hitler's Germany with the Enabling Act in 1933, or France at Vichy with Pétain in 1940 (Carsten 1967, pp. 152–5), parliament yielded all its powers to the head of state and ceased to function. To secure such a result intimidation may be and in the first case was actually used, as also in the case of Mussolini's so-called March on Rome in 1922. And, as in Czechoslovakia in 1948, the threat may be provided by foreign troops.
2. When the assembly is dissolved. Rulers can simply physically close the doors of parliament, barricade them out, refuse to let the assembly meet. This does not always have the desired effect; in France in 1789 the delegates went off to a nearby tennis court and constituted themselves as a National Assembly.
3. When elections are not wholly 'free' and the choice of the assembly is controlled by the executive (Seton-Watson 1956, pp. 167–71). It is true, to some extent, that all choices for the assembly are always controlled by something. The very existence of political parties in their role of interest aggregation mechanism in most societies means that there is a degree of control of choice of the assembly. The only remedy against this, the pluralists would argue, is to found more political parties. But the control of the process of choice by the executive necessarily reduces the possibility of the parliamentary system of compromise functioning until it disappears altogether. Examples here might be the Falange in Spain after 1939 on the one hand (Matthews 1958, pp. 76–7), and in Eastern Europe before 1989 Czechoslovakia with its National Front, the former German Democratic Republic with the Workers Unity Front (SED), Bulgaria with the Fatherland Front, and Poland with the United Workers Party, combining the PDR and the PPS.

Presidential systems collapse more easily than parliamentary systems. They are vulnerable to the disturbance of the delicate balance between executive and legislature, and this happens most easily when collective responsibility of the assembly weakens. In the clash between a single presidency and a multiple congress, if the congress fails to function as an efficient counter-balancing unit, then, necessarily, the system fails to work properly. And it ceases to work at all when one of three things happen.

1. The system may evolve into what with the Venezuelan Valenilla Lanz (1919) can be called 'democratic Caesarism'. In this form of government the state continues to be ruled by a president, and regular elections may even be held, but the system is wholly dominated by the executive power through abdication of power by the legislature, either voluntarily or involuntarily, as has historically frequently been the case in the Latin American republics and is today in, for example, Iraq. So the democratic Caesar is the ruler of the presidential state, and the system is characterised by 'omnipotent

executive power and a subservient legislature' (Stokes 1959, pp. 302, 385). The reason is usually that the congress lacks a real basis of independent support, and so simply does not have enough political 'clout' to counter-balance the force of the presidency. The presidency can deliver all the possible goods, and as long as it can continue to deliver them there is no role for congress; congress merely signs blank cheques in advance by approving the presidential budget, and endorses them afterwards by approving the expenditure. A good test of this is the regular, unopposed passage of supplementary estimates for expenditure already incurred, a feature of the Mexican Congress under its one-party system.

2. The military assume political power, as in Chile in 1973 or in Argentina in 1976. Then clearly the presidential state does not really exist any more because the executive is not elected. In such circumstances Argentines speak of '*de facto*' presidents, though the courts continue to give legality to their decrees and to treat their actions as legitimate (Calvert and Calvert 1989; di Tella 1983, pp. 199–200). However, in 1992 when President Fujimori of Peru proclaimed a state of emergency and tried to dissolve Congress, the majority of deputies met in a secret location, deposed him and proclaimed the senior vice president as president in his place, though without much effect.

3. The executive controls the choice of the assembly. Means of coercion at his or her disposal may consist either of the armed forces, or of another personal armed force as with the formidable and much feared Tontons Macoutes in Haiti under the elder Duvalier. Alternatively choice may be in the hands of a ruling party, which can make use of the coercive power of the state to back up its decisions, though in practice these are unlikely to be challenged.

Personalism, patrimonialism, clientelism

Criticism of emerging states which maintain something less than fully fledged liberal democracy, or which fail to guarantee civil rights effectively, focuses on three characteristics: personalism, patrimonialism and clientelism. The trouble is that even consolidated liberal democracies may suffer from each of the phenomena in some degree.

Personalism represents one means to bridge the gap between state and society. It involves the use of charismatic authority (cf. Weber) to reinforce the authority of state or government, but not just the most spectacular form of charismatic authority.

Charisma refers to the possession by the leader of outstanding personal qualities recognised as such by others. Such leaders come to be the subject of a 'personality cult' which may take extravagant forms, for example Mao Zedong was hailed as a prophet, Mustafa Kemal as 'Father of the Turks' (Atatürk), and Nkrumah as 'the Saviour, Redeemer and Messiah'.

Patrimonialism (or for Clapham 1982, p. 48 'neo-patrimonialism'), on the other hand, refers to the use of traditional authority to reinforce the formal structure of the state. An outstanding example has been Pakistan since independence. Some 80 per cent of leading politicians in Pakistan, including the Bhuttos, come from the old aristocracy. The families own substantial estates and have quasi-feudal relations with those who live in the parliamentary constituencies which form the basis of the 'modern' claim to political power.

In Africa, patrimonialism is often referred to as tribalism. Tribal links and customs are ingrained in the structure of society and tribal links can and do override formal legal-rational relationships.

Clientelism. Patronage is a loose word which covers not only appointment to jobs of office-seekers, but also appointments on their behalf which act to strengthen their political position or to reward their family, friends or supporters, who are bound together in a relationship commonly called clientelism. Such appointments can be embarrassing, as when Carlos Menem of Argentina appointed to office a number of relatives of his wife, and then, after an all-too public estrangement from her, found that her sister, Amira Yoma, his appointments secretary, had been charged by the Spanish police for complicity in drug smuggling. In neighbouring Brazil, President Collor, on the eve of presiding over the Earth Summit at Rio, was accused of corruption by his own brother and in December 1992 resigned under the imminent threat of impeachment.

Well-chosen personal connections can however be of great value if they ensure sensitive offices are in 'safe' hands. Thus Anastasio Somoza Debayle of Nicaragua placed his half-brother in command of the National Guard on which he relied for his ultimate support (Diedrich 1982, pp. 83, 107, 139). In Cuba, when Fidel Castro assumed the title of president, his brother Raúl received the titles of lieutenant-general, second secretary of the Communist Party and minister for the revolutionary armed forces (*Annual Register* 1976, p. 91), and has since been formally designated as his brother's successor. In Communist North Korea 'Great Leader' Kim Il-sung has already been succeeded by his son Kim Jong-il. Though it never appeared probable that Nicolae Ceauşescu would be succeeded by his son, the prominence of his wife Elena gives substance to the description of Romania under his rule as 'dynastic communism' (Freedom House 1989), and in Serbia Slobodan Milosevic's rise to power received a significant boost from the support of his wife Mirjana Marcovic, a professor of Marxism at Belgrade University (Silber and Little 1995, pp. 36, 41–2).

Outside the family circle stand the clients who are bound to their patrons by a set of reciprocal though unequal obligations. As the patrons advance through the system, it is their duty to see that their clients are cared for, and hence at each change of government there is a fierce and undignified scramble for jobs (Grindle 1977).

For the patrons, clientelism is a means to sustain their political support base during the time in which the rallying force of nationalism is in decline and classes have not yet developed to provide bases for political parties.

In new states it may be based on ethnicity, as in the tribal society of Sierra Leone and other West African states, and if so national leaders can go in for 'pyramid buying' of support. By using the established power of local leaders to deliver the necessary support at election times they simplify their task of mobilising political power. It is equally important for its effect on clients, who are thus obliged to deliver that support.

The key features of the patron–client relationship have been defined by John Duncan Powell as follows:

> First, the patron–client tie develops between two parties unequal in status, wealth, and influence. . . . Second, the formation and maintenance of the relationship depends on reciprocity in the exchange of goods and services. . . . Third, the development and maintenance of a patron–client relationship rests heavily on face to face contact between the two parties. (J.D. Powell 1971, pp. 7–8)

Hence the patron–client relationship is unequal and therefore inherently unstable. And in rapidly modernising societies this presents special problems. In the context of traditional village life the fairly simple network of mutual relationships is well known and fully understood. The tendency to instability increases rapidly in the context of urban immigrants, whose desire for jobs makes them vulnerable to recruitment into a much more complex network where any sense of reciprocal obligation is easily lost.

At a national level the most significant problems arise, since the entire network is wide open to exploitation by wealthy landowners and entrepreneurs and by foreign interests. Bill (1988) documents how under the Shah's so-called 'White Revolution' the professional middle class of Iran expanded uncontrollably, leading to rising hostility to the regime and eventually to its fall (Daneshvar 1996).

The importance of patronage is not by any means confined to the allocation of jobs. Pensions and retainers ease the task of getting rid of members of the government who otherwise would impede necessary or desired changes by softening the financial shock of retirement or dismissal (sometimes so successfully that they end up very much better off than they would have been in office). For the sake of appearances they may be combined with some kind of office which though honorific is more or less a sinecure. Many are (fairly) content with the honour rather than the reward. Others are not.

Honours are the most insubstantial and the most versatile of all forms of reward. In Britain an elaborate system of badges of distinction, conferring the right to use certain titles or letters after one's name, serves to recognise by enhanced status the long service of many people who have worked for many years in the routine tasks of government, or who by their efforts have achieved distinction in fields of endeavour which the government wishes particularly to commend. It is a system which uses practically no financial resources beyond the slight cost of the badges and ribbons conferred, and for elaboration it probably has no parallel. But though it derives from the system of real rewards conferred by medieval monarchs, the use of honours is not by any means confined to monarchies. In France the Légion d'Honneur, in numerous gradations, has been democratised in a fashion appropriate to a republic, but is no less valued for being widely conferred. In the United States, the Constitution prohibits the creation of titles of nobility. But it does not prohibit the creation of exclusive distinctions such as the Presidential Medal of Honor. Elsewhere in the republics of the Americas honours flourish too. Argentina has the Order of the Liberator General San Martín, Peru the Order of the Golden Condor, Mexico the Order of the Aztec Eagle, and even tiny Guatemala the Order of the Quetzal, in five categories. In the former Soviet Union and the East European countries honours and medals were conferred in profusion. One of the more unusual of these distinctions was the title of Hero of Soviet Motherhood instituted in 1944 for women who had had five or more children (Inkeles 1968, p. 217). One certainly deserves something for having five or more children.

Interest Arbitration

When reward and sanction are applied not to political control of members of the government and of the elite, but to the social control of the society at large, the economy of force dictates that the principal agency of the government will be the law and the structures particularly associated with it.

Because of the technical nature of the subject, knowledge of the law in most societies is the especial property of a guild of men and women who regulate admission to their profession collectively through examinations or similar means. Even in the former Soviet Union lawyers were self-employed persons (M. Matthews 1978), and where their guilds are well-established and strong, as in the United States, France or Britain, they can attain a high degree of autonomy within the political system.

Since it is from the ranks of these people that those who have to judge cases are drawn, a high degree of conservatism in legal systems could be predicted, and in fact they appear particularly resistant to change, retaining their formal structures even in times of revolution or civil war, unless superseded by martial law or revolutionary tribunals made up of lay people.

There are, therefore, two different forms of legal systems.

The earlier system requires judges to interpret traditional law based on precedent and hence wholly or partly uncodified. This form was once universal, for, as noted earlier, the belief in a system of law seems in most early societies to have come before the development of distinct structures to interpret it. Today its best-known forms are found in the United States and with the Commonwealth countries. However, traditional law is also found in many other parts of the world. The world's oldest university was founded in Al-Ahzar, Cairo, Egypt in order to teach Islamic law, and though it is not found unmodified there today, its use has been revived from time to time in other Arab countries such as Sudan, Libya and Pakistan under General Zia.

With the French Revolution was introduced the idea that the law ought to be the common property of all citizens, and capable of being understood by them. Hence it should be codified, and the 'Code Napoléon', completed in 1806, stands as a monument to the success of this ideal, having been adopted as the basis of the legal system of many other countries in Europe (Belgium, the Netherlands, Spain), in the former French Empire and in Latin America. The Spanish case is particulary interesting, since the Laws of the Indies, first codified in 1682, pre-dated the Code Napoléon by more than a century, and were probably no more difficult to understand (Haring 1952, p. 100).

Code law restricts the role of the judges in interpretation, but leaves them a wide range of powers in the conduct of cases, where the institution of the examining magistrate, who scrutinises every aspect of a case and hears witnesses before the case is formally tried, is particularly noteworthy. Anglo-Saxon common law, on the other hand, leaves the judges free to interpret according only to the precedents set by higher courts, but restricts their power in court by the institution for serious offences of a jury, whose task it is to decide simply on the question of guilt or innocence. Though judges in both systems are in general appointed from within the legal profession by a specially constituted committee or committees of the executive, lower judges in the United States are elected at popular elections, though officially on a non-partisan basis, giving them quite a different sort of popular authority for their actions. The general respect accorded to the judiciary is seen at its strongest in the case of the United States Supreme Court, where the power of judicial review of administrative decisions common to Anglo-Saxon legal systems has been transformed by custom into the additional power (in specific cases where the issue cannot be avoided) to declare acts of Congress unconstitutional.

In all cases, however, the formal operation of the judiciary represents only part of the structures associated with rule-adjudication. Decisions of government, such as appeals, the hearing and decisions of tribunals, and the arbitration of industrial disputes (where such are permitted), all involve the adjudication of rules and are normally performed by political or bureaucratic structures, into which the specialised personnel of the law need not venture. The operation of the police force or some similar structure is essential to bring certain classes of case before the courts. These cases are those in which the government has decided as a matter of public policy that the general good, as it sees it, can only be secured by centralised enforcement of the law. Other cases, involving only the dispute between two persons or legal entities as to their respective rights, will be brought before the courts anyway, though the extent to which this is freely done – itself an indicator of the extent to which the authority of the government is accepted – depends also on the financial cost of justice and the amount of time it takes.

In France appeals against administrative decisions are handled by special courts under a separate code of administrative law, thus clearly distinguishing the public from private responsibility in the matter. In the Anglo-Saxon system, such recourse is through the normal courts. In closed societies, such as the East European states, such recourse is extremely difficult to obtain by any means, attempts to pursue one's rights being met with more or less forcible reprisals, in the belief that any criticism of government constitutes a threat to national security. In fact historical experience demonstrates that long-term survival of a regime and its elite is more securely established by guaranteeing cheap and speedy recourse to the victims of minor injustices, such as seem inseparable from the functioning of bureaucracies as from all human institutions. It is not for nothing that, in monarchies, the prerogative of mercy was seen as the distinguishing mark of a just ruler.

In the former communist countries the popular notion of a legal code was retained and indeed elaborated, but the interpretation of it was placed in the hands of 'people's courts' where lay assessors sat with the judges to determine the guilt of the accused. Since it was widely assumed that the state authorities knew what they were doing in bringing a case before the courts, acquittals were rare. 'Ordinary' criminals, however, though subject often to terms of imprisonment savage by Western European standards, were nevertheless better treated in the former Soviet Union than those whose supposed offence was political.

Summary

Political stability is a dynamic and not a static concept. Systems are maintained in four related ways: by adaptive change, constitutional or legislative, by the use of government power to block demands, by the use of rewards and sanctions to maximise support and miminise opposition, and by delivering services to the public by using government power to arbitrate between interests. Co-optation is used as a matter of course to neutralise political opposition.

If outlets for protest are inadequate, disaffection with a government or regime can reach dangerous levels and lead to ungovernability. 'New social movements' (NSMs), protest groups that challenge the basis of traditional politics, have become a regular feature of modern states, but in general have been accommodated within the existing order or met with adaptive change.

The nature of the legal process, and in particular its predictability, is of great importance in maintaining the legitimacy of government.

Key Concepts

adaptive change, change occurring constitutionally and as a matter of course, through a government responding to the demands made upon it

clientelism, unequal exchange of resources between a patron and a client in return for political support

co-option (co-optation in the United States), the bringing of new members into the political elite by appointing them to formal governmental positions

input control, the use of coercive agencies to forestall demands for change

interest arbitration, the process by which the balance between different power blocs in society is maintained in such a way that challenges to the regime are minimised; the art of knowing when to engineer or to permit adaptive change

neocorporatism, a monopolised and centralised system of interest organisation within liberal democracies, in which the state formally designates and recognises only a limited number of interest groups (Schmitter 1970)

new social movements, protest groups that challenged traditional politics and made identity a key factor in political mobilisation from the 1960s onwards

patrimonialism, the use of traditional authority to reinforce the formal structure of the state

patronage, appointment to jobs of office-seekers, also appointments on their behalf which act to strengthen their political position or to reward their family, friends or supporters (cf. clientelism)

personalism, the use of charismatic authority (cf. Weber) to reinforce the authority of state or government

political socialisation, the inculcation of a political culture and the acquisition of a shared value system

political stability, the reasonable expectation that the existing order of things will be maintained for the foreseeable future

system maintenance, the power of a government or regime to maintain itself

Sample Questions

This field involves practical consideration of issues of authority and legitimacy, and the possible challenges that may arise to them. Questions can therefore be general, as in 'What is political stability, and what factors may affect it?', or specific.

Questions such as 'Discuss the problems arising from the treatment of national minorities in communist systems before 1989', or 'Is there a contradiction between the goals of political democratisation and market-orientated economic reform in post-communist countries?', address key issues of much wider significance, but they will require the student to have a good background knowledge of events since 1989 in at least two East European countries.

Further Reading

For more on clientelism see Clapham (1982) and Randall and Theobald (1985).

For studies of the pressures on governmental officials in semi-competitive states see Grindle (1977) and Okoli (1980). For similar effects in the former communist states see Dawisha (1980) and M. Matthews (1978).

Force and Military Intervention

CHAPTER TEN

Learning Objectives

By the end of this chapter, the reader will be able:

- to assess how far the use of force is essential to the maintenance of stable government;

- to site the use of force in the context of the challenges facing developing states;

- to identify how and why force is deployed by governments;

- to ascertain why the armed forces intervene in politics and how successful they are in achieving their goals.

Civil Order

We have already seen how the state can be defined as the entity holding the monopoly of **force** within a society. This monopoly presupposes that it has been obtained by the exercise of control over rival centres of force within the social system. These centres may either be regulated or suppressed. They can also be effectively counter-balanced, in most, if not all instances, through the process termed here interest arbitration (see Chapter 9). Civil order, therefore, is the state of affairs that enables governments to govern without calling upon the considerable reserves of force which they possess.

If rival users of force are regulated, then they are subject to specific restraints by a code of laws or a system of custom or etiquette, such as those governing the duel or feud in Corsica or Sicily. Beyond this point comes the development of the state in which, as in feudal times in England, the use of force is dispersed throughout many levels, but in each is subject to regulation by that immediately above, and the general arbitration of a code of behaviour recognising obligations to the community as a whole.

If rival users are completely suppressed, then force has to be used to suppress them. In either case, there will remain at the government's disposal a regular corps of special-ist users of force to defend the national territory. This performs a useful dual function. Though the **socialisation** of the regulated community involves members inhibiting their aggressive tendencies with the aid of mechanisms of sublimation such as sporting con-tests, there are always some members who lack the ability to fall in line. Some can be usefully employed in the police or armed forces. These in turn can be used to block unwanted inputs to the political arena. It does not mean, of course, that the demands these inputs represent are either met or dissipated harmlessly, so they retain their poten-tial to influence events when changed circumstances permit.

State building

Civil order however is not arrived at overnight. Since it depends to such an extent on cus-tom and practice, it takes a long time to become established. Building liberal democratic societies in the emerging states has therefore involved special problems. Some, such as ethnic conflict, have their parallels in consolidated democracies. But others have not.

We have already seen (Chapter 1) that it is quite difficult satisfactorily to define ethnicity. Ethnic groups are 'imagined communities' and new states therefore have to seek to get their citizens to accept a new notion of ethnicity. Ethnic conflict in Africa after 1960 following decolonisation (Chamberlain 1999), for example, has been interpreted in two radically different ways. African countries have formally accepted the state boundaries that existed at independence, and for them the problem is that linguistic and tribal groups may therefore be found stretching across two or more states. The remedy is to encourage them to accept the state as it is. Pan-Africanists, among others, have argued that since ethnic groups were divided by artificial colonial boundaries, the rem-edy is the opposite, to move the boundaries. However, successful attempts to do this have involved sometimes savage conflicts, as in the wars between Ethiopia and Somalia (1976–77), Burkina Faso and Mali (1985–86) and Ethiopia and Eritrea (1998–2000).

Latin America, where ethnicity has historically been of much lesser significance, also has artificial boundaries and exemplifies a second problem. This is that if boundaries do not arise naturally, as with rivers or mountains, their ultimate position depends on the relative military power of the states concerned. Brazil has, therefore, got significantly bigger since independence and Ecuador considerably smaller.

A third problem is illustrated by so-called 'stateless societies' such as Lebanon, which first gained independence in 1941 as an accidental by-product of the Second World War, and ever since has been divided into competing communities, none of which fully accepts the right of its rivals to political power. Hence, despite efforts to create a consociational framework, based on power sharing within a tightly defined constitutional order, the state was unable successfully to assert its right to the legitimate monopoly of force, and with the collapse of public order Lebanon, formerly one of the most prosperous parts of the Middle East, became a battleground for competing factions backed by rival regional powers.

There are a number of circumstances in which the sense of ethnic nationalism is likely to increase. First, for example, where a previously authoritarian state democratises, and party structures are weak, demagogic appeals to ethnic nationalism, as in Lithuania, can have a big payoff in terms of electoral support. The 'nationalities question' in the former Soviet Union, it is now all too clear, had merely been suppressed, not resolved (Denber 1992). However, the recrudescence of nationalist sentiments which followed was harnessed by political leaders to cut short the possibilities of transition towards liberal democracy (Suny 1991), leaving at best a form of 'low intensity democracy' (Gills, Rocamora and Wilson 1993). Secondly, with increased international concern for human rights, minorities have not only become increasingly sensitive to slights but also the possibility that by claiming to be oppressed they can invite intervention by regional powers or even superpowers. With emerging regional powers like India seeking to establish cross-border connections between ethnic groups, conversely, a sense of separate identity may easily be generated where previously it did not exist.

The biggest danger then comes from the temptation for leaders to exploit ethnicity for electoral purposes. Where a leader's ethnic base is larger than that of the opposition s/he will strengthen relations with it whenever threatened, as in the case of Premadasa's appeal to ethnic Sinhalese in Sri Lanka or Vajpayee's appeal to ethnic Hindus in India.

Dictatorship

The ultimate defence of a political ruler is to return to the pre-constitutional order and to proclaim a state of emergency. This is quite a simple everyday concept. In any country, from time to time, war or natural disaster creates a situation which, in the interests of the citizens, requires that a government acts without normal legal restraints. The ability to proclaim a state of emergency is so much part of the normal functioning of government that it was used as a matter of course in the USA in 2001 when the first hurricane of the season led to widespread flooding across the South (*The Guardian*, 11 June 2001).

Its role as a response to war, or threat of war, internal or external, is better reflected perhaps in the Spanish term *estado de sitio* ('state of siege'), suggesting a condition in which a government is imminently under mortal threat from a hostile force (Stokes 1959, pp. 393–4).

The ancient Romans had already faced this problem. In their past they had overthrown their kings and had established a republican government. When they were under serious military threat and needed to concentrate their power they instituted the emergency office of dictator. The dictator was given supreme power in the state for a period of six months (Cowell 1956, p. 175), then at the end of that time he went back to being a private citizen.

When the idea of **dictatorship** as an emergency form of government was revived at the time of the French Revolution it was quite widely imitated. Dr José Rodríguez de Francia was elected dictator of Paraguay in 1814, and perpetual dictator in 1816. Juan Manuel de Rosas was formally recognised as dictator of the Argentine Confederation in 1835 by twelve provinces outside Buenos Aires (Wilgus 1963, pp. 65, 261). When he started an organisation to kill off his political opponents, insisted on everyone wearing red cockades to show they were on his side, and had his picture exhibited in all the churches for public veneration, Argentines finally rose against him, but only after eighteen years, and with foreign help. Even Simón Bolivar, deservedly regarded as the hero of South American independence, was dictator of Peru (1825–26) at the same time as he was president of Colombia, and received, incidentally, no salary for either post (Salcedo-Bastardo 1978).

Dictatorship, then, is a republican office which values the forms of legitimacy and is often ratified by plebiscite or acclamation. It originally was and has continued to be justified by its proponents as a response to serious national emergency. It was originally considered to be respectable and only after many decades of abuse and incompetence was discredited. Already, by the beginning of the twentieth century, the term had become pejorative.

Nevertheless, Western Europe had its age of dictators in the twentieth century, and not in the nineteenth, and specifically between 1920 and 1945, during what Huntington (1993a) has called the first 'reverse wave' of democratisation. The redrawing of the map of Europe after the First World War destroyed political legitimacy and left a legacy of conflict. Germany, Austria, Hungary, Yugoslavia, Bulgaria, Greece, Italy, Spain and Portugal all adopted dictatorships in this period. Indeed, despite the Holocaust and Mussolini's war in Abyssinia, the positive view of dictatorship was still not wholly dead post-1945. Not only did Salazar survive in Portugal and Franco in Spain, but the Colonels seized power in Greece in 1967 and came to grief only when in 1975 they were foolish enough to become entangled in a war with another NATO ally, Turkey, over Cyprus. And dictatorship had a great revival in Latin America and Africa in the second 'reverse wave' (c. 1962–85). Though General Idi Amin of Uganda was, perhaps, unique in openly declaring himself an admirer of Hitler, many others, notably the generals in Argentina and Chile, erroneously believed that they were fighting a third world war. Others, like Mussolini, claimed that only through dictatorship could their country make economic progress and keep up with others, but there is little or no evidence that this claim is correct (Wintrobe 1998).

So, to sum up, what is characteristic of a modern dictatorship?

It is, first, something that values the forms of legitimacy, internally involving recognition by an elite group, particularly by opinion leaders – the elders of the state and the military. It may not actually dare to seek mass recognition by plebiscite, but it usually does.

Secondly, dictators always enjoyed the kind of legitimacy they won externally, and today they like to be recognised by other heads of state. Lacking initial internal support as they do, external recognition by peer states is very important to them, especially that of the older, constitutional states, and of the great powers.

Thirdly, the dictator does not recognise the rights of individual people. For instance, Napoleon I regarded the people as being the vehicle of his political programme, as it were, for France. He created the French Empire in the style in which it ought to be created, and with it institutions such as the Ecole Polytéchnique, deliberately to obtain an elite to maintain the system (Ridley and Blondel 1964, pp. 40–1). The idea of moulding the people to need is very much inherent in the idea of dictatorship – it is such an emergency office that all rights are given up to it, and those exercised in the name of the country as a whole.

Fourthly, dictatorship has always shown a tendency to create a new form of 'aristocracy', in the shape of the active military. Because it is a military emergency office, the military tends to become the elite, and generals and colonels hold regional political power, in the way that earls and barons did in the Middle Ages, operating within a military command structure, and becoming a new 'aristocracy', as in Brazil since the inauguration of the Republic (1889).

Lastly, dictatorship creates no regular form of succession. The emergency character of the dictatorship is absolutely incompatible with the idea that dictators can have successors or can other than succeed themselves. Happily, therefore, dictatorships are finite, and since 1989 there has been a marked shift in world opinion away from them and towards liberal democracy.

Police Forces

There are a number of distinct ways in which states use forcible restraints on adults. In assigning to these a number of levels at which force is applied, the first and most effective, though of relatively recent origin, is that of the police.

A police force exists to provide for the use of actual physical constraints by the state to enforce its norms on others, in the belief that society's survival as a community is at stake. It does this by arresting (depriving of liberty) and bringing to trial before a court those who break the formal laws by which society is regulated. The law recognises the differences between offences by assigning stated penalties, but the fact that a penalty is fixed at all means that all are in some degree acts hostile to the accepted order of society, whatever the actual importance of the crime. In theory all are punished appropriately, since the alternative is to allow the will of the individual to prevail over that of society. However, in practice there are two stages in this process: identifying and capturing criminals, and successfully bringing them to punishment, and the efficacy of all police forces, therefore, depends to a large part on the indirect effect the threat of arrest is believed to have.

Hence a great deal depends on what the norms of the society are, and what the successive regimes that direct the state choose to make laws about. Laws for the maintenance of the society or the state should be in a different category from laws for the maintenance of the regime. Though there is general agreement that there will always be some laws to ensure the maintenance of regimes, there is a vast difference in the perceived desirability of regimes, and how far regimes see themselves as being indispensable.

There are two broad types of police organisation in modern states, often termed the 'Anglo-Saxon' and the 'Continental' (Cramer 1964).

The 'Anglo-Saxon' form derives from the experience of medieval England as formalised in the Statute of Winchester (1285) which made citizens collectively responsible for aiding the king's officers in enforcing the apprehension of criminals. At the time when other European countries were developing a regular police force, however, in the seventeenth century, England was reacting to the unpleasant experience of martial law as administered by Cromwell's major-generals. Consequently the introduction of a uniformed constabulary was delayed until the beginning of the nineteenth century, and, characteristically, was tried out first in Ireland (1787). Even after the formation of the Metropolitan Police for the capital in 1829, the rural areas of the counties had to wait nearly thirty years for the formation of a police force to be made compulsory (1856).

Characteristic of the 'Anglo-Saxon' police is that it is loose and decentralised in organisation; its members are limited in their powers, are normally uniformed and identifiable, and in Great Britain and the Republic of Ireland they do not carry firearms except with special training and specific permission. In England the Home Secretary is the police authority for the capital only; in the rest of the country his or her powers are those of an inspector rather than a commander. In the United States police are a state and not a federal responsibility. There is no national police force and a federal investigation agency, the FBI, was not created until 1924. Many cities have their own police forces.

In 1992 there was one police officer for every 275 inhabitants in France, compared with 1 for 322 in Germany and 1 for 454 in Britain (Safran 1995, p. 285). The 'Continental' form of policing is derived from the experience of France above all European countries. There had been a police force in the capital, Paris, from time immemorial, and in 1667 the king's lieutenant of police 'ruled the city despotically and had jurisdiction over beggars, vagabonds and criminals' (Cramer 1964, p. 292). The equation of crime, disorder and dirt is highly suggestive. The police had the power of summary arrest and fining on the spot for infringements of the law, and the Crown retained the right to hold prisoners without trial indefinitely.

The French revolutionary governments, though they began by breaking this system, soon recreated it, and put in charge of the new and extended police organisation a minister of the police 'responsible for the safety of persons and property, for the maintenance of public order and for the security of the state'. Hence in France there emerged three principal forces: a special force for the capital, Paris, under a prefet de police; the Sureté Nationale (now the Urban Police), organised in urban areas of more than 10,000 people under a commissaire de police working under the mayor and prefect of the department; these were merged into the Police Nationale in 1968 (Gregory 1976) together with the Republican Security Companies (*Compagnies Republicaines de Securité* – CRS). This formidable riot force was used in both 1958 and 1968 to defend the Republic against insurrection, real or imaginary, and has been deployed on many lesser occasions besides to protect the government against the wrath of French farmers.

Outside the cities however order is normally maintained by the national *gendarmerie*, technically part of the armed forces. This has at least one company in each *arrondissement* and is responsible for both the internal and external security of the state. It includes the Garde républicaine, which provides security for the president and leading politicians.

The 'Continental' system is heavily centralised, with responsibility for the whole in a minister. It operates not only in uniform but as a matter of course in plain clothes, its members having exceptional powers denied the ordinary citizen, including the power of imposing summary fines. In addition they are armed, sometimes heavily. It should be noted, moreover, that the 'Continental' model of policing, which gives the *gendarmerie* a paramilitary role, often places the police under the control of the Department of Defence, as in Chile and Peru.

It should be added that the influence of the French form today derives primarily not from earlier times but from the unifying effect of the Napoleonic Wars, and the admiration for things French in other parts of the world, for example Eastern Europe, the Balkans and Latin America. It was for this reason that the system was copied by the Russians, who, under Nicholas I, added the dreaded 'Third Section' or secret police. The term 'police' was so distasteful to the makers of the Russian Revolution that Lenin and his colleagues (like the Irish) dropped it altogether, and replaced the police with a people's militia. After many vicissitudes the militia was placed under the Ministry of Internal Affairs (MVD) in 1946. Though decentralised somewhat in 1956 following the general move towards de-Stalinisation, it retained until the collapse of the regime in 1991 the general characteristics of the 'Continental' type. An important difference, however, in the societies' respective attitudes to the police lay in the Soviet assumption of the common responsibility of all citizens to admonish or bring to justice any individual committing even a trivial crime (Cramer 1964, pp. 403–5). This was institutionalised in Cuba after 1959 in three ways. Citizens were organised into a militia on the basis of the city block or area in which they lived. Their behaviour was (and is) monitored by the Committees for the Defence of the Revolution (CDRs), organised on a similar basis. As in the Soviet Union, trials of offenders took place before people's courts staffed by lay assessors. From this assumption of communal responsibility for individual action, it is only a very short step to the political offence, since the essence of a political offence lies not in its visible damage to person or property, but to the invisible assumptions of the society in question.

State Security

If the maintenance of the regime involves the continual use of regular police action to restrain a substantial sector of the population, the legislation maintaining it must be political, and the state can be described as in some degree a **police state** (Chapman 1970, pp. 15ff.). Restraints of this kind however are common in many countries against large groups who are defying the government of the day, such as strikers on railways or in docks, or students demonstrating against what they conceive to be the follies and iniquities of their elders. In South Africa under apartheid, however, the use of police restraint went far beyond this point to involve the persistent regulation of the movement and communication of an unparalleled majority of the population. Pass laws, residence restraint, segregation, were all enforced by the same mechanisms as controlling parking or apprehending thieves. This use involves the conscious moulding of society by the creation of attitudes and behaviour alien to it. It also had an inevitable effect on the attitudes of the majority of the population towards the police, who were seen as an alien force of occupation. Precisely the same processes have been at work in the West Bank under Israeli occupation and it has been clear since the onset of the *al-Aqsa intifada* that Israeli attempts to use the Palestinian Authority as an agent have merely succeeded in discrediting its authority and not in restraining the violence.

The apartheid government of South Africa justified its use of police power in the name of state security. Any opposition to it could be and frequently was attributed by government apologists to the actions of foreign agencies. This is significant, since almost all societies have created specialist branches of their police forces to handle state security matters, and their powers are considerable.

Special police organisations for state security exist to restrain infiltration and espionage activities by foreign nationals who might, using these means, achieve the sort of result normally to be expected only from an overt hostile act of war, or which would enable such an attack to be launched with an effectiveness significantly greater than might otherwise be expected. In the UK the responsibility rests with a Special Branch of each police force, and above all with that of the Metropolitan Police. The Metropolitan Police is accountable to the Home Secretary, who has to authorise wire taps. France's Département pour Surveillance de la Territoire (DST) is also a branch of the Police Nationale. In the USA, with a federal structure and a multiplicity of police forces, the Federal Bureau of Investigation (FBI) plays a prime role both in investigation and co-ordination. The mission of maintaining security offers a lot of power to the agencies concerned. It is now known that under its first head, J. Edgar Hoover, the FBI maintained extensive files on the personal affairs of leading politicians. Hoover's reappointment was one of the first decisions announced by the newly elected John F. Kennedy.

Major powers also maintain two sorts of intelligence agencies. Though they are sometimes combined, the agencies can be divided into two categories: *counter-intelligence agencies*, concerned with protecting the state against attack, infiltration etc. from abroad, and *intelligence-gathering organisations*, concerned with discovering information about other countries. The latter may also undertake covert operations abroad as part of a state's strategy of defending its international interests. Since no formal right to do so is recognised by international law or diplomacy, the personnel involved operate outside the law and in the event of capture are liable to be disowned.

Intelligence agencies therefore have a lot of potential power, even if it is not always employed. The relationship between intelligence and politics varies, according to the tendency of politics to intervene in intelligence and intelligence to intervene in politics. In principle, in liberal democratic states there should be very little or no influence in either direction, and in smaller states in a stable international context, such as the Netherlands, Denmark and Switzerland, this appears to be the case. However, as Table 10.1 shows, we can identify three other main categories in which either intelligence strongly influences politics, or politics strongly influences intelligence, or both.

Table 10.1 Intervention as the outcome of intelligence–politics relations

	Tendency of politics to intervene in intelligence	
	Low	High
Tendency of intelligence to intervene in politics	Low intervention: Denmark Netherlands Switzerland	Political intervention in intelligence: Nazi Germany Stalinist Russia
Low		
High	Intelligence intervention in politics: Israel 1954 USA 1961 UK 1960s	Mutual intervention: most Third World countries

Source: adapted from Bar-Joseph 1995, Table 4, p. 70

As befits a complex nation with a traditional distrust of power, the USA has a multiplicity of intelligence organisations: the Central Intelligence Agency (CIA), the Defense Intelligence Agency (DIA) responsible for signals intelligence and electronic surveillance, and several other agencies under the nominal supervision of the Director of Central Intelligence (DCI). However, though the main responsibility for counter-intelligence rests with the FBI, the CIA also exercises this function abroad, and there is evidence that it has exceeded its powers and intervened in internal matters as well (Mackenzie 1997). In Britain the main responsibility for intelligence rests with the Secret Intelligence Service (SIS) or, since no longer secret, MI6, and for counter-intelligence with the Security Service (MI5). In either case the operation of these agencies is supposed to be subject to the overriding control of the state: MI5 is responsible directly to the prime minister. MI5 is also supposed to be concerned with external threats and not intervene in politics, though in practice the line between the two gets blurred by suspicion of politicians' motives. So in the UK there have been cases of intelligence agency intervention in politics: the 1964–70 Labour government of Harold Wilson, in particular, was the target of hostile activity from self-appointed agents of the security services (Wright 1987; Pincher 1988; Dorril and Ramsay 1992).

New problems come when the powers understandably given to agencies to gather intelligence abroad are misused. By the early 1950s the CIA, initially concerned with gaining information from and denying information to the Soviet Union (Dulles 1964), became increasingly involved in clandestine operations overseas in Iran, Guatemala and Vietnam. In the case of Iran the operation to overthrow the prime minister, Mohammed Mossadegh, had initially been planned by the British SIS but was later taken over by the CIA. Although invariably authorised by the president, these and similar operations in the 1980s, notably the secret war against Nicaragua under the Reagan administration, were conducted under a cloak of 'plausible deniability'. Most of the time Congress wished to see the USA performing well in defending US interests and the prestige of the Agency was correspondingly high in the 1950s (Jeffreys-Jones 1989, p. 7). It was the intelligence failures which contributed to the Bay of Pigs in Cuba and the ultimate débâcle in Vietnam, rather than reports of sabotage, assassination and insurrection (Agee 1975; Marchetti and Marks 1974), which were to lead to the tightening of control over the Agency in the early 1970s and its relative inactivity under the Carter presidency. Particular concern was focused on breaches of the rule that the CIA was not to operate within the United States itself, but claims that it regularly does so have continued to surface (Mackenzie 1997).

Of smaller states, Israel, owing to its unusual strategic situation, has given particular prominence to both intelligence and counter-intelligence (Black and Morris 2000), and Israelis have seldom been prepared to question their use of clandestine methods. The 'unfortunate business' of 1954 was notable however in that it was not only conducted without the knowledge of the then prime minister and defence minister, Moshe Sharett, but in direct contradiction of his government's stated policy. Where perceptions of threat are high, political intervention in intelligence matters is also likely to be high (Harkabi 1988). The more ideological politicians are, the more likely it is that the intelligence process will become politicised. Not only does this make a government excessively dependent on 'secret' sources of information, but it also endangers the effectiveness of the intelligence-gathering agencies by encouraging them to look for 'intelligence-to-please' (Bar-Joseph 1995, pp. 3, 13).

'Secret' Police

A **secret police** is something very different, an organisation that applies the same techniques to the civil population because it fears danger from them regardless of outside influences. The distinction between a secret police and a police force engaged in secret activities may, however, be purely conceptual. The term 'secret' too is misleading. It is not the existence of the secret police that is secret – otherwise it would hardly instil the degree of fear that it does.

In Europe, within living memory, almost all states have suffered from the attentions of a secret police. The power of the Gestapo, indeed, extended throughout the Reich and was felt at all levels (Delarue 1964). The Soviet secret police, under various names, was widely copied, most obviously in the early years of the Soviet dominance of Eastern Europe (Wolin and Slusser 1957; Adelman 1984). The last twenty-five years of the twentieth century also saw several notorious examples from other parts of the world. The Chilean Department of National Intelligence (DINA), under General Manuel Contreras, reported personally to General Augusto Pinochet and was responsible for a long list of atrocities including the assassination of Orlando Letelier in Washington, DC, in 1976. In Peru in 1999 opposition candidates complained that security personnel ostensibly assigned to protect them by the Peruvian National Intelligence Service (SIN) were in fact harassing their supporters. Since the head of the SIN, Vladimiro Montesinos, was directly responsible to President Fujimori, who was running for re-election, these claims were well-founded and have since been confirmed. Other reports of the routine use of torture and the murder of suspected guerrillas and the systematic surveillance of opposition politicians by the SIN confirmed allegations made by the Frecuencia Latina television station owned by Baruch Ivcher and other abuses condemned by the UN Committee Against Torture in a report in May 1998.

A secret police is no longer (if it ever was) a body ancillary to the rule-enforcement agencies – the public prosecutor, the courts, and so forth – but is a rule-enforcement agency, having its own volition as to the assignment of prosecution and punishment. It is directly responsible through its bureau chief to the head of government, regulates its own hierarchy, and is concerned with a wide range of activities in the day-to-day operation of the state which are not disclosed to other members of the community. Its ability to use forcible sanctions is thus limited only by the resources available, and the ingenuity of its members. It is an output mechanism entirely divorced from the input functions generated in the society as a whole. Not only, however, does it act to screen out pressures on the decision-makers, but it can perform an even more difficult task in attempting to create the impression of spontaneous political support from the masses for a policy prefabricated by the elite.

Input control in this sense does not fit exactly within either the terminology of Easton or that of Almond's developmental model of the extractive and regurgitative processes of government (Calvert 1969). Easton, it is true, does make provision for the concept of 'gatekeepers' limiting the degree to which pressures affect the decision-making process, but the context makes it clear he is primarily concerned with the orderly transaction of business as represented by forms, procedures, committees, etc. (Easton 1965, p. 122). Like him, Almond retained the basic assumption that the original source of political power is located in the will of the mass, and not in the ability of the elite to command enough power resources (Almond in Almond and Coleman 1960, p. 7). While this may be true in fact in most cases, and in theory in all, it is not true in fact in all. Input control ensures that only favourable inputs, e.g. supports, are felt in the system as a whole, that is, among all citizens in their political roles.

The other important attribute of secret police, apart from the free use of forcible restraints, is the acquisition and monopoly of a centralised bank of data on members of the community, available for manipulation by the elite for political purposes – that is to say, their own maintenance. The nature of this information is not known to the individual from whom it has been secured. Gossip, misunderstanding and error therefore maintain a status in it equivalent to fact, and may be preferred to it as more exactly conforming to the needs of the state.

The maintenance and extension of this sort of information are greatly enhanced by quasi-military status, such as that enjoyed by the SS in Hitler's Germany (1933–45) or the secret police, the NKVD, in Stalin's Russia (1928–53), both of which maintained paramilitary units as political 'shock troops' for use in actual warfare. The NKVD's successor, the KGB, maintained frontier troops. In turn, these are to be distinguished from military intelligence organisations such as the German FSP or the Soviet GRU – military units on the regular establishment engaged in military intelligence duties. They are also different from the category of paramilitary forces other than secret police (Wolin and Slusser 1957).

Paramilitary Forces

There is nothing particularly secret about the **paramilitary police forces** of Malaysia and Thailand. They had a similar origin in the need to mobilise additional forces to combat terrorism and hence to maintain a force other than the military which could be deployed in counter-terrorist activities and the suppression of 'bandits'.

Nevertheless, they have historically exercised very different political roles, That of Malaysia was a professional organisation, used openly in armed combat against insurgents during the Malayan Emergency (1948–59) (Short 1973, pp. 285–91; Wang 1966). That of Thailand was a paramilitary police force similarly engaged and similarly equipped with sophisticated weapons, such as tanks and machine-guns. However, because of the nature of the political process in that country, it additionally became an alternative power base after 1946 and as such the major strength of Luang Pibul Songkkram. He dominated Thai politics for a generation, and was fully engaged in both the abortive coup of 1949 (Coast 1953) and the successful revolution of 1957.

Paramilitary force can be used against a wide range of possible 'enemies of the government', and in certain circumstances very effectively. Equally it can form the active force of a militia-based revolutionary organisation, perhaps the type example being the *fasci di combattimento* (fighting bands) from which the Italian Fascisti of Mussolini took their name. Hitler's storm troopers (*Sturmabteilungen* – SA) similarly played a key role in destroying his enemies in the early stages of his rise to power. Once he had succeeded they became a danger to him and were in turn annihilated by the rival SS (*Schutzstaffeln*) in the Röhm *putsch* of 1934. The consequences for the unnecessary weakening of the system were particularly well exemplified by the rivalries of the Cicero affair (Delarue 1964), which rendered totally useless much of the high-quality intelligence gained for Germany from the valet of the British ambassador in Turkey during the Second World War.

Military Forces

The last resort of government, in internal as well as external matters, is the military, the 'ultimate argument of kings'. Their employment within the community, however, is restricted by a number of factors: their need to maintain combatant status in the event of foreign attack, the disproportionate effect of their powerful weapons, and their size, not easily accommodated in the absence of special barracks and cantonments in the appropriate regions of the state. These attributes are capable of generating a considerable amount of hostility, as when the billeting of troops on the local inhabitants of the American colonies became a major grievance of the American Revolution. At the same time they give rise to important theoretical considerations which must be considered in the broader context of the phenomenon known as militarism.

Governments frequently resort to using armies against their own citizens to try to maintain public order when all other methods appear to have failed. In January 1989 a state of emergency was proclaimed and Soviet troops sent in to try to halt fighting in Nagorno-Karabakh, part of Azerbaijan (S. White 1993, pp. 163–5). In July 1989 the Chinese People's Army used tanks to disperse demonstrators in Beijing. Casualties were heavy among the unarmed demonstrators. When Slovenia declared its independence from Yugoslavia on 25 June 1991, the Yugoslav National Army (JNA) intervened to secure the border crossings and establish order. In the ten days before an independence agreement brokered by the European Community (EC) brought their withdrawal, 44 JNA soldiers were killed and 187 wounded but there were less than 10 Slovene casualties (Silber and Little 1995, p. 183). The humiliation of the JNA, however, helped its metamorphosis into a mainly Serbian force, and its disentanglement from Slovenia enabled it instead to be deployed to carve out Serb enclaves in Croatia. This had also declared its independence on 25 June 1991 under the leadership of the first non-communist government to be elected in Yugoslavia. However, immediately after the election the JNA had disarmed its defence forces and the serious fighting that broke out in July 1991 was carefully co-ordinated (Dyker and Vejvoda 1996, p. 207). Despite EC recognition, Croatia was unable to regain control over much of its territory and UN forces sent in to maintain peace between the warring parties meant that it was not able to do so until they were withdrawn in 1995.

It should be noted, however, that, effective as the military may be at countering armed insurgents, dispersing demonstrations and even strike-breaking (by substituting for the strikers in the performance of distribution functions), they have the weakness of being too strong. They cannot protect government leaders against a *coup d'état* or assassination, because it is they who are themselves dangerous as a focus for disaffection. The armed forces almost invariably have the ability, if they wish, to take over power and run the country themselves. The question is, not why do they do so, but what stops them?

The Armed Forces and Politics

The mere presence of military officers in a government, even in key positions, does not necessarily mean that it is a military government. We will find it essential to distinguish between military rulers, military intervention, military government and military regimes.

1. **Military rulers**. Monarchs were originally military leaders and long remained by tradition commanders of armed forces. The framers of the Constitution of the United States took the fateful decision to make the president also commander-in-chief of the armed forces of the United States and since that time there have been many examples of the voluntary election by civilians of a military leader as civil head of state or government, often after a successful war. Examples from the United States alone are George Washington, Andrew Jackson, William Henry Harrison, Zachary Taylor, Ulysses S. Grant, James Garfield, Theodore Roosevelt and Dwight D. Eisenhower. In major crises the military virtues are those sought for – the willingness to make quick decisions and the zest for action. Hence a particularly successful military career is seen as a good qualification for leadership, and though General Colin Powell refused nomination for the presidency, he was named secretary of state by George W. Bush. At any one time in the 1990s a substantial number of states have had either military heads of state or heads of government or both (see Table 10.2). By no means all of these have been military governments or regimes.

This creates a wider problem, which goes to the heart of why politics has traditionally been seen as a male preserve. Even at a humbler level, military training, where available, seems to be regarded as an essential part of citizenship for a political aspirant. Obviously a good war record is even better, as witness the effect of his genuine heroism at the sinking of 'PT 109' on the fortunes of John F. Kennedy. On the other hand, the

Table 10.2 Military heads of state and government, 1996

Heads of state:	
Burkina Faso	Cuba
Chad	Afghanistan
Equatorial Guinea	Burma
The Gambia	Indonesia
Ghana[1]	Vietnam
Guinea	Algeria
Guinea-Bissau	Egypt
Mauritania	Iraq
Nigeria	Libya
Sierra Leone	Palestine
Somalia	Syria
Sudan	Tunisia
Togo	Yemen
Zaire	Seychelles[2]
Zambia[3]	

Heads of government:	
Laos	Jordan
Fiji	

[1] Retired.
[2] Seized power in armed coup.
[3] Civilian president; military vice-president.

Table 10.3 Stages of military intervention

Preparation	Action	Consolidation
Alienation of armed forces	Capital sealed off and strong points seized	Negotiation for formation of interim government
Bargaining between major interest groups	President seized and deported	Decree-laws etc.
Ultimatum to government	Manifesto issued	
Decision to intervene: pre-positioning of troops	Curfew and imposition of martial law	

accusation that Bill Clinton had tried to avoid the draft blighted his relations with the armed services and remained a permanent problem throughout his presidency. (Clinton did apply for deferment but then allowed his name to go forward and was characteristically lucky to draw a low number and so escape being called up.) Ironically, despite the emphasis President George Bush placed on his own respectable military record when seeking re-election in 1992, his son, George W. Bush, was elected in 2000 despite having enlisted in the Texas Air National Guard, an effective though no doubt unintentional way of evading active service.

2. **Military intervention**. In his analysis of military intervention in politics, Finer began by pointing out that the armed forces have such a substantial advantage in politics that what is surprising is not that they take over governments, but that they ever relinquish power. Intervention, he argued, will depend on both the *opportunity* and the *disposition* of the armed forces to intervene. Almost all forces have the opportunity, but not all have the disposition, and the relationship between the two is a complex one.

Secondly, he noted, intervention can take place on any one or more of four levels (see also Table 10.3).

- All armed forces act as a lobby. Even in NATO the high spending profile of the armed forces makes them formidably effective at maintaining their position, as witness the failure of civilian governments since 1989 to recover the so-called 'peace dividend'.
- Many armed forces have secured virtual independence from civilian control, but retain the right to assert a military voice in executive decisions. In modern presidential states the minister of war is often a military appointee or a cypher approved by the military, while the armed forces speak though their chiefs of staff directly to the president, whether military or civilian. Military authorities therefore can and do 'call the shots' from behind the scenes, e.g. General Mladic in Bosnia in the 1990s.
- Intervention by direct military action is commonly used to displace civilian governments (or even military ones) through the real or implied use of force, as repeatedly in recent years in Haiti.
- Only rarely, however, as in Brazil (1964), Argentina (1976) or Ghana (1982), do the armed forces choose to supplant civilian government completely (Finer 1962, pp. 70–1).

Finer related these levels of intervention broadly to types of political culture. This presented obvious difficulties, which are common to all attempts to explain political events in terms of culture. Military intervention differs considerably over time in any one country; in 1964, for example, Chile, as a democratic presidential state choosing its leaders in competitive elections in a highly aware literate society, would have been regarded as a country of high political culture; by 1974 it was under military dictatorship and all political expression had been suppressed. It seems, therefore, that 'political culture' is the product of military intervention (and other factors) rather than the reverse. Moreover it does not really answer the question why do the military intervene.

With other writers (e.g. Huntington 1968; Perlmutter 1978, 1980; Nordlinger 1977) we can, however, be more specific, grouping factors for intervention into 'push' factors (militarism among the armed forces, fears of loss of military privileges, failure to maintain military budgets, defeat in war) and 'pull' factors (power vacuum in civilian government, serious economic crisis, corruption and loss of national prestige).

3. **Military government**. A military government arises in one of three situations. The first, actual military occupation by foreign forces, is comparatively rare. The second, more common situation is when the armed forces assume power over their own people and establish a government with the following features: key political leadership by military officers, the existence of a state of martial law, and extra-judicial control exercised by security forces. A third possibility is a lack of central political control over large sections of the country where official and unofficial security forces rule (Sivard 1983, p. 11). This was the case at the end of the twentieth century in Somalia in Africa and in Colombia in Latin America. It can also happen under a military government.

4. **Military regimes**. A military regime involves the indefinite perpetuation of military government. Remmer (1991) distinguishes between four types of military regime, according to two criteria: the concentration of authority in the government and the degree to which military and government roles are fused (see Table 10.4). In sultanistic regimes authority is concentrated and military and government roles fused. These are traditional systems and hence are particularly durable. Paradoxically the opposite form,

Table 10.4 Remmer's typology of military regimes

| | Concentration of authority | |
	High	Low
Fusion of military and govt roles: High	Sultanistic: close linkages centralise power av. 25.1 years	Feudal: military swamped by politics av. 6.5 years
Low	Monarchic: ruler isolated from military institution av. 6.9 years	Oligarchic: collegial rule allows multiple paths av. 16.3 years

Source: after Remmer 1991

the oligarchic, with collegial rule, low concentration of authority and little fusion of military and government roles, is also long-lived. Multiple paths for demands and personal advancement remain open and discontent minimised. Both the other forms, the feudal and the monarchic, are very unstable by comparison. The feudal, with low concentration of authority and the military occupying almost all government roles, results in the armed forces becoming highly politicised and leads to dissension in the ranks. The monarchic, with high concentration of authority and few military personnel in government roles, leads to the leader becoming dangerously separated from opinion in the armed forces. Of course it is possible for a long-lived military regime to evolve from one form to another. In all cases, however, the time of maximum danger to its continued survival comes at the point at which control is relaxed, generally in response to civilian demands which can no longer be contained or repressed.

Militarism

Militarism is the belief that political power should rightfully be exercised by the armed forces. By this, however, is usually meant the army, rather than the other armed forces. Navies, vital to, and therefore of vast weight in, the politics of Britain, the United States, Portugal, Greece, Argentina, Brazil and Chile, have in general acted symbolically through their admiralty establishments. Their political power seldom had much to do with their physical power to coerce, since ships once at sea were effectively out of touch with domestic affairs. Air forces had little independent weight before 1945. They remained (and remain) critically dependent on highly specialised land bases for refuelling and maintenance. Armies formed the ultimate defence in most other countries, and, being land-based and stationed usually close to the capital, could exercise all their power if they chose to do so, and in fact frequently did. They were, after all, equally open to the influence of politicians anxious to obtain their support (Stepan 1971).

There are two types of militarism which must be carefully distinguished. There is **'military' militarism** (militarism among the military personnel themselves) and **'civilian' militarism** (militarism among the civilian population), a distinction first made by Alfred Vagts (1959).

Military militarism is a caste pride, a pride in the glory, honour, power and prestige of the military forces. This type of militarism, however, is not just the normal pride of belonging to a well-organised force, but an exaggerated sense of remoteness and of superiority over the outside world in all aspects, so that those things which the military do not undertake are considered to be things not worthwhile for society as a whole. Military militarism, then, tends to arise in one of two sets of circumstances.

The first is when, for whatever reason, army ambitions become extended to the point of becoming conterminous with the limits of the ambitions of the state itself; that is to say, when the whole end, existence and pride of the state is seen by the army to be its concern and its concern alone. Such was the case in Imperial Germany (Craig 1955), or in Japan after the Meiji restoration, both ambitious to become 'Great Powers' in the fashion that a rather oversimplified view of European history had taught them was the approved method. This was to wage wars of imperial expansion, and the view was oversimplified because it was not necessary in fact to wage war with any real vigour in order to succeed, but only to give the impression of doing so.

The alternative situation is when the military feel that they have been betrayed by the civilians – as in the United Kingdom under Lloyd George when they felt insufficiently rewarded after 1919 (Callwell 1927), in France following the disaster of 1940 (Werth 1956), or in Egypt after the humiliation of 1948, when the government accepted the Anglo-Egyptian Treaty, and the armed forces were so conspicuously and ridiculously ineffective against the apparently amateur army of the nascent state of Israel (Neguib 1955). This belief can easily lead to the conclusion that the army should take over the state to regain its position, as in Egypt.

Civilian militarism is something rather different. It may afflict either the elite or the mass of the society, or in extreme cases both. It is a nationalist pride in crude power – in Vagts's words, 'Self-immolation on the altar of violence' (1959, p. 22) – a feeling that the army is well-deserving of the state, and should be rewarded with the unconditional support of the population on whose behalf it fights. This state of mind, a vital prerequisite of total war in modern states dependent for their deployment of force on conscript armies, has great drawbacks even then.

There have, of course, in every age been people who are exceptionally bellicose. There are thousands more who like vicarious excitement. There are also, in modern times, millions more who in times past have taken part in military service or training; of these some join the ranks of the armchair strategists and others (despite the evidence of their eyes) would be prepared to think the efficiency of a state could be improved by its militarisation. It may not be just nostalgia, of course, for it all depends on what aspect of civilian life they are using for comparison. But civilian militarism goes beyond approval of the military or even beyond applause. It implies extremism in its support, being more militaristic than the soldier in the front-line. There are four main examples of civilian militarism:

1. Extreme civilian support for the armed forces in time of war, as in the First World War in Britain when women pinned white feathers on men in civilian clothes, to shame them, as they thought, into fighting.
2. The belief of civilian politicians that they have special qualities as military leaders, strategic planners or even tacticians. In the Second World War each of the major Allied leaders, Churchill, Roosevelt and Stalin, all assumed military expertise they had not got, though not surprisingly each was, on occasion, right to overrule more specialist advice in the light of political strategy (Vagts 1959, pp. 463–9).
3. The voluntary election by civilians of a military leader as civil head of state or of government, often after a successful war.
4. Support by civilians for military dictatorship, whether or not coupled with aggressive war, concentration camps and so forth.

The incidence of militarism is variable, and though it depends greatly on time and historical circumstance, it clearly has an important relationship to the society in which it is found and hence to that society's political system. Finer argued that the tendency to intervene varied as between liberal democracies, developing states, or the communist regimes (Finer 1962, pp. 86–9).

Today the main problems are to be found in developing countries. The prevalent form of militarism is military. The forces in such countries – whether in Asia, Latin America or Africa – have a pride in their prowess which does not necessarily derive from recent combat, as, in many cases, for geographical or other extraneous reasons, the opportunity has not arisen. Until recently, however, the fact of independence implied an important historic role for the forces. They had the role of guardians of the state thrust upon them, in their opinion, because they saw themselves as the ones who had given birth to it. Secondly, the forces in those countries – primitive as they might appear in the light of modern technological innovations – have an important claim to the principal reservoir of technological expertise within them. The role of the soldier in developing north-west India and modern Pakistan, Iraq and Egypt has its parallels in the Amazonas region of Brazil today. Here the army maintains communications, surveys geographical formations, watches for infiltrators, and teaches civics classes by turn. In Ecuador, Bolivia and Peru, too, the army is often the sole agency of government apparent to the tribesmen, who see it as the agency of miracles in an inscrutable mixture of condign punishment for misdeeds and sudden cures of sick children and animals (see Bourricaud 1970, pp. 313–15). And the military of developing countries have been viewed as the chief agency of national unity (former Yugoslavia, recent Serbia) or even of revolution (China). In consequence, the defence ministers of such states are in a particularly strong political position, which they do not fail to take advantage of as often as they might.

The opposite situation, of course, may be found in the liberal democracies. There the military have been subordinated to the civilian power because of the professionalisation made necessary by technical advances. This professionalism removes the military from the community in a way equivalent to that in which the conditions of service overseas on behalf of an expanding power have removed them in a physical sense. Such remoteness, of course, goes far to end military interference in government, No one would expect, however, that it would be totally removed.

The liberal democracy finds that the military operates at once as the largest consumer of finance and as the most powerful lobbyist. Since Elizabethan times the navy has exercised a powerful influence on politics in Britain, and its maintenance and development have been key issues. But in modern times the sophistication of weapons makes the forces dependent on a range of specialist services of little relevance to civilian needs, while their vast weapons procurement needs call into play the typically 'modern' preoccupation with economics and the organisation of state production for defence needs. The rivalries between needs, especially between land, sea and air, do however act against one another in the call on political resources.

The communist states were in a middle situation. Most communist states were underdeveloped in an economic sense, and so their armed services could be expected to follow the behaviour patterns appropriate to this situation. However, the role of the military as the major power in retaining the communist party in power in nearly all of them was anomalous. Even as an elite the military could not hope to displace the communist party in power, because that would have destroyed the regime's claim to popular support. Moreover the rule of the party was backed up by a capacity for paramilitary force and rendered more powerful by the ability to exercise the state's right to socialise even within the caste itself, and the schismatic effects of the political police. The military could, however, hope to displace individual leaders if they failed to give it due credit and budgetary support. In the USSR Marshal Zhukov supported Khrushchev against the 'anti-party group' in June 1957, and was duly rewarded with a place in the Politburo. He was demoted in October 1957 on charges of 'Bonapartism', and of using his position to weaken party primacy within the military (Conquest 1961, pp. 338–9). General Wojciech Jarusielski used his position as military commander in Poland to intervene to 'protect' his country from direct Soviet intervention. Militarism in the liberal democracy, therefore, tends to be predominantly a civilian attribute, while in the communist state it could be either military or civilian.

Case Study | Military Chiefs in Peru Vow to Take a Back Seat to Democracy

The swearing-in of Peru's new armed forces chiefs on Wednesday took place with all the swagger Peruvians have come to expect from such occasions. But this time, the tone was different. The ceremony may well have been the death knell for the military as a breed apart. The sacking of three armed forces commanders this week by the interim government highlights a new appetite for change, even within the military.

Peruvians have been shocked by the abuses during ousted President Alberto Fujimori's decade of authoritarian rule. They now want the armed forces to respect democracy and stay out of politics.

During Mr Fujimori's rule, the military acted as an arm of the government, answering to the now-fugitive ex-spy chief Vladimiro Montesinos. The campaign against Shining Path guerrillas gave it virtual *carte blanche* to act as it saw fit.

Jose Cacho, Luis Vargas and Miguel Angel Medina, who now head the army, navy and air force respectively, have vowed to support a new democratic era in the armed forces.

Their predecessors – Carlos Tafur, Victor Ramos and Pablo Carbone – were caught on videotape backing Mr Fujimori a year before his fall from grace.

By dismissing the trio, Valentin Paniagua, the caretaker president, has taken the biggest step yet towards braking the military's involvement in politics. Since independence in 1821, the military has run 78 of Peru's 115 governments.

Source: *Financial Times*, 21/22 April 2001

Military intervention

Another section of the now extensive literature on the military role in politics has focused on the nature and origins of the armed forces themselves, and their relationship to the society in which they serve. In Nigeria, for example, the military takeover of 1966 owed much to the persistence of tribal consciousness in the army, among the northerners who felt excluded by the commercially active and politically dominant Igbo (Ibo). The fall and death of William V. Tubman in Liberia in 1980 was born of resentment of the dominant tribe of the interior at the domination of Americanised settlers on the coast. More recently the Serbs and Montenegrins who dominate the officer corps of the former Yugoslav National Army (JNA) have had no hesitation in putting their expertise, backed by heavy weapons, at the disposal of their fellow Serbs in Croatia and Bosnia.

To argue, as some writers have done, that the military act primarily as the armed wing of a tribe, or indeed of a class, is, on the other hand, to underestimate the profound importance of the army as an institution to soldiers, and in particular to the elite who command them (Howard 1955). The majority of armies are dominated by a relatively small, professionally trained officer corps. Its recruits are in terms of their respective societies largely middle class, and hence in many cases are drawn from a wide area. Hence they are bound together primarily by institutional ties. It is through the service as an institution, moreover, that they obtain their access to a system of substantial personal privileges, such as pensions, mortgages, credit, cheap goods, clubs, medical attention, and, above all, government positions, for it is membership of the institution that guarantees at one and the same time the safety of a relatively high basic standard of living, and the opportunity through promotion to gain access to much greater rewards. Military intervention in politics is guaranteed by the need to maintain this institutional structure in the face of competing civilian interests; its persistence is due to the complex inter-relationship between the three levels of the social, institutional and personal interest of the interventors, such that no one of them can be singled out as the cause, nor wholly disentangled from the others (Calvert 1979, reviewing Luttwak 1979).

Despite the serious difficulties the political scientist faces in amassing information about active military personnel in many of the most interesting cases, there is much information available. The need to gather information begins with the pre-recruitment stage in an officer's career. What sort of family background, what sort of education, how he came to be chosen for military service, and from what sectors of society, for what reasons he took up arms as a career – all these are questions of great importance, but most countries lack documentation on attitudes of individual soldiers to set beside Morris Janowitz's *The American Soldier* (1960), itself now four decades old. What can be known is what is partly or wholly in the public domain: how well integrated they are, what sort of regiments they form, and what sort of training process is standard, what their officers are like in relation to them, and whether they have special relationships with the officers of other armies. It is also relevant whether or not they are stationed near civilian communities, and if so what sort of arms they have and how they practise with them, and so forth. For the only states in which the military–civilian relationship can be entirely businesslike are those which have maintained a purely alien army, such as the Turkish Janissaries, or have an entirely alien subject population, such as ancient Sparta or apartheid South Africa. In all other cases the relationship is a two-way one. Nationalism in the citizenry gives the military a key to national sentiment in time of crisis. But the military pay for having an alert militarised populace by becoming subject to the tides and currents of uninformed opinion, so that they themselves become politi-cised and divided, and so lose their power to alter governments at will.

This power is most often exercised indirectly, by pressure from the military authorit-ies on the consitutional authorities to alter either personnel or policies. If this pressure is unsuccessful, the last resort is to intervene. Intervention, therefore, does not come out of a clear sky; like a thunderstorm, it is preceded by obvious signs of discontent, and often by an ultimatum which leaves the government in no doubt as to the army's view. Only if this is unsuccessful does the last stage of the process of disaffection follow, when the high command of the armed forces agree amongst themselves how to intervene and what is to follow. When they do act it will then normally be done in such a way as to minimise any chance of civilian obstruction or involvement until the military phase of the action is over, the existing government deposed and a new interim government ready to take over. In fact the efficiency of a military coup lies in precisely this: that the government can be changed without civilians becoming involved. Where common, the process has become so ritualised that in Latin America in the twentieth century no less than three-quarters of all military coups have been carried out without casualties. Considerably higher levels of bloodshed are to be expected in Africa, where as in Nigeria military intervention had occurred in a context of long-standing rivalry between the Northern Hausa and the coastal Igbo (see also O'Kane 1986). In the Middle East, the strategic importance of the region and the unique significance of globalisation in the form of the international oil industry has entrenched the armed forces in both domestic and regional politics, and the region remains the only substantial area of the world almost unaffected by 'third wave' democratisation.

Though military intervention in this sense is commonplace over much of the earth's surface, only comparatively rarely does it lead to the formation of a military government.

Having military officers in government, or even a military president in a presidential system, does not in itself make a government a military government. Civilians are needed to carry out many of the major functions of government whoever is officially in control and nowhere is this more noticeable than in the economics ministry. Despite the fact that so many military coups are 'justified' on the grounds of the incapacity to manage the economy, almost invariably the person chosen as minister of finance after a military coup is also a civilian.

However, in the 1960s there was a noticeable shift in attitudes and a new phenomenon emerged, starting with Brazil in 1964. Military forces now began to take power with the intention of holding on to it for a period of years – long enough to 'modernise' their countries through economic development. This phenomenon has often been termed **'bureaucratic authoritarianism'**, a term originally invented by the Argentine Guillermo O'Donnell (1988), whose views derive from Marxism and more particularly from dependency theory. Since it is its military rather than its bureaucratic character that really matters, however, the term 'military developmentalism' would have been more appropriate.

O'Donnell's theory envisages three stages of development of political systems. In the oligarchic stage the popular sector is not yet politicised, and so is neither mobilised nor incorporated in the state structure. In the populist stage, the popular sector is mobilised and incorporated. In the bureaucratic-authoritarian state it is then demobilised and excluded. For O'Donnell the bureaucratic-authoritarian state 'guarantees and organizes the domination exercised through a class structure subordinated to the upper fractions of a highly oligopolized and transnationalized bourgeoisie' (O'Donnell 1988, p. 31). Within the state structure two groups have decisive weight: specialists in coercion (the armed forces), whose job it is to exclude the 'popular sector' from power, and finance capitalists, whose role is to obtain the 'normalisation' of the economy, which performs the dual purpose of excluding the popular sector from economic power and promoting the interests of large oligopolistic interests. As part of the exclusion policy, social issues are depoliticised by being treated as a matter of narrow economic rationality, and direct access to government is limited to the armed forces, the state bureaucracy and leading industrialists and financiers.

Though applied in the first instance to Brazil, O'Donnell's model was derived from the experience of Argentina between 1966 and 1973, and, not surprisingly, fits it closely. Having failed in 1955 and 1962 permanently to exclude the Peronists from power by simple military coup, the promoters of what was grandiloquently (but not altogether inaccurately) termed 'the Argentine Revolution' in 1966 sought to stay in power for long enough to achieve that objective. However, the term itself is misleading, in that it is military rule not bureaucracy that was its distinguishing characteristic, and the model does not fit the authoritarian regimes imposed in Brazil in 1964 (reinforced in 1968), in Uruguay and Chile in 1973, or in Argentina again in 1976 (Linz and Stepan 1978). Not only were these states at very different levels of economic development, but in each case, as Collier noted, ideological polarisation was so marked that an adequate explanation had to take account of political factors such as the nature of the party system and the strength of organised labour.

Nor were these authoritarian regimes universal. Venezuela's mobilisation came at the end of its period of dictatorship and was accompanied by a deliberate and successful attempt to establish consensus as a basis for democratic government. The same was originally true also for Mexico, which, though authoritarian, is closer to the liberal-democratic model than it is to the pattern envisaged by O'Donnell, and has been particularly successful in co-opting potential opposition. Both have relatively diversified and well-developed economies.

Lastly the phrase gives insufficient emphasis to the military aspect of these governments, for what distinguished them was not their bureaucratic nature, nor (as O'Donnell argues) the 'transnationalisation' of production (for that has also happened in, for example, Western Europe), but the fact that the process was directed by the army and gained its distinctive features from the army's ability to make use of force. For this reason the present writer has suggested the term 'military developmentalism', a term which stresses its analogies with, for example, the military regimes of Egypt, Pakistan or even Thailand.

Force and Political Stability

Revolution, as will be seen in the next chapter, is often associated with military action and inevitably with military alienation. But it is always a strategic process capable of modification in response to tactical needs. It can therefore be averted by governments by approaching it on an entirely military level, and preventing the combination of the elements which are essential to the use of force against an armed opponent.

No revolution can occur successfully unless it has an efficient leader, an adequate number of followers, a cause to fight for, and means to make its numbers effective. Of these four, the easiest to avoid is the last. The classic instance is the case of the troops that marched through Baghdad on the night of 13–14 July 1958 on their way to the Israeli frontier. For the first time in the history of the state of Iraq they were not disarmed before entering the capital, and the result was the dramatic revolution which dethroned the Hashemite dynasty and established the Republic. If the means had not been available, there can be reasonable doubt that this revolution would have taken place – at least, not in the way that it did (Finer 1962, p. 79).

This poses two questions. When military intervention takes place in politics, how far is this a real expression of popular wishes? Is anomic interest articulation the necessary consequence of the blockage of other channels? It has been the peculiar sophistication of the twentieth century that men have been able to devise methods of creating the appearance of support, and so isolating the individual who might wish to express views hostile to them and their political programme. In the real world, if a man finds the country is run by the army, and he dislikes the way it is run, he may join the army and try to become a general, or he may take a gun and make for the hills, but he is much more likely to stay at home and mind his own business.

Turbulence as such represents part of a very wide nexus of interactions, which in point of fact may only incidentally be concerned with demands on the government. If people are not orientated to expect things from government, they may direct their energies towards getting them from one another, and yet be in general agreement that the government is doing the small minimum they want of it as well as can be expected. Political stability is not the same thing as freedom from violence, and it is not as remarkable a thing as the perspectives of journalism sometimes suggest.

Military government certainly does not mean political stability. In fact it is not even a very good way of running a country. Despite the wild claims that have been made for

Table 10.5 The armed forces and democracy

Conditions	Arguments	Problems
Role of the armed forces and external powers	Democracy is helped by: 1. Absence or weakness of armed forces	How to get rid of them?
	2. Socialisation of the armed forces into democratic values	Difficulty in proving
	3. Indifference of foreign powers to political outcomes	May reflect a country's economic weakness (or strategic unimportance)

Source: Pinkney 1993, p. 85

Chile under the Pinochet dictatorship, the armed forces have been no more successful at running economies than civilian governments. In an age of globalisation, they have had to learn the hard way that you cannot simply order an economy to perform and expect it to respond. Still less were they able to resolve the paradox that the neoliberal prescription of deregulation and privatisation is incompatible with the increased state intervention which military government brings. The most that they could do was to offer heavy bribes to transnational corporations and foreign investors, who at the first hint of trouble took fright and fled.

Military governments are also peculiarly vulnerable to corruption. In a closed society with an authoritarian government there is no effective check on expenditure. The Alfonsín government in Argentina investigated what had happened to some US$20 billion which had disappeared under the military governments of 1976–83. They were successful in locating $10 billion. The rest has never been found, but it represents a substantial portion of Argentina's national debt at the time. A corrupt and inefficient government that is unwilling to satisfy public demands can certainly not be regarded as a prescription for political stability.

So getting the military out of politics is certainly nothing like as easy as getting them in in the first place, despite the fact that it is obviously essential to successful democratisation. The first thing is to take advantage of moments when military governments or regimes falter under the weight of their own failure (O'Brien and Cammack 1985). The second is to have a clear idea of the proper role of the armed forces in society and to be prepared to make selective use of the power of the purse to induce them to accept it (Putnam 1993). It was, after all, a Mexican general who said that he had never met a Mexican general who could withstand a cannonade of thirty thousand pesos.

Summary

In extreme cases social movements can and sometimes do resort to a range of actions with more or less violence. To maintain themselves in power, all governments have resort to emergency powers and are backed by a variety of means of deploying 'legitimate' force in their own support. Dictatorship originated in emergency measures and is always likely to do so. However, apart from its inherent lack of legitimacy, dictatorship is fragile since it creates no regular form of succession.

The capacity to use force however is the essential guarantor of political stability. Governments utilise a variety of means to use force selectively: police, a 'secret police', paramilitary forces and regular armed forces.

The key question is not why do the armed forces intervene in politics but rather why do they not? The answer depends to some extent on cultural factors and the prevalence of military or civilian militarism. Internal factors within the armed forces themselves are whether or not they have both the disposition and the opportunity to intervene. However, although historically military intervention has been commonplace, and still takes place from time to time in some parts of the world, military government is comparatively rare and military regimes have been discredited by their disregard for human rights. Although economic crises may serve as a pretext for military intervention, military governments are generally incompetent at handling economic decisions and easily succumb to corruption.

Key Concepts

bureaucratic authoritarianism, for O'Donnell, a repressive political system characterised by the institutionalised role of the armed forces in control of the civilian population

civilian militarism, a feeling among civilians that the army is well-deserving of the state, and should be rewarded with the unconditional support of the population on whose behalf it fights

dictatorship, an emergency office given all power to deal with an urgent threat; by extension, any authoritarian ruler

force, the use of physical coercion

military militarism, a caste pride in the glory, honour, power and prestige of the military forces

paramilitary forces, (1) lightly armed forces combining military and police roles which are used to support armed forces in counter-insurgency campaigns; (2) by derivation, armed groups operating with impunity in a society where the state has partially lost its monopoly of force

police state, political system in which a centrally organised police force attempts to exercise control over all aspects of political and social life

secret police, in an authoritarian state a rule-enforcement agency, having its own volition as to the assignment of prosecution and punishment

socialisation, formal and informal processes by which young people acquire political attitudes and opinions

Sample Questions

A question such as 'What is political stability? How far is it threatened by economic development and change?' expects the candidate both to be aware of the literature and to deploy examples. Depending on the geographical focus of the course, a question such as 'Why do Latin American (or African) governments have a reputation for instability?' might be a possible alternative, and the question 'Are

newly independent states inherently politically unstable?' is central to the literature on Third World government and politics.

Getting the military out of politics is much more difficult than getting them in. A questions such as 'Examine the problems in any ONE country of your choice of securing the withdrawal of military regimes and the restoration of civilian politics' requires a

Sample Questions continued

certain degree of familiarity with the literature on democratisation as well as some consideration of the practicalities of reining in generals who have been used to giving orders and having them obeyed.

' "Power grows out of the barrel of a gun" (Mao Zedong). Discuss', offers a wide range of possibilities. Given that the quotation is so famous, some knowledge of Mao's theory of revolution (Chapter 11) would help.

Further Reading

On the police, Brewer (1988) is a good comparative study of the police in liberal democracies.

On the general concept of the 'police state' see Chapman (1970). For intelligence and secret police organisation in the former communist states, see Wolin and Slusser (1957) and Adelman (1984). Both annual and special reports of Amnesty International give ample evidence (if it were needed) of the use of force by governments to coerce political opponents.

On the role of the military in politics the literature is extensive. John J. Johnson (1964), Stepan (1971) and Clapham and Philip (1985) deal specifically with Latin America and Decalo (1976) with Africa, though each has value for other areas also. The argument for the concept of 'bureaucratic authoritarianism' can be found in O'Donnell (1988).

Violence and Political Change

CHAPTER ELEVEN

Learning Objectives

At the end of this chapter, the reader will be able:

- to evaluate competing explanations of why people rebel;

- to determine why some rebellions succeed and others fail;

- to assess how likely it is that rebellion will lead to real social change;

- to define revolution and to assess its importance.

The Right to Rebel?

No political system is ever likely to satisfy the needs of all its citizens. However, where substantial numbers are denied what they believe to be their rights over a long period of time, they are likely to seek a justification for using force to overthrow the existing order and to establish a new one. If they are unsuccessful, their actions will be termed a '**rebellion**' and they may well pay for their presumption with their lives. If they succeed, they may become the new government, proclaim their movement a '**revolution**', order major social changes and rewrite history with themselves at the centre of it.

The problem of the citizen confronted with a repressive government is one that has been discussed by political philosophers since Plato. The 'right to rebel' has been considered by many to be the ultimate right available to citizens whose civic rights are consistently denied. But it is a different question deciding on what occasion the citizen may legitimately exercise this right, and how, if it is exercised, all the consequences of the action can be legitimate. There are essentially two different and nearly opposed viewpoints.

According to the view of St Thomas Aquinas, rebellion is justified provided that the rebels can show – after their achievement – that their action was legitimate, that it had involved the use of the minimum possible force by which its ends could be achieved, and that no other resort was open to them (d'Entreves 1959, pp. 161, 181–5). A similar view was arrived at independently by Islamic writers (E.I.J. Rosenthal 1962, p. 97).

According to the later view of John Locke, however, at the time of the so-called Glorious Revolution in England, legitimacy is an attribute fixed before the event. Rebellion is only justified because the government of the day has lost its legitimacy, and the will of the people at large is more exactly represented by its successor. Any action tending to reduce the influence of the people on their own destinies is not legitimate and is to be opposed (Locke 1964, p. 202).

Marxist-Leninists were in an anomalous position. They believed that the overthrow of bourgeois government was pre-ordained by the forces of history, and justified by the bourgeoisie's previous exploitation of the proletariat. On the other hand, once a 'socialist' revolution had taken place, they believed (erroneously, as it turned out) that it could not be reversed and that fellow communist states had a right and a duty to support the new order (the Brezhnev Doctrine). This shows one of the problems inherent in the study of revolution and rebellion. Rebellion creates its own legend or myth, which may have little to do with actual events. The Russian Revolution of October 1917 was not a mass uprising of the proletariat but a well-planned coup carried out by some 300 soldiers, and Marx greeted the Paris Commune of 1871 as the first example of the rising of a self-conscious proletariat, though in fact the *communards* were drawn from all social classes.

The reason for the myth, in the case of a successful revolution, is to support the legitimacy claim of the new government, and in the case of an unsuccessful rebellion, to denounce the action taken as a deviation from the prevailing norms of society. All systems of political thought except the anarchist agree that if a government is legitimate it has the 'right' to suppress those who use force against it. Where violence is 'normal', then the use of force against violence is also 'normal'. Not surprisingly, therefore, there is a clear relationship between the ability of a government to use coercion and the amount of political violence with which it is likely to be confronted. But the relationship is not a linear one (see Figure 11.1).

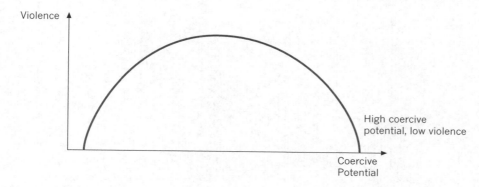

Figure 11.1 State coercive potential and political violence

Source: Duff and McCamant 1976, p. 119

During the Cold War years there was among policy-makers in the United States a competition between two explanations of political unrest, which we can term 'poverty' and 'communism' (Feinberg 1983). This reflected not only the growing global involvement of the United States but the ambiguous position of the United States in supporting authoritarian regimes simply because of the strategic position of the countries they controlled.

There is a great deal of empirical evidence that poverty is strongly associated with social unrest. Colburn (1994) considers that revolution is now exclusively only a problem for poor countries, since countries which have higher levels of both economic development and social mobilisation are more stable. Huntington, however, pointing out that 'the relation between modernization and violence is complex' (Huntington 1968, p. 39), argued that it was not poverty itself which caused unrest but efforts to modernise. Yet if modernisation did not take place, anger would inevitably grow and unrest develop.

Others argued that the United States in setting an example was already doing all it could. Rebellion, therefore, was being fomented by a world-wide communist conspiracy as a method of undermining the global reach of the US government, by embroiling it in conflicts such as Vietnam. The remedy was to spend more money on arms and troops, which inevitably left less for foreign aid and economic development. To the extent that communism was a globalising doctrine there was some justification for this view, but though the two explanations were not in fact opposites, they were presented as such.

Why Do People Rebel?

There is a great deal of anomic activity in any society which is not articulated, the goals of which are not clear in political terms, and which if it does not succeed, cannot obtain subsequent approval. 'Direct action' and civil disobedience tread the shifting borderline between the legal and the illegal. But they do not really endanger the existing government or regime. If they did, they should expect to be suppressed by an efficient government determined to maintain its own power.

People rebel because for one reason or another they feel disadvantaged compared with others, whether in wealth, status or political power. This is termed **'relative deprivation'**.

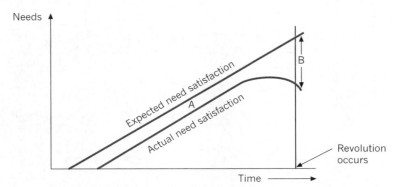

Source: Davies 1962, p. 5

Figure 11.2 The Davies J-curve

They become rebels, however, only if they take a conscious decision to try to improve their lot and see no other way of remedying their situation. Even then, unless their rebellion is focused on politically achievable objectives it is unlikely to succeed.

J.C. Davies argues that revolution is most likely to take place when an intolerable gap opens up between what people want and what they actually get (Davies 1962), and illustrates a common form of this with his well-known 'J-curve' (Figure 11.2).

But people vary a great deal in what they find tolerable. Rebellion is only one possible response, moreover; alternative responses include accommodation, negotiation and passive resignation. While the Seattle riots, protesting at the remorseless spead of globalisation and the dominance of large transnational corporations, caught the headlines, the majority of the public in the United States continued to shop in supermarkets, buy industrial food and drive cars fuelled by imported oil. Only a minority support organisations dedicated to trying to change this state of affairs by peaceful political action.

It is widely assumed that political and social change are bound up together. Unfortunately this is not the case, and it is therefore very important to distinguish between terms. For the political scientist, the first concern must be with political change: change in government or in regime by the use of force by its own citizens (cf. Tilly 1978). This may or may not be an act which is a prerequisite of deep-reaching social change. Historically the overthrow of a government was itself termed a 'revolution'. However, for many years there has been a tendency for social scientists to restrict the term 'revolution' only to social revolutions, those rare historical events in which the fall of governments is followed by profound social change. Hence writers as diverse as Edwards (1970), Pettee (1938), Brinton (1952), C. Johnson (1964) and Skocpol (1979) concur on one thing, that only movements involving such change qualify for the glorious title of revolution (Calvert 1970a, pp. 121ff.) Yet as we shall see, without a political revolution, a social revolution cannot follow.

There is much less agreement on just how many instances there are of what have been termed 'the great social revolutions' (Edwards 1970), but there is almost universal agreement that there have been very few of them. Those that would be generally accepted include England (1640–59), America (1774–89), France (1789–95), Mexico (1910–20), Russia (1917–29), China (1949–78?) and Cuba (1959). Perhaps a dozen more would

Table 11.1 The great social revolutions?

Date	Country
1581	The Netherlands
1642	ENGLAND
1688	England
1775	UNITED STATES
1789	FRANCE
1910	MEXICO
1911	China
1917	RUSSIA
1919	TURKEY
1933	Germany?
1949	CHINA
1952	Bolivia Egypt
1958	Algeria
1959	CUBA
1968	Peru
1969	Libya
1974	Portugal
1979	IRAN NICARAGUA
1989	Czechoslovakia, East Germany, Romania, etc.
1991	RUSSIA, etc.

be fairly generally recognised – these range from China (1911) and Turkey (1923) through the Nicaraguan and Iranian Revolutions of 1979 (Brinton 1952; Leiden and Schmitt 1968; Calvert 1990a, p. 4) to the events of 1989 in Eastern Europe and, perhaps, the collapse of the Soviet Union itself in 1991. Many might add the rise of Hitler in Germany (1933). But they would not include long-term evolutionary changes, such as the rise of the gentry in Tudor England or the Meiji restoration in Japan, in which the element of violence is minimal. In Table 11.1, those more generally recognised are capitalised.

This leaves us the problem of what to call the many political revolutions which occur each year and have no important social consequences, most commonly since either they do not seek to obtain them or they have been carried out in order to pre-empt social change and not to achieve it. These events, which are referred to by a variety of names – palace revolutions, coups, etc. – result only in a change of government and if not accompanied by regime change are unlikely to be seen as a breaks in the social order, but they are nonetheless very important to students of politics (Calvert 1979).

The limiting case of successful political violence is political assassination. This is, of course, universally regarded by governments as a very serious crime, since it threatens them personally and not just the stability of the political order. But outside government there is a tendency to think that in itself it can change nothing and therefore has no political importance. However, this is certainly not the case. With the possible exception of John F. Kennedy, all four US presidents who were assassinated are believed to have been killed for political motives. In some cases an assassination has had profound political implications. On 20 December 1973 the Spanish prime minister, Admiral Luis Carrero Blanco, died when explosives planted in a Madrid street blew his Dodge Dart over a five-storey building and into the courtyard he had just left. The Admiral had been the most trusted adviser of General Franco since 1941 and the General, who was already in poor health, had trusted him to ensure the survival of his regime and the succession of Prince Juan Carlos. Instead the Council of the Realm appointed the reactionary Carlos Arias Navarro, who disliked Juan Carlos and vetoed measures for liberalisation of the regime which might have eased the transition to democracy after Franco's death (C. Powell, 1996 pp. 60–4, 68–9). So assassination can at the least result in political change, and so can other forms of anomic activity.

On the other hand, **violence** on its own does not necessarily have much political significance. Fighting at football matches went on for years before it was politicised and so became an issue for political debate. Broadly speaking, our main concern therefore is with what Russett *et al.* term 'domestic group violence' (Russett 1964). This is violence that arises within the domestic context and does not involve foreign intervention; involves groups rather than individuals; and either its objectives or its scale or both are such that it affects the political system significantly. Sub-revolutionary violence takes three main forms.

1. **Demonstrations**. Demonstrations are anomic groupings of people moved by a single common interest, controlled either by their own agreement or by leaders, with a limited target of applying pressure to part or whole of the political system and a fairly low level of accompanying violence, at least in the early stages. They may occur anywhere within the territorial limits of the state. For example, over the years French farmers have gained a high level of organisation in defending their interests by road-blocks backed up by the threat of violence. Should uncontrollable demonstrations occur in the capital itself they could be sufficient to bring down a weak or discredited government or even topple a regime – as in Argentina in 1982 following the defeat of the military government in the South Atlantic. Otherwise they are best regarded as short-lived interest groups (see Chapter 6).

2. **Riots**. Demonstrations, however, must be distinguished from riots, which are uncontrolled movements of frustrated opinion, undiscriminating in target. In the countryside such movements are sometimes given the French name *jacquerie*. Riots in cities show great differences in their political effects, but seldom pose a serious challenge to a

confident government sure of the support of its armed forces and police. In Colombia in 1948 the capital was out of control for three days of unrestrained violence and looting (the 'Bogotazo') without the president yielding to it. In Greece in 1965 extensive riots took place in Athens, but had no result in terms of change of government or regime. The riots of 1967 and 1992 in the United States helped discredit the incumbent power holders, but the frustrations they expressed were speedily absorbed into the normal pattern of presidential campaigning. However, where, as in the United States, there is free sale and distribution of firearms, a new element enters the picture: the possibility of long-term urban violence. Without firearms, this cannot exceed the level of sporadic incidents at weak points in the presence of city government – in dark streets, waste-lots, or deserted buildings not subject to regular police patrol, for example. The introduction of firearms clearly amplifies the possibilities considerably. It is sobering to recall that in 1964 Yugoslavia was at the bottom of Russett's list (Russett 1964, p. 100) for domestic group violence, together with the United Kingdom. By 1999, with firearms available to contending groups, there had been more than thirty years of armed conflict in Northern Ireland, while Yugoslavia had disintegrated in civil war and so-called 'ethnic cleansing'.

3. **Terrorism**. Terrorism is the use of force to impart fear with a view to bringing about political or social change. In the quite recent past it has been endemic in at least parts of most of the countries of the world. The nature of terrorism, which may in fact be either spontaneous or organised, is that it is widespread and effective across the political spectrum in securing publicity and influencing public opinion. However, terrorism is a strategy born not of strength but of weakness in political terms, and it seldom if ever results in a change of government without the assistance either of external intervention or of a mass uprising.

It is true, as is often repeated, that 'one man's terrorist is another's freedom fighter'. Hence terrorism is an extreme example of an essentially-contested concept, and its practice tends to polarise a society to an extent that renders it extremely difficult to return to normal politics. A purely military solution is rarely possible without unacceptably high levels of force and widespread violation of civil liberties; in Spain, the Basque separatist organisation ETA is still able to carry out attacks. On the other hand a negotiated solution is also not easy for a democratic society to obtain. It took years of negotiations to arrive at an agreement between government and armed opposition in Guatemala in 1996 and the agreement had to be monitored by UN observers to have any chance of success. In Colombia in 2001 fighting continues between government forces and an armed movement which is well armed and well equipped through the revenue from the narcotics trade but seems to have lost all sense of political direction. An earlier agreement in 1985 foundered when those fighters who had taken to peaceful politics were selectively assassinated by hard-line paramilitaries.

Revolution and Political Change

There are, therefore, many reasons why people rebel, but all these actions fall short of revolution. Revolution is violence plus political change: it brings about a fall of government or a change of regime. As long as violence falls short of this point it is a means of interest articulation and aggregation, though of a nature in the long run incompatible with the maintenance of ordered government. It corresponds, therefore, to levels of activity within the regular political system: demonstrations being similar in action to pressure groups, riots to the parliamentary aspect of the political party, and terrorism to the mass organisation attempting to build a groundswell of political support. It therefore can be politically significant in application to regular processes as well as those of violence. The key factors that differentiate revolution from rebellion, therefore, are leadership and organisation – that is to say, its political attributes.

This raises the question of how to assess resultant changes in the long term. Any theory of the development of the political system first has to deal with a number of snags. For one there is the problem of identifying the conceptual boundary of the political system in application to the real world. Then there is the problem of delimiting the period within which development is to be considered and its relationship to earlier political formations in the same area. Thirdly, there is the question of how the units of development are to be measured. 'Development' is itself a complex of concepts only some of which can be reduced to expressions in terms of quantifiable indicators. If there is no general agreement what the system is, or how long it has lasted, there is not likely to be much that can usefully be said about its development.

This is the problem facing Almond in his essays on developmental theory. As has been shown, he goes some way towards considering the third, avoids the first, and leaves practical application to the reader. Using the concept of revolution used by him elsewhere (Almond and Coleman 1960) it seems likely that the major discontinuities, and hence the 'start' and 'finish' of his conceptual systems, are in the major revolutions, in periods of social rather than political change. This concept of discontinuity is clearly inapplicable. Two things stand in the way of its acceptance: the prevalence of political change through violence, and the prevalence of violence without political change. For if neither violence nor political change is separately the mark of discontinuity in a political system, no combination of the two can effect such a discontinuity. To put it in terms of an example, the French Revolution marks a discontinuity in the history of France, but not in its political system, which continued to exist throughout since it was broken neither by the violence employed nor by the changes of government which occurred during it.

If sub-revolutionary violence forms a 'normal' part of the political process, the process of political change that results from it, or from the actual transition between governments, may be distinguished from it. Under the umbrella term 'revolution' there are four concepts to be distinguished.

1. A **process** by which social changes occur, leading towards political change through violence or the convincing threat of violence.
2. At least one political **event**, in which a government or regime is actually changed.
3. The **programme** that a post-revolutionary government pursues, which has links with both process and event.
4. The **myth** of revolution, the symbolic value it holds in the integration or disintegration of the community. The special quality of the myth, which seems to be embodied in the sociologists' concept of social revolution, is that it suggests in aggregate that political order is at once permanent and discontinuous, since it owes its final form to a species of consensus between conservative and radical interpretations (Calvert 1970b, p. 4).

An integrated model of this kind recognises most usefully the functional role of revolution in society. It rests on conflict: the conflict between demands and supports, the conflict between elite (decision-makers) and mass (the public), the conflict, above all, between the political system and the social system as a whole. In the flow pattern of such a model, revolution forms one kind of interaction among the many patterns of positive and negative interchange between these last: the maximisation of demands (or negative inputs) and the minimisation of supports (or positive inputs).

In the political sense, then, revolution is first and foremost an event, and may be suspected in any violent change of ruler by subjects. There are obviously vast variations in the surrounding events, but in the actual change a certain rigidity is apparent. Certain attributes can be recognised as being important, and can be used therefore for classification.

To begin with the event implies the use of a certain amount of violence by revolutionaries, opposed on occasion by a quantity of force on the part of the regime. The fact of success implies that the revolutionary violence has attained a point which can be termed the minimum necessary force (MNF). This point is crucial to the differentiation of revolutionary from sub-revolutionary activity. Failure to reach MNF implies the failure of the movement in question; excess over it, it may reasonably be hypothesised, will result in ancillary phenomena in the political or social consequences of the event (Calvert 1970a, p. 32). After all, those revolutions which have been associated most closely with developed social phenomena have been those in which the government overthrown exercised power at so low a level that any force used to overthrow it was proportionately almost infinite. The force employed is a measurable quantity, measurable either as the number of troops mobilised or as the number actually deployed at any given moment, multiplied by their capacity to use force and the degree of their spatial concentration.

A revolutionary event must occupy a certain time period. Within this three time phases can be distinguished: a period of *preparation* integral with and related to the social process of disaffection; the action itself, which can be termed the *assault phase*; and a period of *consolidation* with the promulgation of the post-revolutionary programme (Goodspeed 1962).

The nature of the assault period is the determinant of the transition itself, and the duration of it – usually brief – is a second criterion for classification. The reason is that the superiority of power to be obtained by the revolutionary force has to be effective during this period, or, more specifically, during a period, termed the critical time, which in a successful revolution falls wholly within this period. Beyond the conclusion of the assault phase, it should be noted, the use of force is no longer directed specifically at the defeated government, but as in the case of any other government of whatever age, against all possible and probable enemies of the new regime.

A third attribute is the level on which force is deployed, that is to say the extent of the geographical space over which the action takes place, which can be termed the arena. This action must be related to the force available if MNF is to be achieved, and the option may exist for initiating hostilities on either of two levels, or on any level, depending on resources. In order of power required, revolutionary action may be directed against the executive, the government, the capital or a province. Each brings its particular hazards.

The immobilisation of the executive requires speed and secrecy of planning, but the least actual force.

Capture and overthrow of the government involves a number of personnel, some of whom are of little importance, but others of whom have authority without formal rank.

These have to be rapidly and accurately located and captured, and synchronisation of action becomes a major consideration if reinforcements are not to become a hazard. Failure to do so results in the sort of consequences that followed the breakdown of the plot to overthrow the government of Abraham Lincoln, which was successful only in so far as it resulted in the death of Lincoln himself (Havens, Leiden and Schmitt 1970, p. 43). A major social revolution of such a type was the Bolshevik seizure of power in Russia in November 1917.

A movement directed at securing control of the capital involves a number of considerations, but that of force is obviously most important. Since it assumes that a complete superiority of force will be achieved in the key administrative area of a country, which will not be challenged in the critical time by forces brought in from the provinces, it is the form normally favoured by military movements. It is effective because it gains control of the area from which the people at large expect leadership, and that on which the communications net is centred. It was also the scene of the French Revolution of 1789 and hence of its many nineteenth-century imitators.

The seizure and exercise of governmental functions in a province, which requires the most force of any type of revolution, is intended to put pressure on this area indirectly. It can therefore start with small beginnings, but depends on remoteness from the centre of power to attract superior forces before government troops arrive to engage it. It can then hope, if the government does not yield, to strike at the capital and put it out of action directly. This is the principle behind the guerrilla warfare that led to the Chinese Revolution of 1949 and the Cuban Revolution of 1959.

For obvious theoretical reasons, the Marxist writers on revolution advocate movements in which large-scale mobilisation occurs of the masses. Since Marxists have traditionally been opposed to the coup, for fear that a military leader may use it to seize power (termed Bonapartism, after Napoleon Bonaparte), they have laboured under the necessity of maintaining unusually high force levels in their attempts to gain power. Lenin himself was prepared to adopt the coup as an opportunistic short-cut, however, with outstanding success (Goodspeed 1962, pp. 70ff.) Significantly, none of the so-called communist 'revolutions' in Eastern Europe after 1945 took place independently of the presence of a large occupying force of Soviet troops.

Reliance on peasant guerrilla movements, advocated by Mao Zedong (Schram 1963, pp. 202–88) and Che Guevara (Guevara 1967, p. 15), appeared in both China and Cuba to succeed through direct pressure in bringing about the collapse of central resistance. However, in both cases other factors have to be taken into account. In China the collapse of the Kuomintang came only after eight years of war against the Japanese, and the power vacuum left by the Japanese surrender. A similar power vacuum was largely responsible for the success in 1945 of the Communists in Vietnam, and the followers of Sukarno in Indonesia, their government being established in each case before the return of the colonial power and thus able to provide a geographical base for guerrillas' resistance to reconquest (Kahin 1974, pp. 392–5). In Cuba, the guerrilla war formed the pretext for a massive urban uprising, and it was the combination of the two, and not just the guerrilla campaign on its own, that led to governmental collapse. It was the fact that the Cuban revolution occurred in an area that was already acquainted with revolutionary movements on all levels which pointed up its regularities, and made possible the assimilation of Marxist revolutions to a general theory.

It should be added, however, that difficulties lie in the way of precise application of force analysis (even retroactively) which have nothing to do with the type advocated, but are purely practical. Information about troop numbers and movements is classified information, and by the time security has been lifted, the recollections of witnesses may be unable to rectify the propaganda versions of numbers engaged. In any case, actual numbers of forces employed are rarely used, vague expressions such as 'regiments', 'companies', 'detachments' being capable of multiple interpretations, even assuming that they were regular formations up to their roster strength. It is for this reason that Lewis F. Richardson chose to set the precedent of measuring the impact of violent events in terms of 'magnitude'. The magnitude of an event is simply the total number of casualties caused by it, as measured on a simple logarithmic scale (Richardson 1960, pp. 6–7).

What sort of statements can this analysis enable us to make on the nature of actual revolutions? First of all, there is from observation alone no clear link between economic development and the absence of violence in politics, though it is clear that there is some link. Comparison on the one hand between Argentina and Uruguay indicates that a highly developed agricultural country, backed by a substantial industrial complex with money to spend on social and other services, does not necessarily enjoy peaceful politics, or even civilian government. Comparison on the other hand between Chile and Mexico suggests that it is not necessary to have a large-scale social revolution in order to achieve equality and social justice. Personalities in power are very important, as the destruction of civilian rule in Chile after 1973 demonstrates.

The presence of violence, however, imposes its own necessities. In particular, given the need to adapt to changing times, military intervention all too easily becomes essential where it is normal. Otherwise the operation of a system in which political change is achieved substantially by violent means cannot be continued in face of the non-participation of the monopolists of the means of coercive force. Contrary to the impression that violence is a sign of instability, governments seem to change sometimes more and sometimes less frequently in countries in which violent politics is the norm. It does not seem to make much difference in either case how the change is achieved provided that it is seen to have occurred. A dictator who changes his cabinet frequently may fulfil the desire for new faces as effectively as the process of frequent elections in other countries, and the value of federalism where it operates, or elective local government where it does not, must at least partly be the facility it offers for frequent lesser changes and the channelling of the impulse into manageable form. But evidently not all states value leadership changes, preferring to demonstrate one leader of accepted skills or outstanding personal qualities, such as Mao, Nasser or Kenyatta.

Thirdly, it should be noted that the impulse towards violence results in frequent and fairly simple coups, sometimes following one another in a sequence. The 'great social revolutions', as Lyford P. Edwards named them, such as the French, English and Russian, and even in some states the American, were composed in part of coups and in part of other acts of violence. As discussed above, the relationship between these coups and social reform is contradicted on both sides, but Haiti, Panama and the Dominican Republic all offer equally dramatic examples of sequences which took place without bringing about social change (Calvert 1970b, pp. 181ff.).

The difference is often attributed to a particular combination of social circumstances, which impelled into power a set of moderate social reformers who succeeded in arousing expectations and making the burden of the past intolerable, without at the same time taking steps sufficient to satisfy resultant demand. This was the pattern of Brinton's (1952) comparative historical study of the English, American, French and Russian Revolutions. In it he drew parallels between the four periods studied, each of which had

Abdurrahman Wahid warned – as the threat to his presidency grew ever more pressing – that hundreds of thousands of his followers would march to Jakarta if he was ousted. Yet when the cleric was sacked last Monday, in the culmination of a well-flagged piece of political drama, the streets were empty.

Mr Wahid had attempted to deliver on his warning, declaring a state of emergency and trying to dissolve parliament, at which point Jakarta braced itself for turmoil. But as legislators voted him out of office, the city that since independence has seen a series of violent protests and demonstrations in 56 tumultuous years of dictatorship and more recently democracy remained peaceful.

Only a few thousand well-wishers came to Mr Wahid's farewell speech in Jakarta's Freedom Square. 'We felt a great sense of relief that the democratic institutions in a new democracy worked rather well,' says Richard Gozney, British ambassador.

Megawati Sukarnoputri, Mr Wahid's deputy, was elected the fifth president at the start of the week after Mr Wahid was voted out of office – Indonesia's most peaceful transition of power since independence.

Observers have applauded the smooth functioning of Indonesia's political institutions and the restraint by street demonstrators and security forces.

In spite of his threats, Mr Wahid's erratic style had helped pave the way for a peaceful transition by ensuring that nearly all of the country's most powerful groups were united against him. The antagonism between the former president and parliament was evident in the first weeks of his rule. But during his presidency, two groups in particular became central to Indonesia's peaceful transition. The first was the military, which has had a key role in the country's politics since the 1950s. The second was Mr Wahid's main power base, the world's largest Muslim organisation, the Nahdlatul Ulama, which claims over 40m members.

After Mr Wahid came to power in October 1999, generals grew to see him as a bumbling civilian politician who interfered in the internal affairs of the military. By January this year he was seen as a dangerous man trying to use the armed forces for his own ends.

'A combination of interference in internal affairs and then weakness in handling critical issues' led to the erosion of support in the armed forces, says Bob Lowry, a military analyst with the International Crisis Group (ICG), a Brussels-based think-tank.

Indonesia's armed forces are still trying to reshape an image tainted by allegations of human right abuse and corruption under the 32-year rule of autocratic former president Suharto, which ended in May 1998.

In late 1998, Indonesia's armed forces committed themselves to a phased withdrawal from civilian politics and their allocated parliamentary seats. Military officers, who rarely speak in public, say the move back to the barracks will need to be managed gradually. But Mr Wahid, keen to appear a reformist, tried to speed the process and was seen to insult Wiranto, the former armed forces chief, who commanded fierce loyalty among the troops.

The military was finally united with the police, their historic rivals, by the issue that was to bring down Mr Wahid – his plan to call a state of emergency. Both institutions strongly opposed the plan. As Mr Wahid considered dissolving parliament, 70 tanks and armoured cars parked opposite his office, pointing their guns in his direction.

In hindsight, they need not have. Even within the Nahdlatul Ulama, support for the former president was eroding. Solahuddin Wahid, his brother and a Nahdlatul Ulama board member, said the organisation did not support massive street protests. 'We don't have the training, we don't have the money,' said Mr Solahuddin, 'and we couldn't guarantee there wouldn't be anarchy.'

Violence still wracks the Moluccan Islands and Aceh provinces, and separatists are fighting soldiers in Irian Jaya, so Indonesia cannot yet claim to be at peace. But a crucial test in its experiment with democracy has proved a surprising success.

Source: *Financial Times*, 28 July 2001

FT

been characterised by a move towards political extremism. He concluded that the Russian Revolution, too, might in due course be expected to enter the period he termed 'Thermidor', the winding-down of revolutionary fervour and consolidation of a new and more efficient state system.

But moderate reform does not necessarily result in the rise and successful accession to power of extremists; it may, and often does, result in a counter-coup by irate conservatives. Besides, history abounds with examples in which moderate reform satisfied demands of a potentially revolutionary character: the passage of the Great Reform Act in Britain in 1832 was one. Even if extremists accede to power, they need not necessarily follow their first reprisals with an organised reign of terror designed not only to destroy their enemies but to cow others into submission (Calvert 2000; see also O'Kane 1996). Terror was used in Iraq and Egypt (Khadduri 1970, p. 137 and note 5), but the Nicaraguan Sandinistas (FSLN) abolished the death penalty and sought to maintain a dialogue with their political opponents. The presence of a threatening external enemy, however, does appear to have been a factor in cases in which terror has been adopted, despite the great weakness of the internal opposition, but external enemies have acted to exacerbate suspicion that this weakness was feigned (but see also Walt 1992). The numbers however are small, and the suspicion remains that revolutionaries by nature expect to find hostility, and if they do not, they tend to create it in order to justify their philosophy of violence. There is, after all, the temptation to extend an apparently easy (because successful) method of achieving power into a means of maintaining it.

There must also be taken into account the panic reaction of people who do not wish to be 'liberated' from the traditional ways that they know, which, after all, are basically the means by which they have been taught to survive (Fromm 1960). In such circumstances even leaders may be nervous about unpredictable changes of opinion, the more so since revolutions do tend to occur in 'waves', either because others find the ideas they propagate congenial or because their success inspires imitation (Katz 1997; cf. Huntington 1993a).

Revolution and Social Change

Among modern writers, there are four main interpretations of revolution to be found: historical theories, psychological theories, sociological theories and political theories.

The very limited number of examples of the so-called 'great social revolutions' has strengthened the tendency to study them through the method of comparative history. But with very few examples to study, separated by time and space and with very little in common with one another, lengthy descriptions yield few useful generalisations and the results have been meagre. Since the Second World War the emergence of new states has been accompanied by the occurrence of new social revolutions, but as the number of cases available for study has expanded, authors have still tended to study them in the same traditional context, using much the same criteria. Thus Leiden and Schmitt (1968) basically repeated the work of Brinton taking as their case studies four examples that had either not previously been studied in a comparative context or had occurred too recently: Mexico, Turkey, Egypt and Cuba. In a theoretical introduction they did however recognise the work of social scientists in seeking to derive from such case studies some more general propositions which would be useful in application to other cases.

Barrington Moore (1969) is not really concerned with modern societies or the theory of revolution at all, but the way in which pre-modern societies had evolved in the way they had. His book, which was widely popular, uses six case studies, contrasting the experiences of Britain, France and the United States, with those of Japan, China and India, and throughout lays special emphasis on the importance of landownership and the role of the peasantry. Moore, moreover, does not hesitate to assert that violence and coercion have played as much of a role in the formation of Western democracies as in the making of communist states or the rise of fascism: the differences between them, he asserts, can be found in the different nature of their revolutionary experiences.

John Dunn (1989) uses eight case studies: Russia, Mexico, China, Yugoslavia, Vietnam, Algeria, Turkey and Cuba. Though treated on the basis of secondary sources and hence on a rather high level of generality, this book is informative, and the introduction and conclusion do challenge many of the traditional generalisations about revolution in an interesting and provocative way. Dunn describes the variety of methods by which power has actually been achieved. But he does not link the achievement of power to the nature of the outcome, except in the sense that both are recognised to be authoritarian.

Unlike earlier 'comparative' studies, such as those of Brinton and Dunn, Theda Skocpol (1979) does not examine each of her case studies in turn and then sum up her findings. Instead, following a theoretical introduction, the first part of her book is a very detailed comparative treatment of three revolutions: the French Revolution of 1787–1800, the Russian Revolution of 1917–21 and the Chinese Revolution of 1911–49. The Marxist concept of class relations and class conflict forms the basis of the analysis in each case, though she differs from earlier writers in attaching more importance to the way in which revolutions modify political structures. This has important implications. First, all previous theories of revolution, she claims, are voluntarist; people have the ability to influence outcomes by making decisions. However, she sees the causes of revolution in structural terms and hence non-voluntarist; people are constrained by social movements and cannot consciously influence outcomes. Secondly, revolution cannot be understood simply on the national level. International as well as national conjunctures have to be favourable for a major social revolution to occur. But international conjunctures alone are not a sufficient explanation, so there is no support here for Immanuel Wallerstein (1974) and the world systems' theorists. Thirdly, classes are not the sole actors, and states are not simply the agents of the dominant class. States are both potentially autonomous and coercive. In fact, influenced by Ellen Kay Trimberger, Skocpol's concept of the great social revolutions is one of 'revolutions from above' led by elites in the name of the masses. Though social revolutions arise from mass action in the pre-revolutionary situation, the programme of reform that follows them is seen as imposed by elites operating not only within the limitations of the domestic context but within the international conjunctures of the world economic system, in particular the structures of the world economy and the changing range of models available for borrowing. These are important, not because they influence the people, but because they influence their rulers.

Psychological theories help explain the motivation of individuals in revolutionary situations, but are not really appropriate as modes of explanation of mass action. Early writers focused on the actions of crowds, but today at least these play a limited role. The role of 'relative deprivation', stressed by T.R. Gurr (1970) and William Gamson (1975), is undoubtedly significant, but as noted above is not easy to apply given the wide range of behaviours that occur in response to a feeling of deprivation. Nor can it be assumed that leaders and followers share the same motivation.

Sociological theories of revolution assume that the stability of society depends on the social order continuing to fulfil the requirements of its citizens. If it fails to do so, consensus on the values of society is lost, and with the failure of consensus the way is open for a mass rejection of the existing order. Thus for one of the first of the comparative writers, Lyford P. Edwards, revolution was of social rather than political significance, and this led him to play down the elements of physical violence and transfer of power. 'The overthrow of the monarchy and feudal system in France was not caused by the French Revolution', he argued (1970, p. 7). 'The Revolution simply made evident the fact that the real power in France had passed into the hands of the middle class.'

George Sylvester Pettee introduced as an explanation of revolution the term '**social disequilibrium**'. Employing the language associated with the US sociologist Talcott Parsons, society is here seen as a fundamentally stable system. Equilibrium is that normal state of society to which it will tend to return after crises or disturbances. If it becomes so unbalanced that this is impossible, major social change will follow. However, societies are constantly changing. If the equilibrium point is moving, how is it possible to determine when a society has become so disequilibrated that fundamental change is inevitable?

A more systematic view is that of Chalmers Johnson (1964, 1966). Johnson adopts as his provisional definition of revolution that of Sigmund Neumann (1948–49, p. 333): 'a sweeping fundamental change in political organization, social structure, economic property control and the predominant myth of a social order, thus indicating a major break in the continuity of development'. He then develops a typology of both insurrection and revolution in six rather oddly assorted categories. These involve the use of four criteria: the targets of the activity, the nature of the revolutionaries, the goals of the revolution, and whether it is planned or develops spontaneously. The categories are:

1. **jacquerie** – a mass rebellion of peasants with the limited aim of redressing grievances;
2. **millenarian rebellion** – urban or rural, a rising in the hope of a radical change in the world in which all will be made anew;
3. **anarchistic rebellion** – a reaction to modernisation opposing governmental authority and seeking to return to an older order regarded with nostalgia;
4. **Jacobin communist revolutions** (*sic*) – these 'are the "great" revolutions', and the French Revolution is given as the classic example of this very small category;
5. **conspiratorial coup-d'état** – a sudden seizure of state power by a small group of plotters;
6. **militarised mass insurrection** – a mass-based, countrywide campaign to overthrow a government by guerrilla warfare.

The weakness of this classification is obvious. The first three involve mass action and much spontaneity. In the other three categories, elites lead masses and plan action accordingly. But there is no obvious reason why these six categories and no others have been selected. Indeed many of the examples of the first three (jacquerie, millenarian rebellion, anarchistic rebellion) can hardly be regarded as revolutions at all, since they failed to bring down governments, let alone change the social system. The typology's value lies in its perception of the social background of revolution, and the essential unity of forms of violent political change.

Political theories of revolution focus on the conflict between government and opposition. Tilly (1978, p. 193) defines the *sine qua non* of revolution thus: 'A revolutionary outcome is the displacement of one set of power holders by another'. The present writer would term it a revolutionary event and hence prefer the definition used in his *A Study of Revolution* of 'a change of government (transition) at a clearly defined point in time by the use of armed force, or the credible threat of its use' (Calvert 1970b, p. 4). But in practice it is the same thing. Instead of using the terms 'process' and 'event' Tilly distinguishes between 'revolutionary situations' and 'revolutionary outcomes'. He sees the revolutionary outcome as the product of the emergence of multiple sovereignty in what he terms a revolutionary situation.

In doing so he correctly recognises the fundamental point about revolution, that it is the product of a contest: whether the outcome is no change, a coup, a silent revolution or a great revolution depends on circumstances and the amount of power mobilised by the contenders. No view that seeks to explain revolution solely from the point of view of the government or solely from the point of view of the opposition will therefore be able to explain properly what is going on.

There are, Tilly argues, three causes for the emergence of multiple sovereignty:

1. the appearance of contenders or coalitions of contenders advancing 'exclusive alternative claims' to power;
2. a commitment to those claims by a substantial sector of the public; or
3. the unwillingness or inability of the government forces to suppress the contenders or those who support their claims.

Tilly correctly recognises (with Gurr and others) that the greater the use of force, the more probable far-reaching structural change becomes, and he hypothesises (though he does not carry this argument very far) that the more change that occurs in the first short stage of consolidation, the more likely it is that the changes will be extensive and permanent – these are, he suggests, the 'great revolutions'. Like many other writers, however, he tends to support the widespread and incorrect assumption that the converse is the case by the comment: 'Military coups almost never produce any significant structural change . . . because they involve minor rearrangements among extremely limited sets of contenders'. Yet, as he goes on to explain, where such a contender achieves power and makes an alliance with previously unrepresented social groups (Turkey, Japan) then far-reaching change is possible.

Consolidation

Finally, therefore, revolutions can be said to be **consolidated** as the new order assumes a bold degree of permanence. When this term is used, it refers not to the process or the event, but to the programme and the myth of revolution. Both are established as permanent essentially by the passage of time, not by the development of a specific institutional structure. There are no specifically 'revolutionary' institutions, only institutions designed to carry out the revolutionary programme, and the routinisation of these is the process of state formation itself. All modern states contain institutions owing their origin to a revolutionary event and a new programme. Hence there are close parallels between the processes of revolution and democratisation, in that both are preceded by crisis and involve lengthy periods of consolidation.

The nature of the new system-balance however depends on the forces it brings into unity or counterpoise. This in turn is necessarily dependent on the social milieu or the initiation of the revolutionary process. The precise form depends on the number of major interest sectors within the ruling elite. If there are only one or two, turbulence remains almost inevitable for the future, while a multiplicity brings the problem of coalition against the possible independence of the instruments of power, for example the army or the police. A tripartite division seems very nearly ideal from the point of view of stability (Calvert 1969). A strong tradition of personalism in the ruling elite can lead to the overwhelming desire for a Bonaparte, the most dramatic form of the democratic Caesar, but otherwise the routinisation of charisma seems to be less a feature of post-revolutionary times than the routinisation of concepts. Individual action can still play an important part, however, in the acceptance of forces and the way in which the rise of new ones is received.

On the other hand, the similarity between post-revolutionary times and pre-modern politics must not be over-stressed. This recollection of the past is dominant in the minds of those establishing the new government. It is their concept of what a government should be. Those who rebel against it are as always few compared with those who seek guidance on forms and precedents. But the event of revolution is only of marginal importance in creating this problem; its myth obscures the lesson that in every age governments are continually evolving to meet new challenges with new responses.

The Revolutions of 1989

Can there be democratic revolutions? (Can there now be anything else?) The obvious place to start is with the revolutions of 1989 in East-Central Europe and the former Soviet Union. It is already hard to realise the extent to which Western observers had internalised the claims of Marxism-Leninism in the Soviet Union that socialism (as they defined it) was irreversible (see e.g. Kirkpatrick 1982). This view had given rise to the so-called Brezhnev Doctrine, the policy stated by the Soviet leader Leonid Brezhnev of using Soviet military force where necessary to maintain communist governments in Eastern Europe. Yet there were three good reasons for doubting the claims:

1. They were inherently unlikely – no system yet devised by human beings has lasted indefinitely.
2. Even within the area covered by the Brezhnev Doctrine governments had been ousted by force or the convincing threat of force in Russia in 1953 (Calvert 1970b), in Hungary in 1956 (Lomax 1976, pp. 115–16), in Czechoslovakia in 1958 and in Poland in 1971, 1980 and, most recently, 1981 when, fearful both of the power of the unofficial trade union Solidarity and of the Soviet threat, General Wojciech Jaruzielski had taken power and imposed martial law.
3. If communist revolutions had not been reversible it would not have been necessary for the Soviet Union to deploy forces in support of East-Central European governments in 1956 and 1968. The fact that they did so confirmed that they believed that those governments could be overthrown.

They were right. They had been overthrown. But both the Soviet Union and the West had a common interest in misrepresenting what had happened in Hungary and together they created the myth that was to shape the events of 1989. 'In the West, the uprising was presented as a nationalist uprising against communist dictatorship, while in the East the communists saw it as an attempt to overthrow socialism and restore Western-style capitalism. Both these viewpoints ignored the real issue of Hungary – that it was a social revolution aimed not at restoring a previous regime but at creating a radically new social order, one that would both be more democratic than the capitalist West and more socialist than the communist East' (Lomax 1976, p. 17). Both Nagy in Hungary and Dubcek in Czechoslovakia (Tigrid 1971) were idealistic Communists who sought to democratise the Stalinist system they had inherited but not to replace it, and, more importantly, in each case the movements they headed were mass movements of workers and peasants and not small cliques of intellectuals. Despite months of interrogation Nagy refused to say that he was anything other than a loyal member of the party, and the abrupt announcement on 17 June 1958 that he had been tried and executed for treason raised more questions than it answered.

Both international linkages and the 'demonstration effect' were in reverse to influence the actual course of events which led to the revolutions of 1989. When the president of the USSR, Mikhail Gorbachev, stated in Prague in April 1987 that in future relations would be based on a foundation of equality, it opened the way for change. Relations between the ageing Gustav Husak, Czech leader since 1958, and the Soviets were clearly tense and it was no surprise when he stood down as party leader early in 1988, though he retained the ceremonial post of president. In May 1988 Janos Kadar, who had been party secretary in Hungary since 1956, also stood down.

But the chain of events that led to revolution in East-Central Europe began in Poland in 1988 when protests broke out at a new round of price increases. By August the strikers were demanding not only economic reform but political change, including the re-legalisation of Solidarity, and at this point the government agreed to discuss some changes provided the strikers went back to work. When the results of the negotiations finally became known, however, on 5 April 1989, they went even further than the strikers had originally hoped for. Not only would Solidarity be legalised, but elections would be held which would allow for opposition representation in the Sejm, the lower House of the Polish Parliament. Though under the agreement the opposition was only allowed to contest 35 per cent of the seats in the Sejm, in the event Solidarity won all of them (The Observer 1990, p. 25). The parties previously aligned with the ruling Communists then changed sides and in August a non-communist government took office led by Tadeusz Mazowiecki.

In Hungary Kadar had already permitted the most liberal regime in East-Central Europe. With his retirement a movement began for the posthumous rehabilitation of Imre Nagy. In June 1989 Nagy's remains, located among 324 unmarked graves in a Budapest cemetery, were given a state funeral attended by more than 200,000 people and he was officially rehabilitated by the Supreme Court on the same day as Kadar died. Negotiations had by then already begun with the opposition. In October 1989 constitutional changes ended the primacy of the Communist Party, which was formally reconstituted as the Hungarian Socialist Party. Early in 1990 free elections returned a non-communist government.

There is no doubt that events in Poland and Hungary represent a process first of political liberalisation and then of democratisation. Can we also regard either of them as a revolution? Both were brought about in response to pressure from below. This pressure came from the mobilisation of an opposition demonstrating publicly. In each case the incumbent government resigned under pressure. The new government was subsequently to legislate for far-reaching social change. The only question seems to be whether or not the governments overthrown fell as a result of a convincing threat of the use of force and where that force was to come from. In arguing that they did, it is necessary to set the events in the wider context.

It was the decision to re-open Hungary's Western frontier in May 1989, however, which had the unexpected, and probably unplanned, consequence of allowing not only Hungarians but other East Europeans, to pass freely to the West. Erich Honecker had presided over the most reactionary government in East-Central Europe since 1973 but though life in the German Democratic Republic (GDR) was grey and spartan, East Germans were able to receive television in colour from West Germany and were able to draw their own conclusions. Soon East Germans were disappearing so fast that Hungary was forced briefly to try to close its border again. (If they had continued to leave at the rate they did in October East Germany would have been completely deserted in less than five years.) East Germans however simply made for Poland and Czechoslovakia instead. On 1 October the Honecker government first agreed to allow them to travel on to West Germany, then tried to stop them, with the result that protests and demonstrations broke out in East Berlin, Dresden, Leipzig and other major cities. Gorbachev's visit to East Berlin on 7 and 8 October, though peaceful enough, was followed by rapidly escalating demonstrations, now openly directed against the regime itself.

The crucial moment came with the demonstrations in Leipzig on 16 October. We know that the question of using force to suppress the demonstrations was considered but abandoned when Egon Krenz, the most junior member of the Politburo, argued that it was useless and likely to be counter-productive (Ash 1990, pp. 61–77). Two days later, on 18 October, Honecker resigned and was replaced by Krenz as chairman of the ruling Socialist Unity Party (SED). It was the Krenz government that decided that they could no longer hope to stop the population from leaving and on 9 November took the decision to open the Berlin Wall. It was speedily demolished stone by stone and turned into harmless paperweights and garden ornaments. Because of both its symbolic nature and the publicity which ensued, from then on no one in East-Central Europe could be in any doubt about the scale of the mobilisation or that the Soviet Union was no longer to support communist governments if they failed to try to gain the support of their own peoples. There was, therefore, a convincing threat that if they were denied, force might follow.

Dissidence in Bulgaria had been very limited. However, the regime which had been headed by Todor Zhivkov since 1954 was also very fragile. First of all Zhivkov himself was 78 and had been publicly reprimanded by Moscow for not taking steps sooner to reform his government. Tension with the large Turkish minority was already high, and in addition, improbably, in one of the few areas in which criticism was believed to be safe a 'green' movement called 'Eco-glasnost' had already mobilised supporters. It was they who on 3 November 1989 first held a pro-democracy demonstration in Sofia. The numbers were small but the fact that it took place at all was sensational, and the day after the news came of the fall of the Berlin Wall, Zhivkov resigned. Under Petar Mladenov the Communists made a belated attempt at internal reform, but with new opposition groups being formed and demonstrations growing in size, on 10 December Mladenov conceded the end of the party's leading role and offered free elections. Talks then began with the opposition on the new constitutional structure and elections took place in June 1990. By then elections already held in East Germany had resulted in a massive turnout in favour of West German political parties, with the result that, following successful negotiations with the government of the Soviet Union, the two Germanys were reunified on 3 October 1990. Not only had there been a close relationship between events in Germany and changes in the Soviet Union/Russia, therefore (Stent 2000), but the disputed area between them, the Baltic states, was to pave the way for the disintegration of the USSR itself (Muizinieks 1995).

In Czechoslovakia the new leader of the Communist Party, Milos Jakes, had already presided over some limited Soviet-style reforms in 1988. The government had also ended jamming of Western broadcasts. A demonstration had even been held in Prague in August to commemorate the twentieth anniversary of the crushing by Soviet troops of the 'Prague Spring' and Alexander Dubcek (Tigrid 1971) was interviewed by journalists. But the government had taken a hard line against a demonstration in January held in memory of Jan Palach, the student who killed himself in protest at the Soviet intervention, and in response to the demonstrations in East Germany as late as 12 November Jakes had warned that similar demonstrations in Czechoslovakia would not be tolerated. However, during the summer significant moves towards liberalisation had continued and the use of police at a mass meeting in Wenceslas Square on 17 November was followed by a rapid escalation of protests. The newly formed Civic Forum, led by the playwright Vaclav Havel, demanded the resignation of Husak and Jakes. On 24 November the entire Communist leadership resigned. Faced with a general strike, the interim leadership agreed to a coalition government and free elections; the new government took over on 12 December and on 28 December Havel replaced Husak as president.

When it came, the change in Czechoslovakia was peaceful but the mass demonstrations and the general strike gave all the evidence that was required of the weakness of the government in face of the popular determination to get rid of it. It had been a long time in the making, but in the end had taken place within a few days. Events in East Germany, Bulgaria and Czechoslovakia, despite the lack of bloodshed, could be called truly revolutionary. In fact the change in Czechoslovakia was immediately called the 'Velvet Revolution', a term which, like the 'Revolution of Flowers' in Portugal in 1974 (Sunday Times Insight Team 1975), correctly recognised both its peaceful and its revolutionary character.

The revolution in Romania was far from peaceful. It began when the government ordered the arrest of a Protestant pastor, Laslo Tokes, who had dared to challenge the dictator Nicolae Ceauşescu over his treatment of the Hungarian minority. Troops fired on a protest meeting in his home town, Timosoara, on 17 December, killing several hundred protesters. Open rebellion spread to other cities and to the capital, Bucarest, itself. Martial law was declared. However, military officers refused to enforce it and joined the uprising against the troops of the hated secret police, the Securitate. Ceauşescu tried to flee to safety. Captured, he and his wife were put on trial on 25 December, condemned to death and immediately executed; the trial and execution were both shown on national television the following day.

Ironically for all their suddenness and violence, there have been doubts about the revolutionary character of the events that led to the fall of Ceauşescu. The key question is the status of the successor government, the National Salvation Front (NSF), a coalition headed by Ion Iliescu, a member of the Communist Politburo. Its credentials as a process of democratisation are also suspect. Some have suggested that what happened was in fact a pre-planned coup which simply took advantage of the mass demonstrations to oust Ceauşescu. If democratisation followed (and Iliescu was still in power in 2001) then it was as a result of other changes in the world context.

There can be no doubt, on the other hand, about the revolutionary character of the other changes. In fact the collapse of the GDR is a classic confirmation of Skocpol's argument that revolutions occur because of the weakness of the state rather than the strength of the opposition (Horn 1992). The key role, however, was played by Mikhail Gorbachev. It was his decision to reform the structure of the Soviet Union itself through the policies of *perestroika* and *glasnost* that drew attention to the weaknesses of the client states. It was his foreign minister, Eduard Shevardnadze (now president of Georgia), who gave notice that the Soviet Union would no longer invoke the Brezhnev Doctrine. Since the fall of the Soviet Union itself admirers of Ronald Reagan have claimed that it was his policy of stepping up US defence expenditure that drove the Soviet Union to try to compete and so to collapse. But it did not try to compete, and in any case the Soviet Union had sustained far higher levels of defence expenditure during the Great Patriotic War (1941–45) and emerged as a world superpower.

There are however other lessons of the events of 1989. First of all, contrary to popular belief, coups are quite a regular feature of revolutions. As Meisel says: 'Revolutions do not happen, they are made – planned, engineered by some determined group' (Meisel 1962, p. 15). This may not always be the case (Romania in 1989 is an exception, perhaps) but instances include many now generally regarded as 'great social revolutions'. The coup of 1952 in Egypt, which overthrew King Farouk, brought to power a nationalist military government but one which within a short space of time had embarked on a programme of radical political and social change which was revolutionary in its impact on North Africa and the Middle East. A badly planned coup led to the fall of the Fourth Republic in France in 1958, and its replacement by the Gaullist Fifth. It was a carefully planned coup and not a mass popular rising that overthrew the provisional government in Russia in October 1917 (Goodspeed 1962), the 'October Revolution'. It was an abortive coup that was the pretext for the final collapse of the Soviet Union in 1991 and the re-emergence of Russia as an independent actor on the world stage.

As Table 11.2 shows, there were at least two successful coups in 1989: in Paraguay on 3 February, and in Sudan on 30 June. The armed forces dominated Panama throughout the year, nullifying elections on 10 May and installing new governments on 1 September and 15 December. Before the coup of 30 June the armed forces in Sudan had already forced the president to change his government on 5 March. Two political leaders were assassinated, and in the case of President Mouawad in Lebanon there were undoubtedly important political consequences.

There were also quite a number of unsuccessful coups. Those countries affected included Chad, Haiti, Ethiopia, Guatemala, Burkina Faso, and the Philippines, where US intervention helped maintain the government of Cory Aquino in face of a serious military revolt. It was of course US intervention in Panama that installed the government of President Endara, which was formally sworn in on a US Marine Corps base on 21 December (Calvert 1990c). It may of course have been the case that he had been elected president in the elections that had been nullified on 10 May. On the other hand he may not. As in the case of the election of Cory Aquino herself, there is no way of telling.

What evidence there is suggests that the incidence of successful political violence varies world-wide with some regularity: between 1900 and 1960 the five-year moving average of the periodicity of revolution in the twentieth century ranged between four

Table 11.2   Governments overthrown by force or the convincing threat of force, 1989

Date	Country	
11 Jan	Montenegro	Fall of leadership
12 Jan	Vanuatu	Fall of President Sokomanu
3 Feb	Paraguay	Military coup
5 Mar	Sudan	Army request new government
24 Apr	Jordan	Riots; Zaid Rifai dismissed
10 May	Panama	Elections nullified
30 Jun	Sudan	Coup ousts Sadiq el-Mahdi
24 Aug	Poland	Mazowiecki elected
1 Sep	Panama	Provisional government installed
5 Nov	Lebanon	Election of President Mouawad
7 Nov	GDR	Fall of Stoph
10 Nov	Bulgaria	Fall of Zhivkov
22 Nov	Lebanon	Assassination of President Mouwad
24 Nov	Czechoslovakia	Fall of Jakes
27 Nov	Comoros	Assassination of President Abderrahman
6 Dec	GDR	Fall of Krenz
9 Dec	Czechoslovakia	Fall of Husak
15 Dec	Panama	Noriega head of government
22 Dec	Romania	Fall of Ceauşescu

Source: *Keesing's Record of World Events* 1989

years in 1939 and nineteen years in 1947 (Calvert 1970b, Table 10, p. 202). This suggests some wider influence from the international environment. What was the context of the changes that took place in 1989? In particular, how far was the year notable either for generalised political violence or moves towards democratisation?

Latin America was the region in which there were most significant moves towards democratisation during the year. Free elections were held in Argentina, Brazil, Chile and Uruguay. The Argentine election resulted in a peaceful transfer of power to the opposition. A fairly free election took place in Paraguay following the fall of Stroessner. Venezuela held its first ever provincial elections. Nicaragua, where a free election had been held in 1985, continued to be harassed by the US-backed Contras, and US influence was able to frustrate the efforts of other Central American states to bring peace to the region. In the process a great many people died (Pastor 1987; Rossett and Vandermeer 1986; LaFeber 1993). In North Africa free elections were held in Tunisia and a referendum restored the multi-party system in Algeria, though too late to bring peace. In Southern Africa there were important moves towards peace in Angola and Mozambique and independence for Namibia in 1990. In South Africa itself the resignation of P.W. Botha opened the way for the freeing of Nelson Mandela and an opening to the African National Congress (ANC). And in Cambodia the Hun Sen government entered into talks for the first time directly with the non-communist opposition.

There were also important moves away from democracy, however. The Chinese government crushed opposition in the Tiananmen Square massacre, and several days later (24 June) Zhao Ziyang was forced out and replaced by Jiang Zemin. The vicious civil war in Sri Lanka continued under the newly elected President Premadasa and on the night of 13 November the leadership of the leftist JVP were killed and their bodies burned on piles of tyres along the road from Katunayake airport. Though Benin formally abandoned Marxism-Leninism, President Mugabe in Zimbabwe reaffirmed it and cold-shouldered the delegates from the more liberal governments in East-Central Europe. And in Equatorial Guinea Teodoro Mbasogo Obiang Nguema, who had seized power in August 1979 and extended his term by seven years in 1982, was re-elected in an unopposed direct election in June (*Keesing's* 36727).

We conclude that though shifts in world opinion may be reflected in changes in individual countries, they certainly do not guarantee that change will occur. Revolutionary change is primarily a matter for the citizens of the country concerned. It is they who have to bring together the essential combination of leader, followers and material facilities, and direct the movement towards the political objective of gaining power and using it to change the social structure. The problem for the promoters of democratic revolutions is that the use of violence will bring about a reaction, and that even if it does not do so, their legitimacy will be permanently compromised. By abolishing the death penalty (27 December 1989) the NSF government in Romania signalled clearly that the Ceauşescus should be the last to die, and some believe that despite their many crimes and the huge death toll that had already taken place they might have been spared had elements in the Securitate not made a last-ditch attempt to try to rescue them.

Summary

People rebel for a variety of reasons. For a rebellion to succeed it must have leadership and sufficient support, have well-defined political goals and enjoy access to material facilites. However, the seizure of political power, though significant from a political point of view, is not enough to ensure that a rebellion will achieve its objectives.

Like democratisation, revolution proceeds by stages. It comprises a process of disaffection, one or more events in which political power changes hands, a programme of action for the new government, and a myth of what it was and what it set out to achieve. Few revolutions are successful in this sense and fewer still come to be recognised as the 'great social revolutions' that have transformed society. Such movements invariably have international as well as national origins and consequences.

Key Concepts

consolidation, process by which a new political order or regime comes to be generally accepted as normal; the period during which this takes place

demonstrations, anomic groupings of people moved by a single common interest with a limited target of applying pressure to part or whole of the political system

rebellion, an unsuccessful attempt to use force to overthrow the existing order and to establish a new one

relative deprivation, the perception of lacking what others have

revolution, a change in government or in regime by the use of force by its own citizens

riots, violent, generally uncontrolled manifestations by a crowd, often undiscriminating in target, and perceived as public disorder; but may be a term of abuse applied to a targeted challenge

social disequilibrium, for functionalists, the absence of a stable state

terrorism, the use of force to impart fear with a view to bringing about political or social change

'Thermidor', for Brinton, the winding-down of revolutionary fervour and consolidation of a new and more efficient state system.

violence, the unregulated use of force

Sample Questions

Questions in this area are most likely to call for a review of the available literature. Thus the question 'How far does the pattern of the French Revolution of 1789 still influence our understanding of politics?' invites discussion of the various models of social revolution propounded by Brinton, Edwards, Moore, Skocpol, etc., while a topic such as 'Was 1989 a year of revolution?' invites the candidate to apply these or similar models to events which are still current. Alternatively in an individual case the question may arise of how far the social changes associated with the period can be seen to have been effective (e.g. in the case of Russia/the USSR).

General questions on political violence may invite the candidate to consider possible differences between the incidence of violence in different societies or states.

Further Reading

Calvert (1990a) deals with the principal debates on the origin and meaning of revolution; see also Calvert (1970a).

Comparative historical treatments and analyses of revolution include Brinton (1952), Moore (1969), Dunn (1989), Skocpol (1979); all deal exclusively with a selection of the so-called 'great social revolutions' but Wickham-Crowley (1993) casts his net wider. The main sociological approaches were foreshadowed by Edwards (1970), Pettee (1963) and C. Johnson (1964, 1966). Gurr (1970) and Gamson (1975) seek to probe into the psychological causes as well. Goodspeed (1962) lays special emphasis on the military aspects of political change. For more on the political explanation of revolution see Calvert (1970b) and Tilly (1978).

On the question of external influence and involvement in revolution see Walt (1992), Calvert (1996) and Halliday (1999). There is a vast literature by now on the fall of communism in Eastern Europe, ranging from current accounts such as The Observer (1990) to theoretical analyses such as Kumar (1992) and Linz and Stepan (1996). Mason (1992) gives an excellent guide to the revolutions in Eastern Europe after 1989 and LaFeber (1993) to the turmoil in Central America. A good guide to the politics of East Central Europe in the 1990s is Agh (1998).

Bibliography

A

Aborigade, Oladimeji, and Mundt, Robert J. (1998), *Politics in Nigeria*, Harlow, Longman.

Adelman, J., ed. (1984), *Terror and communist politics: the role of the secret police in the communist states*, Boulder, CO, Westview Press.

Afrifa, A.A. (1966), *The Ghana coup*, London, Cass.

Agee, Philip (1975), *Inside the company: CIA diary*, Harmondsworth, Penguin.

Agh, Attila (1998), *The politics of Central Europe*, London, Sage.

Albrow, Martin (1970), *Bureaucracy*, London, Pall Mall and Macmillan.

Alexander, Robert J., ed. (1973), *Aprismo: the ideas and doctrines of Víctor Raúl Haya de la Torre*, Kent, OH, Kent State University Press.

Allan, Graham, and Skinner, Chris (1991), *Handbook for research students in the social sciences*, London, Falmer Press.

Allardt, Erik, and Rokkan, Stein, eds (1970), *Mass politics: studies in political sociology*, New York, Free Press.

Allen, C.K. (1947), *Law and orders*, London, Stevens.

Allison, Graham T. (1971), *Essence of decision: explaining the Cuban missile crisis*, Boston, MA, Little Brown.

Almond, Gabriel A. (1968), 'Comparative politics', in David L. Sills, ed., *The International Encyclopedia of the Social Sciences*, New York, Free Press, pp. 331–6.

Almond, Gabriel A., and Coleman, James S. (1960), *The politics of the developing areas*, Princeton, NJ, Princeton University Press.

Almond, Gabriel A., and Powell, G. Bingham (1966), *Comparative politics, a developmental approach*, Boston, MA, Little Brown.

Almond, Gabriel A., and Powell, G. Bingham (1996), *Comparative politics, a theoretical approach*, New York, HarperCollins.

Almond, Gabriel A., Powell, G. Bingham, Strom, Kaare, and Dalton, Russell J. (2000), *Comparative politics today, a world view*, 7th edn, New York, Addison Wesley Longman.

Almond, Gabriel A., and Verba, Sidney (1963), *The civic culture*, Princeton, NJ, Princeton University Press.

Almond, Gabriel A., and Verba, Sidney, eds (1989), *The civic culture revisited*, Newbury Park, CA, Sage.

Althusser, Louis (1984), *Essays on ideology*, London, Verso.

Anderson, Patrick (1968), *The president's men*, New York, Doubleday.

Apter, D.E. (1965), *The politics of modernization*, Chicago, IL, University of Chicago Press.

Apter, D.E. (1987), *Rethinking development: modernization, dependency, and postmodern politics*, Newbury Park, CA, Sage.

Ardant, Philippe (1991), *Le premier ministre en France*, Paris, Montchrestien.

Arendt, Hannah (1958), *The human condition*, Chicago, IL, University of Chicago Press.

Arendt, Hannah (1963), *On revolution*, London, Faber and Faber.

Aristotle (1968), *The Politics*, trans. and ed. Ernest Barker, Oxford, Clarendon Press.

Aron, Raymond (1967), 'Social class, political class, ruling class', in R. Bendix and Seymour Martin Lipset, eds, *Class, status and power*, 2nd edn, London, Routledge and Kegan Paul, pp. 201–10.

Arrow, Kenneth (1963), *Social choice and individual values*, 2nd edn, New York, John Wiley.

Ash, Timothy Garton (1990), *The magic lantern: the revolution of '89 witnessed in Warsaw, Budapest, Berlin and Prague*, New York, Random House.

Auty, Phyllis (1970), *Tito: a biography*, London, Longman.

B

Bachrach, Peter, and Baratz, Morton S. (1962), 'Two faces of power', *American Political Science Review*, **56**, 947–52.

Bachrach, Peter, and Baratz, Morton S. (1971), *Power and poverty: theory and practice*, London, Oxford University Press.

Bahro, Rudolf (1978), *The alternative in Eastern Europe*, London, New Left Books.

Bailey, F.G. (1969), *Strategems and spoils*, Oxford, Basil Blackwell.

Baker, Gordon E. (1966), *The reapportionment revolution*, New York, Random House.

Ball, Alan, and Millard, Frances (1986), *Pressure politics in industrial societies*, Basingstoke, Macmillan Education.

Baran, Paul A. (1957), *The political economy of growth*, New York, Monthly Review Press.

Barber, Benjamin (1984), *Strong democracy: participatory politics for a new age*, Berkeley, CA, University of California Press.

Barghoorn, Frederick C. (1972), *Politics in the USSR*, Boston, MA, Little Brown.

Bar-Joseph, Uri (1995), *Intelligence intervention in the politics of democratic state: the United States, Israel, and Britain*, University Park, PA, University of Pennsylvania Press.

Barnard, Chester (1938), *The function of the executive*, Cambridge, MA, Harvard University Press.

Barreiro, Belén (1999), 'Judicial review and political empowerment: abortion in Spain', in Paul Heywood, ed., *Politics and policy in democratic Spain*, London, Frank Cass, pp. 147–62.

Beck, Ulrich (1992), *Risk society: towards a new modernity*, London, Sage.

Becker, Gary S. (1976), *The economic approach to human behavior*, Chicago, IL, University of Chicago Press.

Beetham, David (1987), *Bureaucracy*, Milton Keynes, Open University Press.

Beetham, David (1997), 'Market economy and democratic polity', *Democratization*, 4, 1, 77.

Bell, Daniel (1961), *The end of ideology: on the exhaustion of political ideas in the fifties*, new rev. edn, New York, Collier Books.

Bendix, Reinhard, and Lipset, Seymour Martin (1967), *Class, status and power*, 2nd edn, London, Routledge and Kegan Paul.

Berger, Peter L., and Luckmann, Thomas (1972), *The social construction of reality: a treatise in the sociology of knowledge*, Harmondsworth, Penguin Books.

Bernstein, Basil (1973–76), *Classes, codes and control*, 4 vols, London, Routledge.

Bill, James A. (1988), *The eagle and the lion: the tragedy of American–Iranian relations*, New Haven, CT, Yale University Press.

Binder, L. *et al.* (1971), *Crises and sequences in political development*, Princeton, NJ, Princeton University Press.

Black, Duncan (1958), *The theory of committees and elections*, Cambridge, Cambridge University Press.

Black, Ian and Morris, Benny (2000), *Israel's secret wars*, Emerysville, CA, Avalon Travel Publishers.

Blau, Peter, and Duncan, Otis Dudley (1967), *The American occupational structure*, New York, John Wiley.

Blondel, Jean (1969), *An introduction to comparative government*, London, Weidenfeld and Nicolson.

Blondel, Jean (1973), *Comparing political systems*, London, Weidenfeld and Nicolson.

Blondel, Jean (1985), *Comparative legislatures*, London, Sage.

Blondel, Jean (1987), *Political leadership*, London, Sage.

Bogdanor, Vernon (1983), *Democracy and elections: electoral systems and their political consequences*, Cambridge, Cambridge University Press.

Bosanquet, Nick, and Townsend, Peter, eds (1979), *Labour and equality: a Fabian study of Labour in power, 1974–79*, London, Heinemann.

Bourricaud, François (1970), *Power and society in contemporary Peru*, London, Faber.

Bowles, Nigel (1998), *Government and politics of the United States*, Basingstoke, Macmillan.

Braybrooke, D., and Lindblom, C. (1963), *A strategy of decision*, New York, Free Press.

Brewer, John D. (1988), *The police: public order and the state policing in Great Britain, Northern Ireland, the Irish Republic, the USA, Israel, South Africa and China*, Basingstoke, Macmillan.

Bridges, Edward (1956), 'The reforms of 1854 in retrospect', in William A. Robson, ed., *The civil service in Britain and France*, London, Hogarth Press, pp. 000–00.

Brinton, Crane (1952), *The anatomy of revolution* [1938], New York, Vintage.

Brittan, Samuel (1976), *The economic consequences of democracy*, London, M.T. Smith.

Brodbeck, May (1968), *Readings in the philosophy of the social sciences*, New York, Macmillan.

Broder, David S. (2001), 'A shaky budget', *Washington Post*, 2 March 2001.

Brogan, D.W., and Verney, D.V. (1963), *Politics in the modern world*, London, Hamish Hamilton.

Brown, Archie (2001), *Contemporary Russian politics*, London, Oxford University Press.

Brzezinski, Zbigniew, and Huntington, Samuel (1964), *Political power, USA/USSR*, London, Chatto and Windus.

Buchanan, James M., and Tullock, Gordon (1962), *The calculus of consent: logical foundations of constitutional democracy*, Ann Arbor, MI, University of Michigan Press.

Burk, Kathleen (1990), 'The international environment', in Andrew Graham and Anthony Seldon, eds, *Governments and economies in the postwar world: economic policies and comparative performance, 1945–85*, London, Routledge, pp. 9–29.

Burns, T. and Stalker, G.M. (1962), *The management of innovations*, London, Tavistock.

Bury, J.B. (1956), *A history of Greece to the death of Alexander the Great*, 3rd edn, London, Macmillan.

Butler, David, ed. (1959), *Elections abroad*, London, Macmillan.

Byrd, Peter (1987), 'Great Britain: parties in a changing party system', in Alan Ware, ed., *Citizens, parties and the state*, Cambridge, Polity Press, pp. 205–24.

C

Cairncross, Alex (1990), 'The United Kingdom', in Andrew Graham and Anthony Seldon, eds, *Governments and economies in the postwar world: economic policies and comparative performance, 1945–85*, London, Routledge, pp. 30–53.

Callwell, C.E. (1927), *Field Marshal Sir Henry Wilson, his life and diaries*, London, Cassell.

Calvert, Peter (1967), 'Revolution: the politics of violence', *Political Studies*, **15**, 1, February, 1–11.

Calvert, Peter (1969), 'The dynamics of political change', *Political Studies*, **17**, 4, December, 446–57.

Calvert, Peter (1970a), *Revolution* (Key Concepts in Political Science), London, Pall Mall and Macmillan.

Calvert, Peter (1970b), *A study of revolution*, Oxford, Clarendon Press.

Calvert, Peter (1979), 'The coup: a critical restatement', *Third World Quarterly*, **1**, 4, October, 89.

Calvert, Peter (1982), *The concept of class: an historical introduction*, London, Hutchinson.

Calvert, Peter (1983), *Politics, power and revolution: an introduction to comparative politics*, Brighton, Harvester.

Calvert, Peter, ed. (1987), *The process of political succession*, Basingstoke, Macmillan.

Calvert, Peter (1990a), *Revolution and counter-revolution*, Milton Keynes, Open University Press.

Calvert, Peter (1990b), 'Argentina: goodbye to Peronism', *The World Today*, **46**, 8–9, August–September, 170–5.

Calvert, Peter (1990c), 'The US intervention in Panama', *Small Wars and Insurgencies*, **1**, 3, December, 307–14.

Calvert, Peter (1996), *Revolution and international politics*, 2nd edn, London, Frances Pinter.

Calvert, Peter (2000), 'Autocracy, anger and the politics of salvation', *Totalitarian Movements and Political Religions*, **1**, 1, Summer, 1–17.

Calvert, Peter (2001), 'Internal colonization, development and environment', *Third World Quarterly*, **22**, 1, January, 51–63.

Calvert, Peter, and Calvert, Susan (1994), *Latin America in the twentieth century*, 2nd edn, Basingstoke, Macmillan.

Calvert, Susan, and Calvert, Peter (1989), *Argentina, political culture and instability*, London, Macmillan.

Calvert, Peter, and Calvert, Susan (1999), *The South, the North and the environment*, London, Pinter.

Calvert, Peter, and Calvert, Susan (2001), *Politics and society in the Third World*, 2nd edn, Harlow, Longman.

Campbell, Angus, Converse, Philip E., Miller, Warren E., and Stokes, David E. (1960), *The American voter*, London, John Wiley.

Campbell, Peter (1951), 'Remarques sur les effets de la loi electorale francaise du 9 mai 1951', *Revue française de science politique*, **1**, October–December, 498.

Cammack, Paul, Pool, David, and Tordoff, William (1993), *Third world politics: a comparative introduction*, 2nd edn, Basingstoke, Macmillan.

Canovan, Margaret (1981), *Populism*, London, Junction Books.

Cardoso, Fernando Henrique, and Faletto, Enzo (1979), *Dependency and development in Latin America*, trans. M.M. Urquidi, Berkeley, CA, University of California Press.

Carstairs, Andrew McLaren (1980), *A short history of electoral systems*, London, Allen and Unwin.

Carsten, F.L. (1967), *The rise of fascism*, London, Methuen.

Carter, Gwendolyn M. (1958), *The politics of inequality: South Africa since 1948*, London, Thames and Hudson.

Cattell, R.B., and Stice, G.F. (1954), 'Four formulae for selecting leaders on basis of personality', *Human Relations*, **7**, 493.

Cerny, Philip (1980), 'The new rules of the game in France', in Philip G. Cerny and Martin A. Schain, eds, *French politics and public policy*, London, Methuen, pp. 1–47.

Chamberlain, M.E. (1999), *Decolonization: the fall of the European Empires*, 2nd edn, Oxford, Blackwell.

Chapman, Brian (1970), *Police state*, London, Pall Mall and Macmillan.

Churchward, L.G. (1975), *Contemporary Soviet government*, London, Routledge.

Clapham, Christopher, ed. (1982), *Private patronage and public power: political clientelism in the modern state*, London, Pinter.

Clapham, Christopher (1985), *Third World politics: an introduction*, Beckenham, Kent, Croom Helm.

Clapham, Christopher, and Philip, George, eds (1985), *The political dilemmas of military regimes*, London, Croom Helm.

Clemens, Clay, and Paterson, William E., eds (1998), *The Kohl chancellorship*, London, Frank Cass.

Coast, John (1953), *Some aspects of Siamese politics*, New York, International Secretariat of the Institute of Pacific Relations (mimeo.).

Cohen, Emmeline (1941), *The growth of the British civil service, 1780–1934*, London, Allen and Unwin.

Colburn, Forrest D. (1994), *The vogue of revolution in poor countries*, Princeton, NJ, Princeton University Press.

Cole, Alistair (1997a), *François Mitterrand, a study in political leadership*, 2nd edn, London, Routledge.

Cole, Alistair (1997b), 'The Mitterrand legacy', in John Gaffney and Lorna Milne, eds, *French presidentialism and the election of 1995*, Aldershot, Ashgate, pp. 43–54.

Cole, Alistair (1998), 'Political leadership in Western Europe: Helmut Kohl in comparative context', in Clay Clemens and William E. Paterson, eds, *The Kohl chancellorship*, London, Frank Cass, pp. 120–42.

Cole, Alistair, and Campbell, Peter (1989), *French electoral systems and elections since 1789*, Aldershot, Gower.

Condon, John C., Jr. (1966), *Semantics and communication*, New York, Macmillan.

Conquest, Robert (1961), *Power and policy in the USSR*, London, Macmillan.

Cowell, F.R. (1956), *Cicero and the Roman Republic*, Harmondsworth, Penguin Books.

Coxall, Bill, and Robins, Lynton (1998), *Contemporary British politics*, 3rd edn, Basingstoke, Macmillan.

Craig, Gordon A. (1955), *The politics of the Prussian army, 1640–1945*, Oxford, Oxford University Press.

Cramer, James (1964), *The world's police*, London, Cassell.

Crick, Bernard (1959), *The American science of politics: its origins and conditions*, London, Routledge.

Crick, Bernard (1964), *The reform of Parliament*, London, Weidenfeld.

Crick, Bernard (1973), *Basic forms of government: a sketch and a model*, London, Macmillan.

Crook, John Hurrell (1973), 'The nature and function of territorial aggression', in Ashley Montagu, ed., *Man and aggression*, New York, Oxford University Press, pp. 183–220.

Crosland, Anthony (1956), *The future of socialism*, London, Cape.

Crozier, Michel (1964), *The bureaucratic phenomenon*, Chicago, IL, University of Chicago Press.

D

Dahl, Robert A. (1964a), *Modern political analysis*, Englewood Cliffs, NJ, Prentice-Hall.

Dahl, Robert A. (1964b), *A preface to democratic theory*, Chicago, IL, University of Chicago Press.

Daneshvar, Parviz (1996), *Revolution in Iran*, Basingstoke, Macmillan.

Davies, James Chowning (1962), 'Toward a theory of revolution', *American Sociological Review*, **27**, 1, February, 5–19.

Davies, Morton R., and Lewis, Vaughan A. (1971), *Models of political systems*, London, Pall Mall.

Dawisha, Karen (1980), 'The limits of the bureaucratic politics model; observations on the Soviet case', *Studies in Comparative Communism*, **13**, 300–26.

Dawisha, Karen, with Bruce Parrott (1997), *Democratic changes and authoritarian reactions in Russia, Ukraine, Belarus and Moldova*, Cambridge, Cambridge University Press.

Decalo, Samuel (1976), *Coups and army rule in Africa*, New Haven, CT, Yale University Press.

De Grand, Alexander J. (1995), *Fascist Italy and Nazi Germany: the 'Fascist' style of rule*, London, Routledge.

Delarue, Jacques (1964), *The Gestapo*, New York, Morrow.

del Castillo, Pilar (1989), 'Financing of Spanish political parties', in Herbert E. Alexander, ed., *Comparative political finance*, Cambridge, Cambridge University Press, pp. 172–99.

della Porta, Donatella, and Vanucci, Alberto (1999), *Corrupt exchanges: actors, resources and mechanisms of political corruption*, New York, Aldine de Gruyter.

Denber, R., ed. (1992), *The Soviet nationality question: the disintegration in context*, Boulder, CO, Westview.

d'Entreves, A.P., ed. (1959), *Aquinas' selected political writings*, Oxford, Blackwell.

Deutsch, Karl (1966), *The nerves of government, models of political communication and control*, New York, Free Press.

Diamond, Larry (1992), 'Economic development and democracy reconsidered', in Gary Marks and Larry Diamond, eds, *Reexamining democracy: essays in honor of Seymour Martin Lipset*, Newbury Park, CA, Sage, pp. 93–139.

Diamond, Larry (1993), 'Three paradoxes of democracy', in Larry Diamond and Marc F. Plattner, eds, *The global resurgence of democracy*, Baltimore, MD, Johns Hopkins University Press, pp. 95–107.

Diamond, Larry (1999), *Developing democracy: towards consolidation*, Baltimore, MD, Johns Hopkins University Press.

Díaz Guerrero, R. (1975), *Psychology of the Mexican: culture and personality*, Austin, TX, University of Texas Press.

Diedrich, Bernard (1978), *Trujillo, the death of the Goat*, London, Bodley Head.

Diedrich, Bernard (1982), *Somoza and the legacy of US involvement in Central America*, London, Junction Books.

Di Tella, Guido (1983), *Argentina under Perón, 1973–1976: the nation's experience with a labour-based government*, London, Macmillan.

Di Tella, Guido, and Rodríguez Braun, Carlos, eds (1983), *Argentina 1946–83: the economic ministers speak*, Basingstoke, Macmillan in association with St Antony's College, Oxford.

Djilas, Milovan (1957), *The new class: an analysis of the communist system*, London, Thames and Hudson.

Dobzhansky, Theodosias (1971), 'Race equality', in Richard H. Osborne, ed., *The biological and social meaning of race*, San Francisco, CA, W.H. Freeman and Co.

Dogan, Matthei, and Pelassy, Dominique (1984), *How to compare nations*, Chatham, NJ, Chatham House Publications.

Dollard, John, Doob, Leonard W., Miller, Neal E., Mowrer, O.H., and Sears, Robert R. (1939), *Frustration and aggression*, New Haven, CT, Yale University Press.

Dorril, Stephen, and Ramsay, Robin (1992), *Smear! Wilson and the secret state*, London, Grafton Books.

Downs, Anthony (1957), *An economic theory of democracy*, New York, Harper and Row.

Dror, Ythiel (1968), *Public policy-making re-examined*, San Francisco, CA, Chandler.

Drucker, Peter (1970), *A new style of government*, London, Conservative Party Centre.

Duchacek, I.D. (1970), *Comparative federalism: the territorial dimensions of politics*, New York, Holt Rinehart and Winston.

Duff, Ernest A., and McCamant, John F. (1976), *Violence and repression in Latin America*, London, Collier Macmillan.

Dulles, Allen (1964), *The craft of intelligence*, London, Weidenfeld.

Dunleavy, Patrick, and O'Leary, Brendan (1987), *Theories of the state*, Basingstoke, Macmillan.

Dunn, John (1989), *Modern revolutions: an introduction to the analysis of a political phenomenon*, 2nd edn, Cambridge, Cambridge University Press.

Durkheim, Emile (1964), *The division of labor in society* [1893], trans. George Simpson, New York, Free Press.

Duverger, Maurice (1959), *Political parties*, 2nd edn, London, Methuen.

Dyker, D.A. and Vejvoda, I. (1996), *Yugoslavia and after: a study in fragmentation, despair and rebirth*, Harlow, Longman.

E

Easton, David (1957), 'An approach to the analysis of political systems', *World Politics*, **10**, 383–400.

Easton, David (1965), *A systems analysis of political life*, New York, John Wiley.

Eckstein, Harry (1960), *Pressure group politics*, London, Allen and Unwin.

Eckstein, Harry (1973), 'Authority patterns: a structural basis for political inquiry', *American Political Sceince Review*, **67**, December, 1142–61.

Edinger, L.J. (1990), 'Approaches to the comparative analysis of political leadership', *Review of Politics*, **52**, 4, Autumn, 509–23.

Edwards, Lyford P. (1970), *The natural history of revolution* [1927], Chicago, University of Chicago Press.

Eisenhower. Dwight D. (1963), *The White House years*, 2 vols, Garden City, NY, Doubleday.

Eisenstadt, S. (1963), *The political systems of empires*, New York, Free Press.

Eklit, J., and Svensson, P. (1997), 'What makes elections free and fair', *Journal of Democracy*, **8**, 3, 32–46.

Elgie, Robert (1993), *The role of the prime minister in France, 1981–1991*, London, Macmillan.

Elgie, Robert, and Griggs, Steven (2000), *French politics: debates and controversies*, London, Routledge.

Elster, Jon, ed. (1986), *Rational choice*, Oxford, Basil Blackwell.

Eysenck, Hans (1963), *Psychology and politics*, London, Routledge.

Eysenck, Hans (1964), *Crime and personality*, London, Routledge and Kegan Paul.

F

Fainsod, Merle (1963), 'Bureaucracy and modernization: the Russian and Soviet case', in Joseph LaPalombara, ed., *Bureaucracy and political development*, Princeton, NJ, Princeton University Press, pp. 233–67.

Falk, R. (1970), *This endangered planet*, New York, Random House.

Federalist Papers, The (1987), ed. Isaac Kramnick, Harmondsworth, Penguin Books.

Feinberg, Richard E. (1972), *The triumph of Allende: Chile's legal revolution*, New York, Mentor Books.

Feinberg, Richard E. (1983), *The intemperate zone: the Third World challenge to US foreign policy*, New York, W.W. Norton.

Fejtö, François (1974), *A history of the people's democracies*, Harmondsworth, Penguin Books.

Ferguson, Kathy E. (1984), *The feminist case against bureaucracy*, Philidelphia, PA, Temple University Press.

Figueiredo, Antonio de (1975), *Portugal: fifty years of dictatorship*, Harmondsworth, Penguin Books.

Finer, Samuel E. (1962), *The man on horseback: the role of the military in politics*, London, Pall Mall.

Finer, Samuel E. (1970), *Comparative government*, London, Allen Lane.

Finer, Samuel E. (1979), *Five constitutions: contrasts and comparisons*, Brighton, Harvester and Harmondsworth, Penguin.

First, Ruth (1972), *The barrel of a gun*, Harmondsworth, Penguin African Library.

Fitzgerald, C.P. (1976), *Mao Tse-tung and China*, London, Hodder and Stoughton.

Fluharty, Vernon Lee (1957), *Dance of the millions: military rule and the social revolution in Colombia, 1930–1956*, Pittsburgh, University of Pittsburgh Press.

Foley, Michael, ed. (1993), *Political ideas*, Manchester, Manchester University Press.

Frank, André Gunder (1978), *World accumulation 1492–1789*, London, Macmillan.

Frankel, Joseph (1964), *International relations*, Oxford, Oxford University Press.

Freedom House (1989), *Romania: a case of 'dynastic' communism*, New York, Freedom House.

Friedman, Milton (1962), *Capitalism and freedom*, Chicago, IL, University of Chicago Press.

Friedman, Milton (1977), *From Galbraith to economic freedom*, London, Institute of Economic Affairs, occasional paper 49.

Friedrich, Carl (1972), *Tradition and authority*, London, Pall Mall.

Friedrich, Carl, and Brzezinski, Zbigniew (1975), *Totalitarian dictatorship and autocracy*, Cambridge, MA, Harvard University Press.

Fromm, Erich (1960), *The fear of freedom*, London, Routledge and Kegan Paul.

Fukuyama, Francis (1989), 'The end of history', *National Interest*, **16**, 3–18.

G

Gaffney, John, and Milne, Lorna, eds (1997), *French presidentialism and the election of 1995*, Aldershot, Ashgate.

Gallagher, Michael, Laver, Michael, and Mair, Peter (1992), *Representative government in Western Europe*, New York, McGraw Hill.

Gallie, W.B. (1955–56), 'Essentially-contested concepts', *Proceedings of the Aristotelian Society*, **56**, 167–98.

Galtung, Johan (1971), 'A structural theory of imperialism', *Journal of Peace Research*, **8**, 2, 81–111.

Gamson, William A. (1975), *The strategy of social protest*, Homewood, IL, Dorsey Press.

Gauhar, Altaf (1983), *Talking about development*, London, Third World Foundation for Social and Economic Studies.

Gehlen, Michael P. (1969), *The Communist Party of the Soviet Union: a functional analysis*, Bloomington, IN, Indiana University Press.

Gehlot, N.S. (1996), *Indian government and politics*, Columbia, MO, South Asia Books.

George, Susan (1991), *The debt boomerang*, London, Pluto Press.

Gerlich, Peter (1987), 'Consociationalism to competition: the Austrian party system since 1945', in Hans Daalder, ed., *Party systems in Denmark, Austria, Switzerland, the Netherlands and Belgium*, London, Frances Pinter.

Gerth, H.H., and Mills, C. Wright (1946), *From Max Weber: essays in sociology*, London, Routledge and Kegan Paul.

Gibb, C.A., ed. (1969), *Leadership*, Harmondsworth, Penguin.

Giddens, Anthony (1990), *The consequences of modernity*, Cambridge, Polity Press.

Giddens, Anthony (1991), *Modernity and self-identity*, Cambridge, Polity Press.

Gil, Federico G. (1965), *The political system of Chile*, Boston, MA, Houghton Mifflin.

Gills, Barry, Rocamora, Joel, and Wilson, Richard (1993), 'Low intensity democracy', in Barry Gills, Joel Rocamora and Richard Wilson, eds, *Low intensity democracy: political power in the new world order*, London, Pluto Press, pp. 3–34.

Ginsberg, B. (1982), *The consequences of consent*, Reading, MA, Addison Wesley.

Gladdish, Ken (1991), *Governing from the Centre: politics and policy-making in the Netherlands*, London, Hurst and Co.

Glade, William P., ed. with Rossand Corona, Paul Boehr (1991), *Bigger economies, smaller governments*, Boulder, CO, Westview Press.

Goetz, Edward G., and Clarke, Susan E., eds (1993), *The new localism: comparative urban politics in a global era*, Newbury Park, CA, Sage.

Goldenberg, Boris (1965), *The Cuban Revolution and Latin America*, London, Allen and Unwin.

Goldstone, Jack, Gurr, J., and Moshiri, F. (1991), *Revolutions of the later twentieth century*, Boulder, CO, Westview Press.

González, Edward (1976), 'Castro and Cuba's new orthodoxy', *Problems of Communism*, **25**, January–February, 1–19.

Goodin, Robert E. (1976), *The politics of rational man*, London, John Wiley.

Goodspeed, D.J. (1962), *The conspirators: a study of the coup d'etat*, London, Allen and Unwin; New York, Viking Press.

Gorbachev, Mikhail (1996), *Memoirs*, London, Doubleday.

Gott, Richard (1970), *Guerrilla movements in Latin America*, London, Nelson.

Gowland, David, O'Neill, Basil, and Dunphy, Richard (2000), *The European mosaic: contemporary politics, economics and culture*, 2nd edn, Harlow, Addison Wesley Longman.

Graham, Andrew, and Seldon, Anthony (1990), *Governments and economies in the postwar world: economic policies and comparative performance, 1945–85*, London, Routledge.

Gramsci, Antonio (1973), *Selections from the Prison Notebooks of Antonio Gramsci*, ed. Quintin Hoare and Geoffrey Nowell-Smith, London, Lawrence and Wishart.

Gregory, Frank (1976), *Protest and violence: the police response*, London, Institute for the Study of Conflict.

Grindle, Merrilee S. (1977), *Bureaucrats, politicians and peasants in Mexico*, Berkeley, CA, University of California Press.

Grofman, Bernard, and Lijphart, Arend, eds (1986), *Electoral laws and their political consequences*, New York, Agathon Press.

Guevara, Ernesto Che (1967), *Guerrilla warfare*, New York, Monthly Review Press.

Gundle, Stephen, and Parker, Simon, eds (1996), *The new Italian Republic: from the fall of the Berlin Wall to Berlusconi*, London, Routledge.

Gurr, Ted Robert (1970), *Why men rebel*, Princeton, NJ, Princeton University Press.

Gustafson, Thane (1980), *Reform and power in Soviet politics: lessons of Brezhnev's agricultural and environmental policies*, Cambridge, Cambridge University Press.

H

Habermas, Jürgen (1976), *Legitimation crisis*, trans. Thomas McCarthy, London, Heinemann.

Habermas, Jürgen (1979), *Communication and the evolution of society*, trans. Thomas McCarthy, London, Heinemann.

Hallett, Graham (1990), 'West Germany', in Andrew Graham and Anthony Seldon, eds, *Governments and economies in the postwar world: economic policies and comparative performance, 1945–85*, London, Routledge, pp. 79–103.

Halliday, Fred (1999), *Revolution and world politics: the rise and fall of the sixth great power*, Basingstoke, Macmillan.

Ham, C., and Hill, M. (1993), *The policy process in the modern capitalist state*, 2nd edn, Hemel Hempstead, Harvester-Wheatsheaf.

Hansard Society (1976), *The report of the Hansard Society Commission on Electoral Reform*, London, Hansard Society.

Haring, C.H. (1952), *The Spanish Empire in America*, New York, Oxford University Press.

Harkabi, Yehoshafat (1988), *Israel's fateful decisions*, London, Tauris.

Harsanyi, John C. (1986), 'Advances in understanding rational behavior', reprinted in Jon Elster, ed., *Rational choice*, Oxford, Basil Blackwell, pp. 82–107.

Hassan, Gerry, ed. (1999), *A guide to the Scottish Parliament: the shape of things to come*, Edinburgh, The Stationery Office.

Havens, Murray Clark, Leiden, Carl, and Schmitt, Karl M. (1970), *The politics of assassination*, Englewood Cliffs, NJ, Prentice-Hall.

Hawgood, John A. (1939), *Modern constitutions since 1787*, London, Macmillan.

Hayek, F.A. von (1976), *The road to serfdom* [1944], London, Routledge and Kegan Paul.

Hazard, John N. (1964), *The Soviet system of government*, 3rd edn, Chicago, IL, University of Chicago Press.

Heady, Ferrel (1991), *Public administration: a comparative perspective*, 4th edn, New York, Marcel Dekker.

Healey, Denis (1989), *The time of my life*, London, Michael Joseph.

Heclo, Hugh (1977), *A government of strangers*, Washington, DC, Brookings Institution.

Heclo, Hugh (1978), 'Issue networks and the executive establishment', in Anthony King, ed., *The new American political system*, Washington, DC, American Enterprise Institute, pp. 87–124.

Heidenheimer, Arnold J. (1971), *The governments of Germany*, 3rd edn, New York, Crowell.

Held, David, ed. (2000), *A globalising world? Culture, economics, politics*, London, Routledge in association with the Open University.

Herz, John H. (1959), *International politics in the atomic age*, New York, Columbia University Press.

Hewitt, Patricia (1982), *The abuse of power: civil liberties in the United Kingdom*, Oxford, Martin Robertson.

Heywood, Andrew (1992), *Political ideologies: an introduction*, Basingstoke, Macmillan.

Heywood, Andrew (1997), *Politics*, Basingstoke, Macmillan.

Heywood, Paul, ed. (1999), *Politics and policy in democratic Spain*, London, Frank Cass.

Hill, Dilys M., and Williams, Phil, eds (1994), *The Bush residency: triumphs and adversities*, Basingstoke, Macmillan in conjunction with Mountbatten Centre for International Studies, University of Southampton.

Hill, Ronald, and Frank, Peter (1983), *The Soviet Communist Party*, 2nd edn, London, Allen and Unwin.

Hillyard, Paddy, and Percy-Smith, Janie (1988), *The coercive state*, London, Pinter.

Hirsch, Fred (1977), *The social limits to growth*, London, Routledge and Kegan Paul.

Hirschman, A.O. (1975), *Journeys towards progress*, New York, Doubleday.

Hirst, Paul, and Thompson, Grahame (1999), *Globalisation in question*, 2nd edn, Cambridge, Polity Press.

Holden, Barry (1993), *Understanding liberal democracy*, 2nd edn, Hemel Hempstead, Harvester-Wheatsheaf.

Hollander, Paul (1973), *American and Soviet society: a reader in comparative sociology and perception*, Englewood Cliffs, NJ, Prentice-Hall.

Hong Yung Lee (1978), *The politics of the Chinese Cultural Revolution: a case study*, Berkeley, CA, University of California Press.

Hood, Christopher (1995), '"Deprivileging" the UK civil service in the 1980s: dream or reality?', in Jon Pierre, ed., *Bureaucracy in the modern state: an introduction to comparative public administration*, Aldershot, Edward Elgar, pp. 92–117.

Hood, Christopher, and Wright, Maurice G., eds (1981), *Big government in hard times*, London, Martin Robertson.

Hoover, Kenneth, and Plant, Raymond (1989), *Conservative capitalism in Britain and the United States: a critical appraisal*, London, Routledge.

Horn, Hannelore (1992), 'Collapse from internal weakness – the GDR from October 1989 to March 1990', in Dieter Grosser, ed., *German unification: the unexpected challenge*, Oxford, Berg, pp. 55–71.

Hough, Jerry F. (1976), 'Political participation in the Soviet Union', *Soviet Studies*, **28**, 3.

Hough, Jerry F. (1977), *The Soviet Union and social science theory*, Cambridge, MA, Harvard University Press.

Howard, Michael, ed. (1955), *Soldiers and governments*, London, Eyre and Spottiswode.

Howe, Geoffrey (1994), *Conflict of loyalty*, London, Macmillan.

Howells, William W. (1971), 'The meaning of race', in Richard H. Osborne, ed., *The biological and social meaning of race*, San Francisco, CA, W.H. Freeman and Co.

Huberman, Leo, and Sweezy, Paul M. (1968), *Cuba, anatomy of a revolution*, New York, Monthly Review Press.

Huntington, Samuel P. (1965), 'Political development and political decay', *World Politics*, **17**, 3, 386–430.

Huntington, Samuel P. (1968), *Political order in changing societies*, New Haven, CT, Yale University Press.

Huntington, Samuel P. (1993a), *The Third Wave: democratisation in the late twentieth century*, Norman, OK, University of Oklahoma Press.

Huntington, Samuel P. (1993b), 'Democracy's third wave', in Larry Diamond and Marc F. Plattner, eds, *The global resurgence of democracy*, Baltimore, MD, Johns Hopkins University Press, pp. 3–25.

Hyden, Goran (1995), 'Public administration in developing countries: Kenya and Tanzania in comparative perspective', in Jon Pierre, ed., *Bureaucracy in the modern state: an introduction to comparative public administration*, Aldershot, Edward Elgar, pp. 161–84.

Hyman, H. (1969), *Political socialization*, 2nd edn, New York, Free Press.

I

Ihonvbere, Julius O. (1994), *Nigeria, the politics of adjustment and democracy*, New York, Transaction.

Inkeles, Alex (1968), *Social change in Soviet Russia*, Cambridge, MA, Harvard University Press.

Ionescu, Ghita (1967), *The politics of the East European communist states*, London, Weidenfeld and Nicolson.

Ishiyama, John (1999), 'Sickles into roses: the successor parties and democratic consolidation in post-communist politics', *Democratization*, 6, 4, Winter, 52–73.

J

Janowitz, Morris (1960), *The American soldier*, Glencoe, IL, Free Press.

Jarausch, Konrad H. (1994), *The rush to German unity*, Oxford, Oxford University Press.

Jeffreys-Jones, Rhodri (1989), *The CIA and American democracy*, 2nd edn, New Haven, CT, Yale University Press.

Jenkins, J. Craig, and Klandermans, Bert, eds (1995), *The politics of social protest: comparative perspectives on states and social movements*, London, UCL Press.

Jennings, Sir Ivor (1951), *Cabinet government*, Cambridge, Cambridge University Press.

Johnson, Chalmers (1964), *Revolution and the social system*, Stanford, CA, Hoover Institution on War, Revolution, and Peace, Stanford University, Hoover Institution Studies 3.

Johnson, Chalmers (1966), *Revolutionary change*, Boston, MA, Little Brown.

Johnson, John J. (1964), *The military and society in Latin America*, Stanford, CA, Stanford University Press.

Jones, Bill (2000), *Politics UK*, 2nd edn, Harlow, Longman.

Jones, G., ed. (1992), *Heads of government in Western Europe*, London, Frank Cass.

Joseph, R. (1987), *Democracy and prebendal politics in Nigeria*, New York, Cambridge University Press.

K

Kahin, George McTurnan, ed. (1974), *Governments and politics of South-East Asia*, 2nd edn, Ithaca, NY, Cornell University Press.

Katz, Mark N. (1997), *Revolutions and revolutionary waves*, Basingstoke, Macmillan.

Katz, Richard S., and Mair, Peter (1994), 'Party organization, party democracy, and the emergence of the cartel party', in Richard S. Katz and Peter Mair, *How parties organize*, London, Sage.

Katz, Richard S. and Mair, Peter (1995), 'Changing models of party organisation and party democracy: the emergence of the cartel party', *Party Politics*, 1, 1, January, 5–28.

Kautsky, John H. (1972), *The political consequences of modernization*, New York, John Wiley and Sons.

Kearney, Robert N., and Harris, Richard L. (1964), 'Bureaucracy and environment in Ceylon', *Journal of Commonwealth Political Studies*, 2, 3, November, 253–66.

Keeton, George W. (1960), *Trial by tribunal*, London, Museum Press.

Kelley, Donald (1976), 'Environmental policy-making in the USSR: the role of industrial and environmental interest groups', *Soviet Studies*, 28, 4, October, pp. 570–89.

Khadduri, Majid (1970), *Political trends in the Arab world: the role of ideas and ideals in politics*, Baltimore, MD Johns Hopkins University Press.

Kirchheimer, Otto (1966), 'The transformation of West European party systems', in Joseph LaPalombara and Myron Weiner, eds, *Political parties and political development*, Princeton, NJ, Princeton University Press, pp. 177–200.

Kirkpatrick, Jeane (1982), *Dictatorships and double standards*, New York, Simon and Schuster.

Kitschelt, Herbert (1999), *Post-Communist party systems: competition, representation and inter-party cooperation*, Cambridge, Cambridge University Press.

Koff, Sondra Z., and Koff, Stephen, P. (2000), *Italy: from the First to the Second Republic*, London, Routledge.

Kolinsky, Martin, and Paterson, William E., eds (1976), *Social and political movements in Western Europe*, London, Croom Helm.

Kornhauser, William (1959), *The politics of mass society*, Glencoe, IL, Free Press.

Koven, S. (1991), 'The US budget deficit and the economy', in P.J. Davies and F.A. Waldstein, eds, *Political issues in America: the 1990s*, Manchester, Manchester University Press.

Krugman, P. (1994), 'The myth of Asia's miracle', *Foreign Affairs*, **76**, 6, 63–75.

Kuhn, Thomas S. (1970), *The structure of scientific revolutions*, 2nd edn, Chicago, IL, University of Chicago Press.

Kumar, Krishan (1992), 'The revolutions of 1989: socialism, capitalism, and democracy', *Theory and Society*, **21**, 3, 309–56.

Kuzio, Taras (1998), *Contemporary Ukraine: dynamics of post-Soviet transition*, London, M.E. Sharpe.

L

LaFeber, Walter (1993), *Inevitable revolutions: the United States in Central America*, 2nd edn, New York, W.W. Norton.

Lakeman, Enid (1970), *How democracies vote, a study of majority and proportional electoral systems*, London, Faber.

Landman, D. (2000), *Issues and methods in comparative politics*, London, Sage.

Lane, David (1971), *The end of inequality? Stratification under state socialism*, Harmondsworth, Penguin Books.

Lane, David (1976), *The socialist industrial state: towards a political sociology of state socialism*, London, Allen and Unwin.

Lane, David (1978), *Politics and society in the USSR*, 2nd edn, London, Martin Robertson.

Lane, Jan-Erik, and Ersson, Svante O. (1991), *Politics and society in Western Europe*, London, Sage.

LaPalombara, J., ed. (1963), *Bureaucracy and political development*, Princeton, NJ, Princeton University Press.

Lapidus, Gail W., ed. (1995), *The new Russia: troubled transformation*, Boulder, CO, Westview Press.

Larres, Klaus, and Panayi, Penikos, eds (1996), *The Federal Republic of Germany since 1949: politics, society and economy before and after Unification*, Harlow, Longman.

Lasswell, Harold D. (1936), *Politics: who gets what, when, how?*, New York, McGraw-Hill.

Lawlor, Teresa, and Rigby, Mike, eds (1998), *Contemporary Spain: essays and texts on politics, economics, education and employment, and society*, Harlow, Addison Wesley Longman.

Lawson, Nigel (1993), *The view from No. 11: memoirs of a Tory radical*, London, Corgi.

Leftwich, Adrian (1984), *What is politics? The activity and its study*, Oxford, Blackwell.

Leiden, Carl, and Schmitt, Karl M. (1968), *The politics of violence: revolution in the modern world*, Englewood Cliffs, NJ, Prentice-Hall.

Lembruch, Gerhard (1967), *Proporzdemokratie: politisches System und politische Kultur in der Schweiz und in Österreich*, Tübingen, Mohr.

Lenin, Vladimir Il'ych (1967), 'What is to be done?', *Selected Works*, I, Moscow, Foreign Languages Publishing House.

Lenz, Guenther H., and Shell, Kurt, eds (1986), *The crisis of modernity: recent theories of culture and society in the United States and West Germany*, Frankfurt, Campus.

Lessnoff, Michael (1974), *The structure of social science: a philosophical introduction*, London, Allen and Unwin.

Levy, Carl, ed. (1996), *Italian regionalism: history, identity and politics*, Oxford, Berg.

Lewis, Paul G., Potter, David C., and Castles, Francis G. (1978), *The practice of comparative politics*, London, Longman with Open University Press.

Lichbach, M.I., and Zuckerman, A.S. (1997), *Comparative politics: rationality, culture and structure*, Cambridge, Cambridge University Press.

Lijphart, Arend (1969), 'Typologies of democratic systems', in Arend Lijphart, ed., *Politics in Europe: comparisons and interpretations*, Englewood Cliffs, NJ, Prentice-Hall, pp. 46–80.

Lijphart, Arend (1971), 'Comparative politics and the comparative method', *American Political Science Review* **65**, 3, 682–93.

Lijphart, Arend (1974), *The politics of accommodation: pluralism and democracy in the Netherlands*, 2nd edn, Berkeley, CA, University of California Press.

Lijphart, Arend (1977), *Democracy in plural societies: a comparative exploration*, New Haven, CT, Yale University Press.

Lijphart, Arend (1995), *Electoral systems and party systems: a study of twenty-seven democracies, 1945–90*, Oxford, Oxford University Press.

Linz, Juan J. (1970), 'An authoritarian regime: Spain', in Allardt, Erik and Rokkan, Stein, eds, *Mass politics: studies in political sociology*, New York, Free Press, pp. 251–88.

Linz, Juan J., and Stepan, Alfred (1978), *The breakdown of democratic regimes: Latin America*, Baltimore, MD, Johns Hopkins University Press.

Linz, Juan J., and Stepan, Alfred (1996), *Problems of democratic transition and consolidation: Southern Europe, South America, and Post-Communist Europe*, Baltimore, MD, Johns Hopkins University Press.

Lipset, Seymour Martin (1960), *Political man*, New York, Basic Books.

Lipset, Seymour Martin (1979), *The first new nation: the United States in historical and comparative perspective*, New York, W.W. Norton.

Lipset, Seymour Martin, and Rokkan, Stein, eds (1967), *Party systems and voter alignments: cross-national perspectives*, New York, Collier-Macmillan.

Locke, John (1956), *The second treatise of government*, ed. J.W. Gough, Oxford, Basil Blackwell.

Locke, John (1964), *Two treatises on government*, ed. Peter Laslett, Cambridge, Cambridge University Press.

Lomax, Bill (1976), *Hungary 1956*, London, Allison and Busby.

Lorenz, Konrad (1966), *On aggression*, London, Methuen.

Lovenduski, Joni (1986), *Women and European politics: contemporary feminism and public policy*, Amherst, MA, University of Massachusetts Press.

Lovenduski, Joni, and Woodall, Jean (1987), *Politics and society in Eastern Europe*, Basingstoke, Macmillan Education.

Lowi, Theodore J. (1969), *The end of liberalism*, New York, Norton.

Lukes, Steven (1974), *Power: a radical view*, London, Macmillan.

Lumley, F.A. (1976), *The Republic of China under Chiang Kai-shek: Taiwan today*, London, Barrie and Jenkins.

Luttwak, Edward (1979), *Coup d'etat, a practical handbook*, 2nd edn, London, Wildwood House.

Lynch, Frances (1990), 'France', in Andrew Graham and Anthony Seldon, eds, *Governments and economies in the postwar world: economic policies and comparative performance, 1945–85*, London, Routledge, pp. 54–78.

M

McCauley, Martin (1993), *The Soviet Union, 1917–1991*, 2nd edn, Harlow, Longman.

Machiavelli, Niccolo (1950), *The Prince and The Discourses*, intro. Max Lerner, New York, Random House.

MacIntyre, Alisdair (1983), 'Is a science of comparative politics possible?', in A.G. MacIntyre, ed., *Against the self-images of the age: essays on ideology and philosophy*, 2nd edn, London, Duckworth.

McKay, David (1997), *American politics and society*, 2nd edn, Oxford, Blackwell.

Mackenzie, Angus (1997), *The CIA's war at home*, Berkeley, CA, University of California Press.

Mackie, Thomas T., and Rose, Richard (1991), *The international almanac of electoral history*, 3rd edn, London, Macmillan.

Macpherson, Crawford B. (1977), *The life and times of liberal democracy*, Oxford, Oxford University Press.

McQuail, Denis (1969), *Towards a sociology of mass communications*, New York, Collier-Macmillan.

Mair, Peter (1987), *The changing Irish party system*, London, Frances Pinter.

Mair, Peter, ed. (1990), *The West European party system*, Oxford, Oxford University Press.

Major, John (2000), *John Major: the autobiography*, London, HarperCollins.

Mannheim, Karl (1946), *Ideology and utopia: an introduction to the sociology of knowledge*, London, Routledge and Kegan Paul.

Marceau, Jane (1980), 'Power and its possessors', in Philip G. Cerny and Martin A. Schain, eds, *French politics and public policy*, London, Methuen, pp. 48–78.

March, James, and Simon, Herbert (1958), *Organizations*, New York, Wiley.

Marchetti, Victor and Marks, John D. (1974), *The CIA and the cult of intelligence*, London, Cape.

Marcuse, Herbert (1972), *One dimensional man*, London, Sphere Books.

Marsh, David, and Rhodes, R.A.W. (1992), *Policy networks in British government*, Oxford, Clarendon Press.

Marsh, H.D. and Stoker, G., eds (1995), *Theory and methods in political science*, Basingstoke, Macmillan.

Marx, F. Morstein (1967), *The administrative state*, Chicago, IL, Chicago University Press.

Marx, Karl (1962), 'Letter to J. Weydemayer' [1852], in Karl Marx and Frederick Engels, *Selected Works*, Moscow, Foreign Languages Publishing House.

Marx, Karl, and Engels, Frederick (1940), *The German ideology*, London, Lawrence and Wishart.

Marx, Karl, and Engels, Frederick (1962), 'The communist manifesto' [1848], in Karl Marx and Frederick Engels, *Selected works*, Moscow, Foreign Languages Publishing House.

Mason, David S. (1992), *Revolution in East-Central Europe: the rise and fall of communism and the Cold War*, Boulder, CO, Westview Press.

Matthews, Herbert L. (1958), *The yoke and the arrows*, London, Heinemann.

Matthews, Mervyn (1978), *Privilege in the Soviet Union: a study of elite life-styles under Communism*, London, Allen and Unwin.

Mayer, Laurence C. (1989), *Redefining comparative politics: promise versus performance*, London, Sage.

Meadows, Donella H., Meadows, Dennis L., Randers, Jorgen, and Behrens, William W. III (1974), *The limits to growth*, London, Pan Books.

Meisel, James H. (1962), *The fall of the Republic: military revolt in France*, Ann Arbor, MI, University of Michigan Press.

Melville, Thomas, and Melville, Marjorie (1971), *Guatemala – another Vietnam?* Harmondsworth, Penguin.

Merritt, Richard L. (1970), *Systemic approaches to comparative politics*, New York, Rand McNally.

Mezey, M. (1979), *Comparative legislatures*, Durham, NC, Duke University Press.

Michels, Robert (1969), *Political parties: a sociological study of the oligarchical tendencies of modern democracy* [1915], New York, Dover Publications.

Migdal, Joel S. (1988), *Strong societies and weak states*, Princeton, NJ, Princeton University Press.

Mill, John Stuart (1958), *Considerations on representative government*, ed. Carrin V. Shields, Indianapolis, IN, Bobbs Merrill.

Millard, Frances (1999), *Polish politics and society*, London, Routledge.

Miller, David, and Walzer, Michael, eds (1995), *Pluralism, justice and equality*, Oxford, Oxford University Press.

Miller, George A. (1963), *Language and communication*, New York, McGraw Hill.

Mills, C. Wright (1956), *The power elite*, New York, Oxford University Press.

Milne, R.S. (1967), *Government and politics in Malaysia*, Boston, MA, Houghton Mifflin.

Milnor, A.J. (1969), *Elections and political stability*, Boston, MA, Little Brown.

Montero, José Ramón (1999), 'Stabilising the democratic order: electoral behaviour in Spain', in Paul Heywood, ed., *Politics and policy in democratic Spain*, London, Frank Cass, pp. 53–79.

Montesquieu, Charles-Louis de Secondat, Baron de (1966), *The spirit of the laws*, trans. Thomas Nugent, intro. Franz Neumann, New York, Hafner.

Moore, Barrington, Jr. (1969), *Social origins of dictatorship and democracy: lord and peasant in the making of the modern world*, Harmondsworth, Penguin Books.

Muizinieks, N. (1995), 'The influence of the Baltic popular movements on the process of Soviet disintegration', *Europe-Asia Studies*, 47, 1, 3–25.

Murphy, Raymond (1988), *Social closure: the theory of monopolisation and exclusion*, Oxford, Clarendon.

Myrdal, Gunnar (1972), *Asian drama: an enquiry into the poverty of nations*, New York, Vintage Books.

N

Needler, Martin C. (1963), *Latin American power in perspective*, Princeton, NJ, Van Nostrand.

Needler, Martin C. (1990), *Mexican politics: the containment of conflict*, 2nd edn, New York, Praeger.

Neguib, Muhammad (1955), *Egypt's destiny*, Garden City, NY, Doubleday.

Neumann, Sigmund (1948–49), 'The international civil war', *World Politics*, 1, 333.

Neumann, Sigmund (1965), *Permanent revolution: totalitarianism in the age of international civil war*, London, Pall Mall.

Neustadt, Richard E. (1964), *Presidential power*, New York, Signet.

Newell, James L. (2000), *Parties and democracy in Italy*, Aldershot, Ashgate.

Newton, Ken (1997), 'Social capital and democracy', *American Behavioral Scientist*, 40, 5, 575–86.

Newton, Michael T., with Donaghy, Peter J. (1997), *Institutions of modern Spain, a political and economic guide*, Cambridge, Cambridge University Press.

Niskanen, William A. (1973), *Bureaucracy: servant or master? Lessons from America*, London, Institute for Economic Affairs.

Nollert, Michael (1995), 'Neocorporatism and political protest in the western democracies: a cross-national analysis', in J. Craig Jenkins and Bert Klandermans, eds, *The politics of social protest: comparative perspectives on states and social movements*, London, UCL Press, pp. 138–64.

Nordlinger, Eric A. (1977), *Soldiers in politics: military coups and governments*, Englewood Cliffs, NJ, Prentice-Hall.

Norris, Pippa (1987), *Politics and sexual equality: the comparative position of women in Western democracies*, Brighton, Wheatsheaf.

North, Douglass (1986), 'A neoclassical theory of the state', in Jon Elster, ed., *Rational choice*, Oxford, Basil Blackwell, pp. 248–60.

North, Robert C., *et al.* (1963), *Content analysis*, Evanston, IL, Northwestern University Press.

Nugent, Paul (1996), *Big men, small boys and politics in Ghana*, London, Pinter.

Nurmi, Hannu (1987), 'Political succession as policy succession: why so much stability?, in Peter Calvert, ed., *The process of political succession*, Basingstoke, Macmillan, pp. 203–22.

Nutting, Anthony (1967), *No end of a lesson: the story of Suez*, London, Constable.

O

O'Brien, Phil, and Cammack, Paul (1985), *Generals in retreat: the crisis of military rule in Latin America*, Manchester, Manchester University Press.

The Observer (1990), *Tearing down the curtain: the people's revolution in Eastern Europe*, London, Hodder and Stoughton.

O'Donnell, Guillermo (1988), *Bureaucratic authoritarianism: Argentina, 1966–73, in comparative perspective*, Berkeley, CA, University of California Press.

Ohmae, K. (1990), *The borderless world*, London, Collins.

O'Kane, Rosemary H.T. (1986), 'Explaining African coups d'etat', *American Political Science Review*, 80, 232–47.

O'Kane, Rosemary H.T. (1996), *Terror, force and states: the path from modernity*, Cheltenham, Edward Elgar.

Okoli, Ekwueme Felix (1980), *Institutional structure and conflict in Nigeria*, Washington, DC, University Press of America.

Olson, Mancur (1965), *The logic of collective action: public goods and the theory of groups*, Cambridge, MA, Harvard University Press.

Osgood, Charles E., Suci, George J., and Tannenbaum, Percy H. (1957), *The measurement of meaning*, Urbana, IL, University of Illinois Press.

P

Page, E.C. (1992), *Political authority and bureaucratic power: a comparative analysis*, 2nd edn, Hemel Hempstead, Harvester-Wheatsheaf.

Panebianco, Angelo (1988), *Political parties: organisation and power*, Cambridge, Cambridge University Press.

Pareto, Vilfredo (1965), *Works*, ed. S.E. Finer, London, Pall Mall.

Parker, Simon (1996), 'Electoral reform and political change in Italy, 1991–1994', in Stephen Gundle and Simon Parker, eds, *The new Italian Republic: from the fall of the Berlin Wall to Berlusconi*, London, Routledge, pp. 40–56.

Parkin, Frank (1971), *Class, inequality and political order: social stratification in capitalist and communist societies*, London, McGibbon and Kee.

Parkin, Frank (1979), *Marxism and class theory: a bourgeois critique*, London, Tavistock.

Parkinson, C. Northcote (1958), *Parkinson's law, or the pursuit of progress*, London, John Murray.

Parry, Geraint (1969), *Political elites*, London, Allen and Unwin.

Parsons, Talcott A., and Shils, Ed B. (1962), *Towards a general theory of action*, New York, Harper.

Partridge, P.H. (1971), *Consent and consensus*, London, Pall Mall and Macmillan.

Pastor, Robert A. (1987), *Condemned to repetition: the United States and Nicaragua*, Princeton, NJ, Princeton University Press.

Paterson, William E. (1987), 'West Germany: between party apparatus and basic democracy', in Alan Ware, ed., *Political parties: electoral change and structural response*, Oxford, Basil Blackwell, pp. 158–82.

Perlmutter, Amos (1978), *The military and politics in modern times: professionals, praetorians, and revolutionary soldiers*, New Haven, CT, Yale University Press.

Perlmutter, Amos, ed. with Valerie Plave Bennett (1980), *The political influence of the military: a comparative reader*, New Haven, CT, Yale University Press.

Peters, B. Guy (1989), *The politics of bureaucracy*, White Plains, NY, Longman.

Peters, B. Guy (1999), *Institutional theory in political science: the new institutionalism*, London, Pinter.

Peters, Gordon (1986), *American public policy*, Basingstoke, Macmillan.

Peterson, Paul E. (1995), *The price of federalism*, Washington, DC, Brookings Institution.

Pettee, George S. (1938 reprinted 1963), *The process of revolution*, New York, Harper and Brothers.

Pierce, J.R. (1962), *Symbols, signals and noise: the nature and process of communication*, London, Hutchinson.

Pierre, Jon, ed. (1995), *Bureaucracy in the modern state: an introduction to comparative public administration*, Aldershot, Edward Elgar.

Pierson, W.W., and Gil, Federico G. (1967), *Governments of Latin America*, New York, McGraw Hill.

Pincher, Chapman (1988), *The Spycatcher affair: a web of deception*, London, New English Library.

Pinkney, Robert (1993), *Democracy in the third world*, Buckingham, Open University Press.

Plamenatz, John (1970), *Ideology*, London, Pall Mall and Macmillan.

Plant, Raymond (1991a), *Modern political thought*, Oxford, Blackwell.

Plant, Raymond (1991b), *The Plant Report: a working party on electoral reform*, London, The Guardian.

Polsby, Nelson W. (1975), in Fred I. Greenstein and Nelson W. Polsby, eds, *Handbook of Political Science*, Vol. 5, Reading, MA, Addison-Wesley, pp. 257–319.

Pool, Ithiel da Sola, ed. (1957), *Trends in content analysis*, Urbana, IL, University of Illinois Press.

Powell, Charles (1996), *Juan Carlos of Spain, self-made monarch*, Basingstoke, Macmillan in association with St Antony's College, Oxford.

Powell, John Duncan (1971), *Political mobilization of the Venezuelan peasant*, Cambridge, MA, Harvard University Press.

Pryke, Richard (1981), *The nationalised industries: policies and performance since 1968*, Oxford, Martin Robertson.

Przeworski, Adam (1992), 'The games of transition', in Scott Mainwaring, Guillermo O'Donnell and Samuel Valuenzuela, eds, *Issues in democratic consolidation*, Notre Dame, IN, University of Notre Dame Press, pp. 105–53.

Przeworski, Adam (1995), *Sustainable democracy*, Cambridge, Cambridge University Press.

Przeworski, Adam and Teune, Henry (1970), *The logic of comparative social inquiry*, New York, Wiley.

Pulzer, Peter G.J. (1975), *Political representation and elections in Britain*, 3rd edn, London, Allen and Unwin.

Putnam, R. (1993), *Making democracy work: civic traditions in modern Italy*, Princeton, NJ, Princeton University Press.

Putnam, R. (1995), 'Bowling alone: America's decline of social capital', *Journal of Democracy*, 6, 1, 65–78.

R

Rae, Douglas W. (1967), *The political consequences of electoral laws*, New Haven, CT, Yale University Press.

Rae, Douglas W., and Taylor, Michael (1970), *The analysis of political cleavages*, New Haven, CT, Yale University Press.

Ragin, C. (1996), 'The distinctiveness of comparative social science', in A. Inkeles and M. Sasaki, eds, *Comparing nations and cultures: readings in a cross-disciplinary perspective*, Englewood Cliffs, NJ, Prentice Hall, pp. 74–89.

Randall, Vicky, ed. (1988), *Political parties in the third world*, London, Sage.

Randall, Vicky, and Theobald, Robin (1985), *Political change and underdevelopment: a critical introduction to Third World politics*, Basingstoke, Macmillan.

Remmer, Karen (1991), *Military rule in Latin America*, Boulder, CO, Westview Press.

Richardson, J.J., and Jordan, A.G. (1970), *Governing under pressure*, Oxford, Martin Robertson.

Richardson, Lewis F. (1960), *Statistics of deadly quarrels*, London, Stevens.

Ridley, F.F., and Blondel, J. (1964), *Public administration in France*, London, Routledge and Kegan Paul.

Riggs, Fred W. (1964), *Administration in developing countries*, Boston, MA, Houghton Mifflin.

Riggs, Fred W. (1973), *Prismatic society revisited*, Morristown, NJ, General Learning Press.

Riker, William H. (1982), *Liberalism against populism: a confrontation between the theory of democracy and the theory of social choice*, San Francisco, CA, W.H. Freeman.

Robinson, Joan (1969), *The Cultural Revolution in China*, Harmondsworth, Penguin Books.

Robson, William A., ed. (1956), *The civil service in Britain and France*, London, Hogarth Press.

Romero, Oscar (1985), *Voice of the voiceless: the four pastoral letters and other statements*, Maryknoll, NY, Orbis.

Rose, Richard (1971), *Governing without consensus, an Irish perspective*, London, Faber.

Rose, Richard (1996), 'Ex-Communists in post-Communist societies', *Political Quarterly*, **67**, 1, 14–24.

Rosenthal, Erwin I.J. (1962), *Political thought in medieval Islam: an introductory outline*, Cambridge, Cambridge University Press.

Rosenthal, Uriel (1978), *Political order: rewards, punishments and political stability*, Alphen aan den Rijn, Sijthoff and Noordhoff.

Rossett, P. and Vandermeer, J., eds (1986), *Nicaragua: unfinished revolution*, New York, Grove Press.

Rostow, Walt Whitman (1960), *The stages of economic growth: a non-communist manifesto*, Cambridge, Cambridge University Press.

Rostow, Walt Whitman (1971), *Politics and the stages of growth*, Cambridge, Cambridge University Press.

Rotberg, Robert I. (1971), *Haiti, the politics of squalor*, Boston, MA, Houghton Mifflin.

Rouban, Luc (1995), 'Public administration at the crossroads: the end of the French specificity?', in Jon Pierre, ed., *Bureaucracy in the modern state: an introduction to comparative public administration*, Aldershot, Edward Elgar, pp. 39–63.

Rousseau, Jean-Jacques (1958), *The social contract and discourses*, trans. and intro. G.D.H. Cole, London, Dent.

Rubenstein, Alvin Z. (1965), *Communist political systems*, Englewood Cliffs, NJ, Prentice Hall.

Rueschmeyer, Dietrich, Stephens, Evelyne Huber, and Stephens, John D. (1992), *Capitalist development and democracy*, Cambridge, Polity, p. 6.

Runciman, W.G. (1963), *Social science and political theory*, Cambridge, Cambridge University Press.

Rush, Michael (1992), *Politics and society: an introduction to political sociology*, London, Harvester Wheatsheaf.

Russett, Bruce M., ed. (1964), *World handbook of political and social indicators*, New Haven, CT, Yale University Press.

Rustow, Dankwart (1970), 'Transitions to democracy', *Comparative Politics*, **2**, p. 362.

Rydon, Joan (1956), 'Electoral methods and the Australian party system, 1900–1951', *Australian Journal of Politics and History*, **2**, November, 82.

S

Safran, William (1995), *The French polity*, 4th edn, White Plains, NY, Longman.

Sahlin, Michael (1977), *Neo-authoritarianism and the problem of legitimacy: a general study and a Nigerian example*, Stockholm, Reben and Sjögren.

Salcedo-Bastardo, J.L. (1978), *Bolívar, a continent and its destiny*, Richmond, Richmond Publishing Co. Ltd.

Sartori, Giovanni (1970), 'Concept misformation in comparative politics', *American Political Science Review*, **64**, 4, 1033–53.

Sartori, Giovanni (1976), *Parties and party systems, a framework for analysis*, Cambridge, Cambridge University Press.

Sartori, Giovanni (1994), 'Compare: why and how; comparing, mis-comparing and the comparative method', in M. Dogan and A. Kazancigil, eds, *Comparing nations: concepts, strategies, substance*, Oxford, Blackwell, pp. 14–34.

Scarrow, Susan E. (1996), *Parties and their members: organizing for victory in Britain and Germany*, New York, Oxford University Press.

Schapiro, Leonard (1970), *The Communist Party of the Soviet Union*, 2nd edn, London, Eyre and Spottiswoode.

Schapiro, Leonard (1972), *Totalitarianism*, London, Pall Mall and Macmillan.

Scharf, Thomas (1994), *The German Greens: challenging the consensus*, Oxford, Berg.

Schattschneider, E.E. (1961), *The semi-sovereign people: a realist's view of democracy in America*, New York, Holt, Rinehart and Winston.

Schmitter, Philippe (1970), 'Still the century of corporatism', *Review of Politics*, **36**, 85–96.

Schmitter, Philippe (1981), 'Interest intermediation and regime governability in contemporary Western Europe and North America', in Suzanne Berger, ed., *Organizing interests in Western Europe*, Cambridge, Cambridge University Press, pp. 287–327.

Schmitter, Philippe, and Karl, Terry Lynn (1993), 'What democracy is . . . and is not', in Larry Diamond and Marc F. Plattner, eds, *The global resurgence of democracy*, Baltimore, MD, Johns Hopkins University Press, pp. 39–52.

Schonfeld, William R. (1976), *Obedience and revolt: French behavior toward authority*, Beverly Hills, CA, Sage.

Schram, Stuart, ed. (1963), *The political thought of Mao Tse Tung*, New York, Praeger.

Schumpeter. Joseph A. (1943), *Capitalism, socialism and democracy*, London, Allen and Unwin.

Sen, Amartya (1986), 'Behaviour and the concept of preference', *Economica*, **40** (August 1973), 241–59, reprinted in Jon Elster, ed., *Rational choice*, Oxford, Basil Blackwell, pp. 60–81.

Seton-Watson, Hugh (1956), *The East European Revolution*, New York, Praeger.

Seton-Watson, Hugh (1977), *Nations and states: an inquiry into the origins of nations and the politics of nationalism*, London, Methuen.

Shils, Ed B. (1962), *Political development in the new states*, The Hague, Mouton.

Shin Doll Chull (1994), 'On the third wave of democratization: a synthesis and evaluation of recent theory and research', *World Politics*, **47**, 135–70.

Short, Anthony (1973), *The communist insurrection in Malaya, 1948–60*, London, Frederick Muller.

Silber, Laura, and Little, Allan (1995), *The death of Yugoslavia*, London, Penguin Books and BBC Worldwide Ltd.

Sivard, Ruth Leger (1983), *World military and social expenditures*, Leesburg, VA, World Priorities.

Skilling, Gordon, and Griffiths, F., eds (1971), *Interest groups in Soviet politics*, Princeton, NJ, Princeton University Press.

Skocpol, Theda (1979), *States and social revolutions: a comparative analysis of France, Russia and China*, Cambridge, Cambridge University Press.

Skocpol, Theda (1994), *Social revolutions in the modern world*, Cambridge, Cambridge University Press.

Smith, Adam (1982), *An inquiry into the nature and causes of the wealth of nations*, New York, Liberty Fund.

Solomon, S. Gross, ed. (1983), *Pluralism in the Soviet Union*, London, Macmillan.

Solovyov, Vladimir, and Klepikova, Elena (1992), *Boris Yeltsin, a political biography*, London, Weidenfeld and Nicolson.

Sorenson, Theodore (1965), *Kennedy*, London, Hodder and Stoughton.

Stacey, Frank (1978), *Ombudsmen compared*, Oxford, Clarendon Press.

Stanyer, Jeffrey (1976), 'Irresistible forces; the pressure for a science of politics', *Political Studies*, **24** (3), September, 237–52.

Steiner, Jürg (1972), *Politics in Austria*, Boston, MA, Little Brown.

Steiner, Jürg (1974), *Amicable agreement versus majority rule: conflict resolution in Switzerland*, Chapel Hill, NC, University of North Carolina Press.

Stent, Angela E. (2000), *Russia and Germany reborn: unification, the Soviet collapse and the new Europe*, Princeton, NJ, Princeton University Press.

Stepan, Alfred (1971), *The military in politics: changing patterns in Brazil*, Princeton, NJ, Princeton University Press.

Stevens, Anne (1992), *The government and politics of France*, Basingstoke, Macmillan.

Stockman, David (1987), *The triumph of politics*, London, Bodley Head.

Stodgill, R.M. (1948), 'Personal factors associated with leadership: a survey of the literature', *Journal of Psychology*, **35**, 35.

Stokes, William S. (1959), *Latin American politics*, New York, Thomas Y. Crowell Co.

Sunday Times Insight Team (1975), *Insight on Portugal: the year of the captains*, London, Andre Deutsch.

Suny, Ronald (1991), 'Incomplete revolution: national movements and the collapse of the Soviet Empire', *New Left Review*, **189**, September/October, 111–25.

T

Talmon, J.L. (1961), *The origins of totalitarian democracy*, London, Mercury Books.

Tapper, Ted (1976), *Political education and stability: elite responses to political conflict*, London, John Wiley.

Tarrow, Sidney (1989), *Democracy and disorder*, Oxford, Oxford University Press.

Tarrow, Sidney (1994), *Power in movement: social movements, collective action and politics*, Cambridge, Cambridge University Press.

Taylor, Michael, and Laver, Michael (1973), 'Government coalitions in Western Europe', *European Journal of Political Research*, **1**, 105–48.

The Times (1974), *The Times Guide to the House of Commons*, London, Times Newspapers Limited.

Thomas, Caroline (1987), *In search of security: the Third World in international relations*, Brighton, Harvester Press.

Thomas, Caroline (1992), *The environment in international relations*, London, Royal Institute of International Affairs.

Thomas, Caroline, and Wilkins, Peter, eds (1999), *Globalization, human security and the African experience*, Boulder, CO, Lynne Rienner.

Thomas, Hugh, ed. (1959), *The establishment*, London, Anthony Blond.

Thomas, Hugh (1966), *The Suez affair*, London, Weidenfeld.

Tigrid, Pavel (1971), *Why Dubcek fell*, London, Macdonald.

Tilly, Charles (1978), *From mobilization to revolution*, Reading, MA, Addison-Wesley.

Turner, Bryan S. (1988), *Status*, Minneapolis, MN, University of Minnesota Press.

V

Vagts, Alfred (1959), *A history of militarism, civilian and military*, London, Hollis and Carter.

Valen, Henry, and Rokkan, Stein (1974), 'Norway: conflict structure and mass politics in a European periphery', in Richard Rose, ed., *Electoral behavior: a comparative handbook*, New York, Free Press, pp. 315–70.

Valenilla Lanz, Laureano (1919), *Cesarismo democrático: estudio sobre las bases sociológicas de la constitución efectiva de Venezuela*, Caracas, Empresa El Cojo.

van Mierlo, H.J.G.A. (1986), 'Depillarisation and the decline of consociationalism in the Netherlands, 1970–85', *West European Politics*, **9**, 1, 97–119.

Veljanovski, Cento (1987), *Selling the state: privatisation in Britain*, London, Weidenfeld and Nicolson.

Verney, Douglas V. (1961), *The analysis of political systems*, London, Routledge.

Vincent, Andrew (1991), *Modern political ideologies*, Oxford, Blackwell.

Vogt, Evon Z. (1969), *Zinacantan, a Maya community in the highlands of Chiapas*, Cambridge, MA, Belknap.

von Beyme, Karl (1985), *Political parties in western democracies*, Aldershot, Gower.

W

Wahl, Nicholas, and Quermonne, Jean-Louis (1995), *La France présidentielle: l'infuence du suffrage universel sur la vie politique*, Paris, Presses de Sciences Po.

Wallace, Michael, and Jenkins, J. Craig (1995), 'The New Class, postindustrialism and neocorporatism: three images of social protest in the western democracies', in J. Craig Jenkins and Bert Klandermans, eds, *The politics of social protest: comparative perspectives on states and social movements*, London, UCL Press, pp. 96–137.

Wallerstein, Immannel (1974), *The modern world system*, New York, Academic Press.

Walt, S.M. (1992), 'Revolution and war', *World Politics*, **44**, 321–68.

Wang Gung-wu, ed. (1966), *Malaysia*, London, Pall Mall.

Ware, Alan (1979), *The logic of party democracy*, London, Macmillan.

Ware, Alan (1987a), *Citizens, parties and the state: a reappraisal*, Cambridge, Polity Press.

Ware, Alan, ed. (1987b), *Political parties: electoral change and structural response*, Oxford, Blackwell.

Weber, Max (1965), *The theory of social and economic organisation* [c. 1919], New York, Free Press.

Weber, Max (1974), *The Protestant ethic and the spirit of capitalism*, London, Routledge.

Weiner, Norbert (1967), *Cybernetics*, Cambridge, MA, MIT Press.

Weinstein, Martin (1975), *Uruguay, the politics of failure*, Westport, CT, Greenwood Press.

Weller, Patrick (1985), *First among equals: prime ministers in Westminster systems*, London, Unwin Hyman.

Werth, Alexander (1956), *France 1940–1955*, London, Robert Hale.

Werth, Alexander (1965), *De Gaulle*, Harmondsworth, Penguin Books.

Wheare, K.C. (1963), *Federal government*, 4th edn, London, Oxford University Press.

White, Stephen (1993), *After Gorbachev*, Cambridge, Cambridge University Press.

White, Stephen *et al.* (1990), *Communist and post-communist political systems*, 3rd edn, London, Macmillan.

White, Theodore (1965), *The making of the president, 1964*, London, Jonathan Cape.

Wickham-Crowley, Timothy P. (1993), *A comparative study of insurgents and regimes since 1936*, Princeton, NJ, Princeton University Press.

Wilgus, A. Curtis (1963), *South American dictators in the first century of independence*, New York, Russell and Russell.

Wilson, Graham K. (1990), *Interest groups*, Oxford, Blackwell.

Winch, Peter (1958), *The idea of a social science and its relation to philosophy*, London, Routledge.

Wintrobe, Ronald (1998), *The political economy of dictatorship*, Cambridge, Cambridge University Press.

Wolf-Philips, Leslie, ed. (1968), *Constitutions of modern states*, London, Pall Mall.

Wolin, Simon, and Slusser, Robert M. (1957), *The Soviet secret police*, New York, Praeger.

Woodward, Bob, and Bernstein, Carl (1977), *The final days*, New York, Avon.

Woodward, Kath, ed. (2000), *Questioning identity*, London, Routledge in association with the Open University.

World Bank (2000), *World development report 2000*, New York, United Nations.

World Commission on Environment and Development (1987), *Our common future (the Bruntland report)*, Oxford, Oxford University Press.

Worsley, Peter (1967), *The Third World*, 2nd edn, London, Weidenfeld and Nicolson.

Wraith, R.E., and Simpkins, E. (1965), *Corruption in developing countries*, New York, Norton.

Wright, Peter (1987), *Spycatcher: the candid autobiography of a senior intelligence officer*, Toronto, Stoddart.

Y

Yanov, Alexander (1978), *The Russian New Right: right-wing ideologies in the contemporary USSR*, Berkeley, CA, Institute of International Studies, University of California.

Yates, Simeon (1998), *Issues in social research*, Milton Keynes, Open University.

Yin, R.K. (1989), *Case study research: design and methods*, rev. edn, London, Sage.

Yin, R.K. (1993), *Application of case study research*, London, Sage.

Young, A. (1994), 'Lessons from the East Asian NICs: a contrarian view', *European Economic Review*, 38, 3–4, 964–73.

Z

Zaslavsky, Victor (1980), 'Socio-economic inequality and changes in Soviet ideology', *Theory and Society*, 9, 2, 383–407.

Periodicals

Annual Register of World Events
Congressional Quarterly Weekly Report
Daily Telegraph
Financial Times
Guardian
Keesing's Record of World Events
Statesman's Yearbook
Sunday Times
The Times

Index